Love Letters

Love Letters

SANDRA LEIGH SAVAGE

iUniverse, Inc.
Bloomington

Love Letters

iUniverse books may be ordered through booksellers or by contacting:

iUniverse
1663 Liberty Drive
Bloomington, IN 47403
www.iuniverse.com
1-800-Authors (1-800-288-4677)

ISBN: 978-1-4620-5068-0 (sc)
ISBN: 978-1-4620-5070-3 (hc)
ISBN: 978-1-4620-5069-7 (ebk)

Printed in the United States of America

iUniverse rev. date: 08/25/2011

Contents

I'm not in anyway, saying good-bye at all. I'm saying hello. Please sit back and enjoy hearing about how wonderful I think you both are, in my very first "Love Letters". This is just stuff I wanted to share with you both and the world. I'm not in that horrible place anymore. My life has moved on and I'm moving with it. That I want His Grace, to show how much I treasure the uniqueness I have within. I didn't understand this, until the end of one of the worst years of my life in equal to the year he died. I went into isolation for a year. Because of that year in isolation, I wouldn't have been ready for my waiting new life. The LORD has bigger plans than I have for myself. When I was suicidal a few months ago, I was so sad, so full of sorrow, but not knowing, it was the beginning of something great and majical. As I sat in my car, as my tears flowed down my hands, I reached for the door handle to get the hose, and in that instant, of the moment of my suicide intent, my cell phone rang. It was the LORD Calling me. He showed Himself in Blinding Light. When my life was Saved that night, He showed me a new world that I couldn't reach without Him and His Serenity. From His Words, as He gives them to her, He breathed into her, saying, 'you should do something with your writing.' God has used her in my life. Just like He did both yours with me. She's one of the most important person in my life. But I couldn't have her until I had you two first. You both gave me my Christian roots in how to be a Christian girl-friend, and the LORD has uses both your skills and Rewarding for you to give you each such a wonderful life. I'm learning to love all over again. I'm stronger. Regarding you both, I haven't for one second loved one of you more than the other, just in a different way. Your friendships gave me my insight in self-knowledge. Just so you know, I'm being well taken care of. God has blessed us; you, you, and her and me. I've waited a lifetime for her, and now, our long awaited reunion from another's sobriety brought us back together with many twists that makes us unbelievably connected. When I left the sanctuary a long time ago now, it took everything away from me which He was using that to strengthen me. Moulding me for my new sunlight to take over with the help of the LORD. He has connected us in such a creative and unique way, I can't even explain it. It's not of this world. Through my awaiting tunnel, God showed me my words. I hope you both are going to be proud of me when you read them. Knowing that your lives made such an impact that it'll be recorded in history. I'm learning new things about myself, that was hidden in me for so many years, my entire life. It's like I'm being sewn into a new life, for me to become the woman I'm so striving to be. To see beauty in myself and not to compare my life to others anymore. I'm learning to love my uniqueness that I've been planned for a very long time. Waiting to come out and gain my new strengthened relationship with the LORD. I couldn't of done it without Him and you and you. He's the most important in my life. And so much has happened to me since the beginning of my journey in 1997. He once again, takes Credit for giving me a total-life-destiny-change. Using sobriety to bring us all back together, with a shit load of twists of 'fate' if you want to. Nothing I've never experienced before . . . . just *mind-blowing* experiences. I love you both and I hope you have a new and freshness to me and my new life. You both have inspired me and I hope to send you both tons of "Love Letters". As I start my new life, in a different ways from what I originally thought, I have gained two amazing, loving good friends in you and you.

You *know* you are special when you can safely and with much effort, reach for your dreams. I think this world needs to reach into *their* imaginations more and bring to life *their* dreams. We need to clean up the mess past generations have left, and begin where they left off and watch the next ones carry on their missions and jobs of responsibilities. I'm always talking about how everyone should make their dreams a reality and sometimes that's the fantasy, and I don't completely know that some people *aren't* meant to reach their dreams, but some are. Even though most of the time, people seem out of balance and need to find their clarity, I don't have any answers to that question. Why does God choose them ? over you? . . . . right? . . . I don't know why, but I know He wants you to be happy. But it's just my opinion. Why *can't* you be one of the chosen ones? and let everyone be in knowing, that everyone in this world deserves happiness and not the cruelty some people inflict on you and your life. Whether you want to be an astronaut or a writer or something you've always wanted to be, reach for your dreams. One day, you could be one of the few rare woman astronauts, maybe you'll be the first woman to land on the moon who can take your dreams to outer space and journey where no others have travelled. Or, you can write to your dreams and live the life that you can only dream of. To write anything and go anywhere in print?, bring it on. Or you want to be a special teacher, who will love her students and take pride in their learning and make the future in it's future scientist who discovers the cure for cancer. I hope you reach for your goal, I would be extremely proud of you. Some will have such an obtainable dream, that's so easy for you. All it took was this, or that. But where you find yours, for you in anyone you are. Hard work would follow you everyday, but if this is your joy, your hope, your destiny, hard work should come easy to you. Labour, make your body dreary tired, for later, you can rest. If you want to become something bad enough, and *really* reach for it, then I totally believe that God will Bless you and for what you need to do to enquire for your dreams. It may be extra hours at the end of your day. *Thirst* for it, *hunger* for it. Become the best *you*, you can be. *Don't let anyone tell you, you can't do it*. Believe in yourself. Know your knowledge within. Know you can achieve that, believe in yourself, but mostly, believe in the LORD. Be a special and unique role model to the next generations. Make a mark in the world for yourself. Why not? Live your dreams everyday in your minds eye, daydream them, plan for them, prepare for them, sleep them and live it. And when your dreams come, you'll fly better with a destination and resting place where you can and see better for your paths to lead you to your future. Your vision will be clearer as you smear off the clutter in your way. Remember my LORD everyday and maybe invite Him to your dream state, and so you should. Become something great in the LORD. Have His Power within you. Always remember, you'll journey through many different and swirling paths that may seem like the long way around things, but sometimes you need those lessons to teach you for your destiny. I challenge you, to continue on your significant life accomplishments. Live as though the next moment is gone. Live, as you can only live your destiny. So, become an astronaut, become a great role model full of dignity and respect. Lift the lids that have been capped or closed, and open up to what life brings to you and the lives around you. Follow your path and shine as you leave your sole to the rest of the world.

"Incredible Woman"

For John and Alison

Allison;

As I prepare for our night together, as I prepare everything so it's perfect for our love, I light the candles, and slightly fluff the sheer curtain that covers our bed. I put love songs on to sweeten the mood. I run the bath water to a warm touch. I slip into my red satin nighty that covers to mid-thigh. The one that will make him flip like he's a shiny new dolphin jumping for attention from glistening salt water. Then I brush my long brown hair that he loves so much. I must prepare for the words I have to place in sequence to make this perfect night work. I look in the mirror and make sure my make-up is perfect. I love him, with such passion, and I once again dig in deep, and hang on for the ride of my life. As he's near to me now, I hear his thoughts, the title waves of emotions that will capture you and rip at your soul. Love each other as if there was no more tomorrow. Make love, every night. Shut the world out of your private world and escape and execute your night together. As he said himself, I'm an incredible woman. I think everyone should love like this in this lifetime as I am with this man. John is the man for me, to cherish him, to embrace hisself and to never expect something he's not. He's here.

John;

'Oh my gawd woman, you drive me crazy! I so want into you, like the highest drugs of ecstasy. Your sensual and feminine smell makes me pour myself all over you, like hot wax burning you and making you squirm in my presents. Conquer to me. I'll break every law that I have to break, to have you. I'm going to explode and I scream for you NOW! . . . . breathing sexual heaviness. You are all my loveliness, dedicated to my sweet royalty. I want to explode all through you . . . . to become dust inside your hot sexual skin that's on fyre in my grasps. As I rub energy in paralyzing doses. I want to eat you like a tiger rips his fleshly meat and becomes your conniver. In however long it takes, forever will I wait in you, for us to rapture time in our love. Fantastic size wants in. As I breathe in her scents. He runs his hands down her like running water, curving her form, and ravishing her. Mentally supplying something not expressed breaths into her pours. I want to seize your property, own you like an anaconda in his jungle. To devour you like a bugs sting. To travel across the universe to hear your voice, as it echoes in my silence. I'm gonna give you galoreity, in plentiful supply. Alison . . . . rip me, to our secret escape. Take me away. To cachinnate into our loud echo into the astral worlds. I want you, so much . . . . as he rasps into her throat. May we express our words of passion, as I say, 'please let me in . . . . *now,* for I need to feel your heat. For it to swallow me, for me to travel in you and become starlight. Let your inner liquid flow out of your pulsating bush. Become liquid on my touch, that makes me become music flow from within your mountains. You're a harp playing as you are a lullaby to hush a baby. You float like music in the air, that is the breeze that breathes on me. 'Love me, forever baby.' as I whisper in her ears, so only she could hear it. She stutters in breaths, for she's a zombie to my voice.

How You Shine throughout my eyes. Brilliantly, everyday, with every word. I love when You make me high. We become one. You put me in this kind-of-a-state that of everything around me is vocally mind-blowing. Words fall like rain into me, and You Rainbow it out, like my brain is going to speed away in my squeals of imagination. I believe in me when You control me. It's a kind of mysterious unknown. You *are* the Philosophical in my valleys. You let me feel so much. So many dominos You play with in my head. How revelations about my sentences come into me and they explode. How I call out for people into the wind around me and catapult them into my whishes. I can only hear You when I'm high . . . to one hundred percent. You are my Calmness in the night when You Speak. You are the Ghost-Opener into my mind majic. You are the Flicker in my lamp, that shines everything for me. You are my Merry-Go-Round, we ride like children around and around, with slow motion covering the sky. You create me, when Here Comes The LORD. See, that is crazy, such intenseness that I go into this kind of hypnotizing-state-of-mind, paralyzed, in Your voice when You Call me to fulfill my . . . well, you know, our final destinations. I feel weepy in the LORD, when I'm in our zone as You create writings. You gave me my independent speaker in me. Where was I reading from? From the Palette of Your Hand? You carry my fingertips to their words. You speak through others to me in vocal with written instructions, the words that flow from me like a delicate fragrance of feelings and thoughts pushed through me with a volt of electricity, and then caboom. The splashing of the waves on the keyboard. The deep breaths I breathe, as to carry out Your Word. It's like slicing me open and trying to figure out a puzzle that only one person can play. To fit that into that and that into this. I'm like this picture and some of the pieces I can't figure out, but then You come and Rescue me and Place in the roots that call for me in my silence. The palette waiting for it's paints to create something of wonder and mystery. Some might say, intrigue to mix-and-match that colour with that colour. Does that make sense? So, I fix it over and over to get it just right. Be my every word from beginning to end with breaths in between from heaven. How You've Breathen Your straightest of lines that keep the words I show on a shelf. That You made in me. I want to be someone's poetry, to be remembered. To find shelter and comfort. The words you invent in me is anything I want. To expand, to say horizons, and sunsets to make your world beautiful. May they be a sunset on the most intimate day of your life. I bring imagination to the new world of my words. As I continue to fill up space and fill you and fix your realignment with your mental well-being. To visually tell you a story but for you to read in our way of cooperation. To stimulate your thoughts to lull you to sleep. Or to wake you to your new day on a cloudy Cape Cod day. To build you up and to make you think. To search for you, to find where you'll open my "Letters". So, cuddle up on your couch, settle into a good book. Will I tease you? Will I make you cry? Will I show you His Love? I hope the answers are yes. I hope that I can mix-and-match here and there and you'll stay on, and pay for another great poetic sentence, for you to swing on the vines that I'll take you on. I hope you can keep up to pace for the long run of this wonderful journey I've stumbled on. Turn off your phones, curl up with your soft blanket, turn on the reading lamp and come on! As I swing my hand to encourage you to read the stories of my life and for you to get to know how words can just, be.

"Manna Bread"

Oh my sweet Manna Bread. You're going to be so beautiful. You're going to be next to perfect in my eyes and I'm going to love you *so much*. I can't *wait* for us to find each other. I've been screaming to your soul for years now. I call out your name into the night, and hope that God is listening to my prayers for you. I pray and hope that you'll be in perfect health because I want a very long life with you. I've even dreamt of you. I see you coming up to me and jumping in my arms and licking my entire face. You'll say, Mommy, I've been waiting for you too. I'm going to sit down in the center of the floor space, crossed legs. You puppies will be smelling me like just any other person, then, I'm going say, in a singing voice, "Manna Bread. Manna, Manna Bread . . . I pray that when I speak your name, you'll know my voice and when I call your name for the first time, you'll know my voice in an instant and instantly, you'll know who you are. Manna Bread. And then that's when you'll run to me. Upon when you hear this "Love Letters" for the first time, you'll understand every word. I think about you almost every single day. I think about your adorable face and the sound of your feminine voice and I hope I'll know it when you bark at me. I've been praying for you, for you to be a very special and such a good girl and I pray that you're the only choice I have. I hope that I show you unconditional love. And in that statement, I promise to take care of you, to make sure you have a happy and long life with me. And when we have playtime and training time, I'm going to record us and post our special pictures on our facebook, so everyone can see how wonderful you are and how happy we are together. In the meantime, as I sit right now, waiting and writing, it feels like forever, to get from now, to then, my sweet Manna Bread. I can't wait to get you. I've been planning for you in my heart everyday with God and my LORD. He knows how badly I want you my sweet girl. But I'm not ready yet, but when I am? . . . I'm not going to even hesitate to come and find you. I'm so serious about you,Manna. Whenever I see a golden retriever, I glow from within. And I think of you, every time. I love you so much and I hope that because of this "Letters", your soul will find me and bring me to you. And when I bring you home, you'll run and find our room, and you'll see your bed, and then I'll chase you, or, if it's been a long day, I'll carry you into our room and place you very gently, in your bed. When I work, and when you're laying beside me, that you'll listen to me read out loud my regular routine, and that I be your comfort when you're sleeping and that my imagination will set off yours and you'll have really cool puppy dreams. You'll run and jump in the water and retrieve your stick, and you're swimming back to me and you bark in delight when you need me to repeat to you about your pro so po graphy, to show your personality to everyone there. Then you end up on a really big field and you run and run and you jump on me and tickle me with your soft pink tongue. And when you're dreaming and running, may I have the video recorder to catch every twitch and laugh at your dreams that I've created? I want to remember every second of your life. I can't wait to bring you home and train you. I can't wait to get to know you're soul in your foolish side that's going to be trademark. I hope that we create from our relationship, to show me new stories, new ideas. Manna, I don't know you yet, but this is everything I want for us as the team and the perfect matching from the LORD, that He not only bless my life with you, but so you too, can have a rich life full of love, compassion, and tender love, to bring you out and make you famous.

Throughout our journey together, I've figured out that I was destined to be your daughter like you were meant to be my mother. I know the power of your love for me. It goes beyond this world. As I know this love because I feel the same for my children. Without you, and dad, I'd be homeless and living under bridges . . . . but God saved us, with you. For you *did* see me in a line up and pick me, because I found you from heaven and grew inside you, showing you who I'm supposed to be. You have taught me about being strong in myself. You've given me good, solid Christian morals, that I honour as a part of me, and I hope and pray, that you know how strong my relationship with our LORD is. He has called me and I hope you can be proud of who've I've become and who I am. And through that faithfulness that you showed Him and me *watching* you develop your relationship with Him, I found me. Throughout this journey for me and my self-discovery, every day, you have showed loyalty to the LORD, and He has blessed you greatly. I stayed, for many years in the secretness of my world. My solitude became my independence. And now, I am Found. I find peace in something I've been searching for. For years his death was suffocating and it was so difficult not to be disengaged in my inner life being the vessel that the LORD was Calling me. Now, I have the inner power to write and I wait for the mystery, for the next breath of what comes next for our journey. I want to make up for all those unpleasant years, but without them, I wouldn't be who I am today. I hope that my words in this one-of-a-kind "Love Letters" express that because of you, I wouldn't have been able to give *my* children *their* destinies. Our hearts are playing well together now and even though we are VERY different in some areas, we were chosen for each other, to be stubborn in ourselves and to be humble in front of God. I know, that there was so much hardness sometimes to break through the barrier of steel with me and we both know, I didn't understand, until now. You should be very proud of me with my new found strength as a woman, and as a woman in, Christ. When I was so ill after Andrew died, I was lost in his death for a long time but you were there for me, and I will NEVER, forget that. You are my saving grace and I couldn't have reached this part of my life without *you* being my mom. Mom, I love you, till we reach yin years. May I find comfort in knowing that throughout my days, I will know that your love will never be forgotten or misused or misunderstood. Yes, some days, for both you and I, there has been struggles for power and being ourselves. But underneath, is just normal everyday, mother-daughter love that God has given us to always remember on those hard days we each feel on our own. When you go to *your* House of worship, know, that every time I write something down in my writings, I'm in *my* House of worship. I will never forget where I come from. I've lost many battles on my own, but in Him, He's won everyone of them. If you ever doubt in my devotions to the LORD, read every page of this book and know that He gave me Every Word. He placed them in the order they're supposed to be. He's taking very good care of me. One day, my secrets will come out and you'll know all that you need to know and understand my relationship with the LORD. I'm learning to Listen, and See. To discern and learn. Thank you for being there for me and my children. I will never forget how you stood by me, in my darkest days of sorrow and despair and I hope you never know what I went through. You are so strong in God, and when you know who I am, I pray you'll have faith and believe.

I have never been silent in my own war. I'm battled and scared from so many wounds upon my heart. I'm always twisting and thriving to get freedom. I'm afraid to say out loud words for they bring up major interruptions of your soul and who you are. Why can't I be free without having trashes against my skin that covers my fragile heart? My hearts, that I carry for each one of you, you hurt me. Why? I only speak from love from my perspective. It's selfish to believe that I too, can say words out loud. I'm so stunted in my worldly ways, whereas in the heavens I'm free and to full height. I'm sorry if I've offended you . . . . In my little world where I sit and bathe in my thoughts and feelings. I'm afraid to show who I really am. For I will be scolded in hot and boiling words that will burn me open and make me scream for mercy, to all my pain, as it piles up within me. I'm wounded . . . . again. I say what I think, and I'm taken down by a heavy power, that I would be blown over whereas you are steady and stern. I sit under you as you pounce over me like I wasn't even there. I'm the playground that runs the tracks, to be someone else's sole imprint, that covers my whole spirit. I never want to speak again to the soul that breaks me as I hide inside. I'm a ball that can not be bounced for if I do, I'll roll down the steep hill and as I rolled down, no one would chase after me. I would just sit at the bottom, and watch cars drive by and never see me. I'd be part of the mud from the puddles from the other nights rain. When I was in yours, just a few days ago, you scolded me into who they think I should be. Just once, I blossom into showing you who I am, and I'm not wanted. Like a fyre spreading and burning all the woods so that nothing is to be left in it's path. As I repeat in my head, to try and connect with you is an invisible force field that shields away demons and monsters. They hunt me, chase me, and stab me over and over again . . . . they pull me by my hands and arms, they bound me to slide and ricochet me on the ground. Pulling me a fast speeds, ripping apart my flesh as blood pours out onto the moving ground. The mystery of when it will stop is in the world of the unknown. Okay, I have to get really down as I stumble to the next bit, and I'm running barely at any speed to get away from the hell that you placed far, deep down, that is vile in him over there. You insist that you're going to ruin me. To make me gasp for my last breath and you squeeze life from me and swallow it into your wretched horns and breath of evil, of your compost of rotting flesh. To sit in your decay. So now this is what you've brought to me mr. devil. I sat in your darkness and your shadows, and you made me feel bad, to feel horrible, as you played with me and dug your claws in me and threw me around and chewed me and made me get dizzy when I'd crash against the walls of your containment of mind environment. Where you laughed and teased me, and dangled death and guilt and plentifulls of sorrow and despair. You will never regain strength to rapture my soul, for I am of the LORD, and His power, is a lot stronger than your power, you slime, disgusting pile of manure. Who has e-coli spreading throughout your body and the maggots feast on your live leather skin. I hope He beats you, with a flogging whip and shreds and peels off layers of your snake skin. I will never let you grab me with unaware sight. I never want to have to deal with you again. I laugh in your fallen angel and squeal in delight that you're in the fyre and the deep pits of hell, where you'll burn in forever and let you bathe in heat and sweat and see murderers and rapists, where screaming in agony will never end. He will never, feed you, to quest your thirst.

For once upon ago, from being my greatest loves, are now my greatest fears. I have to see him today . . . you know who you are. For once he was my superhero, and now . . . . well, now, I have to see him again. Not only do I have to face him, I have to face everyone. And for all those who've judged me so harshly. When no one knew how dark I was, the state I was in. They saw what they saw, not behind closed doors, ... how insane I was. I hid it so well, that no one knew on how sick I really was. Back then, I needed everyone so much for it was a very dark time in my life. And now, I have to shake myself out today, and attend the funeral. Go in there head-on, strong, and looking great. But right now, my heart is very heavy. I hate confrontation, in any way, shape or form. Hate it. I'm going to be going head-on with many confrontations later today. Not very excited about today, at all. I just have to put my this day onto my LORD, because He and I have to Carry me. I need to be strong and independent. Just like always and everyday. I'm certainly not going to give any hugs for free today. I only hug who I want. Avoid direct immediate eye contact . . . . ya right . . . . *like that's* gonna happen. Everyone is going to be looking at who will be there. We're all gonna be looking for each other. Well, *I* will be anyway . . . . got to know where NOT to look after the service. I have to talk to the aka's. I can NOT, NOT go to them and show them my respect and love. The other option came into my head for about one split second, in not going. What would that show? . . . that I'm weak, and disrespectful to the deceased and their family. I have no other choice or option but to attend the service, and hold my head up, like a prince of the deer. It's not just them though. It's everyone, who don't like me, and who snickered behind my back at my weakest points of my life. I just shake my head and hope I don't have nightmares. I have to see him and her. Again, in my pain. I feel as though there was again, sadness and a very heavy heart. I have heaviness in my finger tips, and I'm totally creative and able to feel what I need to feel so I can get through today. Emotionally, I'm beat up, mentally, I'm so tired, and I'm so scared for later. But, like I said earlier, just have to buck-up and be a woman. I hope in my sleep I find my strongest shield to over up my heart. I pray that I'll be brave. But I don't feel very brave right now. I wish I could roll up into a little ball and go into another year of hiding and isolation. But I don't want to go back there again. It was very difficult and I came out of a very dark and year long depression . . . that I never told anyone about. I hid everything, from everyone. I was alone for a long time. I survived suicide and then was given my gifts to make it through the rest of my life. I remember the loneliness I went through, and the rejection I felt, through feeling betrayed, and abandonment, and I came through some pretty nasty shit. I needed my LORD, everyday. I became stronger in Him, enough for Him to totally give me a life make-over. I don't want to feel that lonely ever again, but the fear of death consumes me everyday now. I worry about my friends and family, and their families. It consumes me. It haunts me everyday, that something could happen to anyone I love, just like him. I remember that time. That's my worst fear, death of my loved ones. How I hope I don't have any regrets, someday, maybe one day. I can't believe our friendships have come to this . . . to the fear of facing anything. I'm not quite there yet in myself. I'm very fragile right now, and I'm very scared for my fragile heart. But, I have to get through it. I have to remember to breathe and to be totally "on" when I walk into that beautiful sanctuary. I want *no one* to see *any* weakness in me. I know that sounds very selfish, but I kind of have to be. How I have to sit across from you, as you smile to my heart, and I had to look away from your gazing eyes to see how I was. Angered in my soul, when it was over, in slow motion, waiting for me to get up and run from your presence. I need to delete you, from every trace you have of me, to show you my pain, as I try to hide behind a thin pole, so you don't see my pain. Only glad I only had to see you and not her too as it intensified my pain level. I hope you saw my raw pain that

8

you caused for so many unreturned pasts. I hope when you look at the image you have, you see me avoiding your attempt to see me happy. For it will never happen. I will never be at peace in my burden of love that satan has placed in me. All the past words I've said to you that has no meaning to your life. You play like a violin. You played your notes in perfect tones and the music coming from the end, flow in your way, not myn As I try to shield myself behind my; *please God, make me invisible so I don't see him.* The poems, the letters of unresolved feelings that you never knew everything. I fed your ego for a decade, bringing you into my life that would go to another. How I have to see you again under the roof of the LORD, and as I stand in His sanctuary. I have to hide myself and run like a bullet from your eyes and smile. How I would have to listen to your laughter and see you happy in another's arms, that was supposed to be. You'll always own a part of me and my heart. I wish I could press nothing and send you away. As I try again to say goodbye and to never see you again, for it to stir up dust in the air, that I try to cough out into the big atmosphere to disappear forever. I pray all the time when you have to come into my sight, where I wish I didn't have to go. But life doesn't work that way. LORD, wash to the seas, wash the dirt under and in the crevasses and wipe me clean and let me start afresh. To wash me in salt water and sterilize me and make me whole and forget him and to hope I only have to see the situation three, that's right, three times a year, which makes it not any easier. Let me come into Your presence LORD. Keep me guarded in Your Light and Shield me from them all who destroy me in front of my back. I don't want to suffer anymore, or to live in shadows of darkness that plagued me for so long. Please make this rhythm a new beat where I can grasp the handle and pull myself up when I fall all over again. To know that in this path, I would have never known, who You are and who I am, in You. Still, in Your House, I still bow my head and pray for that's why I'm here. How I once held his hand as he guided me through a heavy crowd. How he didn't let go until we were done. How we once danced and when I heard his heart beat. I'll never forget my undying, and his unpledged love given in return. Will I never to hear your voice again until I can see you safely in heaven and all in love has gone away, when I can run and welcome Home where I can live freely of my love of forever and peace in Heaven. So many unresolved feelings and words of pure hurt on my heart. When you said you didn't believe in me. When you said you didn't trust me. When you took a hammer and used the teeth to open my chambers and helped me to become who I am today and *who* I am. I hope one day, I can walk into the House of worship, and stand under His Cross and be free from latent and not visible to him, so I'm not seen. To not be looked around in his eyes, as I make my way around and say I love you to whom do love me in return and who's love doesn't hurt. Who I don't oppress or show myself as unrestrained manners. To always know that I wasn't the one, who would be the right one, and I pray, one day, I'll be free of *this* burden of love.

Seeing you today, I thought would be lighter than it was. I can only love you from a distance and seen-and-not-heard. I am invisible to your everyday life. You go to work and then go home. Loving you is one of the hardest things I've ever had to do in my life. How I needed today *not* to not fall to pieces in front of you and the rest. How you looked so perfect today. You looked polished and you looked so handsome. You are so beautiful in my eyes. I feel such guilt for loving you, and the sacrifices I've made for you in my heart. My heart beats black tonight. How I went into isolation to pray for Mighty Strength today, for seeing you was crushing. I leaned my weary and tired body with my head resting on my closed fist, praying, for my LORD to give me strength in hiding and I needed to get through this mess in my heart. When you look at that, of me, I hope you see my agony and pain, for I had to sit right across from you. Us, and you as you and me as me and the rest . . . with a mirror on the centre of the table. When the day, this horrible day, ended for me, and after I walked away, from such an intence heartbreak . . . . did he watch me? I'll never know, because I never looked back. The aftermath was suffocating. There was no peace in my resting dreams, only dreams of your face . . . . that you invade me, and you're so selfish with my heart. You don't appreciate my love for you. You've hurt me, with such intencity, that my soul was weighed down with darkness. My face was with such pain. I don't want this love anymore, but every time I see you, and then walk away later, I mourn you all over again. I pray all the time that I hardly have to see you. You're words took *everything* from me. You sucked me into this vacuum and I had to go against its wind to get out to have a new life. There was *nothing* I could do. I was so hurt. It crushed me into isolation. I'm working on trying to NOT love you anymore. The pain of loving you, and knowing that I'll never be her in your eyes. When I have to walk away from you, from your always smile for me, and the light that comes on, and the side-ways looks, just stomps on me and kicks into every point in my body. There was no shield for my heart today. How after when I see him, I sleep and dream of him, when I awake, I'm weary and tired and depressed and sad and lonely. I cry for hours. You are my heartbreak. When we danced, and I listened to your quickened heartbeat I've never felt more true, than that moment was. The pain of my heart makes it a rush within me and I can't do anything or deal with anything today. How, 'only in a perfect world' wasn't meant to be seen . . . how it erased like slashes across my naked skin, and gashed my heart open. I didn't ask to love you the way I do. I love you, and that's never going to change. May these words tell you who you are and that's why I'm seen-and-not-heard. The words I've put together in a rhyme; Would my wounded heart, piece back together again? LORD, forgive me as I whish death upon me . . . . as I wish to push a knife through my body . . . pierce it through my sorrows . . . my aches, my pain . . . would you miss me if I died? If I closed my eyes, would I fade away? Should I stay till the end of the day? . . . and then another and another? Just let me fade away into the sunset . . . I wish I could live there. Is that heaven, LORD? As I scrape these words from the grounded in grains that sit and make the machine not work. Clean me, take away my pain from this love, and I beg for my release from my prison of his locked clasp that he shows me every time he sees me. I love you when I see you, ... I love you, I just need a moment. Unlock me LORD, free me. I pray for freedom and one day, He will Grant me a Pardon.

I want to tell you how much I love you. I will love you till yinyears. I will be in your arms forever. It's almost like you're a fantasy now. Are you real? I want you to know, how much I love you. I whish I could love you now, for all I know now. You taught me so much. You're still teaching me. I see it now, because my life has given me gifts I wouldn't't have had if I didn't't experience your death. I don't know your last thoughts. Did you think of me? Did you think of our wedding day? Did you understand the vows differently than I did? What day did you actually die on? What was it like? I wish I knew these answers. And so many more. You are my inspiration. But I know that God's whishes for me, were greater than mine. And that meant that you had to go Home. I had to find me for you and for us. I know you're here with me. You grazed my neck. I trust in my LORD to know, that you're here with me a lot when I write. You capture me and hypnotize me in whispers and voices, they put me in a zone and I just type. The words just pour out of me. You invade me. It's my love for my Christ. Who suffered for my sins and teaching me to carry another's for them. I did. I carried your death as my cross. I wore the burdens well. I entered hell and satan had fun. He tortured my soul. I was his reigns. I saw things that only evil should see, but then, I wore it well and I played along for a long journey. It was when I was in isolation, that I grew new Strength and was learning new things away from church. I was becoming myself. When I survived suicide, when I learned of my gift. And the gift of my writing and the always-wanting-to-start-my-own-book. But I couldn't't be here without the loss of my husband. I battled many battles. But I needed to learn so much. I wouldn't't be unique, like I am now, with all the education I took, which is paying off in my books. I wouldn't give you such recognition you should get. I would never want others to know that your life was in vain. That your life was with great turmoil, and for you, as the only one, ended this journey, but to enter a bigger one with more purpose than we can understand. God's purpose is always first. I understand now, why He called you Home. To show me shit with joy at the end of it. To learn that life is about tests and lessons and good and evil . . . . death, in all shapes and sizes present themselves to you, whether you want them to or not. Whether it was a senseless, and could-have-been-treated ailment—heart attack, murder, and that includes suicide. Death is ugly. It's dark and dreary. Devastation is your everyday life. With such intencity, that you can't breathe. You cry, for hours . . . . you can't breathe. There's only two facts in this life, as you come in, you go out. That's a fact. Everything in between is where you become of one. You live among millions, who also have a purpose, to make this world spin. Whether you're evil or a dedicated Christian, you have a purpose . . . . NOW, that doesn't mean you can just go out now and be bad . . . NO, just that people are who they are for a reason. If you didn't have evil, you wouldn't have princes. Life is about lessons, about learning, about teaching, about sorrow and utter despair, and about happiness. True happiness is when you can say that you love your job like others famous people have done. I don't have all the answers to life, but I've lived enough of it, that I know what I'm talking about. I haven't lived a lot of different lives. But I have lived myn. Maybe I have less shit than you do, but my shit is *my* shit . . . . it belongs to *me*. I'm living my life as I'm supposed to. I'm listening to my calling. I'm obeying very well. I hope that one day, you'll be walking or have been walking the walk you're supposed to too. My sweet Andrew, you lived your life the way you were supposed to. And *your* death has proven to show *my* destiny. Your love lives on and is now a part of history as one of the greatest love stories ever told. That you were my prince charming when you breathed a new breath. Together forever will never mean anything other than you. I hope everyone in life gets a chance to live love like this kind. Who won't let one day go on to the next without showing love. Sometimes life is shitty and you don't want to love, you have to reach for the LORD and He'll pull you up. Sometimes shit happens for a long time . . . and you feel that He's not listening to you, when in fact He is. You just have to shut up and listen. You have to give your whole self to Him. You have to appreciate yourself first, before you can *really* appreciate someone else. In my whole life, now, I can piece it together and bring it all together. But I couldn't have lived that life if you were here and we both know that. You dying was supposed to happen, it is written in history, and your death has had purpose. No one can ever take your place or share your life and death. That it was written in The Book of Life. And I've gained so much strength from that. That our lives are intertwined into each others somehow. How can this person know that person without this person and this person? . . . and so on. How a simple decision that you make, can change an entire life. It can alter destinies . . . by a simple decision that you make in your own life that will affect someone else. Just a simple decision . . . . snap! . . . your destiny, changed forever. That our memories take us on journeys that carry on into our next life. I love you, Andrew.

You tell everyone else how much they mean to you and your life. You tell them 'I love you' but what about you? Don't you deserve to be loved too? Look at your life, examine what you've come through. Your trials and tribulations. Your joys and triumphs. Sometimes you forget about you in the busy-ness of your life. Whether you're a mother, a father, a grandparent, a friend, sometimes you forget about you and your needs. Whether you're single or in a relationship, you still need to learn to hug yourself and say I love you to you. My journey of and through my self-awareness has been a long road. I've had to learn to separate myself and see myself from another's perspective. I've come through hell, and during my off years, I've shed many tears of despair and sorrow, and I want to tell you that there is an end to misery. You just have to wait it out, learn from your experiences and move forward. There are so many heartaches in life, it's how you jump back up and shake yourself off and start over again. My relationship with the LORD has proven to be my salvation. I was faithful, and I never left my love for the LORD. I often told myself that if Jesus can carry His Cross for the whole world, I can carry one. The cross was very heavy and full of heavy burdens. No matter what you're going through, be tight with God. I know that's easy for me to say in not knowing what your circumstances are, but I've survived suicide. I'm a witness to the LORD and how He worked and how He works in my life and the lives around me. Recently, I wondered what the lives around me would be like if I wasn't here. Lives change by others and we're influenced and everyone in life affects your life. Just by a single decision, a simple reaction, anything can influence you and your life. Just think about that. Not only life changes you, death changes you too. My path and journey has included loss and devastation. For many years I couldn't function and live a normal life. I took death very hard. I felt alone, and went through the days of my life in a puddle of guck and horrible experiences that have shaped me into what I've become today. By being strong though, and keeping my faith close to me, even though so many nights when I would cry, and beg in sobs for God to let me die, in any way, to end my sufferings, and my pain. I was suffocating with life and I wanted out. But I just couldn't commit suicide. I made a promise a long time ago, and I had to keep it. I also couldn't bare the thought of someone finding me dead. I just couldn't live with myself with that decision. I walked through shit and slime and had to feel my way out of the darkness that hovered over my life. For a whole year, I went into isolation, and I learned so much about my LORD and how He's helped me so far. Sure there were days where I wondered if He was there or not, and He proved to me He was. He saved my life . . . many, many times throughout my off period. I had to become strong in Him and to know myself that I've come through my darkness and now I can live my life the way He'd want me to. My family and friends were there for me at every turn, but sometimes I just felt that something was still missing in my life. I wasn't full. I'm so grateful for my friends and you know who you are, for helping me learn important lessons in life. I needed to learn . . . . everything. I didn't know how to be a friend. Now I know. But I needed those friends before I got back together with my wonderful best friend, who's taught me so much about myself. I didn't know what it took to be a real friend, but now I do. To get to be where I am right now, I owe so many people. I've learned who I am, what I'm supposed to be, where I'm supposed to go. I have a direction now. I was so lost for my entire life and now all those lessons, all that education, with me learning more about my illness, I've finally become a person that I can be proud of. For all my supposedly 'failures' have turned into so much success. I owe everyone whose showed me, me. I've learned to love again. To finally reach a place of contentment of being me. I've always wanted to be someone else, always envied others and never wanted to be me. But recently, God has showed me how wonderful it *is* to be me. I'm always still a work in process, from where

I've come from in my mind. Total life changed experiences. I can now look at myself in the mirror without tasting self-loathing and self-hatred. I see a face of another person in the world needed to find her path and move forward with a lot of love for many things. I've struggled my entire life with self-image. I've lived boarder-line anorexia. I'm a secret eater. I eat all the sugar I can, then I won't eat for a couple of days. At some point during this entire life struggle, which I still struggle with on a daily basis, I've learned that I'm weak when it comes to food. I still haven't been able to shake that part of my life. It's a daily struggle, but I'm working on it. Another struggle I live with is smoking cigarettes. I have to conqueror that weakness, and I'm working on it, but now, if I have a cigarette, I don't beat myself up about it. Everyone has weakness in their life . . . and food and cigarettes are myn. It's just how you mentally and emotionally react to it. When you come through so much in your life, you learn different coping mechanisms. Everyone is very different. I have my way of coping and you have yours. No one is right or wrong. It's just the way you deal. Some chose things that aren't the smartest, but this world is filled with many interesting people and different ways of coping. Some chose drugs and alcohol, some chose driving really fast, some chose to lay down and sleep, some choose drawing or painting, or listen to loud music. One thing I've come to appreciate myself for is that I know myself enough to know, that how I cope, is very different from others. You have to find yourself in your lessons of life. Every single person is an individual and no two are alike. Even twins are different. Even they have their own differences. But I'm no pro. Everyone is different, and God has created us like that. No one could ever replace you. Learn that you are created differently. You have a destiny, a direction that you must follow to get to where you need to be. You have to meet the people you're supposed to meet to live your life. To become who you're supposed to become for the next generations to follow you. Everything happens for a reason. Whether it's a wrong decision that has consequences that change someone else's life to get them pointed in *their* correct direction. See what I mean? Everyone has *their own* journey. No one can replace you, remember that. Live your life to change the world. Be you, love you, appreciate you. Look in the mirror everyday and thank God for your life, and if you want to make it better, make different choices if needed. Just remember, your life, is precious to your loved ones. They love you for you and would be devastated if something bad were to happen to you. Just like I've had to learn and recite to myself over and over in my head. I've chosen to live, and turn my back on suicide, and love and love some more. I hope my life has shown you another way of thinking about things. I hope my words have comforted you. Sometimes, you just have to walk in shit to get to Glory.

"My Journey on Being a Christian" October 3rd, 2010

My journey of being a Christian has been both very difficult and trying, but it's the best thing in my life. Everyday my focus is on Him. He's showed me a new beginning everyday. He's transformed my entire life. Every decision is based on Him. Well, I try anyways. I'm not perfect by any means, and sometimes I make the wrong choice in His eyes, but I try to live to the best ability as possible. To live as a Christian is all I know. I've never lived another life. I was brought up in the church and every Sunday we went to church. My grandparents /on my mom's side/ were very solid Christians. As a family, we had solid morals, beliefs, love, discipline, respect of elders . . . . you know, the foundation of Christianity. I myself was a very rebellious and mischievous child and teenager. I was a kid. When I grew up into being a teenager, my faith became my own, instead of just my parents or grandparents. I became my own person in Christ. I started thinking differently. Taking things more seriously and testing my abilities against Him. I always tried to 'do it on my own'. I needed to be strong in myself before I would be strong In Him. My greatest need for my life is to be strong within myself before leaning on other people. I had to do it myself, and God knew that. So, He let it happen, but He was always close by for when I needed Him. Just recently, I needed to ask Him for His strength. I was in a very difficult situation, and I had no strength. I prayed for a shield for my heart, but I didn't get that, although I did get enough strength needed to get through it and for Him to help me walk away from this horrible sadness. Being a Christian makes you realize the world around you, and all the sadness, grief, sorrow, desperation, happiness, joy, and teaches you right and wrong. It's harder I think to live as a Christian more than not. But that's only my opinion. In my faith, there's a burden of many loves I wish I never had. My heart gets broken a lot. I fall in love very easily, and when it comes to an end, more often than not, I'm broken into a million pieces. But, I'm also very strong so I quickly pick myself up and shake it off and carry on to the next thing. My faith is all I know and I'm very lucky to call myself a Christian. There are many people in this world that aren't allowed to be a Christian and they're not free in their belief. I'm one of the lucky ones. I love my God/Jesus/LORD. The Father, the Son, and the Holy Spirit. My faith is my entire existence. Even though I struggle for independence and try to rely on my strength first, I know that my LORD will be there every time, even when it feels like He's not even remotely close to me. I have to learn though, and that's what every parent goes through with their children. It's no different than God showing us our way. One of the main beliefs in my life is forgiveness. It's one of the hardest things that a lot of people have problems with. When someone does you wrong, the first instinct is to get even or pay them back for hurting you. You strike out and lash at them, and always remember what they've done to you. Forgiveness, I think, is the hardest thing to do. Some people are just evil. But if we didn't have evil, we wouldn't have good and compassion. If you've been wronged by someone, just walk away. Find within yourself peace with whatever's happened to you or someone you love. I know how hard it is to forgive. I said some horrible words in my day. To many people in my life, to people that I'm supposed to love. Once you say them, you can never take them back. You don't know if that person is weak or strong. My words dug deep, and knowing that I can never take them back, breaks my heart. You don't know what's going to happen tomorrow or even from second to second. Learn from my mistakes. Yes it feels great to get your feelings off your chest, but I must warn you . . . you can never take them back. If something happens to that person, many of you will live with great remorse. Some of you won't, of course, but this is what my Christianity looks like. Fix your relationships with tender words, love and compassion. Things happen in life. You don't know what tomorrow will bring to your life. To forgive myself from those horrible words I said to my loved one? . . . has been a very long road. But, I know I can't live with that guilt if I want to continue living. So, I've had to forgive myself for that horrible anger that I showed. I'm now at peace within myself and I can appreciate myself and love that the LORD has taken that burden from my heart. I'm learning new things with myself and about myself that I would have never learned if I didn't say those horrible words. Forgiveness is not only for others, but for yourself as well. I'm proud to be a Christian and I pray that the LORD will be with you throughout your unique life walk.

"Nympholepsy"

A frenzy of emotion, as for something unattainable. If you have this, you'll completely understand, but I want to write to the person obsessing over something/someone you can't have. For me, this would have to be mixed with self-control. There are many situations that I've been in and I've needed self-control. Self-restraint is so important, and if you're looking to solve something and there's only a one-way arrow, no one understands but by those who have shared in this emotion. When I need to be strong and need to have both of these attributes, I pray, a lot . . . tons. If you're a child, then it's different, but if you're a grown adult, pull yourself together, have yourself under control. If you cave, depending on the situation, you're digging your own hole but if anyone understands the importance of this lesson, it's me. When you have this, you have an ecstasy of emotions that transports your mind into a crazed fiend and enters you like an evil spirit, who tears your body to shreds. This is to me a spell of violent mental excitement. To go into a deep cleft, into a coldness of isolation. To have complete separation from others who don't know what it means to have nympholepsy. You fall, so deep, so fast, that there's no way back. Your emotions are crazed and uncontrollable. You have no need for your emotions, but it sucks you in like you're sucking on a cigarette, and you're controlled by this force of breath. The wind swishes you around like a cyclone. There's nothing you can do, you just have to float with it as though you were in a vacuum of quarantine. So have self control, I beg you. Do you do that on purpose? Do you chase around that hole that will make you fall into this pit? The ecstasy that controls you in this moment, of excitement into another pit and when you fall through that hole, you drop into another bowl and you reach for nothing because it's not there to help with your grasps and it's smooth so you can't grab it. So you wave your arms around and then, you drop into the next bowl, where you're in a title wave and everyone's screaming and grabbing at your hair and they push you under the water so you're suffocating and drowning. You flail around your body to get someone's attention. Then someone steps on your head and pushes you through that hole and you drop onto a plank and you're so tired from the upper bowl that you just fall to your pile on the plank that now you must get up . . . get up, and you're being pushed, even though you can hardly walk. What did I know? Where was I? Where am I? The next thing you knew, you were paddling a canoe and I was in the tapered end. I gasp for breath. Then I blink my eyes and I'm being smeared around your hands and you're being so violent, and I'm being pierced with needles . . . I have to wake up! I scream to myself . . . WAKE UP! So, being in this type of predicament is almost fatal so I better stop writing like this, so you won't get lost in your emotions. To avoid confusion this is joining of letters to make you understand the crossways of different accurate ways I've placed you, to get a message to you. Do you understand? That you'll be homesick if you do it that way . . . if you do it this way . . . hahaha . . . you can't be serious? So when it comes to emotions, try not to get lost and not be restrained under such cruel initial start of the race you must run, no matter what. Take hearten and encourage the comfort they give you and don't bleed all your information into the microphone at the front of the stage, where you'll need to bring it. Be all you can be, and wherever you go and or what you do, do it with passion with no stopping exceeding your accomplishments with so much intence feelings. There, I'm done. Hello there.

It Is Written, It's Done, ... Right?. I feel as though my heart has been torn out and handed over to the next person to rip me apart and shred me. I sweat out the sadness to regain composure to my real life. To see others lives being lived, and see happiness, yet in my own life, I'm sorrowed. Jealous of a life I could have never led. It was/is not mine, so I go on, pretending I'm happy for them, but yet here I am, spreading out my unfulfilment life. They spread it and flatten me out and I have only one choice. To live myn or through them. I don't know why I am who I am. I have no answers for myself. To always question, why me? To live in my darkness and cover my unwilling face to the world. To be the boomerang that has no destination, but just to come back to you. No one wants *my* life. I have to find my fulfillments and act on them, but aching to jump out of myself and live as though I want to live. The world is a big place and I've been chosen to live this life. I know I have a purpose, like she does, but who am I? Who am I supposed to be? To see others lives through my jealous eyes that keep growing bigger. To learn lessons, to speak truth, to walk under the LORD. In knowing, that my life brings me emptiness trying to be fulfilled. I live through the mirror of elsewhere in this roundness and see what others have, and know, I can never have that. All my pain and hurt is another's joy. To know they don't care what happens to me. Why should they? I'm just another face in the crowd to be ignored and walked on. To be someone else's fantasy, to be used and abused. To be thrown out as like with the trash. Just a piece of old food going rotten. I am their garbage. I try to be strong, but sometimes life just hands you a lemon to be squeezed out, with the drops of juice falling to the ground to be wiped up and forgotten about. Gone forever, soaked into a dirty rag and washed out and being vanished forever. To know I can never be her. To not travel her walk. To see her face and know, it's not my life, it's hers. To see her life transformed into a piece of art, waiting to be seen by everyone, into the beauty that she is. Her long black hair, the smile that could be spoken of in times of the future, with knowing that she blows like a tree in the wind and spreads her wind flowing through your hair by the ocean and flies forever across the seas of vastness. The sorrowness of knowing I have to not show her my sorrows of my life, when all I want is to be an unspeakable beauty from a book into the visions of your mind. Her eyes sparkle in the eyes of the picture frozen, captured in forever of time. To capture places around the roundness, to far away places, to freeze a moment in time, that's for her only. To live in captivity and see the failures, to regain strength to live a life that's not hers and my own, to have her electricity of execution of unspeakable beauty. She's been shocked into this life and let her beam in the peaks of life. For her, her words are her expressions, and myn are words put together to show the unknownness of our separate lives, thrown together for the spirit of my feelings. To feel what I feel is a curse of sorrow and despair. Being me is somewhat of a mystery of journeys travelled. She prowls after him, with the soul of a beast within and preys him and shines through his eyes. The pride she must feel in being herself to me. Her lines of her face is heaven in his life and her laughter is her love for him. Your name means part some meaning and reference of the Trinity, which doesn't't surprise me, knowing that your beauty within you is a breath. Your eyes of wonderment surprises me. You are a freeness of a forest and you travel inside of the woods and to find you is in a way far away land. Your freedom is not myn. Envy is that evil place I travel to whenever I'm sad. To see you so happy and you are rich in the sunset of my eyes. Your creativeness is exquisite and your talent is brilliant. My path under the LORD is also creative, mixed and matched words that allow me to be free of expression, but I'll always dabble in the enviness of my heart. Life drives you like a powerful beast taking control of your reigns. You're my friend and I love you. Your life is your life and I continue to live as myself, in my own destiny and maybe one day, be free as you are in you. You're so alive in aspirations and goals which I try to find myn too. You have a style like as a gazette running in the mist of a cloud of mist to invisibility running in rays of sunlight. Out of sight I am invisible. Just another entity living in another part of the lands. I cry to the LORD to give me my own smiles for myself, which is hard to find. My pain is visible to the invisibleness of others lives. The stars shine down upon you, whishing you happiness that you deserve. The hole from heaven looks upon us all, and all your angels are providing you the life journey path that's supposed to be yours. Your face is my sweet poems of sadness that stretches throughout the time. The whispers of my heart signs it's signature of despair through the silver lining to you. Knowing you're successful and wealthy in spirit. You echo within me and let me know that you came to me through creativeness. My silence is my peace of hurts and pains of pangs of my heart. You sparkle like the night stars and glitter in the night, like a firefly finding it's place of landing. May your dreams never fade into blackness or sink into a blackness hole. I feel free now in my release, and you'll forever live within me.

You are majic in my eyes. Your beauty is engulfing as it shows Your heart and shines through Your voice of an angel. That carries the flow of sound into the air that helps the butterfly to fly. How the music dances on it's strings to make sound appear in your soul. This song belongs to You in all Your majic. May the notes of a singer bleed through Your skin and lift you above the clouds and lays you on a pillow of clouds and glides you along the sphere like a child sliding on ice. It circles you, encases your whole being. My poem has ended on your heart lines from with I share my truth. May I be open to hear Your Deity instrument, as Your trumpet blows to get my attention to wake again. This poem is dedicated to You my LORD, my God . . . . how You teach me to fly . . . to fly to another place, far from here. It takes me to a majical time, where the clock remains still. You are the mountain standing in frozenness so we can see Your peaks and Your valley's. Where You once were as you walked in human form. How this ground remains Your carpet. Your divine Character pronouncing Yourself to Your services of mercy and grace. Always carrying through various duties in the operations of Your universe. How my simple wight, a living being, walks on Your sacred ground. A vision of extraordinary beauty of perception through my eyes given to; You, my Aeon. How I stand in pensentness under the greatest of skyscraper views. This is my beatingness that is encased in Your hands, that fall from heaven and land on my pillow. You are my Accomplishment under the next test, as I blow a whistle in my head to get my attention. How words swirl in my head as like cotton candy wraps around so it can water in my mouth. You are my picture in my head that casts a spell of words to spill out of my finger tips . . . that create images of glory in Your captivating stories. You tell them through me. You spell out the word throughout my touch to each letter. I write as though I am painting a rainbow, and colours fly through each line and sparkles fly around your dizzy head. May you be captured and stamped in your spot in . . . everything you do? Of course He'll help you slide down to your childhood, and let sand flow through your hands and watch the stars fall in so small grains that this world is anothers in my hands. As they shuffle in around your palm before freeing them to their world to under our feet. Where they wait for you to pick them up and halt them into the air to fly to another landing place so they can carry on and make you happy. To exchange times from tomorrow unto today where I can sit in my stance and meditate in the upper area, as they throw me in the air and we all fly our own separate ways and fall to the ground and meet our new strangers. Start a new one on that one now and I keep rolling and nothing is blocking so I can't stop. But I keep trying. Boy, what's in my head eh? A little hungry passion that I call my home and my whole. It's lit under my belly lifting me to more and another hight. As I stoop on Your Ezzle and paint the next life's pictures in living colour and filled with splendour. But I don't want to go outside the box here and take you to another world that you don't know about or know it. As I sing oooooooo breathe, haaaahaaaa, I don't know which directing they went in, I'm sorry. I think I'll keep rolling to stop when I get there, make it go to there and I'll concluded in speech with great emotions and matching emotions that don't just happen, I need a reason for saying it. So, in light, what I'm trying to say, is that You're my Aeon, LORD. You make everything happen and this is here and this is my world.

From the moment I first saw you, I fell in love. You sat on the stairs and leaned back, with a huge smile on your face. And from that moment on, you were him. I remember running and jumping into your lap when you met us for the first time. You leaned back to the next stair up and your smile lit up my heart. Your beautiful thick brown hair that was perfect in my eyes. That was the first time I saw you. I go back in time and remember. For our story starts from then on. You played with us, you always let me put my hands in your back pockets and follow you around, shaking you both forward and backwards in jolting movements. Hiding your slippers in the freezer, and you'd laugh every time. You were my hero, and then, I started growing and maturing and I also remember the darker side of our tumultuous relationship. I never understood why, you were angered at me, and, for so many years I always thought you were mad at me. I felt like I was the brunt of your anger and words that wounded my heart for a lifetime but live in forgiveness. I had to feel angry, which was a part of you, so I could figure us out and why I was seeking attention and began lashing out with others that would continue to hurt me. I wanted to fill the void when you left me and that day you told me I could no longer hold your hand, and I didn't understand, and that's when it all started and began all the anger we held and we yelled it out, and then used anger to love me, for I wasn't your little girl anymore. I was growing up. As I became a woman, I started watching you as a man, as a husband, as a father, as a Christian. I began to see a good man with a tender heart. I got to see the softer side to you and your love. So I kept giving chances out like they were candy for a bunch of children. And one day, I needed you to rescue me . . . you saved me from violence. Then, one day, *the* day, the most tragic day of my life, you carried me up the hill to start my new life in my new agony and pain, suffering and turmoil. You then couldn't save me. I remember that *one* time I saw red, from being insane, in another state, when I saw evil, you listened to my horror story and changed it to green . . . and you've never let me see red again. I was crazed with new anger and a vileness that lived in my heart, and I took it out. That must have been heartbreaking. I kept you far from me for a long time. But, one day, I received new eyes from the LORD, and I looked at you in a totally different light. I prayed. For a long time. Sometimes, you always seem to get lost from me, who doesn't quite understand my pain, but I know, for a fact, that you love me. As a mature adult woman, who's praising hers for a job well done. You never left us. You were loyal to us. You had dedication for us. I will *never* forget that. When I look for someone to love, I look for someone with as much honour as I have for you. Everything you stand for, everything you've given me, you are the first man I honour, before anyone else. Sometimes I forget to show my love and devotion to you, but always know, I love you, more than you can even understand. One day, you'll have to make your journey Home, and every time I think of having to say good-bye to you, I can't even bare it. We fought, tooth and nails a long time ago, and sometimes we don't make sense to each other and we still have our little rants under our breaths. We've come a long way together, as I was a young child to a woman of Him, the LORD. You're always there when I need help from you and you always run to my rescue when something's wrong. For you were meant to be myn, chosen, who got to live in this role of my life. And when you say, I love you too sweetie, when I mask my cry.

You captivate my heart to the full extremes. I'm writing to you, please read me. I've waited a long time for you. We're perfect together. You knew the answer to my entire life. You knew it. You delivered that answer with perfection. I'm so happy you found me. Now I get to empty my heart to my complimented soul. To empty all my love. To open channels not yet heard. Your intelligence is lightening and my creativeness is my form. We are the only ones that can be us. Take me around our world. Show me your dream if I show you myn. You hold me with such passion and demanding attention. I ooze into your mould, your chiselled body. I want to write you my heart . . . for you to carry it as a "Love Letters" close to your heart and carry me all day. I will always be with you. We have the strongest connection, here is the LORD. I love that you love Jesus like I do. To know that we can go to church every Sunday, to meet new friends. To pray with you, to know that you're there for the right reasons . . . like me. You looked at me like you knew me for years. Not even one hesitation when you saw me. And then we talked for hours. Starting our life together. Knowing this summer, we created something so beautiful for the start to my new life with *my* new man. I've been praying for you, for a long time. I knew you were myn when you knew the Trinity. Only you would know the answer, because you were looking for me, and I waited patiently for you, with some garbage on the way. You believe. You have blind faith. I like that. I have to let go with you. I have to give me to you. I have to believe in trust with you. And you have to have trust in me too. You believing in me and my gift is critical, and I wait for that answer. I'm so excited to see you later today. To be in a totally different element, together, for the first time. I can't wait. I miss you. I can't wait for you to read this for the first time and see where we started from. I get to write my poetry writing again. To flow into your soul and tear at your heart and flood into it. To learn new places within my contrast. To see deep into his eyes and forget about this world and transform into another. You are my fantasy. I have made love to you, within my heart walls, that had to see total darkness so I could love you the way you need to be loved. You are my "Love Letters". Forever will I write words of love and passion in your ears, and tell you of a new and profound love. I hope to share a long life of unconditional love and intence passion. Thank you for coming into my life when even I knew I was ready. God's perfect timing, right? You are my reward. I never lost faith, I never lost my LORD. I prayed from truth and dreamed of you and your life. Who would you be? What do you look like? So many things are making sense . . . . October 18th. You are just so coruscate. You sparkle in my matching beams, that bounce off each other that shines an explosion-rainbow of stars and galaxies. So many questions. I have so much sadness in me, that lives in me and is a part of me. My pain is who I am and shaped me to the new person I became. Are you strong enough to carry my heavy heart? With my new happiness and joy? Will you love me for all the pain I carry? Are you the man of my dreams? Are you are my missing piece of my heart puzzle broken in half? You have started sowing up my heart and let me heal with a deep scar . . . to know that I've finally found you. How you've given me some more of the life needed to be led, as we parted ways and you stopped believing in me, but I'm doing more with Him, but you gave me hope, and I'll never forget our last night together, as you held me in your arms and listened to my tears and you leaned over and hugged me.

"You Don't Remember Me Do You?" October 21st, 2010

You helped carry me through the darkest time in my life. You loved me with such strength and dedication. Your strong devotion to our friendship will never go unnoticed. No one could have gotten me through those days but you. Your part in the tri-of-us was you. You can never be replaced in my life. You're special. You have this gift of such strength of love. Why else would God choose *you* to be a labour and delivery? You carry a silentness to your heart. My life carries so much sadness. I can never know how sad it was for you to carry me through to when I became strong in isolation. I abandoned life, because my heart was crushed and I suffocated and died for a period of time. You sewed my rags with such love and compassion, and now I'm rich. I had to find myself away from everyone in the LORD. He carried me when I wouldn't let anyone else. He saw my rawness and the sores on my heart that were bleeding within. I was the walking dead. You tried to understand me with everything you had. Your love for me will go down in history. You were called to me from God, and to cry to me that you would go another round with me if you had to. For loving me, that much. Every life has a purpose and they were chosen to live that particular life. No one else could even imagine living the pain you've lived with in being my friend. My pain, my sadness, my tears, to loose another person, is my life. Love has taken me far and I live a very vast imagination life. Being me means that things happen differently, with such power of intenceness, with pain as the side-effects. I sometimes feel that this world isn't where I'm supposed to be . . . my passion is in heaven and the astral planes of the other-side-world. I've been judged for my love my whole life. Now, I'm basking in how unique I really am. My life has a great purpose, and God has blessed me for never leaving Him. I love my blessed gift from Him. I get to love even more intently and I'm finding happiness. Those first words you ever spoke to me, when I was no where anybody could reach me. I'm so glad you were chosen for me to reach me and talk me down from the cliff. For so long I always referred you to a team, and now you're an individual. Someone who needs to know that they were chosen from God to bless my life with a very special chosen friend to show me what true female friend-love means. You were supposed to happen in my life and I love you, for everything you bring to me, for your devoted friendshipness, and for loving me, with such intencity and your needed strength to hold me back from running away again, that will be forever recorded in history. And now we have cherishes in common, and you can understand love in a new and developed way. That you were destined to be you and no questions to ask if you're going to glorify God in your role in God. Your tender heart as you showed me your tears of aching love for a friend, and it's been a while now. I met you at a time that I was the only one like me in the seven of us, but I didn't let that stop me from becoming needing attention. How I looked to you for advice and unconditional love and devotion. How you opened your home to me over the years for important study. I'm so glad you came into my life, for you gave me another special and cherished friend from the same store. How I love her, but this is for only you. How when I asked you how it was, and you said it was alright and I said then you're doing it wrong. How you've made me laugh and understand a love that I needed so badly then, to being well and healthy, and living a new life, because of you two and you as you. May my love for you be published as my first, who am I to her? I love you, my special friend, vv.

23

Why is it so hard to write to me, but not to others? For all my life, I've always looked down upon myself because that's what I've been enlighten. Not intentionally, but in my eyes. Why couldn't you be more quiet? You're not that one, the quiet one. I'd ask can I help you?' The answer was always no. Seconds later, she'd call to do exactly what I offered to do. So I felt unworthy, unloved. Always pushing me at arms length. I seeked as a rebel. I was seeking attention from any body for the lack I felt in me. We never understood each other. Absolutely, other people in the world had more problems than me, but I lived my life, because it was myn, my life, and I had many problems as a child. To finally accept who I really am inside? Also, the main point, to spread the LORD's love for me and to send out messages to the rest of the world. I always compared myself to another person and never accepted myself for, myself. I wanted to push myself aside, to outcast myself and to be moulded into anyone else but myself. I acted like a chameleon to whomever I met. I would agree to everything someone said and if I didn't know them, I'd nod my head up and down and then if I didn't agree secretly, I'd just walk away smiling and in pleasantness. And I'd secretly shake my head and keep my view quietly. I still do that to some degree but with a very select few get my real opinion, but I share it with caution. I hate confrontation, and I hate to make people mad at me. I had to figure out life, my way. I still seek attention from my important people in my life. But sometimes I don't share my thoughts in fear of rejection to my whishes, or have someone change my mind to what *they* want, and usually I cave and do what they want, in secret whishes that they accept me. In so many ways, I'm not independent at all. I'm still in many ways, a child in pain looking for acceptance. I have many regrets in life and I always need to please the people around me and I feel that if I disagreed with someone important I would just walk away instead of saying something I would regret and could never take back. I love very easily, because I made a mistake one day of telling the most important person in my life how I really felt inside. I'll never get over it. Even now, I'm still trying to find my voice. It may still be a small little voice, but at least I'm finally finding it. And now, when I do speak, people hear me and don't shut me down. For many years, I asked myself, do I have a voice? Can anyone hear me? Sometimes it would be yes, and other times it would be, a no. Now, I have my words, and feelings going into my words. I wish I had what I have now, in all wisdom and know her more. More intimately, more deeply. After she died, I got to know her better. Through my grief, my sorrow and despair, I now hear her voice within me, calling out to me, hoping my voice is heard, living a life that was from her. I pray to my LORD and ask for wisdom, and continue to live through her. When I look at her picture, so many unresolved feelings left unsaid, but what should I do with that ? besides just live my life the best I can. I have to reach deep within me to feel and I have to have another state. Fining my voice is also finding my unresolved feelings. I love her, I really do, but I now have to somehow preserve my life and try to make her proud and make something of my non-ordinary life. I'm sorry for confusing you and being distracted with the word her, but you can never know who is her, and maybe one day, I'll forget, like I have now. So thanks for reading and soaking your eyeballs, no matter how many, into my wordvoice. As I read the words of unfinished love.

Maybe *you're* my missing piece. You're my best friend, my confident, my lover of heart from real and only friendship that is out of this world. You're the reason I had to suffer first. I had to find my way through darkness for me to see light. You changed my world. I was lost, starving, hungered within like a rage ravaging me alive. You're my edge of love. My love for you is like the knife that slices through you and sheds blood. I see me through your eyes and it's beautiful. It's nothing I've ever experienced throughout my entire life. Your laugh makes my heart shine brighter through my eyes. I see the light now. Whereas before you entered my life from far away but so close, yet I couldn't reach you. When you walked towards like the most openness of eyes opened and heart. You gave me new love. To know and share our LORD, our Gracious, Miraculous, yet it is written, entrance as you stepped one after the other. I dance with our connection. You are my best-friend-obsession. Are you there? Yes, I am. You have come into me like a dominant force that pierced through my soul. You were my leap of faith, and my faith has served me back. I had to shed many tears to swim to you and I reached for your hand and you saved me. I see through you like you are a mirage on a hot day when you thirst for water. You are my illusion of reality. You radiate love like a microwave with high levels of high frequency, an awesome phenomenon, and now my reality. I need and hunger for your chaos, for one more moment with my *best* friend. You have given me some of the best days of my life. As she shines through you to teach me, about life, love, forgiveness, moving forward, letting go, and more intencity to live forever within me. I never knew life this way before. I didn't know I was worthy of anything higher than a piece of dust. You've transformed my whole structure of my heart. You accept me, and I don't have to hide, behind the mask I wear daily for the world, but I let you into my fort and you hold me in your strong devotions. You're not scared of me like the rest of the encounters of my life. Your words shoot into me as a dagger would it's target. Waiting for me to grab it and aim it back. We are Godly Unique. We are a sole example of what friendship is all about and all the poets recite in their poems. I grow because of you. Your 'hard labour' teaches me, a special individual that you showed me with the presents from God Himself. There's a reason why He chose you for me and me for you. And we learn more about His will for us, His great will, for us to be reunited. His will is more majestic than I have ever known in life. His purpose for your life, for our angel, your gracious and miracle of a mother, is much better than what we could have come up with. She needed to let go of this life, so you could teach me new love. Love seems so little when I say it to you. What would I have done without you? I can't even imagine forever without you. I thank you, my sweet glowing loving friend obsession. I love you, more than this earth can ever give me for you. Maybe you're my puzzle, and I'm supposed to be fit for you. Only you, in human form, knows me so well that you can dictate me, my thoughts, my feelings, my emotions, like you're reading my scribes on my heart. Through His help, you have become my writer of my words. You show me through example and then only you can unroll me and know my truths of my life. I wish we skip off the ground and run into the sky and reach heaven and run and leap with them forever and eternity. One day, in the future, I will hold your hand as we transform into our other selves and sing and dance forever. "Are you there?" . . ."Yes, I'm right here."

Sobbing, now what do I do without him? You? I have reached to the pits of hell. My heart is beating, but it's tortured with plaguing sadness and so many tears and sobbing. To blur through day after day. To know I would never see your sculptured jaw, to know that with every word more tears are shed of missing you today. You can do no wrong today. To never touch your face to say love words and pour my love into you as you fill me up with fragile and intence love and passion of emotions that we entered each other and became one. I was for you, you were for me. Sobbing, I failed you . . . in so many ways. To know what I did to help you make your final decision of your life. To know I can never take back those words I said to you. I'm so sorry. So many tears are falling. To have our babies to stay here for. To know I'd have to live without you. For such a long time. Without your smile to look at when I'm sad, to never hear your voice again except from our wedding video, and that's all I'd have of you for the rest of my life. it's an, I—miss—Andrew—day—today. To only have memories of a life I didn't know how to live properly in knowing how to love you the correct way. To live years without you where the tragedy and catastrophic event in my life. The guilt that made my life a burden of love, that I could never leave my children in that way. To live through the darkest of evil. I suffered through many nightmares. I'd see you and we'd live happily with our children. I got lost in grief for twelve years. I don't remember most of those years now. It's lost just like I lost, Andrew. You . . . my love. Your touch will never run down my cheek in lust and we'd never again get lost in the night together. The words by songs played in the background when we'd explore in our new love and lust. To only have memories now, as I travel back in time and make love to you the way I remember you, and begged for you today in our privacy with an indivisible being, that entered me and longed for you. Then my tears ran down my cheeks. Living those dark days. I'd live everyday in vile compost. I didn't know how to love anymore . . . my heart was rotting in poisonous situations that plagued my mind. My everyday was stamping it's image of living with the words I said to you before you died. To know you heard every word, and knowing I helped your death happen. That a life was lost because of me. How I was so sad, depressed with tragedy thoughts. I'd have dreams almost every night of you and me happy together, then in another dream following it, you died all over again. My dreams were my nightmare. I'd thrash in my sleep. Many nights suffered in insomnia, of crying, of sobbing throughout the night quietly as everyone else slept in peace. To know I had to live for our children. I had to survive suicide every night. Sob through the night and get so tired I'd finally fall asleep after the kids went to school, but have another nightmare of killing my son and hiding him for three days under my bed before I told my mom . . . . This is what happened to me after you died. I couldn't escape anything from you and your death and what I did to you. To swear, that I'd never change that. No one can take my guilt away that surrounded your death. To know that you died alone. To watch my children grow up and watch everything while you lay sleeping in your dead body. I went to your grave faithfully days and months after we buried you. To have to know that that bump is still there, on his unmarked grave. I'd lay on the empty titled grave that I wanted to dig up and lay beside you and die and ask you to meet me at the Doors. To know the last thing you heard from me was; anger, bitterness, hate, revenge, and lethal venom. To know for a fact that this is it for you and your fragile heart. You can not take any more of life and what it had to offer you. To never know your last thought you ever thought. How I could imagine it and I'd go with you. To live my fantasy of death only in fiction. I remember my sadness. I remember that I did some things that could have led to family tragedy. I hallucinated, and strange things would happen to me at night, and it would terrify me, and I had no one to talk to. I wasn't able to grieve the way I needed to. I'd hide my solitude from night time during the day time. I was lost. I learned hard intence lessons. I was lost in the truth and I tried to figure it out for a few years following your death. I was blessed with two very special girlfriends, who showed me the way until mirror came back in my life . . . . To live everyday without you. But know in my heart that you gave me our children and you had to trust me, or, let me pay. To pay me back for being a bad wife to you, because I didn't know how to love you the right way. We got lost in life on most occasions. Then I was your reason for the next change in your life to lead it to an end. I'm not that person anymore. I learned my mistakes Andrew. You're showing me the way now, because I've suffered. I've done my time and now, I'm able to find you and beckon you to me with just a thought, and I forget the past and live with you as my angel and you and God show me the way. And now, I'm focused on life again. On our children and on them. And learned how I could continue on our love through words and watch our children grow up and become adults, and I carry your joy, a part of you lives through them and because of your life, they're going to and they have changed the world. Maybe you needed to hear what I had to say, to show you my renewed strength for my children. But to always love you for the person you really are and to show me my way to today. I've gotten stronger. I'm a woman of Christianity. And I also know that I would have never been able to give my children what my parents have given them. I can only think of it as an act of unconditional love and the many sacrifices they made for the three of us. So then, I remember that your death led us to live a life. I can never know how they helped me and my children. They gave us a life we would have never had if you were still alive, and that's when the rule of life kicks in and takes one of us out to teach us how to live and move on. That I can smell scented smells again. I can see again, but I have a fragile heart now. I have tremendous fear of someone I love dying and me going into that darkness again. It's my deepest fear. But, mirror and I figure it out together and I make it through smoother now through a rough patches. And now I've found my writing. I often wondered, Andrew, and knew instantly, the way we were, and your death would have caused a hole entire life for me and the kids if you stayed alive. I'm not glad you're gone, but I've accepted that it was meant to be, that it was written in the Book Of Life, and to now accept the reason I had to survive suicide. I had to find my life. Your death showed me. Your life showed me. I try to forget our bad and love you now, with you in heaven, and me here, and find a peace within myself, and find my Cross and say a little prayer. My relationship with the LORD is always brilliant, but He still tests me and I have to prove myself every time. And every time I pass, I'm blessed with gifts of friendship and relationships that are filled with devotion, sacrifice, dedication, and with a little rock in the boat. Then I hear love songs. And I think of you, for the past, for all those memories you gave me. I'll probably never get married again, and I'll never have any more children, and I never would have found mirror, and I would have never found my writing passion and the future surrounding my writings. You gave me the best kids. They've had a good, Christian upbringing. I get to watch them do their firsts. But I keep you close to my heart as I watch a graduation, begin to start thinking about love and for them to discover that there is no answer to why love is the way it is. Over the years at certain moments I'm okay and really happy, and other moments aren't so good and it's rough for a while, and it's hard to get through. My heart is raw, scraped up and full of scabs, but I have a strong soul and a strong will for life. And my life is my children. In loving them, I still get to love you in the same way that love is, invisible but there. I've had two dreams of you recently, and today I miss you, then our girl came home and told me she missed you today too. What she was feeling transferred over to me. This has happened twice now with us that she'll feel a certain way inside and because of our connection together, she ricocheted it to me and so I felt the same way in her ripple effect. I get to love your connection with me. You were missed today.

I must be a major disappointment to you. I'm not like that in many ways, and it must show you that when you used to see me. What's she going to do this time? What's next? Always judging me and I'm sure it's very easy to do. Reminding me in the past on a daily basis that I'm not allowed to feel. Always silently cursing me under your breath. I hear it. You made sure you tell me that I'm a bad person, in not what you wanted me to be. I guess, I'm not allowed to say this to you too right? Oh ya, that's right, I can't say this or that because you said so. Reminding me that I'm an only wanting to be seen if in-a-good-mood. Always reminded me every time. Always competed with me. Who's had everything. Always an arms lengths distance, right? That I have to be the mature one and stop bad blood. To always have constant conversation of how I have to forgive you for making me feel like shit. That I have such intence feelings about everything that happens to me. To remember who had control over my life. That you used that to show your chest puffed out and feathers cocked, showing me, who's the boss. How your uncompassionate heart showed me in full sight of the errors, but hid yours. How you used my heart. You showed me no mercy in forgiveness. How your love has poisoned me. How your control had my control. How I must have shamed you, deep inside, that you'd never share with any soul living because it's so dark. How can I feel like that? Easy. I look at her reflection everyday. Deep within, right? How I've learned many things about you. About your secrets you carry inside that you've probably never told anyone. How you stole from my heart. Held with tight fists, throbbing to be set free. How you put limits on me and our friendship, and how you know exactly know how to put the lid on me. How you crush my spirit with your actions towards loving me. How you love to tease me and erase my lines on the board to nothing. You never see me. You show me often how you love another more, but another secret you can never share with anyone. It's shown to me often through the distance from another place. How your love for me has rules. I'll love her today if . . . . she does this today, and walk tip-toe past me like they were sneaking in the night and 'hope she doesn't see me.' You must lie to me when you say that to me. You're so good at it. How your friendship robbed me. You steal compassion and turn it to me and blame me for what's happened. Make me guilty for your guilt. You're good at your games and I've learned a lot from them. How you know everything but show your ness to show me how I'm worthy to kiss your royal feet. How you keep me in your palm with control of a friendship way back. How I had to control my anger for all these years. To show you your wrongs in the world. To show me daily how invisible I am. I waited for you, but you never come. How your love shaped me, and moulded the form. How even now I have guilt for showing my anger. I'm so angered and to shed the blood spilling feels good. I guess you don't understand. Hence my secret anger. I'm your secret, right? Will I love her today? Only time will tell. How your love showed me despair and deepest darkness. How I announce to the world my heart and you have nothing to say. I'll pass by her tonight and show no love. How you've shared being a coward. How your sugar was my self-esteem. How you owned me. You must laugh at me secretly. What a fool she is. You've shown me that I am unlovable and I'm unworthy of your love in friendship and of your trust. Holding everything over my head and dangle in front of my face and know I can only have one choice. Have I let you down so much? Haven't I shown you mercy? Why don't you love me? That must be your secret. How your friendship to me, poisoned a future of not letting go of a friendship so deep into who I've done now in our relationship. Your head games of playfulness and violent slams makes me never want you again and what your life has become. One day, I'll move on and if it's wrong and you're wrong in me, then know, to hide your identity in my poems, with show two. I'll always love you, but one day, now, I will never play your move again. Shhhh, it's a secret, my secret.

"Our Canvas"

I feel empty as like I felt the day after when I did it to him. My thoughts still haunt me from my venomous words, that say that your taste buds show their power under my finger tips. No self-control is my rollercoaster ride that never stops. If you weren't shown, how can you know? You treat my thoughts as though you're going through a pile of paintings. I can skip this one as you pull it forward, I can skip this one, and all my situations are just skipped by with no thought as to the drawing on the canvas. All there is here is a powered glue gun. Plug me in and pull the trigger and watch me spill onto a surface and leave me there and use me for your own pleasure. I feel empty and sad that I feel like shit . . . again. There is no shortage of this in here. It's everywhere and what can I do to release my pain? Put it in the plug and let it do it's majic. Let it fill me with self-loathing, self-hatred, and just sit back and watch whatever happens to her next. You draw what you want, like your illusion, and your fantasy of being a perfect image of what you really want. You don't want my pain. You don't want my thoughts. You don't want to know my hell. Let me empty in silence and I put my invisible cloak on and walk past the crowd that makes me not breathe oxygen. If I could just close my eyes and disappear, I would. If I was the enemy, I'd ask you blow me up as like a terrorist attack. How much I'm sure you wish I was a crispy crème with oozing goodness, but I'm not. My darkness is my daylight and I wear my masks well, most days. How I wish I was attached to life support and I've been in the coma and now it's time to pull the plug . . . and then flat line. There's no joy or happiness for public but for me, it's the best gift ever given to me. I'm better able to decipher how I feel now, but yet to be able to subtract it. As it sits on a shelf waiting for it to be used in your ingredients. How I wish I could just jump off your shelf and run in a hole like a soldier runs for his fox-hole waiting for my battle to win me and take my life. I don't even want to cover my head. I stand up and I stand for your bullet. I give up. I give in. You are not my warm blanket or soft bed at night, you live in the darkness of my daylight. I fight to warn you off, but my shield has your punctures and it's now weak. I recite your motto with a white flag in surrender. I will obey to my master and never let my own have control. Show your pit of hell and let me lie on that and sunbathe. To know I can never let my tears show to you for you would wipe them up like a spilt egg. Swipe it up and trash it. It's so easy to hate myself in your cover. It's so easy to loathe myself with your picture on my walls. Your sins have caught up to me and now they're being poured into my heart shaped canvas and you over spill. It's like a chemical that poisons my blood and then I fall to the ground in a twisted fragment detached from my whole. I lay down with uncontentment and pain inside. I am not your sunshine. I am like the rain that clings to you as a cat and water. You dry off as soon as you can as your hair clings to your dripping face. I am not your pride. I am not your joy. I am your jolt of electricity that electrocutes you. As this is why they walk by like I am not even there. I am saddened by the loss of what I need the most, but they can not give it to me, it comes from another. Let my words reside in you and less be remembered, that you don't remember and wipe your slate clean for the next days work. I'm just a blank canvas, waiting to know how I feel today. I can not go down any further than you've made me from being down there in the pits of hell. It will never shine, the sun in our friendship again and the words can't stop.

It has showed me, in great detail that it doesn't support. I reach for it, everyday, but it's squash, like its shoving me through an old-fashion-drying-machine you lay flat and ring out. The non-support is a twisted mess of unloved chaos. It chewed me up and wretch me out of your stomach. It flushes me and I can't do anything to stop it. My heart is in smithereens and hey, don't even notice that my blood has stained the walls. Things are happening that I don't even want them to know about. Unless it's you, it's not me. It always come first right? There's no softness that I can fall on. It don't even recognize my pain. I am *not* true to you. It has not shown any way of peeling back my layers and finding a rotten core. A core that can no longer make new. Inside I am your nothing. Just a person. Just a face. Someone you tease, play and want to know. My heart is bleeding and you can't fix it, or you don't want to fix it. Oh ya, you don't know *how* to fix it. I become the conversation on non-existents. When I hear it, I leave and become feelings of despair, alone, in my isolation. My head becomes my twin-enemy. I get higher than what I can handle away from it. I want to run, far away, my only way is my escape. My Comfort is my quiet Isolation away from it. I don't know you, you don't know me. Maybe it's better that way. Maybe it's better that he doesn't know how smashed my heart is, that he made me that way as you shine from your stupid existents from under the heavens. So flushed your torture, I breathe in. We're not equals. You're the equations of my not adding up corrections. I am the equation that you don't understand and their history is waiting for me. I'm always looking for approval but I don't get the equal sign. I'm the book binded so tight it can't enter the book or wanting them to read inside me. When I look into the night sky, I see the porthole to my direction and I envision in to the tiny line I have to be to be able to transfer, but this life, and all it's pain and suffering can't fit through it. It don't want your help anymore. Just leave me in a back alley and leave me for the nocturnal and the night. Someone will pick me up and throw me into the trash bin. At least I'll be seen and taken care of. How I don't feel or sunshine now. I am the rain I hate and bitter cold that will end my life. My life doesn't make sense to you and you'll never understand me. That I know. I'm not worthy of knowledge from it, when it don't question me or show intent on listening to me and my heart. I don't want to call out for it, for it's the reason I'm dead inside. I am the accumulation of knowledge of knowing your secrets that they never wanted me to know . . . but I do . . . . Do you know what that means? Do you hear me scream at you? Can I transport my cries into You, LORD? I want to beat you with my pains of my insides. To show it what them created in me when I was insane. One day, to stand on Your steps and cry into You, LORD, so I can be engrained in You and live and you breathe the pain you've caused me. So, fix me and let me plant new sprouts in myn, but you don't know how to, and I must remember that. My mist travels throughout but by the time it reaches you, it's evaporated into nothing. I fix and grab a hold of my mirror and she makes me better because my mirror is the only one who can grab my heart and holds me. You are not my mirror, satan, you are the flush to my naked and raw spirit. I only see the ghost of nothing and the beginning of my high. So satan, take your rotten feelings that you play with me with, take your disgusting dispute-vomit face and place it where it causes you torture, and let God place on you the nefarious and let you suffer in His pain.

"You gave me a life that would have been aching with emptiness and I would have hungered for you for eternity if you hadn't entered this world through me. Only you can live your life. Find your way, and let her see life."

You're not a little girl anymore. You've grown up and now you're coming into being a woman. You're about to learn about love, with everything included. Loyalty and communication are the most important. Then you change inside and everything that mattered in this world, just doesn't seem good enough to the point of exhaustion. Learn to be a woman of God first before you give yourself to any man, but sometimes, if the right man comes along, then you can change from him. Learn him. Stand up for yourself in an assertive but positive and always in a Christian way. As your relationship grows, you're going to grow too. Live life, my sweet angel. Don't let 'worry' win your heart. Learn from others' mistakes. Like me for instants. Always be *you*. You don't have a twin, and I didn't have twins for you to be only you in this world. Change it. Make it beautiful through your eyes. Make a stamp for your life and make it imprint. Always be curious about the world. Be one of those people who makes a difference. Be you. Be your father and me through you, and your lens. Be the microscope for others, in a humble bow. Yell out for the world to hear you. Explore the world. It's your playground. Learn from them and lead a knowledgeable and wise life, my daughter. Be proud to be a woman. Show it. Take care of yourself. Eat right and if you learn more about food, learn and enjoy cooking and eating it. Don't look back when you remember. Be very respectful to every culture. And God would never want you to disrespect your distant relative from Adam and Eve. Would you want them to disrespect you? Feel that same way to them. When you love, love all the way. If he's the one, then give your whole heart to him, and if he's a good and solid Christian man, he'll never want to hurt you, with good intention. Forgive easily. Fighting with your mate is inevitable. It's going to happen. Learn how to talk to each other and be fair when talking it out. And when it comes time to make love, be you. Be a woman with him. Share your wants and desires to him and escape with him to your private spot in the universe galaxies. Be sensual. Don't expect more than what he comes with. If he's a doctor, don't expect him as a plumber. If he's a missionary, don't expect an artist. Whatever he is, let him be it, with freedom involved. Be strong on your own. Pray. Pray that you become the woman with a vocation. Stand proudly like a buck, but in a doe's body. Stand up for yourself. Speak. Don't be meek and mild so much that people walk all over you. Be brave in that way. Show them another perspective, yours. In humbleness find your voice. When you're sad, be sad, but then pick yourself up again and move to what's next. Hang on though, sometimes the rides can pull on gravity and knock you down. When it's time to move on, move on and learn from that experience. Don't forget the past, because it's your helper to make you a stronger and better woman needed to go in time with your life. You are you. If God wanted you to be anyone else, He would have given you another name. You have a destiny and with His help and you developing into a strong Christian woman, you're never going to live empty. Find your destiny. Yours. When you dream, dream big and in style. If you live in humbleness, share with others. Take my pride that I carry for you, and take me with you as you live your life. Live with errors because they're going to help you for the next thing. If you need to be strong, lean on Him. He'll never leave you. If you feel distant from Him, it's you, and your strife. Be the strongest you can be, but when it's time to feel sorrow, feel sorrow. Let it out. Cry it to the LORD, reach out your arms to Him and take Him into your saddened heart and soul, and let Him comfort you on your weakest days. When you remember in your life, hold onto those memories and cherish them and bring them with you wherever you go. When it's time to laugh, laugh and pee your pants. Celebrate life when needed. When it's time say good-bye, say good-bye, but if you need to, embrace it for it's another stepping stone to your next domino. Be a good sister. Be his strength when he needs it. Help him, be his rescuer. Be his pillow when the world is his cement. Cry for him when he's in sorrow and pick him back up and show him the way through your eyes. Let him not forget God. Lead a non-regretful life. Never ever, say something hurtful to another in anger. You can never, take back those words. Words hurt. They can be fatal. If there's nothing more important, my daughter, say 'I love you.' If you feel the need to hate, then you're doing it wrong. But one day, forgive. Figure it out in yourself, then give it a burial. Be unconditional. Let love run your life. Whatever you do, do it for the LORD and humbly bow at His feet and thirst for it. Be great in your eyes. Accomplish what needs to be done. Sometimes, you'll step away from the path and try to make it alone in effort. Be cautious when taking a step away from the path. Learn His voice and when someone is wise with you, listen. Others need for you to come in their lives, and you need them in your life. Everyone has a purpose who will come into your life. Be watchful, curious, learn, love. You don't know their situation, and you could change their entire lives when you don't even know it. Be wise for them. Give to them. You gave me a life that would have been aching with emptiness, and I would have hungered for you for eternity if you hadn't entered this world through me. Only you can live your life. Find your way. Take yourself by your hand and wrap it around yourself and I am your blanket. I will never leave you. If you miss me, all you have to do, is close your eyes and I'm right there.

When you read this, you'll be on a plane or in your new home for a little while. Maybe you'll think of me, maybe you won't. As of right now, you are in God's Hands. I have NO control to do anything for you except pray, every second of everyday that you'll come home, safely. I do know, that within you, there will be a change in you when you return. I will never see who you are, ever again, and before you need to change so you can change the world, you need to know all of these words that follow. In the waiting process of who you will become, I will love you exactly the way you deserve and to apologize to you. You need to hear and read my heart for you. And then when a new heart is born, I get to love him for the rest of my life. So, in this letter, it is me saying good-bye to my young boy who've I've loved so much, to the man you're going to become. I always knew you'd change the world. Even when you were inside me, I'd always say, while holding you in my hands, he's gonna change the world one day. And now, you're off to do exactly that. This letter belongs to you, my first born, the first love of my life. I love you, my precious son. You're a young boy now, but you're coming home, a man. And in not knowing what's to come, I say; To my future, to *his* sons and daughters, I say hello to my future. To my love affairs I'll hold when you come to us. All our love will be overwhelming. I can't wait to see who you are, my future grandchild. As a whole as a family, I must say to the future, in thoughts of waiting for your return and say; we're going to love you so much. I'm gonna be a cool third generation. I'm gonna love you so much and if there's more to love?, bring it on. **But, not yet**. In *this* time, it's not time yet. Teenagers they must be first. Please wait. Because *my* babies are still in high school. My first born, is in grade 11 and he's 16. He just got his braces off about a month ago now. What a killer smile he tortures me with. He's so beautiful, and tall and cool, hip, in style guy he is. His bangs stand straight up with gel and his feathered dirty blond hair, ugg, to die for. So handsome. He is a solid Christian man. He grew up in a Christian home. Went to church faithfully. Recently, he had to raise money for his trip to Costa Rica, and he raised every cent himself. I'm so proud of him, I can't even tell you. I can't even imagine how he's feeling inside. Whether he's really stoked, and so excited? Or if he's like, ya, okay. Cool experience. I haven't really asked him that question yet. Maybe I should, totally. I want him to know how proud of him I really am for this historical moment in his life. I'm so frightened for his safety, but I know, I have to let him see life. To see other cultures, to learn about his world. His precious little soul in my womb. Waiting to be born, so he can change the world. I've become a new person because of your him. At present, he wants to become a mechanic and own a really nice motorcycle. High quality. Only the best for my son. I want you to know, how much you mean to me, my beautiful and precious son. You were my first born and you are my son. There's a special connection to your first born. He was so stunning. The day after you were born, I laid you on our hospital bed, and you lay there sleeping, and I just looked at you. Every part of your new little body that in a flash of an instant changed everything about life and love. He was my first whole love that wanted me as much as I wanted him, and I need him. I hope he hears every word, and carry's it with him. You gave me new life, new love. Let my love be in public eye. See? I love you, my intimate part of my soul, my son. He's had a hard life without having his dad around. I'm very gentle with both kids on this matter now in their life, but this is when you need to deal with it so you won't carry it around for the rest of your life. Maybe I can fight it out of you, ordering you to grieve properly. It's a tough topic so take care of his heart in that way. I've made my biggest mistakes as a wife and as a mother. Many regrets that one day will come and, I can mend with him . . . together. Open him a little bit more towards me and him. He's very guarded, and I hope to be his armour one day. To be the arms he can run to when in pain and sorrow, or joy and triumph. I get to watch you become a man. I wouldn't be who I am without you and you've showed me how to love, the truth. You became my new life in truth and responsibility. You made me a mommy for the first time. My first Mother's Day. My following life after that. The best decision in my entire life was to move back in with your third generation. It gave you a life that I couldn't have ever given you on my own. I'm glad you had them to help raise you to make you into the man that God wanted. For your life to be the best it could be from what it comes/came from. For you to find your true destiny. I hope you've found peace in your heart towards your childhood. I was lost to you. Only a pretend mommy, who was so lost in grief and deep despair . . . and I wasn't there for you *most* of the time. I will never get that time back with you or your sister, but I hope I can make it up to you and your children by always being there, whenever I can, and just shower all of you with wisdom, knowledge, and the most purest of loves. You are the love of my life and you own my first heart. I have many hearts. Each person gets their own, but this part belongs only to my son. No one can enter that one. I found a recording of him, my first born child, as a brand new baby, and he's just screaming, whaling, and we recorded it. I'm talking to him calmly and having a fight in conversation with a lullaby hush to hush him. I'd say his name, over and over again like in a song. As I tried to make him suckle. Finally, you would fall asleep well into the night. I just loved you and your dad loved you too. He was fragile and I didn't know how fragile he was until it was too late. He adored everything about being a daddy to you. I hope, when you read this letter, you've forgiven him and found a peace within. I pray that for you my son, a humble peace from such a devastating hurt. You never let me in with that at this time in your life. I love you through all your pain, all your secrets you hide from me, that it's not safe to share right now. I'm searching for you and I hope one day, you will trust me and know all that love that you didn't know existed for you. I cry for you at night and in my darkness. Because you don't know, really, on how much I love you and how much you make me shine. When you "hug" me, I soak it in, like a waterfall running down me and calming me from a stir. I treasure every second of those precious seconds with your arms around me, just enough to feel pressure around my back. That's all you can give me right now, and I *love* what I get. You're my boy, you're my son. I may not add up too much in my eyes, or even in your eyes at the moment and I know you got the shitty end-of-the-stick *most* times, but know I felt heaviness every time you thought I'd forgotten you and when I had forgotten you. I'm sure those were difficult times for you, thinking I didn't love you as much as I loved your sister, but you're *DEAD* wrong with that one. It just worked out that way unfortunately, and I hope one day, you can forgive me for being a shitty mom to you. I hope as you age past this "Love Letters" that you remember them and know that I made many sacrifices that I will never tell you or your sister, and that my illness, gave you a better life, and that it was a gift for the future . . . when needed, and as you read these words, may they comfort you. That I loved our late night talks when you'd be laying down and when I'd pretend to leave, you'd be abrupt "no" and you'd reach out your arms at lightening speed to keep me near you. All those times you cried for me and I couldn't save you. Well, I want to. To show you . . . my love for you, the only 'air' I can ever breathe in so you intoxicate me. While we were in our separate lives in the same roof, I was being prepared and so were you, to be strong, on your own, to always have hope for a future with just us three. And why shouldn't I have this dream? Of one day, have just the three of us again. To continue on from when your father died. To take a step towards getting a schedule back, from when you were a baby and I'd get you up and dress you, feed you, play with you. To jump ahead fourteen years, to regain the motherly role in your late teenage life. I can't wait to be free with you, to show you a mother you haven't known for a very long time. Hopefully to become your friend, and maybe one day, a beautiful and once-in-a-lifetime embraces to follow. I want to feel you, that connection that's just waiting for us to leap into a new life, for both of us. For you to finally know why I love you so much, and that I've been wanting to scream to you. I'm your mom! . . . love me back! For the first time, in our new way, to carry on from when you were just a young little boy. I have so much to give you, you just have to receive it. My love . . . . My Eric . . . .

I'm scared for our friendship. I feel we have a cracked and fractured heart towards each other. I'm very scared and I feel opened up and left to rot. I heard you say it three times. I knew at that moment, our friendship had changed. Your planner changed. I see that, with a broken heart and retreated into my isolation with sufferings and joys. My body tingles with fear of loss of something so sacred and rare and unique and wonderful. Whether it's this big, or that big, let me in, and now you're almost gone to me in your eyes. What would I tell? It would be my greatest nightmare if she ended us. I would be a pile of rubble getting flattened onto gravel rocks. I would die all over again if I lost you and your friendship. You're my BEST FRIEND. No one deserves that title with me but you. You showed me about love shown in the right ways. You opened my heart and set it free. I would be lost forever if you left me. How something so right, go so wrong . . . . How those repeated words keep reciting it in my head and for me to even imagine never seeing you again, I would die from a broken heart. How I would blame me, for such a stupid word that wasn't typed and then deleted. The air of my breath would be captured in my newly death in life, and live on and be successful, but only in the LORD. I would lean on Him through the next darkest days in my next living day. I would become nothing inside, worthless and a piece of shit and feel it in silence. You are the doe that sings and runs her leanness beside her doe, leaping with butterflies and flying off sparkles of dust. You are my healing place. When I'm broken, you have the glue to piece me back together, when I'm broken from a fractured heart and I can't split us back to when it was just us. Life came calling and wants and needs was gone in an instant. Back into silence of being an only living soul. Living through a blur of a time of ago, would be a catastrophic event in my lifetime. Misfortune and a failure of keeping something so yintimes that would live in me like part of my flesh. I would spit in my face in vain if I lost you forever. I would loose my self in the grains of sand on a cloudy day and get drowned out of the oceans and be lost to you forever would be unbearable. I would be ruined. No smile could wake me up like you can. And I once again value the hatred of yellow of knowing that I let it out and now I live in clouds and thunderstorms. How I could sunbathe in hell for ruining us by my vile and poisonous tongue. How hail is blowing against us with it's gusty winds with storms never ending. How we'd be floating alone in this hard life. How my world changed in an instant. Snap . . . aaaannnd, gone. Our soul uniqueness would be gone, disappeared in the storm as we reach to reach out but is blown in it's circle. How I would become one. To never touch a delicate soul in my lifetime . . . to only reach and get memories would make me go mad and frantic. Always in agony with all the poisonous ventricles surrounding my blackened heart and growing thorns. I would die without you. My dreams would die and I would become nothing. My new love would have a burial to never to be resurrected again. These words would burn in my eyes and blind me from shining glass. I would cease and come to an end. Love would never be the same. I would loose. YOU'RE MY BEST FRIEND. Please don't leave me . . . just like everyone else who's loved me, leave because of myself in look who've I've become. My heart is only open because you're blessed. You have a gift of knowing me as like no one has. Will we say more? Are you there? . . . I don't know, and I'm right here.

"Catapult"

November 18th, 2010

You're gone. Just like that, like a puff of air rushing through milking it's way into the galaxies. You were here for only a second before you were shredded from my body. Under the ocean I look up and know I can't make it there without you. The sun beaming down onto you. As the leaves breeze from around you. The ocean carries your dangles in their waves crashing on the shore of life. Then, the floor beneath us shakes, and shakes me up and puts a stir on me. I'm in their circle of wind and I wait for it to stop. You write my heart, with Him directly connected. "Um, yes, is the LORD there?" and tells me what to do. Showing me the floor I need to walk on first. He shows me into The Room and lets me stay, but only in my dream . . . . For real life just isn't wasting time. I'm called back to my shores, but it's only an image, frozen. It was given to me for only but an instant. Cracked in rocked gravel that falls from the other side and just lies there. This can't be happening to me again. I wish to be your sliver with wings showing me the way out. How you are a magnet that searches for then connects and press me on with a touch, and when you touch the mirage it echoes *in* your touch. I'm washed up on the shore and feel heavy as I leave the water with deep intentions to stay. Then a swoop from above and carries me to another place and lets me catapult me with claw scraping my new pathway. I'd be on my own, not shimmering with light and light blue. I am a dream of your conscience. Living someone else's dream that will never be myn. She has let me go. My other half has laid down as I fling around a globe but not laid to rest. To reach the height of expulsion, into my next air. Your spirit floats adjacent to me. As we smile to our eternity we stretch out and swirl in our candy store. I land on solid rock. Ouch!. I forgot. I can only float for only a while, then I'm ravaged again to the mid air journey. I reach for imagination as I take you into a make-believe fairyland. But I can't, because it's hot out and I'm so thirsty. You make me feel eased when in your presence. And you spill all emotions and feelings and you make me free. I bow before Him and share my deepest darkness in my soul and breathes new life into me, He reaches me every time. I speak from my heart and I tell all. Only in my . . . . whoosh! I'm caught in a title wave and under someone's surf. Tell my story and I'll tell yours? As we both say everything we've ever said to each other in our scrolls and they unravel before us. Our laughter, our tears, our sorrow, our pride. Things changed in your noun. I swallow my newest life and create until I become a million sand grains that lie under your shale. Millions of yins away from now, will be us again in the cycle of everything. When the big circle gets stirred up and grinded to who we need to be again. Crushing us into another new life to meet again only to be rowed until the end will come a million miles upon yins of rope to roll up. This one comes from that one, that one comes from this one and we unroll because it's too big for the sky of forever. Any colour, any shape, if there even is any, and lay it under you and run down the hill with the confetti spilling into your hair. But wait! . . . I'm not done yet . . . Don't you hear me? . . . so I speed away into the yens of riding free with no fear of falling, lifting him and spinning him around as we sore to the Deity and asks if we can have another forever . . . of course He said yes. He knows we're not going anywhere far where He can't see me. Oh, I was wrong, oh, I was right. Trying to figure it out is the blow-dryer of a giant size blowing our hair and our cheeks puff out because the wind is so strong, so let go. Be anything, and thank goodness for some more.

I write away, clicking the next letter beside each other making another word with meaning and emotions. As my thoughts are racing to form another sentence, I'm eager to see the next thoughts. I rebel against my wanting schedule and try to write anything inspirational. I miss passing stroke after stroke to make something anew. As I imagine standing under it's archway to overlook the city's streets, as it stands in glory all on it's own. You show your point to the sky and know, you're number one in all the world to me. How I long to stand on your public viewing point. Right now, you are a picture, a statue in my beautiful room, how I love you and you're unique and you stand tall on your spot. The breeze blows my long hair in the spring winds with the smell of your everyday air, but to me, it's new, fresh, and dazzling. Your splendorous and magnificent wonder in your life is in my imaginations, and I go to you often in my daydreams and when I see you in real life, I'm going to run to you, embrace you and fall all over you. How my dreams are coming true one day. You are my mystery. You are my arrow that points in the upright position, and when you point your arrow in my direction, I will be your target. How many love letters are there to you? How many more have you inspired ? in poems and books? How you bring love together in your view of architecture and bricks made to make something beautiful. How I grab you and soak you in, but only from a picture hanging on my wall. How the winter cold comes to you and doesn't share with me, but in the spring nights, the lights you have light up the city and you make it wonderful. How your structure stands so famously and everyone knows you and who you are. You are nothing but silent as you stand in your place. You know where you belong and you are home. You can't wipe any tears that may fall but you catch them and make another dream come true. The trees stand in your face and loving beside you with a pathway that many have stood under, have stood beside, and have stood on your deck. Love is your title in the pages of history. Your beauty is the structure of metal that is your person. I beg of you, take me away to you, take me to your desire to bring together, but even as I stand alone as you do, I love as you do. I wonder, the people who raised you from ground up, who they were, how they felt, who left their mark, who is engrained in you. May your rivets tell a story. The men who hammered, the time difference from then to now. How many you have carried up your stairs to have you sway in the wind. How you are so special and romantic. How you endured almost being demolished, but spoke out and now you stand, in every right, where you belong. You are a reminder of the revaluation that royalty opened you up to the entire world. How many secrets you must have, and to be a fly on your elements. To scratch my name in your painted surface as your peak of observation to show the ground many feet below you. How your tower was become from the iron lady. How in those days so much saved you *because* you're a lady and you spoke from your heart. One day, I will go to my iron lady, and bow on your decks and feel you under me, in front of me, and all around me. You show graciousness in your majesty. You wear your crown with brilliance. I will walk under your arch to the entrance to look at the history of your story, and I will stand with an awe in the air. Tears will flow from my cheeks and know, that I have finally met, the lady of my heart, my soul, my dreams, my imagination. I love you when you invade my visions of standing in your presence, and how you complete me in the view of my *La dame de fer.*

How you have so effected my life. I write you, over and over and over again. One word you would type in reflection in what I've written. Is it a mistake that I loved you? When I'm away from you, I try to forget you live, and turn you away, in so in to oppression you. Is that the word? Yes, oppressive I made you. Well, glad to be rid of that, I'm sure. Great! No more her to get in my way of my life. How foolish of me. But, you are such a good spirit despite all of this. I don't know why I love you. I just do. An intence connection on my side of this one way love affair. That my imagination brought you here every night. I don't know what happened in me every time I saw you. I keep it close to me and not share much. All those letters, poems, and now giving you a burial. You showed me my strength and my destiny, so all those letters were preparing me for what's to come for me. To show my heart to everyone, so show my emotions. And that is my life. And always intence. I have to have it immediately, that's just how I live. To grieve one and plead my love and devotion. He fell in love. I was lost forever. My heart just *fell* out of my body. I found out on a balcony he was now engaged. I couldn't pray that day. I knew it was over. My dream was gone forever of living in his world. Then for him, to say those words that I left. I found isolation, insult. I was forgotten and unwanted and unloved, by so much that made us inseparable for so long. It's come to this now? I'm once again ready for your punches, so knock me down, show me how you're a man, showing me my errors I'm sure. Bitterness lives in my mouth but all I can show you is love. How you showed me on being my friend without another connection. To be loved by you was an honour. You showed me love for many years, as my friend. Showed me what *real* Christian men are like. To show me a place of honour I hold for you. I know, a million percent, I would feel safe in an extreme emergency being with you. You are such a good man. When, even still, when I'm asked of good Christian men, you're all on my list. You sat, and read and listened to me. You are the epidemy of gentlemen. And I'll never stop loving you, even a glimmer you won't see it. I can't look at you without echoing those crushing and suffocating words. That you didn't know me at all. I crawled into a pile, and lived in misery, for a whole yin. But, I found a new and brand new strength from the LORD and within me. I found my destiny through loving you and loving you was worth it to me. You're a good man. I'm glad you're happy and you're life is important to me and I treasure you and your goodness. I'm happy now too. I found my joy. I found out who I am. I found out my LORD. I found my feelings and emotions and I'm able to express them well. To plant a seed, a word, a sentence, so you know how much I loved you and you'll always have a piece of my heart and I'll never get it back, so I've asked the LORD to heal it. To end my sufferings when I have to see you, to not look at your face and continue to haunt me. To make me run from you so fast that I *have* to run from you. You suction my soul right out of my body. Such force of pressure I forgot to breathe. I have to run in the opposite direction before I let you see the pain in being separated from you. I can't look at you and I wish you were invisible on those gusty days. I want to be invisible, I don't want to be here LORD . . . I scream in silence. Don't look, just make it through, then run. Don't look at me. You make my heart sore. I lean on my LORD, and I fight myself to be strong, but I don't get strong. I become a vulture meal. Don't talk to me. I went to another place that I want no one to see. The pain I suffered in knowing you thought the most horrible thing of me. The tears, the longing prayers whishing for them to come true. How you used to play with me and get my goat. All those teasing moments. I was your focus never meant to happen. How I looked at you, in so much love. All I wanted was something that was to never happen. Someone else owned that spot. To see your daily smile. To love such an amazing Christian man who doesn't know the word 'no'. That's his best quality. Such a pure love that he pours out to everyday. To love. To help others. His only fault is he didn't love me back. I'll never live with another regret. I loved you as only I could, but it didn't fit your puzzle. Both noun and verb. I see the best in you and it wasn't meant to be said out loud. How my love songs never come true. The only dance. When I'd run them through and your smile was always present for me, dangle . . . dangle . . . dangle. To have this piece in dedication to me, to know I loved you for a purpose, for you to hold my life. I take comfort. For my emotions are strong. I live in them and I can't get rid of them. Don't look happy to see me in the second you look up and there I am. Look away to your other side. I don't ever want to see you again, but some will take that well. And I'm sure you're glad to be rid of me. Like the other one does too. Blessed be the day that she walked away. I tuck in my head and hide. I ask the LORD, again, to give me strength to see you so I have to prepare. I can't wait for the day I don't have to worry. How I whish to not know your sights. How my love for you will be recorded in history so know that your life has a purpose. For me to write another beautiful "Love Letters" to show you from this perspective of someone you never really knew in the end. To show you the burial I had to have in your honour. But knowing you doesn't understand that. Knowing won't cancel. It won't bring back my heart given so freely of choice. Not given the option to choose. I give you *this* piece of me. To let you know how I wanted to love you yins day ago. But only from a slide show motioning your life in front of me as all I hear are crackles, due it's not my life. To pour out and shed in the light of the world. To only share my words of the past that I'll never forget. I'll love you forever and not even *you* can stop me. Why would you? I only whish for one to love me this much of a connection I haven't yet found again. To readily know that you have a second heart that comes from your love. But I loved you first. It's just another side.

How You've created in me such poetry and flow onto the next following. How I reach for You when I'm struggling in isolation. Such emotions to deal with. How I love my Number Three. It surrounds me in love and dedication and devotion. "Can You hear me LORD?" I need to plug in our plug. In direct Light in the shield of my shade. To listen to me while I hid in secret, and blew it all out of me. My Best Friend who knows everything. I say with a stiff upper lip. I'm serious about my Trinity. I know, I'm a total crazy and out. You let me be so inventive, so creative, so opened up. I reach for the sky and You give me Glory. You give me words of a poetic sentence. You are my Inspiration and You're my Goodness. You are my It. I would say good-bye to my angel to go with You, if in a spot. I live in faith, everyday. I plead the same. For He is Good, and Pure in His love for you. When we separate, for any reason, I always come back. I bow in weakness and ask for Help. I surrender to You when I'm desperate. When I feel crushed inside, I touch You. To see on my Day, I can only imagine in my dreams what's going to happen to me. Will I fall on my knees at Your Feet immediately? Or will I be separated from You, because of my terrible sins? I will never forget what I've done to some in this world. Will I hear the voice I long to hear on That Day? I see him and I run to him and take him in my embrace and he hugs me back. I say hello to everyone and make our way to the LORD. Hang out with Him for a while then go see my House. And there they'll all be waiting for me. How I get to get permission to become an angel to watch over them as they lead theirs. And then like spend forever playing and traveling. Live in my City of celestial elders. Grab your hand and bring you to me and wrap my arms about a thousand times around you, then I'll have a question and we'll go hang with Jesus for a while and sit at His Feet and listen to Him tell His story of when He lived on earth. I get to meet the man I'm most scared of being in the time of need. To never again have discomfort in skin and pains. Then after we listen to Jesus' Story, we ask permission to fly around the universe for a couple of hundreds of yins. How I'll never let go of your hand when you reach me. I can't even imagine no forever without spending it with you. Please, you have to be there on my Day. I've waited for so many years in a timed life to see you when I'm dying. To never feel pain again. To never have to cry for sadness due to some new tragedy I'd have to live through, so the next step could be taken care of. Where I'd run to you and we'd walk down every street. I'll never feel guilt again. I'll be free, forever. I'll be free of remorse and deep sorrow. Such regrets. Like slivers piercing my skin in every second of every day. To never have to echo in my head, I'm worth it, I'm really worth it, no questioning, it's gone and I'm in Perfection. My thoughts will be renewed with Goodness and no evil. No tug-of-war inside my head. I live with only my imagination when I think of Heaven and the Royal City. It's only been in movies and books and in the most beautiful spots on earth in pictures. Some of the most beautiful poetry in the history of man written on paper, but nothing . . . can grasp of what It's really like There. When at any Time, I can call out for God and He answers me when needed, but still knowing that nothing can get passed Him and to love him in open, grateful in my old heart to see him again. To grab his hand and to NEVER let go. To forget how to love him with my earthly heart and love within a ghost.

If I were to beat myself up tonight, this is what I'd say; Ya, like he'd ever consider going out with me. Not even approachable. He's the second best looking man I've ever seen in my entire life. With your language in tow. You're so gentle to me. You listen to me and you bend over backwards for me. I can only fantasize. You're beautiful mane with pinecones visions ahead. So chiselled in stature. So put together, business man . . . with a heart. So handsome as he just strolls in, like a knight-in-shining-armour. I dedicate this to you. When away I forget, but then there you are and I forget to breathe. The hands that put me at peace when I go . . . . Let them never figure it out, as I say my peace. I linger as you tell me I'm sick. As I tell you my story, you don't know what to do, but you give me constant love and compassion. I tell you what I don't them. To have such an amazing heart. The puzzle fits. She is a gazelle in beauty in my jaunting haunts. So radiant as she enters as she's dressed in red. Perfect in his eyes. So lucky. But, no one will ever want me. I'm not perfect. I'm broken and fragile. Who, but him, could ever love me like that? Only him in reincarnate form. But, . . . that'll never happen again for me. I get to watch it surround me as I know my puzzle will never be filt. Knowing, I have to prepare. As you comfort me I say. Nothing is complete or making sense. I know. It's supposed to be that way. I sit, vulnerable. Isolation and quarantine is my home, I know it well. Let this be the Letters that doesn't fit together and lets talk about some stuff. So, k, what kinda' stuff right? I guess I have to pick the next topic . . . ? Well, I know a lot about pain and suffering. The agony I've been through. My heart was smashed and bleeding and gore spilt all over the road. It was just trashed. It took a very long time to recover. I know a lot about isolation as I did it. But I learned a lot from isolation. Sometimes I long for it, so I can let go of my dark side and put it away for the next play. How I let music write for me, but so does the stillness. But not now do I ask for the notes of music lead me into the next thing. I want to think of the most randomist thing to bring me to the next ray and where it could take me. The doors were shut so fast today LORD, not even a chance to survive the crash of today. So hard for me to think of today as a success. I failed at everything I've done. No 'brownie points' for you. What can I do right? So, I write. Words are very powerful. Be careful of your words. Words are my life, and everyone is my disability or ability. Everyone is different. But when I'm in disability I learn to be strong, and in my ability I learn to be stronger. I never know what kind of day I'll have today. It's always unpredictable. No warning to warn of the title wave. I guess I'm intimidating enough to cast fear. What would you do if the sky was to fall upon us? I'd reach up and watch my LORD call me Home, but only if they were too . . . only. If I only had one day left. Oh the past words taking ahold of my feelings in the music that was through my childhood coming into becoming a woman . . . of something. I don't know yet. It looks more and more hopeless sometimes in my dreams. But I have to believe He has a better plan for me than I have for myself and I just don't see it yet. So, I just have to keep breathing until my time limit stops. I wanna go forward and see where He takes me. What else can I learn LORD? Show me the Way. Let my dreams come true. I pray for my future. That one day, you'll be seeing me. That I may have many riches and many successes. To change the world. To finally be someone who matters.

"My Dreams"   November 26th, 2010

This is why I need to write. As directed to follow; I've only dreamt *it* in my head now for the past few years and more recently, in my dreams, but I've seen my house, at least some of it anyways. The lines are very clean, contemporary style. White walls, white carpets, with a fireplace on the left side with a protruding mantelpiece and floor. Very white and lighted where needed only. I've been dreaming of houses and rooms upon rooms I've dreamt of throughout my lifetime. So somehow now, it must be coming true. But, if it doesn't happen like that with the secret room, it's okay. We live in Maple Ridge in a very quiet spaced out neighbourhood. I have a nice backyard. Fenced in, hiding in my trees. Where I can play with my dog and have her bark and not worry about people complaining. We then come into our lovely kitchen with my favourite feature, tied with it, it's an island and stainless steel appliances. Matching the rest of the house style. I love to sit on both back decks, whenever I want to, and have free freedom. To be writing full-time and know I must work everyday. As my career and hopefully be under contract and just write and write for at least five hours a day, or until Done. I can't wait for that part, I can't wait for all of it. To be paying a well deserved and really wanted mortgage. I've wanted this and it's taken me far in the last decade of my life. But when I get out on my own, I want it to be all the way. Along with control on everything that's a factor in my life, along with that, I'm changing my diet, and my new diet is going to be fantastic. Try to down some of my own cooking and I can't wait to cook in my *very own* kitchen. To start fresh with new everything? That's what I want more than anything. To be able to clean my own house on a sunny day with my music turned up without worrying about parents. I'm going to love my bedroom. Its really big with a very nice on-suite. Big master bathroom, with a separate bathtub/shower. The shower has to be nice. Rocky-looking flooring and tiling, glass shower stall with a walk-in-closet. It's going to be unbelievable. To conform into a whole new person to them, to everyone. I don't know what that looks like yet, but when it does happens, I'll have to dig my heels in and try to hang on for the ride with them, right beside me. To see my son being a man, buy his first motorcycle, to witness my daughter transform into a woman and have a career. I can't *wait* to live with my children. Along beside me and my children, as mentioned above, I can't wait to get the most beautifulest, Golden Retriever. She's going to be just unbelievable. Can't wait for those days that are so far in front of me right now. Like it's never going to happen. I just have to keep writing everyday. Write with purpose for all my dreams I want to become a reality. This is it for us. If I fail at my writing, this dreams, this huge dreams, will only be that, a dream. If I fail at this, then everything's over for us. This dream will never happen. I *need* to write, it's a *necessity* in my life. I want to work for my mortgage and my future life. I want to be a successful writer/author to many books and to live my wealthy and Christian lifestyle. I want to go shopping and buy whatever I want, whenever I want. For so many years they heard from me, 'I'm sorry hun, I can't afford that this month.' I *never ever*, want to say that to them ever again. You want a leather jacket? Oh, okay. Lets go. You wanna go to Red Robin's again tomorrow night? You want to see that movie? Oh, okay. Let's go. Then, when it happens then, that I've been praying about and working towards, and by this time and that time in the future, I want to be debt free. I've waited my whole life for this moment. A new life for me and my kids. Very excited about that. To figure out my new schedule. To get to unpack in *my* new home. I'm very excited about that. I'm living for this future now. I'm preparing myself. To learn a whole new life that will be shedding in my life when we all move out. A different life. For us *and* for my parents. Let them be as a couple with no children to worry about. I know they love us. We love them and that's not going to change just because we live in different addresses. I love my parents, and I need my parents. I just want another life that's been waiting for me, calling out to me, reaching it's arms out to me and when that time comes, it'll embrace me and teach me more life lessons to learn from. For my kids to be free from someone else's dictation. To learn how to be a full-time mom is going to hard sometimes. It's going to be a whole new experience. See, this is my dreams. That's why, I *have* to keep writing.

This is just going to be gibberish babble talk . . . . say whatever comes in my head. So, I'm really proud of my kids. They're both excellent children. I pretty much got the best two in the world. I'm bias though. The other day I went and talked to my son for about fifteen minutes. Then when I went to leave him he immediately left the living room and followed me down to my suite, and when I sat on my couch he sat on the stool to my immediate left side. I had to walk around my coffee table. He didn't even move when I got up. It was awesome. I got to spend more time with him today when my mom and my daughter went into the store. We figured out that if I write once a day in this book, I'll finish my book by next July 2011 sometime. Speaking of next year, the very popular vampire series, will be coming out with the next part next year, so I'm really excited on collecting the series to the end. That author is my inspiration. I hope my books come to life too. That would be so excellent. I'd jump all over that. So that makes me want to be a better writer. To be my unique self and bring life to my books, just like she did in her series. I want to become a famous writer, to be known world wide. To have a lifestyle that fits my life dreams. Travel, a large home, dogs, money in my bank account. I wonder if anyone's ever melted a brain to liquid form. That would be so weird to look at. A bowl of brain juice. I wonder if you'd get smarter if you did that? Maybe I've discovered a cure to something. So, if you're a scientist, I'd love to see that happen and let it be the cure to cancer or something miraculous. Melted brain juice. I'd love to be a scientist. To know what they know? So much details of information, it just is so fascinating to me. So, I wonder who you are. Are you a male reading my book? Is it entertaining? What made you pick me as a writer, and not the first book you looked at? Has anyone told you how handsome you are? For you to know that is so important. You have some meaning to everyone in the world. You were chosen to live your life for a very specific reason. You have a purpose for this life. Maybe you're a doctor and you save lives everyday, or you're a pastor and your faithfulness to the LORD is your imprint and one day, you'll save a life by making a phone call to someone in need. Maybe you're a teacher, who *really* loves their job and loves teaching children, maybe you're a chef, who takes pride in their work, who cooks to perfection and cares about his customer. Maybe you're a photographer, who's job is to take pictures that could affect another's life through visual projection. Maybe you're a stay-at-home-mom/dad and your love for your children touch them so much that they're whole destiny sits in your hands. As you sit and read these words, think about your life, think of everything you've come through and you're still on your journey to change the world. *This* is my imprint on *my* life. I've been blessed by your eyes, and that is my success. If you spent money for this book, you have changed *my* life, because without you, I wouldn't have the success I'd want to achieve. To entertain you and keep you wanting more from me as a writer. To spread Light to a dark world. To maybe share inspirational stories from my own life that could maybe help you in some crazy way. I always knew that I wanted to help people in some way. I just never knew that *this* was the way. I feel somewhat responsible to you now, that you keep reading the words I keep writing. I'm here to warn you too. To express how important loving another person is. It's a challenge to love some people in your life, I know, and I don't know *your* situation, but if you love, then you're complete. It's all about love. All you never know when it's the end. Every second into the future is a mystery, and no one knows from second-to-second. Make every second count with your loved ones. Make sure you're solid in who you are to other people. Be you. If God wanted you to be a super star that the whole world knows, you would have been. He made you to be *you*. If you've hurt someone close to you, have patience with yourself with getting through your situation. Be strong and maybe ask for the LORD. No pressure, in your own time if it's supposed to happen. Maybe your life is lead by another religion other than my own; Christianity. Maybe you're a Buddhist. Maybe you're Muslim. I can reassure you, I'm not a Bible thumpin' kind of girl. Just know that God loves all His children and that includes you. My life has taken me on a rollercoaster ride. I'm sure you've had quite the life too, eh? Just because we don't know each other, doesn't mean I can't spread my care to a complete stranger to me. If there's one thing I know about myself, I have a lot of love to give away. But each person gets their *own* part of my heart. Some think I love too easily, maybe that's true in the case of me. But I'd rather love than hate. It's so hard to live this way sometimes. I always live with guilt, in thinking that I didn't love them enough. I have so many regrets in my life. But if I didn't make the choices I did coming through everything, I wouldn't be writing this book and I'd probably be homeless and living on the streets. So, I learned to appreciate many things now that I never did before. What a life I'm living. So many lessons I've learned. Such strength I've found in myself and in the LORD. For my life though. Your life is different from mine and it's not a competition or my story is better than yours. Think of it this way, there will never be another Einstein. He's the only one. Same to you. I hope I clearly sent my opinion, but in no way telling you to be another person. You are irreplaceable. I hope you're able to travel in your lifetime. Why not man? I can't wait to travel. And you're going to help me do my share of traveling if you've bought this book. Make the world your playground in safety. Some of you won't listen to that warning. Lots of you are daredevils. As long as you love what you do, do it. I really want to say this to you, and I hope you take these words in wisdom; I know that life is life and we all have to do things we don't like doing, and it sucks, but I would hope that you work at a job that you love doing. I'm a firm believer that you should do a job you love doing, if you're lucky enough, you already have this option. Some of you aren't even close to be at this place in your life, but I hope one day you can be at a job you love. I think the world would be a better and happier place for everyone included. I hope you love lots in your lifetime. It's worth it. Because you never know second-to-second. Life can be snapped up. Make every second, everyday, count.

If I were to self-loathe myself tonight, I'd say something like this; I feel pretty down right now. Maybe I do deserve to live in misery. It's like a twisted and wired fence. I feel like I'm becoming something I don't want to be within myself. I so try to be the best I can be, but I guess I'm not doing as well as I thought. Snap! Just like that. We're being stolen apart from each other. It's not the same anymore. She's changing right in front of me and she's already gone to me. She's in love. Her calendar has been changed into a new and wonderful world of being in love, that her heart has new priorities. And that's what's supposed to happen for her, and for us. *spiritual perfection* the number 17. So I went onto online, to search up the number 17. I thought the information for this number was and is fascinating. It has importance in both of the math realm *and* Biblically. It is in both worlds in this one and that. So I guess God *is* trying to tell me something, on a night, I once again, thought about suicide. So I guess I do have importance from Him, even though I know He loves me. He woke me up. Smacked me across the head. On most occasions, I always have a constant war going on in the way I think and between goodness and then some peril thoughts about myself, since it is, a self-loathing night it is, and all I want on most days is just peace with one hundred percent. Take and subtract the No/Yes constant bickering in my head . . . always a tug-of-war of destruction of something in my life. Well, if I erase the words I said on that terrible and fateful day. Where it all vomited out of my mouth to him, when he was dying. I'll never get over that. I will never heal from that. Words are everything. And now and still with my delicate heart, something little said in meaning to go to another person other than myself, for someone to say something that to them isn't nothing at all, what I'm saying, is I'm very fragile. Handle with care. I'm so glad I have my writing in times like this for me to let me vent and escape the freezing. To be able to express and expose myself in rawness hunger for so much. I just have to keep remembering to lean on my LORD and listen to Him when He gently reminds me of me being a part of this world and I have a purpose. To share my love for God/LORD/Jesus to you, so maybe you can find a connection that's rare to just *you* and Him. To open up and . . . let's go to another world before I continue on with the story. So, just hang on. You're to look at your errors of your ways, and hang your head in shame? That's not what I meant to say . . . I meant to say, come on, you can do it. Be strong in your life. Don't let others tell you no. Be strong in your morals and your spiritual beliefs. Always believe that His purpose for your life, is bigger when *He* controls it. I just bathe in Him and lather my senses. And my senses are opened up and I'm able to hear Him. That's the only reason you're reading this. He used my entire lifes experiences and rolled them all up and threw me the vessel I had to go through to find this all out for myself where I'm able to be free in expressions. Only with You LORD, will I open up everything. And when I share, you won't interrupt? . . . or quiet me, when You know I need to talk about stuff so I can carry on. And when I talk out loud, in the night-time of silence and breezes, I break out of my shell and when I get out and I live in, still the guilt I've carried for most days of my life so far. It's due to the unfavoured days to the said sentences. In trying to always . . . and I'm remembering I'm always crushing myself in bathing insults. So LORD, as You know, I need to have a purpose in my life, to have a reason for being here and not being able to be There.

As you live in the world, you live in me. Torturing me at every thought. Ravenging my spirit and soul, ripping me through and throw me at yins per second and it never stops. I wish it didn't live in me lashing out at thunderous amounts of speed and whipping in agony pushes, thrashing me to nothing. You steal from me. You scare me with tragedy endings and it robs me of happiness. No more to give, I have no immune system left. No barriers left to fight with. How could I write a "Love Letters" to 'him', right? He steals from me and creeps me out. Puts evil with a spin on it. Like email he texts me at every second he can in his day. And makes me feel bad towards my love. I live in depression and self-peril. It's my danger and enemy. It reminds me every time I look out and look in. I can't stop it from entering me. Then the other side is so soft and compassionate, loving so much. My Holyness grabs me and shakes me out and shows my magic, sparkling, pixie dust over me, and then I write. Showing *my* control in my life. Letting my dust work word-for-word. Poem-by-poem the alphabet comes out. How the intricate details are always hidden from light because I don't want you to see. My hiding place is where I go to in need of feeling sad. I let my sorrow flow from my windows onto the suction gravity that steals a river. When I look out and look in, you remind me of my uglyness of my evil twin. Maybe she cryes for me when I'm out of site, she waits to see what today brings, but she doesn't live in the juice. The rain that fills me and then rocks the boat and tips me over and I can't get back up again. I have no levees from the ocean. But then reality sees me leaving and brings me back. Showing me the way to the next door and when it opens, I have to be ready. And then I see your face in the lives of those we love. You torture them as you live in a form and spit on their faces. your tongue is of a ton of razors and lick them like kittens lapping their milk. Rotating yourself and slicing them open. Just because you want to. To me, you'll never be anything. I won't even capitalize your name. I love hating you and you know who you are, the devil in my invisible energy. The darkness that thinks he owns the world because of his destructiveness. you laugh in faces of goodness and taunt them with your power. The heaviness you place on my fragile heart and you know that, so you play your part well. The intimate feelings of rapture you place in their emotions and feelings, how they are your violin. They feel like ill inside. How you hide beneath pond scum and mask your face to look like normal in skin but you live in the juice because of how it's structured. you translate in rudeness and infested in slimes poison. Emotional pain is your passion and equilibrium. you think you can defeat us. We are your aroma in your horns. It is your bouquet of wines from your branches of tentacles that reach for us when we call out for the LORD. One day, you'll be frying in *your* fire of all things. I have good knowledge of darkness. And I want to bring Light to a darkened world by evil. I want to put you in a prison and make *you* screwed. you have no good to you, you are merciless, you have no power over God and you know that you evil bastard. you are completely evil and you use things against and you should be destroyed for eternity. you give me no benefit in dealing with general tense and I hate that feeling. I don't appreciate your participation in life. ou are obsessed over your grab in her hair and yank her around a ring of razors teeth. It's hell or Him, and I know that what's coming out of this is obviously I go running to my LORD. Pain is your ecstasy. Release is my Gain.

You hold me in a spot where I feel comfortable enough to tell everything. You listen to me when I'm opened up. You help my thoughts become it's freedom. You assist me in putting order in my crazyness and is just there for me when I need a place to go. You are my freedom. You wheel me to the places I wish to be there in a blink. I try to feed you with love and wings. Sometimes you take control and show me where to go. When I think of you, it's all good. I have to take care of you so you can take me to where I need to regain composure for life that just shows up and sucks it out of me. You give me tranquillity in my time with the LORD, as He enters our surrounding peace. Your space is my outer emotions. It's where I cry and talk to God. It's where my words come from and you're my saving grace. I'm sorry when you get sick. I try to take care of you the best I can with major assistants. When you don't work, I become nothing and I sink way down until you're better again. Because of your existents, I have a life. Without God watching out for us, my life would cease if I didn't have you. I have to trust us as a pair and together. We have to work together and everything has to be in order. I had a question the other day about you, and I told the truth. You share the power with help and a hand from God, that He blesses you and takes care of you through sacrifice and unconditional love. Whenever you're broken they help fix your brokenness. I pray that you're okay now and ready to start driving again and be my horse. You soak up my sadness and remind me as you sing to me through words from Above. We've gone far you and me as we go far to places that remind us of another life. You don't mind that I don't go everywhere when I enter our space. You listen to me as I belt the volume out and travel with me along with the visions of what it's made of. A reminder of the grandeur ahead. Oh, just over here, oh, just over there . . . look at that! I can look out and see everything that is around me as pressure is there and on. We've been so good. I pray it stays that way. It's a lot of dedication. Being with you inspires me and it brings me peace through Him in your silence of your calm. This is where He screams to me what's to come to learn about and I could only hear Him in you. We're connected in a very special way. In you, I hear my Destiny. Your Perfect Number stares at me every time LORD. That's awesome and I hear You and Jesus Christ walked in the room and Whispered in my imagination, type it and send it. The expansion of my life, as my life found me. Find me . . . . find me. Be a Candyland and I find; unique. Continue to call out for me as I will come to you very soon. I'm always in a hurry, and it's because of you that I can put your invisible knowledge of a predicted time. And float in my river's edge. Please continue to speak to me LORD as I try to be polite as I speak in another language from the dialect that is different from breath with notes. That's pushed out with force from compressions. From a love that lives on forever. I do owe you. You gave me my destiny. You helped me to find it, in a heap of a mess first though, then I'm able to speak it in another language of understanding of *my knowledge*. Carly short, you show me. When You show me Your gracious Perfect Presence in my sights. Showing me again my fight. To show me Light that I need to see for myself, not now. As you show me your feathers that stroke the tail. As You pulsate around my body and make me vibrate language in writings showing you how she makes me feel. To open my thoughts and shine His Light through your darkness. Watch. Be ready. Do your Research.

I write to the half-being you are to me. I don't know you anymore. Your heart and mind and life is something that was taken from us when destinyes changed. Then, half remained, and through thoughts, you've become a hidden cave. In your new ways towards us, do you really think that you're going to get your way with this? How dare you think that *that's* going to happen . . . . but then I remember how it is now. To know now, how you've become so destructive and you are true to you, and under great restrain I say, you really do live in your little world and live an imaginary life. You're wrong! You're so wrong on everything you've said to me since that day. Let's see how I can be poetic in the anger state I'm in. But then again, I have to remind myself that you're disabled in everyway to me. Your juices ran out and left nothing. But how can I be hard like this when I'm so dedicated to God? It's a really tough spot to be in. How can I have an intent-on-trying with, within you? I wanted to have a relationship with you, with this side of and from you, whether your side was a lie, then I walk away forever. I'm never looking back if this is going to happen. I took anything I could get. How you hide, like me, for we shared something most of the world did with each other, and how our relationship has gone stale and our time has come to an end, and I wait till you strike again, to show you, how you've disappeared when you were struck. I wanted to hold on to anything, but understanding why it left in the first place. So, if I'm going to say good-bye, then I'm going to make it worth it. I'm glad the last thing you heard from me was 'I love you' so many years ago when that day took you away from us. Your goodness was pure and you loved me and protected me. You were so young when you were taken from us. As the river edge comes to my side, I say good-bye. I have to let you go now. I wake up to conditional, and it's your call, and it's not you. But then again. I'm sorry for all the trouble I caused you in our earlier days and I how I teased you. How we were bad and did things that now, it's a mistake, and we should have never done them. How we'd go downstairs and danced to our music and listened to our songs and now I remember them when I need you to confide in. And you just kind of took it from it. I wish we had more time together but I'll always treasure our time, and the passing of time, how I could have turned to you in my deepest despair. How I know you would have coddled me and be the one for me to call at three a.m. Hey, maybe *you're* my guardian angel living half way. I don't know how that would work unless you walk in both of our shoes. Strangers don't know us. No one knows the life I had to live with only a part of you, when and where now, I don't know and understand most things. You were so young. And now I wait to grieve your absence again. Give it a burial, finally. I turn my back on being rude and walk away with a new outlook on my good-bye to the owner of age first kiss. I'm glad we had wa wa. We went out a lot together. With all the bad, we also did good together and I'm sorry that it felt like you were kept giving. How will I mend from loosing it all in one day? And more one day . . . etc. I only love your part and save the rest for later on. I remember the water fun as we swam our way to the top. You gave us a part of your history and you will last throughout in generations that follow you. You trusted us for the care and love, and we will forever remember. I will defend your honour as I say my final good-bye to you. I will never turn back in the future, you're in another life and I hope I'm showing you what I've endured in my bereavement. The outcome is good.

"Cat and Mouse"

Even still, I come into your presence and I'm fulfilled with all your glory. You are such a little child in your spirit. It spills into my senses, and makes me zoom around like we were characters in a cartoon, where anything can happen. So you're the mouse and I'm the cat. But in this story, you sit on my back and we leap from this elevator ride that is like a giant long rollercoaster, with rainbow stripes with zigzags with bold and bright colours whizzing by us at lightening speed . . . whoosh! Weeee, this is fun! As I scream back to the mouse jumping up and down as we spiral out of control. We catch our balance and grab for each others paws and laugh and sing out of tune. Then suddenly, we come to this quiet meadow. Where deer are playing and laughing with the bunnies and the singing birds that are chirping us a song of glee. Are you having fun? I say in a whistle-high-pitch squeal. All the animals are gathered in a circle and they're playing. We get back on the rainbow road and start bumping into the walls and we laugh as our eyes pop in and out as like a slinky that can only happen here. We collect points as we find the boxes that lead us to our next adventures of playtime. We look at each other and in your delighted squeak, you get to choose. Oh yay! Then, all of a sudden, we're both struck with a bolt and we become miniature and we have to dodge the big, giant elephant stomping and making us run for our lives. We grab a hold of the elephants skin and we crawl up as he's swaying his body from side-to-side. We desperately cling on for dear life and with my trusty claws I struggle for our lives as cartoons will not be over because it's majic here. I reach the top of his back and something startles the elephant and they start running in their group. You haven't stopped yelling and I haven't stopped laughing and I have to pee. We're bumping up and down and our fir is standing straight up due to extreme wind conditions up here. Come on silly, lets fly! And then we let go and spun out of control and landed on the ground and now it's only the two of us. Okay . . . now *blink*! Mooooo? Excuse me mouse and cat, what are you doing here? And you yell, we're jumping!! Ya wanna come? And we start laughing. The cow says, na, it's okay, I'm gonna hang out with Poohy and Pyglette, but thanks. Let's go say hi! We run at top speed and spinning through the air since, here we go! Poohy and Pyglette were sitting on a raft sitting on a diving deck, sittin' back and laughing about Tiger's new adventure. And look, here comes the Tiger now. He was bouncing on his tale. We looked at each other and said our goodbyes to everyone and go on our merry way. Okay . . . *blink*! We fell down. Where are we? Our eyes got wide when we saw where we were. We were miniature again. We looked out of the window and saw flashes of large unknown faces. Where are we? We asked each other. Then the lights were strobe lights and we were in this huge building and the lights are dim. We were tumbling and falling and I opened my eyes wider when I saw that. As I pointed to you to look around and see where we were. We were in a pair of dice. Outside the noise was loud and muffled. YAYYY!! As the muffled sound entered my ears. Finally we stopped jostling around in our glass cubes. Okay . . . *blink*! We open our eyes and we're in this huge mansion. We look around at all the gold and crystals and dangling jewels. There's a lot of people sitting over there, so, come on! We ran side-by-side until we reached the crowd of children and listen to that man. This man was sitting in a chair. A young child screeches in delight . . . Jesus, Jesus, tell us again!!

I sit and wait as my future plays itself out in front of my eyes. Let it open my mind and I wait patiently for something wonderful, majic to happen. Majic! It just happens so fast with us. Hypothetical situation; give me everything, control of their lives, owing what? . . . give it to me. I take over and wait until no point with no. I have to do this and that. Hard labour. For the both of us, but I'll teach. I love you . . . unconditionally, no matter what, and I'll never leave you. You are safe in my possessions. They're *my* feelings now. Now go, do your wonderfully deserved life. I will be her honey on cornbread. I will show her *my* world now. Let this one live forever in your memories and row on. Let her live a life she's never known . . . for me? Another life to change paths and exchanging independence. I will be her lighthouse now, that now belongs in my reside. Let me dwell her imagination as I carry her to another leaf. This will be her new reality, to touch something she's never touched before. *I* need her now. She's my hand, part of my imprint that is engrained in the fingerprints that give her life. She's my butterfly and she's going to spread her wings from being a caterpillar, emerging from her cocoon and let her fly in the sunlight and be free. I can do so much for her pyscy. She'll have unlimited imaginary visions that need to come with her. I will take care of her. She can be someone they respect and admire, forever, and it lives on for generations. Please, I beg of you, she needs to be mine. We'll work, play, love, be sole, be together for a mirror facing a mirror. I stand strong for her and I will fight for her. I'll put my gloves on and see you in the rink. But I know inside that you want to let go. How can you not? What a transformation I'm able to create in her. She is my laughter, tears. I'll be her favourite song that she'll sing until I can no longer hear her. In our old days, we'll be walking hand-in-hand to our next journeys together. As us and as mothers. Our LORD will Reign in our lives and of our children and in our home, like missing the strongest chain and become only as strong as your weakest point, which I'm the hot metal burning the edges together so they can never break and fall to the ground. She will never fall in my presence. I'll catch her every time. Unlucky in love and life she is my chair and my legs will hold her up. I will never show her anger due that I'm soft and gentle and I want to show that part of myself so she can carry it on. It's always her after what's most important to me, she's my missing family nesting eggs that they wait for me to come back and feed them. I am a rock, with minor fissures, but I heal very quickly and whatever she needs, I will provide. I will be her towel when she needs to let out a river on something that I fix and she only is a drip. I'll take her hands in mine and lift our hands to our faces, and pray to God to continue to live in our lives and that He heal her brokenness. I will be her stream of calmness when she feels like a hurricane. When she's swirling out of control, all I have to do is touch to her like a feather under my tips, and then still . . . instantly. She will no longer feel dizzy. I will happen without any delay. Her soul will forever be untroubled. Where she feels tristful I will be her gentleness and always protect her and hold her right against me and make sure she's whole before I let her go. To show her our own, unbelievable miracle when we were lost in grief that brought us, us. To show the world that it won't conquer this strength of mercy, compassion, loyalty, devotion. And let us live forever in our occupancy, with hands welded together with rainbows and the anticipation for our permanent residency in our LORD's place.

I want to totally transform myself. To become whole for the first time in my life. I feel a new power that is connected to His stars that belong to my person. To only show God all of me and my unhindered past life to rebuild my fragile ness to be empowered in their eyes. To finally be important to *me* and letting the old me die away, but use my past to renew my future. I found Akasha and I've found my Power. To realize and to hear the new invention to speak it's way out. To understand fashion, to change the world to show my past bullies. To be the beautiful swan emerged from slime. Better me me, I plead from God to help this new life You've breath. To myself; no, I'm stronger than that. *Fight* to get out. I just realized myself under my LORD. Die, like you live. Be dramatic, tragic enough for the world to remember that, to the moon like you're calling to yourself to hear my cryes for Home again. Scream on top of the moon, breathe Me out and spread out over the next Centuries to become a poet. To be here though. To be then. What's to happen is a mystery . . . to a hundred futures. Oh that's such a relief, ah, not another one. Thank You LORD, to never know the truth through secret passages through communications as You ride in a Limo. That's so cool LORD, can I catch a Ride?! I'm listening! Be my Organizer LORD and Reign over their rules. Speak through me to You. Translate and I love You. You create me and live in my soul. If I'm in love with her, am I looking in my reflection? You're my Power and I need You to show me the way. Let it be a love that no one could ever understand to the next galaxies with stars showing their way to the next hole, to re-gain structure to live in another path to show another entity their purpose, so they can fulfill *their* destiny to change another's, to change another's . . . and the world lives on until God has decided it's to end. Then another world will exist and *it* will never end. The end will end everything in Anything. Anything goes in His One Soul, that needed to love and He gave Himself in Raptured Blood. Now He is where He needs to be. To show you, the way needed, you need to travel and be free in your love with those who deserve it the most. Who I am is important. My faith is my One and Only. He is my humming in my ear drum letting it be well aware of Your Presence and the Life of Books as You continue to press down and reading becomes protocol . . . the Records of the Scrolls. To you, become whole with yourself, be yourself so when you read yours, you'll know what to do instead of following. Listen to The Voice when you make a decision, but sometimes your mistakes guide you, lead you, be put in your splendour and feed on, as seeds, ready to be growing. To hear the hum to remind me of Your worlds You've created. The words will be read over and over to discriminate. To be heard as Distinguished Tones. To blow Your Trumpets so I can hear You when You call me Home. To be connected to something I've always wanted, a Permanent Home, with jewels and gold and royal furniture that Sit's a King. To rush over the warm crystal floor and under me is a bridge over the galaxies, with twinkling stars that shine as diamonds sharp to shine in His Lights. It's arch is high to march the ships beneath them, and sing for Him as its Harmony with It's combination of tunes with ribbons streaming down under Your Microphone. To the whole worlds You've created as we all hear You calling us and we answer and follow Your voice to Home, where everyone is gathered in a long line priming their hair and clothes, dripped in honey raining to the worlds below as they untransfer their majic to water when we look.

"Undercovered Love"

Undercovered love, spread out throughout the astral planes. Please don't go baby. In my imagination this is what we're doing in our universe that's yins miles. Your beautiful brown mane blowing in the breeze with my long red tangles around your see through ghost. We enter this magnificent outdoor cathedral with the outside as the roof. We hook our arms around together and walk down the isle, staring into our eyes that shine in sparkles and we don't need speech to know anything, as we wrap and float into the grandeur sky-room as one. So many spirits busy upon their lives as another world is made. We float and dance under the walkway as if we were under water as it uncases us. In a thought, we were alone. We were in another form. It was a huge open field with three feet of winded bladed grass the colour of healing. There was a blanket as we both landed from our feet. He pulled me down to his side and he grabbed my face and gently kissed me all over my face and he softly kissed my lips and it began a new love affair, I kissed him back as I rolled through his mane and pulled him closer and he pulled me to lay flat on my back. He rolled on me and we rolled around in pure intimacy. I caressed his back and we were all over each other. Our kissing was pressured force with intence passionate growls under our breaths. You roamed your manly hands and grabbed my breast and brought your lips to cover and gently bit me and suckled. As I nurse your manly desires. You come back to kissing my chest and ribcage. You reach my jeans and you look up to me as I'm arching waiting for you to take all of me. You smile with your front sexy and handsome gap. When we enter this form, I wouldn't want anything else. It's your trademark and her birthright. You undo and unzip and I help you remove my jeans so I can show you my underneath. Your fingers, caress me and I begin going into him for every seconds of yin time. Your face and fingers reach deep within me and I grab your head and pull you further. I squirm in your jell. You stroke your pressured hand to cover me as you brought you up to me. I undid your jeans and you kicked them off. He was rock hard. I sat up and put him on his back. I went for his sexual relations and I put him in my mouth and grabbed him in my warm to stroke him hand. He was big. I suggested the year that started this, and we were both in each others face. The wind was refreshing on our sweating bodies. We were just in this, rhythm with each other. I did twice and he is waiting, so I moved. He climbed in. He was knocking on my heart and I opened the door. The feelings drove us crazy and we moved in beat. I grabbed him into me with his moans deep in his throat roaring in heat. I repeated his name over and over and over again, just to make sure he heard me as I wanted to scream of passion into the daytime sky. He was moving faster and I was arching my back and pulling him into me and grabbing him, YES! He pushed himself up and rammed and rammed and rammed and then, explosion! We both sweated into each others pores. We lay in our love making and laughed. We got up and ran as though we were free horses running our domain with yins of acreage. We ran in our nakedness and I jumped on his back and he grabbed me and swung me around as we delighted in our presence together. Our lips would caress each others and our bodies were satin upon touch. We became horses and ran beside each other back to our primary inhabitant and were in the milky way and shining diamond glitters in the astral planes as we floated in as like we were on ghost lingering to cling on you and we glided and we were one again, the only way I wan' it.

"Create Through Me"

Oh no! What happens if I run out of things to say? What would I be then? If all my words left me? Who would I become? My freedom would be gone. I would be lost within my thin walls of my cave of essence. My future poetry would be gone and the world wouldn't know everything about me. I seek shelter in *your* reading my words and hope that you can understand, and relate it to your life, to help you through *my* experiences. Nothing, would take over and demolish me and crush me into a million of yins and shatter me to my core. I would be spilt blood and a pile of rubbish on this dirt road of life. I would take my pills of sorrow and despair again. My self would be non-self to the point of oblivion. Spilt in the milky way and divides into another cemetery. Buried in dirt and the slime and insects of feasting. I would be lost if my words left me, if the LORD left me, I would float aimlessly in the atmosphere where space is only in front of Him. I would plead my case and ask for a pardon and if He could cease my existents. Where there's no meaning to a word that will be our forevers. I would retrieve to recover the forever tragedy that would be me, none other. I love writing. Look what I can create . . . what *He* can Create *through* me. The world would be missing out on something completely new. I *want* to spread His Word. It's my birthright, throughout generations before me. To spread what's embreaded in me, to spill out something to a new generations. To know, that you'll never fully understand my language and question many things. Just know that from that experience, look at what I can do with it. To have worked so hard, for so long . . . to know that every word was placed there. On purpose. I write with such intencity, passion. Whatever you're going through, whatever your situations, know that *you,* have a purpose on this earth. You were created for a Greater Reason. It's like wind blowing past us showing us the way life is and how it goes. Live your life. Love your life, for distant time. *This is my* imprint in life. All my words that have been waiting for me. Find *your* imprint in this lifetime. Find *your* God and love Him with everything you have. Devote time in Him, because He's the One who will show you Home. Be yourself and sing to Him daily, lay in front of Him and He'll fix your desires. My poems that will spread His Word with soft love songs echoing in my eardrums with the most beautiful of melody. You are near me, and I feel You. Be my Song in my heart melody . . . am I already LORD? Be my Beat on drums in a Chant of Your Love. I am a seed. I am planting wise words coming from Above. I will live no other life for the most distant duration belonging to then from now. I hope I will be your whisper for inspiration, to motivate you to be only you. To live *your* life and not someone else's. Make *yourself* rich, from His Direction. To sing my fingertips over my notes of music and poetry. Don't become a life where you can't dance under His sun and moon. Stir us around with your decorative stick and become someone's swallow. Go for the ride but surf your way there. Become a storm, and spread out the sand that's getting to stay on the ground after *it's* swallow. You matter in this lifetime and you wouldn't be otherwise. See what would be missing if all my words escape me? This is me, this is Him, stirring you up, getting your attention. He's knocking, are you listening? It's just my opinion, it's just my words, my song for the people's He's reaching. Once you find Him, hang on. It's gonna be a hell-of-a-ride. Thank You LORD for this "Love Letters". Search and destroy, find them LORD, expel and Force Your way in.

Maybe if I talk about it, it will go away. Blow, in the wind and whish yourself away from me. Feeling heavy is my whole life. I think. Every second of everyday and I don't have an off button. I think about different situations of troubles in my life. How I have to hide. To never happen. It's a cloudy day upbove. And how I can skip onto my future, and I'm so excited about it. So no matter how I feel at any given time, I have to write, and have a purpose and feel heavy in here and I get to become anything I want. I can feel anyway. I can be angry and yell and punch and get mad. I can become disease. But I don't want to be like that. I want to be a guardian angel and live in heaven to the end. So I push them to the core and store them in the never-vaults. I don't even want to talk about it. So I'm thinking of what to write, so why don't I pray? Since I'm sharing everything else. LORD, forgive me. For the sins I have caused other people. To finally ask forgiveness through my words. I did a horrible act to another person in my life. Too many to account for. I know I've asked for Your forgiveness before LORD, but this time it's different. I've done a lot of really bad things and it's because of Him, I never went to jail. He saved me, every time. Then came my future and said of the unquoted yin-long uncoding into it. And now, here I am . . . vulnerable in your judging thoughts. I need to shake it out LORD and give it to You. I pray for peace within myself regarding this past into my future. To carry it as deep code. I ask for Your Forgiveness, and for when I do think of them, I can carry my head high and know You've fought this battle for me already, and I can never speak again. To use my past I need it for the future. LORD, please touch the many lives You have created in Your image. Bless all and be a Watcher in their life. AMEN. Well, I'm feeling a bit better now that I've talked about it. Now I can let it go and move on, right? So now I'm guessing I need to be a writer and entertain you and keep you watched on my page of literatures. To speak another language that you have to figure out yourself, and use your imagination to interpret. Let it take over your mind. Fall into a deep read and follow me. I'd love to show you my imagination. He has blessed me with this and I take it very seriously. I put everything into these pages of interesting everythings. To flow and impetrate future happiness, and success in all what You're going to give me. I can only hope for, but ask for fluency and for my writings to never leave me, because I love creating. Anything can happen in writing. To let my imagination out and let her play as though as were a child. Skip and do games . . . run and jump and bang your head with pumps so you always remember them and let them help you become you. Be important in your reflections, smile at you and love. Because that's what all this comes down too. To show the world, my love. Sure I'm still myself, but I love. To become like a straw that you suck from your milkshake and every time you suck in, more love is gone and refilled. To wish for one day like this to happen; Did you see the column today? Today's advice is . . . and then you read it and you take my advice. I'm not a doctor in any way, but I've lived life and made a lot of mistakes that could have been solvable. But then it's too late. And you can never take it back. I learned that the hard way let-me-tell-you way. I'd give anything to change it, and the only thing I can do to make amends with myself and him, and live my life. To live on and spread good to you. Be wise in your reply. Use knowledge to move forward. Forgive easily. Always love. It's helping you, it's helping me and it's making the world go round-and-round.

To my love of my life. How you came to need me and made my divided womb. They're so amazing. To love the way we needed it . . . you love them wholey and Holy. The unconditional love with no bars. The love of loving and your devoted, how they nurture within us. How they come alive when we come alive. How their love changes you. How I would accept anything that you give me. How you creep into my thoughts and bring my imagination to life. With our crawling all over each other and loving us all. How your deep voice transmit from another world a light-years away, as it echoes in space. I hear you as you invade my privacy. I hear you when you bring alive in my admiration and special love affair with you as my invisible lover. You're not gone, you got better, with a life that can only be a sacred time with just us, in our own time. As your song explodes into my invisible senses that are a rapture to you. To express my motions to you. To carry us off to our dreams. Let that be our bespoke and no one can take us apart, say, I'm spoken for. I'm your lover in physical and with the celestial surroundings. I want to get lost in the crowds with you and become between the atoms. I need you in both ways my love. It should be, I have to let you know how I love you. To sit in the symbol of forever and rest on one of them as the ride carries us. What would I say to you if you were right in front of me . . . ?, I don't know. I'd just stand there, gazing at you like I haven't seen you in a lifetime. Soak in every line of your sole. Breathe you into my head and think with every beat. How unique having no like as I breathe, take rest. I run to you in a millimetre away and become your oxygen. As I'm both human and spirit. Being in just us and break to you that soon I have to choose another life and we have to meet again because it has to be us and through being another us have to search and find us again. Live another and different life. And we find each other every time, but now I have to just wait to finish this one to find you to do it again and again and never end until the finishing breath and ray of sunlight. I have to finish writing, I have to reach for my dreams and I can't do it without you. We're only separated by sight. I stare into your beautiful crystals with a baby royal blue. And you smile and your moustache covers your top lip as you grin to me in a devilish and crooked smile. What are you doing . . . ? Smile . . . . You tell me your secrets, letting them out for the whole world to read them. What do you want to tell me? What? I would be in your way to deliver the needed goods to live. I will miss you till then my pumpkin pie. Don't cry until your eyes are swelled to maximum. I'll be waiting for you with my arms opened wide and I'll show you around and take you to our room. Until then, I will always and forever be yours, share our love, so another can love this way too. To show that this life is. If you let go and sneak a peak in the doors, but then I have to shut you out till your arrival. How you will be forever frozen and in a metal detail, in a finely wrought decoration. How that time for us was so short . . . only a second in the mists of clock time. The size of a piece of the millimetre. I can press rewind and watch you through glass to hear your voice, to see your hair, to see your copied smiles and to hear your voice. To remember how you moved while telling a story, to remember how it was said and in your way. Listen to me when I stop by and say hello. Continue to be inspired throughout this precious time and bring Light to the world. I love you. I'll never leave you, I'm always just a memory away and a blink of your eyes. Dream of me often, so I can see you more clearly as you see me now.

Okay, now is the time to shine brightly as it's the perfect number. Write as though it is my last Letters, and hope that each one is as very different as your fingerprints. May the tips be as like no other words without repeat, as my next story is in sunlight. To show it's heavy beat as you walk down the runway. May you walk with intencity, with a rockin' rhythm. May the crowds erupt in applause as you walk towards the cameras, lights and 'action'. The music is loud, and pumping. Be your own rocket and escape the atmosphere. Show your stripes and patterns. Make your scent bold and beautiful, as they stroll by and they are their muses. May you look around and jump off a snowy cliff. Go beyond the limits and jump off. Be your own show, be helium. Rock out of this world and walk in the middle of the street and make car horns honk at your site. Everybody's cheering so loud, with noisy celebrities dressed up in the nines and you're rollin' in dough. Your colours are loud and make a statement, be sparkly, be shiny, be, just be. Kick balloons and shout out loud for attention. Party like it is the new Millennium and start a new revolution. Become a radical and stomp on the earth loud enough for everyone to hear you. Suddenly, a crack is spreading between your legs and what do you do? You jump in the crack and use your strength to crack the world open and you show it you. Design anything, draw, paint, create, and let it be your rainbow situated high above to bring daylight into daytime. Make it extra bright. Scream out streamers that decorate the streets in random fashions. To feel passion and don't turn it off. Let your picture be taken and be a billboard. Take off at mock speed and take flight around the circle of survival and don't draw on done ideas. Be a big deal, don't just sit there, kick up a fuss and make your pressence shine in a new Light. Be luscious in your daily routine and announce your entry. Make everything amazing and position as like vogue. Be your favour. What have I done? Have I started a flash? Have I encased your mind yet? Are you curious of what's to come? Become a label in someone's wardrobe and live their experience in your own being. Be your own style and point your feet in the zig-zag patterns and in around circles. Open the show, be the ringmaster and start the strobe lights and dance your way to the top. Be your own elegance and layer to not too much. Be the file that makes your claws steel sharp so when you hook on, you make it bleed with your blood and sweat and falling tears and be their favourite. Make it so they don't get it. That's what it is all about, and grow into your own calendar of events. Drive downtown and honk your horns and shoot your ricochet. Live on the edge, and live experiences. Open presents and throw up your hands and let go as you ride the rollercoaster and scream, really loud. Be the life of the holiday parties and jump up and down to the music so that the people downstairs can almost see you through the ceiling. Let your hair down and work till you drop and be happy where your life is. Work so hard, feel good, and let the bath soak up all your stress and be crazy. We're all strategizing and slipping out of routine. Don't ease up too much and don't forget to ring the bell for attention. Crack your whip and make the whipping sound and become the end and make the snap and come out at lightening speed. Ride your horse at free gallop, and don't fall down. Kick it in high gear and ride for your life. Race round the track and win the final race. Wear loudness and be that title of prime time. Spring up and say, no gloves on and meet me in the ring . . . PUNCH! . . . In your face . . . you're out!

"*I* made those choices. Not *you*. Remember that!, as I scream to you. Why can't you hear me?! So I settle in the grave of the next yins that I've been waiting for her to hear me. I know my choice was the bad one, but look what you're doing with me on this side! Listen to me! *My* grave is *my* grave, not *yours*. I had to go first because my tyme was up. I was a mess as a person and you kept me alive longer than I would have given myself. I know my mistakes now as a husband but it's too late for me, not for someone else. I was there with you when you had my funeral, when you stood over my grave . . . I was helping your father carry you up that hill. To start your new life and to learn where I left off. I'm with you throughout this journey you're seeking now. Be who you're supposed to be. Be a great writer. This is what I'd say to her if she could hear me, as my echo keeps coming back to me and I replay it over and over to her as she lay sleeping. You're so close to me only a ripple away. Go, on your way to something so great, I can't even tell you. Don't let my choices get in your way, ever. I knew who I was. A messed up kid who loved the idea of being the worlds most patient man who loved her and now I want her to hear me. I just want to tell her I'm okay. He's taking really good care of me, walking beside me as you use my face to carry on. I've seen everything. Every second of it and I live in agony as I've been haunted just like you. It's only when you learned who you were, was I able to go into the Light, but first you have to let me go on. You love me. You loved me." I don't want to hear anymore for my tears flow and I pull myself together and know that's it's only my voice in my head playing tricks on me. As he resurfaces. As you make me play your song of farewell. We were never meant for forever, and you always knew that. You were so beautiful walking down our isle. Looking like a dolphin jumping out and turned into this person we thought we were marrying, with your smile that could light up a huge crowd. I said those vows knowing, when will I now? Having our children was the best thing I've ever done and I picked you to be my children's mother. I loved you, it's only now you know to what degree. I watch you cry again and again and all I can do is be the sad love song you repeat over and over again but I'm waiving to you but you won't see me. As she listens to one again. Reciting every words because that's her life now. Knowing I've been with her. All the time. For her heart has been so sunken with guilt with what *I* did. I had nothing to say but when I was going to in my past tryes, and to thank my best friend, who he carries everyday. That's all I needed to say. I can't tell you my journey until you get Here. Or you just won't tell me! Don't argue with me, just type. Belong to this. Be a master in your craft. Stop blaming yourself for my death. I can't even talk about that experience for me. I suffered as you suffered, but now that you're better and you've discovered who you are, I'm able to be this for you. You never left me. You chanted my name over and over with tears so big, in such agony of breathing in my death. All your love that you've ever felt for me helped me move on too. Now you can listen to me and write many great books that will be enjoyed for yins. And you can press repeat to your hearts content. Cause that's how you hear me. I was with you . . . . why can't you hear me?! I just want to say I love you . . . really. I love your love gaps. They always made me smile and let you get anything you want. Let me reside in you and live on through your writing. I can't wait to show you so much. Passion, Love, Stillness, with so much Light. So, now, go. Let me rest beside you tonight with your words from your dreams."

So all along, you've been trying to tell me that your name is my favourite number in all of Creation, and I just got it. Where I sit and open up to you as you hang from my mirror, in my face, and I finally got it. Your name is; Trinity. Where I sit and talk to myself, where I come alive in my gifts. I just open and I'm able to. I hear You now, and You enter my thoughts and explode and I'm loaded with shrapnel. And then I have to bleed them out, and I only do this with You where I sit and listen to Your voice. Now I know me and whom I am. I'm not scared. And I feel all this in Trinity. Something I can say in a repeat constant line but never tell anything. I gasp in and jump into my secret world. What I want to hear is only The. I can't tell all my secrets to anyone but you Trinity. Where I'm on and sound enters me and takes control to let the vibe come through the words. I rage threw my sorrow into the night air and let it. I rage it to You. Boy do I ever know who I am. My thoughts take me to places that I only have the language. Funny you did it seconds before. Say what it may. Starts now the beginning of a new one and I need to listen to you whistle the words. Be my words my beloved soul being. That gets to float in and out of my pours whereas I have only one. You feed me and I thirst every time. You speak through some channel on the radio, and I hear Your Transmit. And pass along. Sway in your wind in your sweetest ness. I'm now be and my breath with breathe itself a lullaby. Staying within my boundaries, I'm unable, but then I'm alive again in our soulng. What will their reactions be if they saw us together? They wouldn't understand and I'll be my normal. Is there beaches there? You are my emotions and my positive energy. And in order to finish more must come . . . so come to me, no blocks to shelter me in nothingness. May fields erupt to eject matter and fill up and come to you in motion. Of which you also know that will one day be the worlds main ways. Oh Trinity, I need to tell you this and that but only then will my secret world be a nation speaker. Look at the sky and now the stars are twinkling their songs that all combined together and separated and become brand new songs for us. To spread joy and to help the helpless, so be words of expression that others need to get through something really hard. The power they have over you and your in the creation of new images, mental creation. Let them come alive in images and they live in a vial for science to pick it apart and discover something vital. May the dome and cathedral shelf your every thought to put here. I want you to know all the words to my song. May you sing me over and over, given through my Trinity. I take shelter and when I sit in doom, You reach for me and You come out of Your last place and show me the Way. Never show me good-bye. I can never leave you even though you're only a thought. A thought I take and hook into him, and go on a spontaneous field trip down a bumpy road as we four-by-four over rocks and trees and a stream that will get us wet. When we'd see the white barked trees and they'd stare me down. And hold your hand as we continue our long journey into the darkness. Your ness is the pulsating rate that you pump my heart in your hands and you are. To be Your columns of balance as You hold me. As You are an orchestra of different instruments that arrive in harmony as we walk down the hallway to our room. It's this magnificent field filled with wild horses gazing in their ranges and the trees swaying in the sunlight wind. The sky is of daylight and the moon and stars are in the distant horizon. So, in knowing all this, take me to your dreams from what Trinity said.

This is my prayer tonight. I don't want again to fall into my sunken. As I intensified my pleas to You. I want it *so* bad. I can feel it, it's so close to me, yet it seems impossible for me to reach it. I want it *so bad.* As a hiss through the visual stare to Him, put my wholeness into the body moving fighting it to the Cross. I was shook up and needed to talk to You about it. And was again reminded of the power that sits in me . . . waiting, standing still.again. Maybe the calling to my children isn't finished yet. Maybe they have to live here to see those dreams for themselves, that can only be achieved here. So I can't rush this time we have left. I have to let what's supposed to happen, happen in His tyme, not myne. You know I'm Yours LORD. I'll never forsake You, not here may I stand and shout to the international standard of what normal is. Combination of my secret. Nope, shaking my head, not yet. As I shake my finger in front of you. Live the secret lie I have to live, from people of my love. As I sit alone listening to the words he was talking about. To only be me and not, them. LORD, hold me tighter, hold my tender heart in Your healing embrace, one more time before I wake up and start all over again. So can I finish crying in Your arms LORD before I go? Can You calm me when I'm shaken and violent mind-blowing blown LORD? As I've repeated this dream already. Why again? What's the message? Who is the you need to be? Are you lost? Tell the world how important I am and show results. To live in the reality of how life really works. Life is not a dream, it's serious sometimes and we have to be prepared for the battle that's upon us. Shake up our comrades, and ask them to join the fight. As she fights for me upon request her again to . . . peace on the way. To know that I'll have that ground to fall on, for gravity to be in it's own rules. Am I lost LORD? As I cling on to You as I live with difficultness getting my story out. I want to Hear tonight LORD. Show who You are to them. Show how we work together. How a letter can even exist without You as the Writer. How You show impossible to the impossibleness. I wonder if I asked someone to trade my life with someone like them. What would they do with this information? How would they live it? I'm glad I don't have to find out 'cause I'm gonna live it, 'cause it was made specially for me. Only *I* could live my life, like *you* live yours. Your life started, and there's no trading. Find your reason for living. I'm giving advice again. But I'd rather give advice than not tell you. Maybe you're going through something like I am now, then. It doesn't matter who did what to them, you just have to move on . . . again switch thoughts, as my thoughts have been bolted. Maybe I'm supposed to be like this for you right now. To help you forget so you can get really confused in myne. To almost run out of tyme so I can prepare for what's to come next. The numbers combined I guess creeped in and said, this better be a good one. To show my weaker side, my vunerableness to the inside of my messed up head. Well, to show youuu . . . everything. Not that you haven't seen anything, but this is a different side to me. As I wish I were wearing a suit and tie, but I'm not dressed for company. As he says I'm beautiful. Even in my weariness. Come into my insanity and sit down, make yourself at home. I can show you this, a lovely sparkled sleeveless sweater with gold flickers as like in a diamond ring. As I go where I want it's okay to go. And then the next shake up with ice, sinking right into my veins, giving me pain of freezing throughout, and will shatter any moment. As You send static so I can Hear as You've spoken.

LORD! This is *our* song? No wonder I write the best to this song. What we can create together. Whoa . . . . It's so true. Every word. When the world has something to say because I'm a Christian. I just want to show the world another perspective, from an insider who lives it and connect with someone who understands hardship and loss. I'm not trying to say that you have to believe, not at all. I can relate to sceptics. I get it, He's invisible. You can't see wind, but it shows its presence. Love is an unexplained phenomenon that no one can explain. Love and hate are very visible, in actions. Maybe it's a chemical of some kind. But hey, it's just my opinion. I love feeling love. But when I don't have love in my life, I can't function. It gets ugly in here. But then I play our song, I just fly in You. As You blow Your breathe and become my carriage and sweep me into other particles and matter. Be Freelance LORD. Create majic. So I'm sitting on a picnic bench listening to my music and up came a beautiful golden retriever and started sniffing my feet and body and I was so elated. I started petting her. She licked my face and the owner was calling her off me, but I didn't mind. Hi, he says. Hi. I laughed. What's her name? Her name is, Trinity. Well hello, Trinity. I stood up and looked into his eyes and it was starting a new life. Type . . . type . . . type. Take me to a different place. Take me around the world so I could never stop inspiration, I could put out the flame that You put there. I'm sitting in my saddle on my beautiful wilded tamed horse. In a full gallop. My hair blowing fastly behind me. Going with the horse, flying by objects of posts with wire that were miles in front of us. The rushing thoughts of, go faster. Hear me LORD, psst . . . I can't tell You, people can hear us. Be my roar in screaming distance so they can hear me. Elements in a scene of musical notes that are flying within a grand-master piano. Sitting underneath a vaulted painted white ceiling. He's sitting there, playing his symphony escaping to above and going out. As the cameras come to under him for angles, the song plays as he's in his long tuxedo, his hair slicked back and he's getting into this song. And then comes the climax. The piano was taking a beating as he pressed really hard on the keys until he took it back to quiet and the audience was just silent and eager for the next note. Finally, we were able to fall back into our home and wait for the next vibrations. Think . . . think . . . so guess what? I want to do something with you. We're going to make a peanut butter sandwich. Or something else because of the allergies,. Okay, something you're not allergic to. Okay, go to your kitchen. Go to where you keep your bread and take it out so it sits on the counter in it's wrapping of course. Take out a knife from the area you keep it and place it on the counter. Pick up the bread and take the twist tie off and when it opens take two pieces out and lay them on the counter and rewrap the bread and put it back into the bread location . . . . I'm a writer, I can print anything when, where and there. My head is cluttered with noises. Like a deaf man forever in silence. I don't know what silence is just as he doesn't know what sound is, but both with their own vibrations. May I continue to tell you a story that's just me? You've shown me how drunk I can feel and slur thoughts together, as I stumble to the ground and cuts my lip, then I heard a sound of whistling as a swoosh, and my head is spinning and the world is spinning and I stumble in the darkness and I hit walls as my fingers are getting bashed up. Are you okay mister? Oh yes, just making a peanut butter sandwich.

"Dior J'adore"

December 11th, 2010—You turned 15 today . . . .

No, this has to be fresh and never written before in the history of anytime. It's a girl. You were destyned to be mine. I have my daughter. Your jet black hair turned chocolate brown. Your beautiful grey-blue eyes that are my heart. You found me and I hope I was good to you. You always were trying to get your point across and make sure the whole room heard you. In your love for your voice to be heard and tried really hard try to get it out. Now, look at you . . . you're just stunning, with your personality showing me the way, being my leader in loving you the way you need to be loved, my perfect soul-angel in this lifetime form . . . which is now becoming a woman. I'm watching you grow into this edgy-blossoming boe boe, va va voom . . . . From struggling to speak, now you show your strength in speaking very clearly to me, and I hope I'm showing you your love style. May this always remind you of the power you place over my all-soul-heart. How you sit, waiting for me to love you more and more and touch-me-I-need-you . . . all mine! As you once told me so. You have so many scars from battles that didn't even belong to you. How've you over come them. From a child's 'hi mommy' to 'I love my momme.' From an infant to a young woman. As you stand in glory. You changed right before me from then to now. I can't even wait for you to continue your journey. Born on the day that changed my life and became your life. He left us a gift for which the world will be thankful. To live your life, as you figure out things on your own now in secret that's only between you and Him. To grow with you so I can keep up with the tymes. To not miss anymore. J'adore, my daughter. If only can no longer exist, only, go on love, grow . . . become. I give you my blessings to be free as you find your way, where I can no longer follow with you, as you mature and grow. As you become a maturing midanger, I'm learning so much from you. And you make me a better mom that's for sure. You allow me to be the kind of mom I really want to be. From, never leaving me, when you were a young child, to now closing your door so you can have privacy. I have to give you the best gift I can ever give you, is freedom to be you. You never have to carry burdens for me, for I'm in Good Hands for which He's now carrying you. I have the mother heart, you have the daughter heart, but we walk at the same beat. As I wish to spray my Dior J'adore fragrance upon your skin, you remember me and the love I will have forever. So don't forget where you come from, in every way I can open your eyes to your heart when you struggle from your past. How I named you . . . no way? You were destyned to myn and you were supposed to be. I just can't believe it, how much you are my miracle in staying alive for this purpose was supposed to happen. To not help you through that part of your life, but to help you with this part in your life. To feel you coming out into this sometimes not-so-big-world. God just blew breath into me and made His Purpose and my destiny. You. You are my breath. You are my heartbeat. One day I won't be here but I ask you to lay aside, to let my spirit lead you on this difficult journey of your life. You will lead with Christian power to live your life to the fullest. There are things you must discover on your own. Just like anyone else. I'm a breath away, séance my name and I'll be there. Until then, I'm just a touch away. I'm so excited to see where He takes you and I show my pride badge everyday. May you always remember my love for you. Keep this close my daughter. As I will always say to you even when you're old . . . . if you miss me, all you have to do, is close your eyes, and I'm right there.

"A Cherished One"

Can I? Can I write today? Of all my imaginations, let them spew out and let me create something that's unusual and new. So there was once this cat, who loved attention, who followed his master, Harry, everywhere he went. Well, this one day, Harry, was going to work and he was walking to the train station and I was around the corner. He did his normal thing, stepped around me, got whatever he needed to. The cat got in his mind that every morning, with this one in particular he said to himself, I'm going to follow master and I want to go with him. Harry collected his things and said good-bye as normal to his family and left for work as usual. As my master opened the door to my freedom, I was just behind him and just in the nick of tyme. I escaped that big thing that contains me in this room. Yes! I'm out! Yay, as I start trotting with the pace of my master, and started walking down the street as I just keep following happy-go-lucky. I wonder where he's going? Why hasn't he turned to see me? What a great adventure I'm going on today with my master. We were in this big open space and there were lots of people like my Harry. This is fun. I say out loud, hey, wait for me. Lots of stuff was around me. They were making noise. We stopped and I rubbed myself where I usually do on his leg, and waiting for attention. Master! He look down at me. Finally! Harry looked down at me and stopped in his track, and said Purrcy! He knelt down and picked me up just like he did every morning. But this morning, he didn't pet me, so I followed him. Finally, I'm so happy he picked me up. I said, good morning Master.

2nd half

All of a sudden, we were children, laughing, in an old station wagon, as we were supposed to be going to sleep. We were scared as our young imaginations come alive. Psst, just imagine slimy, creepy, straggly fingers wrapping around the windows. Psst! Look out! I grab you and pull your small body next to my equal, and I said, they're seeping into the corners. As I shake you to scare you and say it in a creepy sound. As I laugh my ass off inside. You'd whisper, stop! And I loved to scare you so my storyes always did. Psst! Did you feel that?! I yelled in my whisper. You begged me to stop, in your quiet whisper as to not to wake our parents. I have another one . . . ! Do you want to hear it? Should I reveal my second memory of just you and I? Remember when we'd see each other at Grandma and Grandpa's house? I wanted to pierce my ears and so we got some bobbie pins, and you took my ear and pushed. As hard as you could, so it would go through my earlobe. From that, my ears got really infected. To reach back to those days man. Pretty cool memories for me. I loved hanging with you. So that was the technical . . . and this is me . . . remembering old tymes of when we were children, headed back into being innocent, from their side. As I sit and let them come out with Him leading, as I run back to our childhood. You, the blond cutie pie and I'm just me. To remember them with fondness is not hard of nothing I can do. They can never take those days from yonder. And I hope you know, far away places still love that part of me, and I cherish you with words from the only Truth comes from. I'm sorry, for missing your life. He has His own Plan and we must follow Instruction. You are my childhood's imagination. Come'on, let's rewind our minds, forget of sorrow and traumas.

Don't drop her, she'll break! Take better *care* of her, I said to my reflection. My mom gave her to me! As I brush pink blush on my porcelain dolls face, I tell her, tell me all your secrets . . . as I remove her hair rag-ribbons. I can't drop her, ever. She would say to me, as I close my eyes and pray . . . I wear fancy clothes wrapped in silk and wearing a royal red cape. Just for you. You sing to me, to sooth me when I say goodnight. As I reach my praying hands up to my face, and prayed out loud, to the sky, I hold you up to swing you around my room, as I make you fly, careful not to drop you. If you could talk, I wonder what you'd say? You'd say, you're my best friend, as I continue to swing my doll around. As I would reach for your heart and remain open, to all hugs, as my arms, they *never* close. My name is, your porcelain doll, and I am special. I can see her . . . when you sleep. At night, I wish I could share all my secrets with you, so one day when you reach for me, and my power, through your love, I hold for her. You trust and believe in my secrets, and one day, they'll be told to you . . . as I whisper to her broken heart. I'm so glad I can tell you all my secrets and you keep them inside and never tell anyone, and I never have to be alone in my silent world. I can send your heart letters to explain my reasons to love you unconditionally through only our hearts. You take such good care of me. To know that you wipe my invisible tears when you share your sad storyes and know that they'll only stay with me. As I continue on to say, if one day, if I brake, if she dropped me, if she stumbled in the dark, I'll still love you, because I'm your porcelain doll. When you sit me on your dresser, I watch you with careful eyes to make sure *you're* not broken too. Did you know your mom watches you pray at night? She comes into your room, and sits by your side so that you're never alone in the dark. She's so beautiful, I see her, every night. When you sleep, I watch her softly kiss your forehead and stroke your hair and whispers in her raspyness tender love and she whispers in your ear . . . I love you . . . I love you . . . , through my emerald green eyes, gazing over her red-puffy-hair. Oh, how I wish I could speak. And I say to you, you whisper for me to tell all my secrets and you stop and wait, as you stroke my hair. As I look back on our childhood, how you've cared for me, ever since I was *finally*, picked up from that shelf so long ago. ~~~This beautiful woman found me. She looked right into my eyes and fell in love with my pale skin and all the rest of me, and she said; *look at her emerald green eyes*. She picked me up, and I knew, this is meant to be, I'm going home. As your mom placed me gently down in the front seat, placed where I would *not* fall, as I'm on a new journey. As we went home, she said; *she's going to take good care of you. She's going to love you and play with your hair everyday.* As her voice was of a million angels, as she was sent to rescue me from a life on a shelf. Her words were loving and *I* was chosen. She pulls up to her home and carefully picked me up and cuddled me in her mothering arms, to inside. *Ready porcelain doll?* She places me on the kitchen table. *Baby! . . . come down stairs angel*! I hear footsteps above my head and she came running to her mommy and ran with open arms, and the mommy said; *close your eyes, and when I count to three, open and look, okay? One, two, three . . .* Her little eyes opened up and lit up. She stared at me. Straight, into my emerald green eyes. She reached for me and held me close to her heart. She took me upstairs to her room and she says; I'm gonna put you *right* here, on *this* pedestal.

Hmmm, I guess I better go check on my little mouse. Who's once again, called to the friend that showed up at our door one day, asking if she knew the way to the place she was supposed to go. Oh, let me ask my Minnie, come in . . . make yourself at home. She was quiet and jittery. I perked my ears up and grabbed my tail to find Minnie. Where did she go . . . ? There you are Minnie. There's a rodent here, and she's lost. I have to go back to my workshop and finish building that trinket I found from the pathway at the front of our nest. I could hear them talking in their female squeaks that I didn't sometimes understand. As I heard Minnie say that, in the squeak she made when she was overjoyed . . . . Over the next months, Minnie was so happy, and squeaky, and I like her new friend. Now, where did I leave my flashlight again? I'll just have to ask her again. As I skittered down our leafy tunnel. As I was nearing our dome room, they were laughing again. I miss my Minnie Mouse, but I want her to be happy. Minnie? Do you know where I put my new wires for my newest trinket is? As she laughed at me as did her friend. As I stand there and wait for their laughter stop, I asked Paris, where's your wagon wheel? I want to fix your wheels. I heard her pleased squeak, really? . . . she asked as he skittered away to get it. I quickly scurried to Minnie and said; how is Paris today? Did she like the chocolate blood mousse? Did you leave *me* some of your chocolate blood mousse? . . . I haven't gotten your answer yet. Do you know where my new frayed wires are? . . . as I bent forward to kiss her cute nose with all those soft whiskers. I heard Paris and went to occupy myself as she awkwardly brought me her wheel. And too, Minnie carried my crooked wires in her mouth, and accidentally . . . ya right, nudged my side. I went back to my workshop. I can't wait to surprise Minnie's friend with a brand new, freshly made, remote control, fully chewed frays, wheel that she can press once, instead of twice. She's good to the mouse, so I have to be special to her and if she needs anything from me, she's got it. I don't really fully know her yet, but I know, from what Minnie's said about her, I think I'll love her too. She would come over and help clean by eating the bugs and getting rid of unwanted pine needles, so they'd make pretty girly things and Minnie would collect in a hole that I made for her. She stored them for the winter and to keep warm with her friend. After more time of knowing Paris, I want to help her feel wanted and needed. So one day I went up to her and said in my male squeak, thank you for helping Minnie burrow those seeds. Well, I'm headed out to find more nuts and bolts. I headed out of our hole. It was quiet and still and I was careful. I scurried under a log and found some grub for Minnie and Paris so they could cook it and give them more time together. In a while, I went on my way back to our hole and found them nesting beside each other to huddle together for their own assemblage. Thank You Night Sky, for sending us our lost Paris. She was meant to get lost, I just know it. Night Sky is huge, so it must have guided her here, so that's what I will teach Minnie and Paris. I went by them quietly and took my new finds back to my hole of wires, frayed bits, nuts, bolts, and a new metal piece that took almost two of me to carry, but it's for a good cause. As I snicker under my pant as not to wake the field mice. Thank you Night Sky. As I think back to when Paris talked to me, out of not too many yet, she squeaked; thank you, for helping me with this drafting breeze in my hole next door . . . thank you for fixing my brand new wheel. How can I ever repay you? Be good to the mouse.

"Devoted Christian"

Guess You had to test me again. Guess You had to see my defeat eh LORD? I retracted my prayer when I said, bring it on LORD, as I opened my arms towards heaven, and I closed my eyes and all I could think about was my LORD and our connection. I just wanted so much to have my new power in myself, and to open up and receive You and what You have for me. I want to be me now, so keep blessing me LORD. I don't want the dark side, . . . at all. I want You to heal my life and I give You everything. Cee. LORD, I need You. Please don't forsake me, for I hold the world in my site. To show You to them. I want Your Power. I'm not afraid, as Your Love is the only way to give me life. *This* is *my* power. Writing . . . so with days gone by, this is my thoughts, my prayer to my LORD. To show *you* my Power that lyes inside *me*. To shine, to prove to the world, that I mean something to someone . . . just like you do and you have. I'm not telling you anything to share my secrets. Just my thoughts, that run my life and to tell you that you don't have to be defeated either. To have let earthly feelings control me . . . I'm embarrassed. But sometimes, it's just 'cause we're humans. We have a life that we all need to live. Whether you're a rocker in London, with a ton of piercing, or you're the princess of a royal wedding, or you're a single mom living in a rotten basement suite reading a love letter to *your* LORD. Whether you're not religious, and to you, the devoted Christian. I want to have a part of your life now. And now, the LORD walks beside you, telling you to walk away with a Great Purchase. Ya know, I have many faults and sometimes I whish I wasn't me. But it's those mistakes, that guide you to a better life. We all have earthly feelings that we have to deal with on the way up and out. To feel and see sorrow, heartbreak, to live with catastrophic guilt. And to see and witness triumph and success. But some can't find the way out of the dark tunnel that seems to follow some of us around all the time. I suffered on the saddest day of my entire life. I suffered greatly. I was suffocated in agony and I was being choked and couldn't breathe. I prayed. I begged for death to find me, and take me to him. Every day, was my awake nightmare. To never see you again? . . . I was dead *with* you. I sobbed . . . every day, every night. I was being robbed. You died. Years later though, I found Him and His Glory and I found my destiny and I found and am finding our children's destynyes. I've realized over time, that the reason you died, was for me to find me. I know you're helping me from Home though. You're teaching me even after the grave. From your Green Pasture. Where suffering doesn't even exist. Not like here, where some suffer every day. Some of us will be constantly reminded of the shock waves from glitches in our lives. Who helps us grow, to learn, to love. Some of the population doesn't even know what love is. I've witnessed a lot in my tyme and I'm pretty sure I know the difference between love and hate. But that's just me though. I have an imagination and I don't want to pick a fight with you. I've chosen *this* life for me. And God has showed me many different lifestyles and religions. I'm not a professional in any field, and in many careers later. But my LORD is my whole life. This is just me, showing off my talent. From nothing, to *this*. From someone who's always wanted to trade someone else for my lyfe. Always tried to get rid of myself. To envy. To feel such jealousy. To want what I didn't have. I know one day, it'll be my turn. I have to believe in that dream. I'm a dreamer and in those dreams, there's always my LORD. Learn, grow, but love first, right LORD?

Tomorrow will be our first Christmas. Ever, together. How special and miraculous is our reunion. This year has been the best in my entire lyfe. Besides my marriage, and the birth of my off-springs. The most rewarding, special, sole dependants, independent, and growing year of my entire lyfe. And if all my whishes aren't fulfilled me in any way I was starving. To protect you, I can't share who you are, in printing, in so many words, that you would know who you are. To myn, they would know too . . . to be together, again. With this time, the most that I could have ever expected. I enter you through your windows, with no drapes to close off. As I type and so know, that tomorrow is going to be our first Christmas. Being this high up, I guess my air is running out, and then I read about Zenith, and know that No Other, could have brought us together again. You were some of my main focus on coming through the last decades of our lives. We have so much to celebrate. A love affair of two, come together, and become one and we all work together. To finally find our other hand. It was no wonder we had such a rough time. You were my hand and I was your hand. Now I finally understand things and I'm not confused anymore. I couldn't scratch my head. I made the wrong turn. And then we had to walk, by ourselves, when we were reaching silently and without our knowledge, and with them gone, we only have each other. I can't imagine a world that didn't have you in it. Isn't this something you say to your partner on their wedding day? Are best together, not supposed to make known to make our domain, home. We made our announcement to the world and we're being heard. We become a field of action, and we shook and shuffled the waters a bit till they spilt in words, that was making a couple of calls so the world would be a better place. I can only be, when I know you're backing me, and you've got my back. You'd take and carry a bullet and I'd take and carry a bullet. Your tears belong to me too now. When you cry, I want to be strong, but I cry with you. When you're so happy, I'm so happy. I carry you and you carry me. Right? We belong to the write of us. As I continue to find my fully developed destiny, but right beside you and then we have to jump really high to reach the top and to reach the bottom, we have a children's slide like a water ride and the sun is shining the whole way down, and we head in the right direction. You are my compass. And I wouldn't be where I am today without you, coming and saving me and rescuing me. I was so lost when I found you, and I was missing you so much, from a time from a long time ago, that brought us back together again. It goes beyond love. It's something I've never experienced before, in any human being. And I get lost in when we're together. Are best together? . . . yes. We join together and love our LORD. And without Him, this page could never have existed. And all my love wouldn't have existed. To love the only way I can, and shine in all my words and why *shouldn't* I type glory? This is because He brought us together and made you, you, so you could explain my lyfe to me. In *my* language that only you know the language to. To know that you'll have no knowledge of this letter, until you read, now, in Your tyme. And feed words to recite poetry in your head, but follow like an arrow pointing you the way home as like from an old memory. How could have we found each other if this isn't the write answer? If it wasn't for Him, showing us our future, in our pasts, as we spew our sorrow and joys, and just be able to vent. Our future moments will be recorded, so when we reach our Home, we can play them back and watch them over and over again.

What a trip I had tonight. I went to Christmas Eve church service and saw everyone. Well, not everyone. I was on LORD, and You shone through me in Your House of Worship. When I talked to that man who said he's not a Christian. I leaned forward to him and I said, I'll never believe you when you say you're not a Christian. You know who you are. I'll never believe that. And then I asked another, if he was writing music and he said, he should and that suggestion, it comes from the LORD. I prayed to You big-time tonight. You have blessed my children *double* this Christmas. And now I know how they will feel tomorrow when they both get the same thing, but in this circumstance, it's a great thing. What a blessing my life has become in the last year. And now, two sets are equally loved and to have showed it. To know, that my children, are that important, that both sides loves them. I'm so lucky to have that for my children and I'm going to share that when they discover they have two now and not just nothing. To bring two families together, to make one . . . with such love and devotion to each other. We all love for each other. We're lucky to *have* each other, and this year has brought me in a total turn-around from last year. To learn about *real* love . . . tender, soft. I was so bitter and hard. So much anger and resentment. And now I know tender and gentle. The way it's supposed to be. So much love. And I'm reminded of who I am to You, and how important this Love Letters must get to the people who need You most. And then I remember tonight and the whole day. Getting to spend time with my hand, and what a wake-up-call this entire day has been for me. And know that I and my children are so important to a lot of people. It's just so touching and overwhelming to know how much love they get . . . how we all get from these wonderful people, that I've missed so richly in my life, and how all the ones I love, know it. And to know one day, that all these people are going to be reading all these words. I have to just keep typing and hope I keep you tuned in for the next things to come. To bargain for your attention as I *capture* for your attention for a read. Tonight at church, three of the cutest babies were singing for us. Adorable moments for their parents and adopted aunties and uncles sitting observing the sweetest sounds on earth. Tonight, I watched my matriarch one, with her children, and I watched her with a new love inside me, with such tenderness, that I've never felt before. A love that should have always happened, but it's tyme *now*, and I'm glad I'm learning this now, before it's too late, until we meet again. I can't even talk about it . . . moving on. When I saw her, she had been crying, and I wanted to reach inside her and hug her so tight. I think she misses stuff from her life. Things she feels that she's lost. Clinging to love. I felt so much pure love and concern, and then more moving-forward-conversations and she moved away to home. I was sad for our rushed quick hug and Merry Christmas. I hope I've kept you reading. The words just keep coming, on this wonderful, majical night, from a blessed day whom we did not forget. I was so filled up with Your presence LORD. And my prayer that followed . . . just trippin' on it. I have no problem with my relationship with you LORD. I feel very privileged by knowing Your Name and You are my Highest Favour. I want to thank You LORDGod, for making this night wonderful and I ask that I remain faithful in my service for You, all the days of my life. That I shine Your Light and for people to see It, and reach for It. That you remember the joy that comes from this holiday. Always pray for Him, and He will bless you in uncertain ways.

"Our Christmas Present"

Feel and fell. I feel with a new peace and comfort in knowing You're listening. Let go and feel something brand new. I was showed *real* love this Christmas. You connected me, in a new way. I feel so happy in us, and notice it's a three. This is our fight. That we must face in the power in the number three. We have to face our beat, our song that leads the body to dance in the spot. When I feel free, for the first time, and I'm not heavy anymore, as I fall and tremble, when you catch me, I go limp with fatigue. As I make my sound on the way down. How you've fed me and quenched my thirst for distress and you've both cured it. My fingers will be lead with more purpose, more knowledge about how I've been sunk under concrete and you've managed to break through and set me free. How I've found new love with a new chapter. You are now my lullaby with softness surrounding you with song like from heaven's clouds. How you've opened a new life in seeing me filled with rest and I'm assured. I'm at peace with your open ears and silent heart, in breaking down a brick wall, with only with your help, can I be me, anytime I want. I can remain mysterious to the wondering eye, and to never fully know what these words mean. I wanna be led, and no anchor will keep me in one place until I'm freed with love and confirmation of self. I'm not silenced anymore and I can fly in relationships going on the their failure. It's been saved from evil and unspoken words, of frustration and boiling in spewed anger. How I feed you with the texture of words and live in my worlds of feelings. I don't have to feel around in the dark anymore and the space isn't too small anymore. Whereas I was drowning in love and there was no way out. I was being stuffed in a box and left there to remain cramped with no stretching room. I'm not in the claustrophobic sphere of stale air. A helium balloon as blown up under me and has carried that part to it's explosion. I'm not tumbling down the eternity hills that never disconnect. My freedom. To listen to the poetry that wants to be written at lighting speeds, of when I press down as the music leads the swirls of never ending bars of notes. Of when the person strokes the wires and the voices that speak out to match the music. To let it carry me to another place of somewhere it may exist or may not. But as you read, don't let you get crept out, that you can't recover, as you try not to get scraped up as you crawl to the hill above you as you drag through the rocks and all the sticks. I'm free of the rules that came down with all that. To know I wasn't truly. My arms couldn't carry the burden of my freedom with that anymore. To know that He answered my dying whish, and then to get, in my face, in knowing how much love is around me all the time. To know I don't have to love with confusion. A warfare. The warfare of you and me. I'm not divided between two nations, as I'm laid at rest and start now. To get to know a new me, my new world of reality has changed forever. And I said thank you and showed appreciation. I swallowed humble-pie and squeezed out on them and they hugged a new me. I can swim anywhere in the ocean and lie on a beach now and follow my dreams, as I continue to write. So thank You, for showing me a whole new life that I never knew existed, and new faith that I never had, to know that when I really needed to see the kind of love I needed, you showed me and gave me, to my selfish heart, but was being selfish because I needed to cry out and for you both to hear me and believe in my new identity. The other part of me, can now be free with me, and to let all these words to be shared on both sides. We were given each other for Christmas this year.

Be the best you can be. Know that every choice you make, makes your life upon what it's supposed to be. Work with the ten percent of the stress that's taking up the scars that I've carryed along the way to today and my feelings that I belong to that are only myn. Why live in the wrong way when you can love the write way? Why dance to a song you don't know, when it's calling your name, and blast it out the window and you'll see reactions, which you may not agree with. Dance in your own life and don't limit to the low level of them who said you couldn't do it and you did. Pose in front of the mirror and smile at your reflection and understand who's looking back. Don't let yourself stomp on the wine glass that holds the wine of the root of your taste buds. Be your glass fulled up. If you spill over, catch up and rush to put the glass under it. Fill up again and renew your senses and dance with looseness and flair around like your hand going over a plate of water. And make splashes, as in the woods, does it make sound as it falls? Make the fish jump up to grab your line that will carry you to the next ripple in the waves you've created. Become. Anyone you want with no tops and unlimited access. Be intense or not, but I recommend yes, be intense. Don't rush to end your life. Don't live upto only ten percent. Become a rush that people need to know who you are, and live for pure gold to shine and sparkle in the spotlight coming your way, and let it sweep you off your feet and land in a puddle of mousse and slip you into the clouds of life. The base of your life, will help with your judgement and your next thought into the future you don't know about yet, that if you wrote down, it wouldn't happen in that way, because that's not how life is written. Live in virtue and happiness and let the righteous and quality show in your windows of opportunity, and let your poetry, whether in words, or actions, or signs to show your language. Let you swing and sway and let your body turn loose inside and let the ten percent grow to eleven percent. Live as to a new motto, compared to what? Let the horns out a bit, but be with a glow of goodness with a red light shyne the mists of your features. Don't let aggression ruin what could be. Don't let you become a pantry of a closed closet and not allowed to be pulled out. Be open, become your own beat on the drums as like in a ceremony of some kind of tribal dance. You should accept your capacity and live with the entire volume at maximum. Be a flower at top speed with growth in slow motion to enjoy and be at joy at our lives from with God has chosen for you specifically. You have your own power that you must master at, and shown in approval. Spray your perfume, from your collection and spray yourself with the only fragrance that you can create and invent. Be of a flowery or musk scent as to make it original and remain true to you. Burst forward and lead to perfection of your past and present, which is a gift that should be lead. Run at fast speeds to understand where you need to be so that you can bong on the elastic rope that you live with connected to something that shouldn't be cut to let you go. Be a spring that bounces you back to the coil that you've made so that you can't see what's to happen. So, hang on to whatever you can so when you let go, you know where you're going. Be a book on information, so when the question comes, you know the answer, and people can look up what they're looking for. Be the leader that leads you to the promise of what's to happen and come for you to bathe in, soak up everything and be an encyclopaedia of the million dollar question that you must answer to your selection of words that become your entire empire that awaits your return to your future.

Today . . . what day is it? I continue to wipe my loud tears as they yell their way out of my body. They can't bare to live in this way, so they forced their way out and I sobbed them out into the palm of my hands and your glass container as I held you at my heartbeat. Every night, and this is what I have to say. I can't stop sobbing, as I lay my body over his casket. This is the most tragic day in my entire life, as I sobbed as I watched him go into the ground. They buried him slowly as to make me suffer more, that I couldn't imagine life without him. Oh my God! As I imagine my body lowering beside the inside with his dead body. I'd rather suffocate with his body underground than live forever, for the rest of my life, breathing without him. I remember when he was at the bottom of the grave. My huge tears fell down and filled up all six feet. It was a concrete box with a lid. I couldn't believe it, that he would be there forever, no longer allowed to live in his human body. How could I live without him? Knowing everything I hadn't said and what I did instead. I crouched at the head of the hole and looked down at the yellow flowers that layed on top of the casket and the box I had no choice, and I watched my tears fall and they all splattered on my husbands covered body. My soul was being battered and slammed against the top of the cover to open and beg him, to plead with him and say, take me with you. When I had to leave you, I had to remain in the arms of my father, as he said, come on sweetie, they have to do their job. As he struggled to hang onto my falling into limp body and how he carryed me on the most tragic and catastrophic day in my entire existence. I couldn't walk up the hill, as I ripped away from my father's arms, and went back to the head of my husbands eternity bed and resting place, as he lays in his stillness, and laying in green pastures. To never hear your voice again, to never sleep by your side as now I am a widow, alone in my isolated world, that I took in comfort at night when the world slept and I sobbed to you in the quietness of my jail of sorrow and torment and agony. I was alone. No one understood my pain. I suffered in the pits of hell when I started grieving. To no longer have the love of my life, sitting next to me. And now he rests right beside me whispering my rewards for being a good servant, and will bless me, I pray in great humbleness, my LORD. To miss out of such gladness that *you* can see through the invisible window, that's only, one way. But I dreamt one night, an angel walking towards me, with a bright light shining behind him as he walked towards me, and he didn't say a single word, he just looked at me and then it was gone, and then the following night I dreamt of the angel walking towards the light that shone in front of him. I watched as you walked away and I woke up and I knew something was wrong with you. I had a pit-gut bad feeling about you and I asked if you were okay, and she didn't know either. Then that's when the end of your calling to us, to beg one of us to hear your screams of mercy of the agony you experienced too during that time, and when God got my attention. So much started to happen. So many signs to find your dead body that lays in your car, waiting, calling out to us to pay attention. On the same day, two knew something was wrong, and then came across *devastation,* and the long road to recovery with the children that will be blessings to this world. For me to find my destiny, that your life helped create in my life. I've had to forgive me, and forgiving myself has been the hardest part of my recovery, but now I know, you rest in the Father's Arms and I trust in Him. Your *purpose,* was supposed to. The day I had to bury my husband.

"Our Sky"   December 27th, 2010

To miss you today, and tonight. I want you beside me as I sit lonely on my chair writing you *another* Letter. Another Love Letter that I'm at peace with, that you made a choice for your eternity and forever, so your soul is waiting for me, and I know you are my love. As I continue on to tell you that you are my softness of touch that you get my attention through our language. You are the tip-toe in the lilies of the valley as they open bloom for you and you run to the never-ending sky. You are my tiredness and dreary eye lids as they want to flicker to sleep in your arms that sway me back-and-forth. And sing me my new favourite song, that explains to me your letter back to me for me to understand what you need to release for you to be at peace with my new era of living without you in my form eterntity. It's you that fell into the sky, that you wait as you're going to travel with me and I live for you and show a love that they don't understand yet. And you can't explain it, because they just won't know our parent hearts, that lead every decision. The sacrifice to be a good mother. I hope to see you too, maybe I already have, but have forgotten, but how could I forget something like that? And I think I did see once, through air. I'll be with you one day, and I hope you're going to be there for me to run to. I want to see you through my dreams as I fluctuate. You shift back and forth in my dreams, where you see me, and I look past you and you look at me like I'm suppose to know you, and then I realize that it's you that stands with arms and legs crossed and is close shaven and short hair, clean-cut, and so handsome and beautiful and you come to me and I think, oh my God! . . . , you're alive, then I wake up from my dream. Then I wake to an empty spot next to me, where you haven't been in more than thirteen years. Back to regret not enjoying you more as I could now, with passion to light up our sky. To be our own quay where we can hit the shores whenever we want to. To be a particle of water to go and be everywhere, anywhere. To either glide or swim beside the dolphins as they jump for playtime. But, we can do anything because I'm the writer and I can do things that seem out-of-the-ordinary. So then I can astral but can only imagine what freedom really looks like. To do your first thought, with no fear of reaction, because there will be none and it's a fantasy worlds. To not change anything because I can make up anything. To be tired and soaked in tiredness in how to make you travel to another place in case your stressed or worried or scared or confused. I hope that I can comfort you and assist in helping you make the right decisions that need to be made. Even if they're impossible, you have to struggle and claw your way to the top. That I won't vandal on the way up to outstretch your arms and fill you with the love that I will seal with a kiss. I want to share the time where I carryed your cross and how I stumbled over and over again. I could never stay on solid ground. How I stumbled in my head-on collision to today. To write to you again fills me in every way. Such beauty with songs of high pitch music that matches the lullaby to settle my rattled nerves. I look at you with something beautiful to come from here to there. Play me, stroke me and strum me to the next note. As you play your celestial instrument that doesn't belong to earthly things. And it's with words coming out, to make one of these, to float out and compose on it's own. I can't wait to see you again my beloved, my sweetheart. How I want to announce to all my loved ones how our love happened. We rushed through so much, it seemed we were always in a hurry to get to the rest of our lives. When I see you hun, we have forever, with that, I'll be fyne.

I'm finally free and I can finally let it go into the lyrics of the song love myn. I can only wish you alive in my dragging soul most of the time, that one day, you'll take my hand and help me jump up to where you are as my plane trail trails behind me. It's all about you right now. I don't know why. Maybe it's tyme for me to set you free from me, so you can finally find and go Home first, to prepare me for my eternity with you and we become one, where we know everything, every thought we ever continue to have. As my weight becomes your blubber bubble, and as my heart just whispers hello and I love you. May you know my sorrow in such heaviness that I could no longer take it. But I became strong in the LORD and the one who sneaks around you in the dark. In the shadow that doesn't exist in Him. How deep can we go? Deeper you say? I remember when we were at the bus loop downtown, and we snuck behind the bushes. I was so stressed out that we were going to get caught. I whish now I was as secretively seductive for you and I would have played longer. Heavier? I remember when we made love twice that tyme. It was my favourite tyme with you in this way. How romantic you were back then my beloved husband. I'm finally free to release my love for you, in only the way I can, knowing just us, and our sign through me and my thoughts. How your soul was torn and shattered on *your* journey to heaven. How you must have floated above for days, wondering what to do. How you journeyed as I am now, but notes of music, that feeds me peace in your path to change my life three times. The day I met you, the day I married you, and the day I buried you. The majic powers in these numbers that follow me everywhere. Because of your love, the world will change and live on for forever. I pray that their love songs are as romantic as yours and mine is. How you cradle me in your arms with such love flowing from your heart to mine. How when you caught my every tear, you took them to heaven with you and are now comforting me. As a blanket is wrapped around me, nice and soft. I get lost in your arms and come with me, as I jump in our sky. We don't stop going up and we go through the top to the next galaxy. I have to refeel and regain momentum in our story. Come to me my love and keep whispering in my ears. As I breathe deep and get ready. So I was warned ahead of advance. From the Trinity of all this, is she with the name and I grab at words to recreate the rest of my life, and to share my live heart with his dream heart. Bring to life, something that's just amazing, like your dreams coming true. You trust and the world opens up to let the Light in and this is how it's going to be told. Where will we be tomorrow? Where we couldn't live without bold announcements from the LORD? To bring out the intencement of everything I've ever lived . . . my darling. Can you believe this is happening to us? To be able to share my love affair with the ghost of my husband, of his spirit, of what we would have had if we were perfect that can only live in my imagination. You wouldn't believe it! So many lives are going to change. That came from our, love story. Bring you to life again for a while and put you in the actor and have you stay as we write on stage in front of the cameras. That is only a huge dream that will change lives, and the history of Hollywood. And it's only because you existed my love, do you see how important you are? Even after-life? Rape my soul to remind me of our past so I can write about it forever and to let go of all the words that are dedicated to you, my new and old weighing you down my love. To not be a foreigner in your arms. Be myn, love my soul, love my heart.

My dreams are actually coming true now in tyme in my life. To have to reach down and describe his death in taking a motion movement and I have to relive all that pain from back when you died. To have to write in explicit instruction on your suicide. Of your every movement and words you said as you fell asleep, with your relationship with Jesus. With such intence feelings and emotions, bring to life, what you last did. I have to look at you in another person. I'd have to make up conversation, but since you're beside me, just whisper in my heart and head through the crown. As vision after vision of explanation of all my visions and revelations and explanation to certain thoughts that now were visions upon visions and explanations as to why I had that one and that one, answering so many questions. All the sevens following me and intervening with my Director of Everything and my hand and proving I'm not lying as I'm spilling my storyes. As we share it with everyone and give a new story to the world, and all the choices I've had to make to get this. And this makes me deliciously in the taste of being scared of something that could never happen again in my lifetime on earth. As it drinks me in with intoxication of your last gasp of breath, as it echo's in and sends you on a thousand journeys of this life that never ends. As it sits up there for how long? And then it falls to the last one I'll never get from her, and it fell. That's gotta mean something right? It's the end of a rainbow of short span as to show Him and then go back to everyday life until the next one, of all colours. Will you be the silence that sends me the message of the end of our love? The silence I've lived in for years, and I know the type. And if she calls, I'll be the message machine she talks to, and I will be live feed. I'll just wait till then, until then, I will continue to share my story. To have to keep faith in who I am and trust that this, will never go anywhere, that the next tyme I have to go insane, I'll be able to lean my tyred body against Your wall. We had three hundred and seventy eight days. The Trinity, Your Perfect number, and the sign of eternity. All holy numbers to the end date and I'm a stronger person for loving them, and I've gained strength, and a new love for life, and I don't know what will happen for sure, but this is my prediction. Three. Your Face is everywhere. With just a thought, and its all gone, with a snap of your finger. You had everything, then, in a flash, it's gone. All for making a very fatal choice. Such regret and betrayal. From something that you shouldn't have done, and I'm the killer that never makes a sound quenching from the Truth, which now strangles me and pushes me off of that cliff over there in the distance. To know she won't have that security, when I just said that to you. Will I never hear your angel again? It was so clear. I'm being strangled with a reality that I had forgotten about and now reminded of the errors of my ways that will end forever. But, I'm strong now, but I don't know everything yet, but it's so easy for me to judge me for my wrongs, that slap me across the face to wake me up to nothing hugging you in return. I hate the empty ring, with none voice at the end of the coil to say whatever you have to say to me and then go beyond my life to live yours, and you didn't expect this in return. Sorry, it's too late, no apologized comeback. We are the love song that must come to an end. As the brakes come to a screeching halt and slaps us with that we are human. I beg Him to be perfection, but only He can take that Spot, and tomorrow will come and the Truth will be told to me and a new fear that creeps behind the door and opens and scares you, and you freeze and deep breath, but this breath isn't myn.

"My A Kasha"

I'll tell you if I find something interesting. No, it's not important. Tell her I figured all this out on my own. Yes you did my love. We discovered the world today with each other. That we are connected in such a holy way, that you see it too. That we feel such intenseness as we have our mother-daughter hats on on the same head with different thoughts, but sometimes having the same thought. I feel so much love towards you and we are each other. This is our moment that is unbelievable and I have to tell mirror . . . that I couldn't get a hold of, which fed me more of what I had to learn over the past few days with about a hundred perceptions, from my second daughter, that I've adopted. As you dance your freedom next to me, and I have one more word, which I have three kids. With you included with three there, next door with the invisible door, that comes and has fun with your imagination and can jump from one scene to the next. To feel and have knowledge to so much of the heavenly concert playing in my head. To feed us such information, that we need to write about and let the imagination play, and come up with so many deathly plays. How we keep important information that we need to make it to the next step. You are my idol, you said to me just a while ago. That means that you, have blind admiration for me, which is supposed to be. In me, knowing how you love such a special person who carries many loads, and who has what it is. Laugh, I love you back, my dreams, who have come to lyfe within my third eye and we have figured out your name and there's purpose to death, and we need to live in their deaths. As we unveiled so many things that brought us today, with such importance, that we were being Called to find Him today and him today, and remember where we come from, as we bow to the LORD and wash His Feet, that has Walked where we are now, that He too, had to find The Way. As I breathe in and gasp as if I was having a baby, and laugh at the Power You show us. How other people would frown upon, You have blessed us today with Your Perfect Numbers. We always must be holy upon the world, as you nod at me believing those nods as submissions of facts of You're telling me the Truth. As you snicker and say our lyfe is trippy . . . and I laugh inside for I can write it all down and you'll never forget this day, where you found many answers that you've had questions to. We are here sitting next beside each other as I can record this moment in forever of history of any records, but I think it's records. As interruptions are required to recover for new material and to say, I love you. To not race to the end of our lyfe. To not end us soon as it just happened for us. As you came with me to the saddest spot where you were opened too, so you could find it. How it was wondering who's been there for of the smear across his name that will one day belong to you and your other soul, who shared my womb and grew together in separate containers with my blood pumping through your veins who share my love. You both heard the same voices, but had to fight your way to breathe equal air. My air. I look to the heavens to read my soul twin who's wrapped around my waist and trudge up my hills and stumble down into my valleys. It's such a burden to be chained with you dragging behind, which I once had of your father. I looked around and he was chained to my right ankle and he was dead, dragging behind me. What a dream that I was glad to awake from, as I had to bury him over and over, with you and you right upstairs. As your little girl rested on missing me and I now shake with your reality, which were filled with voices that are now screaming to get your attention, answer them. How?

"Dear Barbie Doll"

This is part of publication and this is the first Letters like it . . . as you experience me, front row seat. Oh welcome, come in, as I pull the chair out as you all sit down. I'm going to take you on a special journey. In other words, welcome to my world. Of creating, from reaches of this and this from above that seals us from them, but they follow us all the time and I'm able to hear. I haven't spoken of my lyfe yet as I live in a mythical and metaphysical worlds that make me up to full. This will make publication and maybe to something that's not invented yet, and I give you a glimpse of the future, with sparkles and sprinkles. I've had to discover, uncover mysteryes as the day went on to now which is still mind-blowing information that is wrapped in pretty huge bows that weigh the parcel down, but what's waiting inside? . . . this is the day I discovered my destiny and build some old characters from my play of my life. With the darkness a part of me, knowing the effect of ripples as it jumps and bites you in your crown to open up to new ideas and wear what materials you were. Blessings? I hear words from deep within me, as you're trying to keep up to my pace of where I'm going with this . . . let's just keep reading. As I touch your head and keep your eyes open as you continue to read this Letters, to my Barbie Doll. Who was my favourite doll to play with when we go way back. When you were standing in non-attention, face-to-face with the enemy, filled with lectures of who you should be in their eyes. You were finding your way, and I just played around you, trying to join in conversation that was only meant for you and them. How you were the chosen one for years to yintime in my mind. How our distance lead me in another path so far away from loved ones to live my life, to find my way. To live without you and others of the like. I grew up. I became a woman of strength. Of power that can only come from Above. I grew up with new friends, and the only ones I had, but now that part of lyfe is over, but I let it live within me for a reminder of where I learned to love the LORD, in Power and Faithfulness. I write and rewrite my life to where it is complete and even though it's full of selfless . . . oh, who am I to say all this? How you yelled at me at the next generations place of living, that I loved as my secret. How I played that joke on you and you said my name in such horrified voice, crushed to live the next second. How your smile and laugh reside inside my heart. How you used to love it way back to yesterday. Loss has taken part of my lyfe and I had to swallow in criminals of the night to regain breath and learn from long isolation to listen, and to learn and to appreciate all my days of my lyfe. Live in my world for a while and you might get tripped out. To know all I know, and to know that one day, it will spill over the Nations and be seed for a new flower in the sunshine. My brain has been shaked and rattled into a new plane and now I live with things that can only come out then. Shake your head if you understand. Oh, you don't? . . . that's okay. Only little left till the end, so how can I grip your attention to read the only one like it? One day, when you see me up on the billboard going down the highway, may you laugh and say, right on . . . yes, she made it. May my lyfe be your bong as like that of a bell, in reflection and you hear me when I say something. For it's with Power that I speak these words. For you to listen and lead the pack forward. Be clear in your speech, so when it's muffled, you'll be able to understand. Listen for the beat that will slide into you and make you sway backwards and forwards and tumble in my fascinations. Please, tell them how far I've come.

I know you love me. I love you and you want to protect me from lyfe. Part of lyfe, is loss. If I have lung cancer or any type of cancer that I go. This is not a suicide letter, this is a loving and tender, I love you letter. If I have it . . . okay, you don't want to go there, and I know you want me to write about butterflies and make you laugh again, like that one time. Tear jerker's are my specialty and spelling out love is like second nature. So, okay, fine, we'll talk about butterflies, but just for a minute, because I need to show you Perfection, with the LORD, in my world of understanding something I can't explain. I whish I knew everything about my purpose here, as the music carries butterflies on His Hands. You're gonna have a hard time with this news, or, okay, maybe I'm wrong, and I'm gonna pray about it before anything happens, so to open my mind again. The voices are calling to me and are instructing me to do something, but I can't make it out. I know that you want to talk it through, process . . . that's your word baby. Powerful word if you think about it. One day, you'll be processing, with answers I don't know and I don't have. Cee, that's why I told you I want to know everything. And not wait for another frickin' thing. But, one day I won't have to wait, and I'll know the Final Answer. Okay, think, yellow, sunflowers, pink, sparkles, field mice and white. You are the song that now haunts you, with those power words spilling a wicked reality, with beats that take you to another place in your head. To be able to create, anything I want, even a suicide letter, but praying over it and just putting my whole soul and Christian heart, that I hope I do have a lyfetyme with you and me, with mistakes and all, write you? Who else could make me make stuff up and stuff? How his death will haunt you in hiding behind the LORD, and make you come to terms with many things that you call your strongholds. That He wants to give you anything, but you have to learn to let go. To be free in your soul that is just aching and I wish I could take all of them away and blow them out the other end of my closed fist, and they'd be gone. I pray for Perfection Healing, and love yourself. You beat yourself with a thousand lashes, and I share your pain, so I'm being slashed with you, in equal pain, suffering, over and over . . . babe, just wanted to say I love ya. Every lick of love we get, goes with us, to There. But, I know, you don't want to talk about it. I whish I could write a love song for us. I wonder what I'd say? My pretty pink and burgundy and gold hiding in a painting so I can discover the artist. To make you cry from all my love, ya know? Not that I want you to cry, don't get me wrong . . . . thinking . . . . to steal a lifetime of making you the Perfect blond that will be yours forever and you'll never have to read a box to get it to where you want. I'd grab your hands and rub them together to create friction for this fiction. Look at that, they're calling to me again, in tune and hiding behind the voices singing. Do you think my dream is real? Does it mean me? The steps of the process that's going to happen very soon, face it, it could happen. As you shake your head and say no, stop it. I know you'd sacrifice so much if I do, and run *yourself*, into the ground before me. Your devotions would show you sickness and worry, and you'd sacrifice so much, and it won't be like that. Says me. You must pray everyday when you beg God for your prayers. I carry your cross my love who cleans with white for perfection. I'll try to be strong for you now after all the times you were strong for me and each other. Don't let it choke you with the guilt I carried for so long, fight your way to breath. Don't let anyone creep in your house and tear down your . . . .

Yes, I am heavy, thank you for asking. Sweep in my zone and sweep me under the carpet as my heart is detached, and I have to create what I'm good at. I have to go deep into the bloody wound and stitch it with no eather. Nothing to put you under the knife as I'm a problem to deal with, with openness that we need to make that our honest spots. I have to relive everything, from then to then, that followed me and tortures me inside the skin I was given and I've abused it. And now, here comes the question. Tell me what you were thinking, in your brain, so I can get the words right. I'm still mending from all that time ago, that was your purpose, so this could happen for me and so I can change the world and make it a better place, but I can't without fans, that blow me over with their whishes and dreams that couldn't exist without them. As they both carry me through this now difficult task I must comply too. With no conditions, as my heart doesn't know which side to belong to. And it's fascinating and out of my control, that takes me to your world of air and no air. We don't have to breathe anymore, and we're freed. We are no longer slaves to this brutal earth planet thing that revolves around such a breath-taking galaxies, but then, there's here, with them. I'm attached to the invisible which I live by everyday as I say what I do and be pushed on, and it's the invisibility that I love so much. As you pull through slowly and constantly, through my pours, criss-crossing each other and blends and I tend to my slowly ending heartbeats. It's all because God knew my path and cee, He led me to you on purpose, so I could and show the world a new way of looking at The Other Life. I hope you're waiting for me. Where there's absolutely no prerequisite except live by Him and His name. I want this in my lyfe. This *is* my lyfe. Christ is my lyfe and bless the LORD. May you take it however, but this is me and my lyfe. This is the only lyfe I've ever known and I live as good as I can. I know I can be impossible, but I have reasons to everything I do. And one day, a long time ago, you were part of that too. Do you show me your footsteps in my fuzzy dreams? Are you calling out to me? I'm trying to answer, but I don't want to be wrong LORD. *And* I don't want to be wrong. Please strum me to the next chorus that will show me my entire life and death. I want to know everything about all the mysteries and answer questions to settle the earth into a calm, but I know that wars need to happen, to show ending on tyme. I will end in tyme with purpose so the next one can move on and so they can find *their* answers, which you did, before your final breath, away from me, to another lyfe that I can't follow you and follow you into a breathless atmosphere, and no blood to bleed because you were in pain. It doesn't even exist There as we fly at lightening speed as whizzes of Light falling beside us over the rest of them and sprinkle angel dust, to clean them and their spirits of worry and tormenting things. That whenever we want to, in our yinyears together we can go see God and bow in front of Him together and look out of the corner of our eyes and smile . . . but what about here? Strongness lives here. I can not take away from them, so I have to keep my body for now, but you all share my heart, because no one knows the power of my love, okay maybe a few people know. How love swallows me in huge gulps and I travel through them and love them, and I can't let go. Especially you and you and you and you and you . . . you get it. May this Letters reach you and show you who I'm speaking to. May you all live a righteous life and strive for, in Perfection the LORD that carries me, and full of emotions on my part, while He walks you through.

"Bumpy Ride"

As I sit and listen to the music that reminds me of you, I dreamt that we were having a baby. I let the words haunt me and run in and hide within my head and spills out another Letters to you to always tell you I love you, and I feel you near me today. I am hypnotized in your past lyfe here with willingness to fall asleep and find you in my dreams and cling to you forever. I must finish what I started for other people are waiting for me to let it all go. I know it may seem familiar, but you looked so good in my dreams like we never left each other in the spirit realms, and how my dreams are light and normal activity for you There. Like just another day where I'm just happened to be pregnant with you smiling at me, just like you did in the beginning of our love story. You'll be with me, I'm sure until you know I'm on my way Home. As I stand letting the water drip down and pour off my feet, I imagine you there with me, as my towel keeps me warm and dry. I have to say I love you, and you're the reason I was born, to live, to experience, to loose, to learn to find me in all this lyfe mess that I can't treat any different from what it is. Both a bumpy ride and a rollercoaster with a hell elevator going up and rocking you in your chair when you're a hundred feet in the air. As you act like a child and spit off the top of the ride and see where it lands . . . in a child's eye. And once, you were a child, born to live a lyfe with great purpose, as with your death. You once ran on this ground and won the race and that's when you felt great as, the chosen one, to your close friends. I will never let your lyfe be a joke or light-heartedness. You were chosen to fall in love with me and to give me your children, to raise them, and love them apart from being husband and wife. I hoped that we could have a long life, but the way I was back then, it wasn't supposed to be that way. My journey was to be me, for all I was and am, as you were. All it takes is one person to change the world. How can I change the world without you? Knowing I have all your children, both here and there. Tomorrow brings new adventures, with ties to the tyme I will last breathe. This is our moment together. Let's show them how powerful our love is for each other. Let's not play hide-and-seek in the woods where I loose you behind the trees with the white bark that scares me enough to grasp the dashboard with nail marks to show my fright. The long roads we drove together, and I whish I could rewind the tyme clock, but I can't and the long journey here has stopped and moved on to another thing. How I loved your storyes, but I whish I was more open to your fragile heart to know that I shouldn't stomp it to a thousand lashes that I went to your grave before you entered forever, and my mind and soul brought a shovel and lifted all the dirt for where you were to lay from suicide in your fields of other graves that is quiet and serene. Where birds chirp and fly in groups, as I sit below your headstone, that says, together forever. I was to condemn you, as I always do, to describe what has happened to you and happen to me but I whish I didn't, but I can't change my wrongs with you expect through my dreams where you visit sometimes to show me you still love me. I will forever write you Love Letters to show you that even through others, it always comes back to you, to let go and prove myself to you, but one day, he'll be special and he must know about you and your journey to death and your life in the hereafter. How your love for music shows me the way, the hearing of the words I whish I could copy and use them as mine, but I can't, so this is it my love. How I show you, forever, and trying to mend from our pain from us.

I had to get lost in my grief tonight, but please can we move on? No, as He answers, and tells me I need to get through this, from love and tenderness. I had to relive your final moves of your life in your suicide. I had to jump into a body I thought maybe it's you. Showing me the way, through a script that I must write for all survivors. In any form, all. Show faces from the one they *love,* from suicide. Show the *reality,* of suicide. The stage of where you were when you died. When you shaved your moustache off and when you shaved your head and hid it under your hat the last day you saw me and I saw you, in the wrong way, on that final day, of my goodbye, not the way I want now. Can I take it back? No, but maybe creating from it, can be a healing tool. I need to get through this again, that has now invaded me and now I'm creating our love for other people to view, and to share all my faults, and to teach people, that you don't have another time. *This is it.* The *last time you see him* . . . and the next time you see him, he's dead. When you find someone you love from suicide, it hits you like a tsunami. It hits you, like a volcano's eruption. Violently. Everything about you shuts down and you're being eaten alive by maggots of the darkness, and they spew you out to feed shit. You never know what can happen from someone else's torment and sorrow over their loved ones committing suicide. I lost myself. For a very long time. It was like I was being brutally murdered everyday, but I kept living through my murders every time. My tears owned me, and they'd make their presence show every night. The sobbing quiet begs and pleas of mercy of my death, that plagued me every night in my dreams of your dead corpse tyed around my ankles, and rotting and decaying bodies, in dark places. I'd dream of his two gravesites and what they looked like, but never knew the details when I woke up, and they'd haunt me during the day, with bags under my eyes from the devil's death over me, how he ate me alive and made me suffer in agony, that I didn't know if I'd stop crying or not. Cry so hard, that I couldn't open my eyes the next morning, so I'd hide in my dark room and put on my okay face, and lived on, where I didn't know where I was going. I'd be hit with fits of rage towards people of who suffered right next to me, but became people I didn't want around me. I'll never know, how horrible it was for my family and friends getting me through this, this darkest lyfe, I can't imagine. I missed my children growing up. I couldn't even brush my own hair during the day, and forgot why I got out of bed? As I scratch my head in my silent sobbing voice. To get over so many years of zombie me, on auto-pilot, and when I had to smile, I smiled, when I had to be queen-shit, I was. Trying to be normal, but I never was. At night, I'd be terrorized by images I'd cee. Ghosts loved to taunt me at night. They'd stand in front of me and wave like an old woman with no eyes, and followed me. They'd annoy me when they wanted my attention, as I'm standing singing to my LORD, surrounded by friends. I think I'm still haunted, but now, I can accept it for what it is now. Surreal was the events that were happening to me, with and without my permission. I questioned God a lot during this dark time, and I didn't hear what He wanted to tell me until now. Suicide is real. It robs you of any kind of joy, unless you're perfect and don't have feelings. Whoever suffers from it, is affected and effected. How I had to live both worlds, both from heaven and also from hell. The warfare I went through as I started following the LORD again after Andrew and I separated, and just when he died. There is, yes, there is another choice.

"Everything"

What am I supposed to say to him tonight? I'm sorry honey, I've been keeping me from you, and I'm sorry. I thought you didn't want to know, and what I have to say, is huge. As I struggle for tonight to happen for us both. As I sit and explain myself, and hope that you'll be sitting with me, across from me. This is our moment, and this is so important. It's about stuff you don't believe in, so I didn't think you'd mind not knowing this stuff. To have to explain why, I have to do what I have to do, and you're apart of this. To be a part of this, you have to stand right next to me, supporting me, us, and tell you what's been happening to me, spiritually, that's created all of this. To never have known that you share my secrets too, and you have every right to know. I sometimes forget how much you want to be free too, beside me and yours. That you'd want this lyfestyle too, so you can't and can have anything, but within reason. To be free of this burden you carry surrounding your father. You need to start letting go of that, talk to me. His first child, his son, who has a very loud, and silent heart. I forget to remember that you need him too, right baby? That your life has been anything but a coater, but may you one day, cee the sacrifices for you, from a parent-heart you will one day know as myn is now. When you know what I have to go through so you can be you in front of me. You need to mourn. And I'll be right there when you come to me, when the tears can't stay inside anymore. How you needed me and I wasn't there for you, because I was lost in where I belonged to. It's tyme you faced your feelings. Regarding your dad. Who needs to cry for the small boy, needing his father, but wasn't given that. You need to believe in me, so I can help you feel, in front of me, and to see my tears of hurt for that chance that could never happen for you. To have to show you my inside, when I have to tell you what I have to do to recreate. What will you think of me when you're alone? I'm still fragile regarding this, but I hope that I can be a strong pillar for you. I'm insecure in other people's knowing and believing me when it happens. How you're belief in me is gonna lighten the load of my heavy heart. How I'm so proud of you. How you've survived your lyfe with what was given to you. How I missed your childhood, because of just stupid choices made in our lives. You told me that you didn't believe in this stuff, so I took it upon myself to not tell you. I'd rather you never knew, than to let you be free in choosing if you believed me or not. How you must feel that I didn't trust you, in us, as mother and son. The darkness I've carryed, should not be carryed on your shoulders. How you've been so quiet for so long, in your own inner isolation. This is myn to carry, to be a strong mom to you as I tell you everything. I've just wanted to keep our safe relationship untouched, for we barely speak, and I wanted to just one day, tell you I've been planning and inventing. That will forever change your lyfe. But until then, I wanted to show you that I'm more than words to you, to show you proof of my worth to this world and how you came from pure love and whish one day as you embrace your lyfe. To show you that I respect you and the distance you need from me, and when you come to me, I give you what I'm allowed to give you. I hope one day, we can live in a our house, and you be you, and I be me, and we all protect each other and always trust in what I say to you. When I tell you all of this, know, that I will not lye to you or keep things from you, to give you little messages of love and to help you find who you are. To help you lesson your burdens from a love that ripped you till now.

I feel very alone right now. It's very quiet here, and it's only two. What does she think? Am I still sleeping? I want to try not to today, as I'm very tired. To reach and capture something I'm working on and I don't know how to reach for my soul today. What's wrong? Maybe again, I'm feeling someone else's feelings from the innards of their soul. How to reach God and figure everything all out to you . . . to maybe tell you a story, and do something different. I'm a little confused about what this is about and how I feel today. Should I just ramble off a sentence that doesn't make sense? To you, do unto me as I do unto you. But that makes perfect sense. Please assist me in my next thing to say . . . no? Well, okay then. This is what I have to say; hear me call your name in the reminisce of my voice in my dream where this no speech or verbal communication. I look at you as I float past you and you stretch your arm to stop me from continuing on the eternity float-fly-by. As it's not a race to see who's fastest. I decided something today, where I won't be as open as I usually am. I sit in quiet and cee what my fingers do in Your name to make this dream happen for us all. To continue on even when I don't have my connection. No music to lead me on the way, just silence, peace and the little noises of traffic and noises of the house. So now what do I say? Maybe I'm to create a new story, that you haven't heard before. So many empty lynes to fill, but what if I run out of words? Would you believe me if I told you some really scary stuff about stuff you don't want to know about? What if I told you, that sometimes, lyfe and fiction are of the truth? That all that stuff about goblin's and ghosts, and mythical and metaphysical beings are walking among us? But of course, then you have the sceptics who don't believe in this. What about your life, chose you *not* to believe? Haven't you seen proof ? upon proof ? that is on the television ? or on the net ? or people who've experienced it ? or the people who've lived it? Do we have to blow our brains out for you to believe? Haven't we been trying to prove it to you over and over and over again? Okay, on to the next. If I have to stop for today, then I have to stop, but I don't want to, because this is the big dream that must come true for me. When you jump up and I pet you, you take me to your world where the only thing that matters is you. You enter in at snails pace and skittish, but you want to believe that it's safe as you enter. You see your other part, as you look into his eyes and make sure it's him. But that's your world, as my world is listening to the voices coming from the television of last-night, with a high of all day. As I look down and see the patterns of the rug that holds all the cold from coming up and you seal me and my fate of frozen. And then shut the door. So, I'm trying to tell you that sometimes, you don't need that feeling of euphoria of relaxation of hearing the voices to tell you what to do. No, no other substances today, as I shake myself awake and alive to rejuvenate my next thoughts to restore a former state. Uh oh, it's coming to a close, to no longer say something of make-believe, and to transfer you to another meaning of the same word. To almost depart from looking at the ness of the word prevaricate without misleading you to believe my beliefs and let you have your own interpretation. But know, I only speak from the truth I know of, from my own lyfe and experiences. Let it just be what it is, like everything else in this world, of feelings, and emotions that I whish didn't exist, but it does, and while I'm doing this, hope in seeking an understanding of this fiction from a non-fiction life, that doesn't make sense, but does.

I have to write about everything my beloved. As we go back in tyme to where we began, that was our dominos as they fell and fall into their correct order. How you live now and how we lived back then. I just wanna get totally wasted right now, I'm having Andrew withdrawals. I don't want to feel this pain I caused again, but I know I must in order to move on and allow more time to mourn him, as I'm not done yet. Am I allowed to whish you in my thoughts? Can you come to me and haunt me and your ghost swallow and make you gulp? All I want is you, back, right now! Can I do this? Alone tonight, with thoughts of you. You were worth so much and I didn't show you. I could go back to blaming myself. All *over* again! Great, I have to go through this again? I have to go through *everything* again? To make this happen, I have to relive my past to help my future, so I'm not really complaining. I should be happy. This is what I want, so going through this again is worth it . . . so let it happen naturally and write as many Letters as I need to, to get through this tyme in my lyfe again. Just write. I want to get more high and get totally bombed and high that I can't think, but I can't . . . I just have to keep writing, when all I want, is to get high and to see Andrew. I have no one to talk to right now, except through words on a screen, where I only want you near me right now. To go back to where we started all of this stuff. Where it all began, all those years ago. Back to where I always want to be with you. You, are the love of my lyfe, who will lyve on forever both with feelings and words and love I never knew existed or never knew about until you. How you fell in love with me, the real me, that I showed you and let you into my world and found out that your world was also messed up. How I wish I could go back and rewrite tyme, where I also tell him not to go, but yet I go there all the tyme with you, but I don't want him to live as I lived, so I tell him all the time, to stop whishing. Who am I to talk, right? Andrew, if you were here, and I could talk to you, I would say this; oh Andrew, I'm so sorry I hurt you so badly. You didn't tell me you were sick baby. How I long for you, to come back to life, to live the perfect life, together. Get me lost again with you, take me to anywhere you want to go. Come back to me, and love me always like you loved me that last time we made love. Make love to me, everyday, every night, I want to recapture those moments and they are frozen and so now I have to relive it for this, for this moment in our lyfe together as husband and wife, to show that marriage goes beyond the grave, it belongs to another tyme and place far away from this sometimes hell, where I would feel, like I can not get any deeper in the depths of hell. Can I ask any super hero to rewind the world again ? like he did for his love in the first movie ? when she dies from an earth tragedy ? and he flew around the world in rewinded fly-by? But I know the answer to that, where tyme never stops, and it can only go forward. Once you lyve a moment, you can never lyve it again. Andrew, I know you can cee this, and I'm begging. How I've had to lyve this lyfe without you, it's been devastating. I didn't know you were sick. What did I know? I was a stupid kid, who didn't know what she was doing in this game, that was my move. I'm sorry for what I said to you on the answering machine on your end. I know, you heard *every word*. I say that with so much guilt in my heart, that is only wanting you, right now, as you touch me to make me itchy to know you're here, telling me I'm doing a good job, or maybe I'm crazy again or something. Andrew and Sandra forever. Breathe words into me and show me the way.

"Dreams"

My dream bedroom; As I walk into my dream-illusion, with the curtains draping over my seventies living room with an antique feel to it. I want a trippy-spectacular Moulin Rouge feel to it. When I'm high, I wanna trip out. With dull and beautiful lighting, bouncing off brass surrounding my bed and mirrors. When I write, I wanna look down to a royal magazine. Open new doors for new and upcoming artists and create new foundations to sponsor. So much could happen for you and you too. Get media attention and bam, public demand. So this is going to assist in all this. So cool. The shield is up and it's hard to receive my message. But I listen again with thoughts of my dream bedroom. Have advertising media coverage on your skill. Maybe be a cover on a local interior decorating's new artist, an architect, magazine cover. Create new jobs and new technology. I could sponsor literacy and sponsor local amputees. I want to travel more than anything other than getting Manna. So I have to be really good when I write to make you read more of me to what my brain says next. So lets go back to my dream bedroom that will get media attention. Give them their dream while I'm succeeding on mine. Not to sound too vain, in knowing what I want. Like when a musician makes a song that has heavy beat, that captures your ears to listen to the end. Please, keep reading for, and as the future has now past us into this reality of make-up words that help you build new worlds to live in when you want to run as fast as possible. Here, pull me in, come closer, as I drag your chair. Close your eyes . . . deep breathe. There, don't you feel better? I smile to relax you into meditation. Hey, it can happen here, this is my world. I wonder what my bedroom is going to actually look like? In my head I can create cool colours or warm colours, just depends on the day. I wish I could say this; In a singing voice . . . Manna! Come here girl! I will look down at her and she looks into my eyes, and I'll say; do you want to go for a walk girl? She'll wag her tail and drool on my feet . . . yes mommy, let's do whatever you said, as she can only hear bark. As I climb down my spiral stairway in a floating lightness as my feet touch squishy plush red-velvet coloured carpet. With a fireplace with a long drape of sheer curtain sweeping over my living room, with my animal print couch with my wall-mounted up-to-date TV, my jungle-animal table with Paris lantern lamps on either side. With my grandparents old TV cabinet holding my alcohol and red wine with an old stained doily with it dipped in glitter. As I walk past my custom made bed platform. With brass bars surrounding it, with my night stand covered in lace stuck-on with hand-made fabric with abstract features. As I put Manna to bed at the foot of my bed then I go to my secret room, that I can't tell anyone about, but where I can only say, it's amazing and fun and what I've been dreaming about for my entire life. There's a big room on the other side of this make-believe wall with framed like a door that looks like a door but it isn't . . . what I'm trying to say is, only I know where to enter. Then I take you out to my own private room where I only go. It's round with a round bed and a skylight vaulted ceiling where it's only red, orange, and yellow lighting. It's where all the majic happens. Cee, I can make anything happen. Okay, now I want to go camping with Manna. So, we go to the bottom of the road that leads us to a campsite with a rocky bed along with a river in a rocky bottom and trees and solid ground for our tent. As we lay in our bed, we talk quietly to tell each other how we loved each other and fall asleep to the river beside us.

As the dust moves so slowly, it forms over a million light years away. As they form to an image as seen by those ones who take pictures from somewhere, where we can look from an image. How does that happen? Have you seen a nebula? All the different ones from God as He just blows and whatever is to be made, will be made, by the Sculpturer Himself. An eagle, an angel jumping out of water with the frozen image of her looking up and her hair flowing behind her with this blue and pink with yellow stars, with all the colours highlighting her silhouette. With Orion's Belt a yinyears away from each other, because space is just so huge. As the angel stands in glory with it's being surrounded by glitters of light as if the sun is shining above it, with so much beauty to look at, I just want to breathe in poison so I can stand and smile and lyve there forever, where the tyme is not periodic. It's just so beautiful, right? It just sits there, with no where to go, nothing to do, but be captured where I don't even know where. How they got to deep space, is beyond my little understanding. It's lit up with burning gases and dust that isn't blown in a wind . . . but is there wind in space? Does God breathe so the standing angel and eagle move and change shape to capture another idol in the next galaxy? It stands at guard and at attention to wait for the next one to come by my eyes and give me an inspiration. The peaks of the highest mountain in the space sky that never ends. How majestic is the tips to reach the never ending upslope with shimmering clouds of dust shedding their particles that stands in glowing light. With their surfaces with texture that if you touch it, it would change with your ghost blows. To the next one, it looks like a tree on fire with the scattered flames extending to the next superoen and on an impossible fire that won't catch on unless God says so. I wonder how big it is, so just let me get this right . . . it's how big? Something my little brain can't adjust to the knowledge that some people are still trying to understand and comprehend. To try to understand the significant of it's non-heavy mass of these stars, if we could jump up and grab one, right from the sky. Get lifted up and take one from their spot, and justify that with it's beauty, we can't mess with it, so, it's up to me to say no to myself to that kind of understanding, of where I want to be. How far does the mass of dust go? It must end somewhere. It's like a sheet of paper that can't live up there, because it wouldn't survive with everything else, 'cause it just can't. Did you know that there is even a heart up there? It's even red. Wow, God, You sure show us eh? The power I want to get across, but only mere words can do the job. I whish I could make a picture to show you what it's like up there. Where I think, there is no sound, minus the screams of explosions when the stars blow up and spread their gases around some more of the yin of space. I wish I could make a sound echo, into the depths of where echoes goes on forever. If I screamed loud enough, maybe it could. Come on LORD, show me more of the place I long to be. To go where no spirit has gone before into the deepest part of space where only I can go. With the old sound of music in my head so I can spill out the words in a loud voice that will bring a new being to me. To no longer turn on a light and waste electricity. The light there is always on and never causes blow-outs from cords or wires. Let it shine and show you something you've never seen before. To be where all colours exist to paint my palette with all touched surfaces that make up from dust. To stand there and count the stars as I can paint with an array of theirselves scattered and put in their arrangement.

I don't know if I should write tonight, but I guess I am. Today was a bad day. It was a bad day to be me, that I didn't know if I should or not, but I couldn't earlier. I had to escape into the television all day and after this, I'm going back. To have to physically stop, and crash for a day or two. I have to recover from today. I probably did everything, actually, I know, I did nothing write today. I want to escape being me tonight. To have to relive this day wouldn't go too well. All around. No escapees on this tyrant. I need to hide with caution on these kind of days. I'd go into details, but I'd rather never speak of my total disconnection from everything today. I'd rather not get creative right now, if you don't mind . . . you do? Well then, I watched an addict show tonight, seeing lots of fame and fortune gone down in drugs and the reality of drugs, where no parent should know, 'cause they're not me. But I know, you'd rather much more talk about having tea at the building, with royal servants to serve you with gold handles . . . oh ya, right, no creativeness, that wants to come to the ice and do a ballet with twists and turns, who glides across like water spilling in slow motion. I have to release my tensed brain that didn't cut nothing but every throat. I was having a seizure without control today. I fell to the ground and I stayed there all day. To be reminded again on it's only just me here, maybe with the LORD beside me? I felt very lonely today, and there was nothing I could do right. I'm so glad I'm high, to where all I can do is write, type, letter after letter. I can write you awake for me, and live in the now, but take me away from myself God! I have to have these days that haunt me and evil spells out instead of joy and happiness. I look in the mirror with a grimace in towards my soul, of who possessed me today without permission, but they didn't care. I want to be on my own so badly. Knowing I can't leave and lyve on my own, the three of us, sometimes weighs heavy on me, and I just want out. I love you, to whom I'm talking to. Of course I love you. I can't even go there right now. Just keep typing. Paper, take me away, to another place, where I'm happy, where I can jump out of my skin and write a play about how lyfe is for some and for others it's great. Where I don't feel now due to my pressure being down. I don't even want to talk to anyone. Just leave me alone to live in my own dump and know that this could never happen for me. To doubt myself from a long time since I haven't. I just want to own my own house, just me and they would all pay rent and no one would own except me, so I have to make sure I can sustain that kind of lyfestyle for a very long time. I wouldn't want to be around me today either. Get in my head, let my head explode with storyes and maybe explore new words, to bring newness to the mind. For I am speaking to a group of people and you're in my head man. So what do you wanna know? Cee, I whish I could wait for what you want to ask about, but if you pray it, one day it will reach me and your question will be answered. Just like me. Well, just a bit to go now . . . excuse me? Have you seen her today? I seem to have lost her. I wonder where she went? Well, cee . . . I don't know what's wrong. She isn't letting us see her today. But something's wrong with her. Let's not bother her today dear. She looks rough, but I know better than to bother her when she's having this kind of day, in which you should be celebrating that we're moving out. No more days like these anymore, under constant foot. I'm glad I'm almost done . . . it's been a bad day today, I just want it to end. I seek out a calming lullaby to put me to sleep that I go into over night and wake up to a new her . . . as my day ends.

. . . . . so then I said, yes, and laughed. The person on the other end was erupted with laughter. I smiled and told them how happy I was that they called me again. Okay then, bye. As you turn on the television to listen to somebody else talk now. So pretend I'm the TV. Stop and keep reading, and that's contradictory in saying that for it's the opposite. Do you see that? As I slop my words past my mouth. Such sloppy writing, eh? . . . think, think, think . . . My finances are troubling me tonight. But I won't go into details, it'll be boring for you. To sit here and use you as my counsellor, so I can get this stuff out, ya know? Gotta keep writing to make the new dough. The head of politics on my new and coloured money that will buy me things. But first, my house, then my dream bedroom and secret room/s. That I want to pay dollar for. Then get the dogs, that I'm going to travel for. Well, that's my dream future. To lyve the way I want to. How I've always dreamed of this style of lyfestyle and I've always achieved for that in my life. Always moving to the next thing that can lead me up in my now, very humble lyfestyle, where I live with nothing of letting me spend over a top dollar in my low budget. I'd be homeless if it wasn't for my parents if I'm speaking humbling. In the Presence of the LORD. For only He knows my future. It's only a dream for me, for now. To cee where my writing takes me, we'll have to cee won't we? Maybe I'll cee Paris, maybe I won't. I just have to keep typing and telling you new storyes every night, to pray for more words from Him, to keep you entertained. And showing you I deserve to have you read my entire lyfe. I love writing. I can't live without it. I have, and it sucked. This is going to shelter us. Starting a new and fresh lyfe. So I can have a lyfe with my kids too. I want them. All to myself now. I've earned this tyme with them. I want their teens in trade for their childhood. Retire, travel, be a couple with no us, together. Just the two of you. You've earned this retirement. You've taken really great care of us, and now it's my turn to be a full-time mom. Visit whenever you want, but call first, and you know I love you, so don't even go there. I want to continue to be on the up scale with this and continue to create, and to get into your heads for a while to let you escape into someone else's problems for a while, right? Do you want some wine from my cellar? I have both white and red wine, help yourself . . . . I sit forward with my face in my palm, with family members and friends all around me, and I can't believe it, to share that I think he's an addict. I wipe my tears away and say, yes, I think maybe she's an addict. I would never lie to them about anything . . . I may not tell them everything, but, no, I would never out-right lie to them. I just think it's best for me that way. This is only me though, not you. How I teach is very opposite than another, and there's a code there. Okay, this could become a fight, so let's move on shall we? . . . . Let's forget sometimes, on how we feel towards another person, and just clean your slate and start new and fresh . . . ya, right, I know that's what you're all saying. I know all about wanting to forgetting what another has done to me. I know, it's super hard, right? But I'm trying this new freedom in my lyfe. I mean, really? But, I *know* how hard it is. It's never too late to make amends. Just my opinion . . . . LORD, I speak to You now and say thank You for today. I spent well tyme with my daughter and son today, so I loved that time. I got to hear my mother and my daughter say her prayers tonight like every night, I got to spend well needed time with my son and got to pray today, like every day. Amen.

Well, I haven't been writing for a few days. I've been roughed up a little bit, and I couldn't process it properly, but now, I'm flowin' again. I've missed you, and I'm just so happy to be creative again . . . so I watched the ballet show, and it was so amazing. Real ballet dancers. I can see why she loves it so much. So graceful and served with perfection, balancing on her toes in that arch I love so much. Beautiful swans. So who of you love to be in love? There's nothing quite significantly longing in their life, other than being a mother for the first and second up to the largest family in the world, than falling and being in love. But it's also the biggest lesson in life. Of those special marriages that violence is not a part of it. Every family is in their own. My father who raised me to be his own, he's the first man that I honour. And then the rest to follow. Sometimes it's hard to find men in my group, who I know, eternally I know in an emergency, I could count on them. In a seconds notice, they'd be right there. I hope that in your lyfe, you can count on the men in your life too. I hope everyone has a friend like that. The women married to these men, are very lucky, in their own unique way, like me and Andrew. Like my grandparents, who loved each other, in such a rare way. I envy that kind of love. Maybe one day God will show my future husband to me and I'll know like I did the way with Andrew, but sometimes, people just aren't that lucky. I honoured my grandfather higher than any man in my life. I only remember being really mad at him twice in my entire life. I didn't really have or established my respect of my grandmother until Andrew died. My beloved, who just couldn't make it in his world. If people want to say to me that he was being selfish, to me, it just wasn't like that. He had so many fractures in his fragile heart and soul. And that's all with that. So painful, you know? Knowing that I was so into me, that I wasn't tender the way he needed from me. I didn't know how to be *his* wife. But now, he's with the LORD and Jesus and all the rest of my wonderful family. And I'm finally able to write freely, most tymes anyways. Sometimes I'm robbed of happiness when I think of Andrew, but sometimes, the memoryes are all I own and knowing he's gonna be right there waiting for me, I have no doubt in my mind. Love for me, goes beyond death. All their love that they had for you, it goes with them, and they carry it with them until they see you again in Heaven. But that's only my opinion. A part of my life is going through something big, now. I have to put all my trust in God, and that's sometimes really hard for me. I struggle with that in my lyfe. But I think a lot of people feel like that. Maybe, maybe not. Depends on who you are, right? It's okay to not agree, unless an emergency and everyone needs to vote, quickly or urgently. Depends on your unique situation. When I'm dire need, I beg to the LORD in weepy pleas and call my best friend and she'll be right there. The truth shall set you free when you really need it. When you're in a situation, where law enforcement pulls you over if you're going to an emergency. Okay, thinking sometimes blows my mind out. Just over takes my mind to somewhere the worst situation happens. I myn as well blow my brains out. Where the most worst thing that could happen . . . okay, now you know I'm a pessimist. I'm the weird and tripped out passenger, with seezuring effects on my brain. So, this is when I bring in God and beg Him not to let that happen, and as tears flow in such a devastating event that would be for me, us . . . . I need to clear my head in knowing there's nothing I can do about it. As I plea to God, in this certain situation.

I love you my mirror, my hand. Being with you has changed everything about me. I'm transformed. I've changed in appearance, my demeanour is totally different when I'm with you. I've changed in manners of character. I'm a butterfly who flies about with you and we fly through everything, clouds, snow, and sunshine. You're the song in my head that I'm keeping repeating over and over again. When I'm with you, everything about me changes. I'm the dandelion that when you blow it into the wind, it's carried to plant a seed elsewhere, where it's supposed to, and that's you with me, don't you see? Your golden mane with my dark cherry red, that sometimes are curly with the tides of the sunshine or straight, that you say, it's five minutes, let's do it. With no care to the world. Then with the body shivers tonight, who's to say what it was . . . but it happened. How we have so much to catch up on, that we're not too bad at. Let's reach up and grab His hand together and see where He puts us down, like when I need you, He has us, and where He'll put us? . . . it can only get stronger with talking, like we've done, let us be a blessing as friends like no other, I'm sure . . . maybe, but . . . You make my load of everything about me, so much lighter than I carry it. You're so special, pertaining to you, which means that I want you to share things with me, but mostly the LORD. Amen, right? You give everything you have, to everyone who is family and we love you, so you can be you with certain and creolize me with the help of the LORD, may we bless His name always. As we strive for what He wants for, and from us. He makes us whole and see, we have to embrace us for who we are, for that's His will. I want to bring you out of your shell, like you have with me, so I can show you someones who've helped me along the long road to find you. Every time I see pink gems in places where I'm at, I'll think of you, full of pink and fuchsia with lots of butterflies fluttering past us and lifting our hair in the spring wind, of freshness of the new season, for you *and* for me. So, this is easy, with coming to my other place of lying down and laughing and playing with hours to spare in our perfect world, eh? When I need my fuzzy blanket, I'm in knowing comfort of love, that spreads throughout here and spread through the air like a summer breeze with some shadows but mostly the perfect temperature. And hey, lets climb those steep stairs together with my own cheerleader, who will support me up and down, when I need help. So when I'm climbing, you're climbing right beside me and that's the way it just needs to be with us. How I love you, how you show me action without restraint into this whole other world that only you can take me too, you unlock me and let me stand, tall and brave . . . . what? Oh, um, well if you knew us, we'd just play along but in our heads, we'd be at the same place and tell you otherwise of their knowledge of us. Our lives are joined together without fail, as we fail on the way to teach us all the ins-and-outs. How my spirit flyes around in myself. Allegiance with such loyalty and full of devotion. Dear God; thank You for her in my life where I can think without dust and spider webs who can only decode me with all my secrets and needs and desires. Of my lost best feature about me, who finds me behind my curtains and opens the room with sunlight and vitamins, that help me with my needs of hunger of a friendship I could no longer live without, for my days were bad and haunting and terrifying, that you smooth out with your hands and down pouring dreams that make me believe for good, and when I'm away from you, I get lost in a world that I just can't open my curtains the whole way. Yes! Thank You LORD.

.

Dear God;

I don't know why You gave me life, but I'm starting to realize that more and more. I only want to use smart words . . . just speak through my heart eh? When I get a letter from my child, it's everything I own and I keep the torn from my first. If I know how much it means to *me*, but to You, God, You got It Goin'. How You heard us three times, with no fainting spells this time, but I have to say, they're pretty cool. I love when that happens to me. It's part of my longing in parts of all of them. Even though I've been told, You've written everything. God, You give me so much that I'm not grateful sometimes, but I'm working on it. Through just one person, who I met as a teenager, could bring me this, so her destiny was fulfilled, and now we get to rejoice together because of it. Because of a mother's love, who gave everything she had and owned to the needy and when she became tired, too tired to go on in this unpredictable life cycle. Because of her, love continues and letting go is okay. That two lives could just change everything for our future. What a sacrifice of humbleness and unconditional love, to everybody . . . that mattered to her. What a loyal servant she was and she stood bold with a soft heart. How You shuffle life around so much, and when You shuffle, I like the mixture. Who knows what's to happen this year. I give You my heart, but sometimes I'm withdrawn and it's hard to cope some days, but then that's when I call my mirror. But God, I love being Your servant, even . . . well, I better not curse myself. When I have a rough load, You always save me. Even when You're carrying me when I feel alone. It's hard to fully understand how You work, because it's so chaotic down here . . . most days, to a lot of people. Father, I just ask You to take away heavy burdens from their hearts and bless their lives, fully and richly. Amen. You've given us pink butterflies and black sparkly beads that we do. Please enhance our day to what You want from me. To give me words of beautiful things to her that makes me feel about a million percent. One day, I'll come Home and see You . . . but I hope my purpose, and their purpose lyve on for a long time, to carry on our honour of maybe the next hundred generations. To research me like all of them. That would be cool. So, I should finish my course eh? I just don't know what could come from this. Questions with no answers the way I want them. I could fight You on this, but I know You'd Win. Maybe someday, this will be documented and in a museum somewhere where the most expensive pieces in the world, and even then, Your Name will be written from my heart, to share with the world. As I bow at Your Feet, and then You'll let me be free and fly to where I want to for as long as I want to. This is Your "Love Letters" God. As words flow as the words continue to beat in me. I ask that You continue to bless me with everything, with Holy water and splashes over my face in a commercial and makes me whole. But I'm not fully whole until that final day of my lyfe here, where I whish to not return for another go for another try, no. This is it, God . . . I just wanna play and bounce on a trampoline that doesn't allow gravity, and just jump really hard, with all that bounce, and send us through the atmosphere and live among the stars and different astral plane worlds and the hierarchy beings. Who can never come here, because that's not their lives, like us, as so many as billions of this kind of creature.

I'm just going to start typing and we'll cee what happens, okay? Okay, let's cee . . . Ya, like I need time to think, but thinking does egg out, weeds and all, get it out, and open me up and do something I haven't done yet.

The LORDS Answer—Habakkuk 2; 2-3 (NIV Bible)

Then the LORD replied; Write down the revelation and make it plain on tablets so that a herald may run with it. For the revelation awaits an appointed time, it speaks of the end and will not prove false. Though it linger, wait for it; it will certainly come and will not delay. Amen

To be able to spread these words around the world? What a privilege to honour my earthly parents. They can be proud of my accomplishments and realize I'm not a child anymore. I'm a grown woman, with needs and desires, with a child for whenever you want her, for when I'm near you, you may not realize what I'm all about and the things I need to tell you about myself. To be able to express my feelings where no one can tell me, no. To know that this is where I can bring into being from construction, of hammering and banging in my veins as I bring to life a story to amuse you and to keep you reading. To show you that my life has a great importance and dire needs to be fulfilled. So different eh? Haven't done a Letters like this before. Father, let them hear Your voice and rejoice in Your Name. Let me show what Your Name means in the Light Of Love. So we close our eyes, our windows into something we can't even imagine. It may linger in anticipation for our smallness here compared to There, and there, and there. Discover the, my hidden knowledge if you whish to understand this secret language of love and letting me be me. I am afraid of somethings, yes LORD, as I humbly ask for forgiveness for being afraid of what comes from this. I hope it spreads Your word from a humble servant, in hopes of spreading peace in their hearts that have hardened like ice that can not be cracked or chipped. I hope Your words of comfort and love, comforts them, like it has for me . . . okay, now, this is what I have to say . . . I whish the world could become it's own Nation, with power, but even in the Bible, it says the LORD strikes down the other armies, so war is supposed to happen, even though I whish for nothing more, just for a moment where the entire world, comes to a halt, and comes together, hold each others hands and be joined by hand, so everyone has to be holding someone's hand and all the wars stop, all the hungry knows they're not alone, all the suffering knows that someone will always be there for them, to stop the abuser from hitting and punching, the guns would stand still and no bullets leave, all the hookers and slaves of the night and day, stop and the masters of them, just became one. That every single person in this world is joined as one. I know that will never happen because that's just how this world works, and it needs just to let it do it's own cycles without being touched in that kind of thing. Enemy will battle enemy, as compassion is what He wants, but it's us who chooses our fate down here. There will always be sickness and fevers from illness, and there's nothing I can do about it. In His Name, I pray for the hurting and the wee ones in despair. May they be honoured when one day when You will call them Home.

I must say, you've been chosen. I can't say from whom it was delivered from, as it's confidential information. The only one is me and them. Let's go out, into this not-so-big world, as fully-loaded Christians, and break down that wall of mass chaos, as we all stood beside each other once many years ago, and we were strong in our faith as sole. That trust is there from His house, and we were perfect . . . with many flaws on this side. We spent all our waking hours together, most of us, in the dark, sharing our secrets and storyes and wishes and dreams. We joined hands and prayed around the grand. As we gathered wisdom for a future unknown then, and how we have grown away from each other. So much can change in a decade, with a few extra. But, we have a strong bond in deep, so if we came together again in a whole different way, and lyve in the once-tight-group love. I'd call a meeting around the grand and ask in a circle of nay's or yes. Say, you all know me, you know how I work, and we all know how close we all were once, and I want to add a few more people to this core and chosen group, to spread His word, together, and help the world know unconditional love from Above, and how strong we are now compared to then. How strong can we be? Only you can tell me. Only you can tell me, if you want to have a lyfe, where you only work because you want to, but to keep up the responsibility due that your role is very important. You've been chosen, to carry His Name, everyday, on your badge of honour in Him. And take care of ourselves at the same time, with earned wealth and each of you have a purpose in this calling that I will have to ask you and tell you the news I have for you all. I'm to share of my year of isolation and finding my lost soul, and learning to who I am, and everything, at the foot of the Cross. I would plan a reunion with just the seven of us, and I would tell them why I really planned this calling. If you want the answer to your questions, and if you *really, truly, in Christian love,* love me, I would invite you to join me on this day, at this time, so I can change your life. I would ask that spouses give permission to attend this event alone, as it started with just these people, but I accept your presence if need be.

The LORDS Answer—Habakkuk 2; 2-3 (NIV Bible)

Then the LORD replied; Write down the revelation and make it plain on tablets so that a herald may run with it. For the revelation awaits an appointed time, it speaks of the end and will not prove false. Though it linger, wait for it; it will certainly come and will not delay. Amen

To you, who *was* this person, and what was his lyfe and lived how he was supposed to? You have been chosen, to serve God, under Christian love, to change the world. To take charge with your Shield and Sword, and march in His Army, and live in a really trippy reality, I implore you to attend, from any distance. Travel with Him beside you and pray as you come to have an open-mind, open love, open friendship, and my love for you. For you who got this Letters, this is the date to follow. Father, I ask that their minds are made up from their love and just a bit curious as to what this new situation that has arised in my life, for all of you and your familys, to swarm around. Let's build a solid, Christian-based new lyfe, together, again, but this tyme to, and with a vengeance. Yes or Nay?

Tonight, I write to *you*, as clear-headed as possible, after being sick for a couple of days. I want you to know, how much I love you, more than life itself. I love you, and it's so much, I can't even explain it . . . try to? Well, if you're a loving, devoted, insecure and humble servant of *our* love, well, I know you love in this way too, so you understand then. It's like an experience I can't explain. It's so hard to describe a mother's-kind-of-love. I could try to explain it, but remember, some of the words may sound not at all like the love I have for you, but I want you to be able to try to understand, like I have to try to explain. My love for you has kept me from my hand taking my lyfe. Without even knowing it, you have saved my fate of my own death, on many occasions. Do you know how hard it was to not to? Sometimes I couldn't even breathe, or I cryed myself into my pit of slumber, and I had to *beg* God, to glue myself to the ground when I was curled up into a ball and huddled in the fetal position. All I wanted was to let death swallow me and drag me to your father. You were my sacrifice that has saved me, except once, but on that one, the LORD called. It's hard being my daughter, I know. While you've had to go it alone most of the time, so have I. I have good friends around me, but *I* still had to make it, *me*. Just like you'll have to do. Lyfe is about tough lessons and the stronger you get, the better you'll handle a rough experience and experiences that you must face in your lyfe. No, this is not a poetic Love Letters, because love is serious, and loving someone you love that hurts you, is the deepest wound to heal. I had to deal with you telling me stuff, and when I cryed, you said you felt bad for making me cry, but baby, I've cryed on this subject many tymes. The pain of being away from you is like me tearing a piece of paper in half with all the jagged edges raw and rubbed down, but it's me trying to ask God to mend me from being torn, but the page is never the same, even when you try to tape it back together. I need *you*, *and* I need my best friend. I'm torn all the tyme, between this lyfe and that lyfe, and trying to build the lyfe we dream of. Being my daughter, I'm sure, has been very difficult. Lots has had to happened for you to speak your mind, and I'm proud of you for telling me and being honest, and with me crying it didn't help, but I wanted to show you how torn I am most of the tyme and what I struggle with, knowing how much you miss me when I'm gone, but it's always on my mind. I struggle, with *so many issues* on being a good mom to you. I hear advice from them and then them, and I never know which one to lyve by. And when I'm on my own, I get lost in this world of depression and sadness knowing I've caused you pain in your life and you miss me when I'm gone. With this in your lyfe, you'll grow into a very strong, independent woman, who knows what she wants in lyfe. You'll be a woman who knows how to make up her *own* mind and not someone *telling* you, how to think or act or do. You'll be your own woman and I'm jealous of that part of you . . . yes, *I'm* jealous of *you*. I can only dream of one day, no one telling me what to do, what to think, what to feel, and most of time, I'm confused on what the right thing to do is. I can only pray, when you become a full, developed woman, you'll be able to do what you want, when you want, no matter what. Even though you lyve in this certain lyfe, embrace being you, be *free* in what you do. Don't let anyone tell you, how you should feel. Don't let anyone tell you what to think, and you don't even know that you are my hidden envy. You may think low of your life, but the world is waiting for you, show it *you,* and live.

I'm going to talk about something that only a very special chosen ones know. It's been a self-assessment night tonight, and was shown my many sins in my lyfe that I have caused on different people. What I'm about to write about, is sensitive nature. And tonight I was shown that I needed to ask forgiveness for it, for them. I need to ask for forgiveness for something I did, a lot of things actually. No one knows this. But in all cases, I plead the fifth . . . oh ya, that's the States. At any rate, I'm asking for forgiveness for pain I have caused in my life. When I was seven years old, I was raped. It was the older brother of my friend. I went over to ask my friend to play ball with me . . . I was so vulnerable to him. My mom was sleeping at home when I went out to visit and play ball with my friend. It was summer so I had my little bikini, like any child wears, no big deal, no ones fault, just the way it was back then. I had my ball with me. I was just seconds away, just around the way. I reached the door and bounced my ball as he answered the door. I asked if she was home as I continued to bounce my ball, and he reached out and grabbed the ball from me and bounced it inside. I remember every detail of where the ball bounced, to the far wall of the staircase in front of the door on the right side, as I remember the staircase going down stairs. I had to get my ball back. I didn't want to get in trouble. As I went in the house, he was turned back-to-back to each other, and that's when he closed and locked the door. The kitchen was at the door and I remember thinking that I wanted to grab every kitchen knife and scratch him up a bit, but he said, let's go downstairs and it was cold, crowded. I remember the pole and the floor mat he laid me on. He asked me or told me that if I show him myn, he'll show me his. And some of the rest of the next details, I don't remember. But it was a while that he taunted me and raped me. I was scared and I told him I wanted to go home, but he wouldn't let me. It was a long tyme before he let me finally get up and right away, he went upstairs and I found my ball and ran upstairs, fast. I got to the top of the stairs and waited for him to come to let me out. I couldn't reach the chain lock, or there was some reason why I had to wait for him. He left to go upstairs to the washroom, and I probably know exactly what he was doing. When he finally came back downstairs, he said something like, don't tell anyone, it's our little secret. I went in that house a little girl, but no stranger to physical abuse, and came out a different little girl. I never told anyone after it happened, and when I did, they didn't believe me. Just as well. There were a lot more dyre situations than mine, the hungry, the daily physical abusers much worse than myn was. So, I just shove it under all that and forget about it. It doesn't need attention like all the rest of the world, I've separated from it and sweep it under the rug like dirt that I want to hide. I detach from it, I'm cold about it, nothing really. Tonight is a self-examining event and I'm remembering all my sins, that are dark and need forgiveness from God. The pain I have caused on that case, I can finally understand, now I get it. I get the pain, and I'm forever going to ask forgiveness, but have to remember that when I prayed for it, You gave it, and now I have to pray it away when the devil taunts me and teases me into darkness again, where I have to fight it constantly, day and night. All the things to the innocent and proved I wasn't a good friend after all. I carry many dark sins that can only go through the silver lining to Him. Where one day I will go and be forgiven for all my human sins that I'd like to be rid of one day and never come back to this earth again. Forgive me Father, for my sins.

I must do this. I must make something today with all my dreams that need to come to lyfe by and throughout this tyme, that has lead me to it. To say hello to the world with another something else to feast upon. I can't bare it, I can't bare the sight of not letting it go on. What am I talking about? . . . I don't know yet, but when I do, I might not tell you, for my thirst for this is inwards and silent so loud, that you can hear me. To pound one after the other, one, two, three, is the majic number, you cee, it's the right one. Just talking gibberish so you don't understand, but why would you want to? It's just writing, of on going sentences so it keeps in tyme with my thoughts of you or them. So what if I don't make sense. Am I always supposed to? Nope, this is my call. I can't just lay there and not do it, as I whish I never saw the antlers in the water for it's of a deer that got shot and died. As the reason is private and secret, for if I tell you . . . I just can't, it's about something I can't tell you, but maybe I can, with being continued contradictory. That is logically incorrect in the opposite ways of which it should be but isn't. It's an impulse and surge of things that don't even exist in this forum for public interests. Just explode in the excitement you whish to show them in their own tyme, for it's gonna happen soon, or, will it? Something that doesn't make it can also be brought down, but can it? What if it goes up instead of down? It can happen you know. Is it the picture you whish to cee? Or is it not? HELLO!! I'm talking to you, aren't you listening? Some people. I don't want to make any element, with it's sphere of activity. Going in this direction, going in that direction, seeking where it's supposed to go . . . where it's supposed to be, but where is that? I want to push away anything right now that not make me glad to do something I don't want to, 'cause I want it down when I need it up. A lot of empty space in the air with the anticipations of breath to let me be etched in printing. Like a drawing in your head to what you see in this meaning. How it's so loud in my head where I want to scream of release of this feelings. Feelings of my bondage of being taped up and bound to slit and shed blood, with no open sores to mend. HELP!! I just want to scream in the wide open for someone to hunt me and bring me to attention and salute me for all the melodrama for the tragedy I have faced in this wild world of what we so call, lyfe, and living. This new mission is an illusion of null and void. As I look up and see branches going in all directions from the root from in the ground, that is buryed with the dirt of the echo of nothing going in the ground. Is this tyme ours or yours? Well, for me, its myn, for only I can see what this is all about, or maybe I don't. Is it too complex for you to understand? If it is, I apologize, but maybe I'm not today, tonight, yesterday and this morning. AAAAAAHHHH!! Am I fading into being a hostage? A brutal takeover in my head? You cee, this is what happens to me, I go into the trance of intergalactic between here and that other place that I've mentions lots of tymes so far, of killing one bird with two stones. As someone once said to me that I've said everything, but I haven't, so I must do that. To wrap it around me so tight I can't move, to so much claustrophobic that I can't beat my thoughts out of this tight ropes that's lassoed around me and my neck like my wild horse who wants to get loose and run, just run like crazy and fast to there, but I'm not here, am I? Am I in my certain harmony? No. I'm in this entity that lives and breathes this poison air surrounding me from the clouds that wait for me to not breathe anymore but only when it's the right now moments, from composure.

"My Dream"

This is my dream. I want to own my own house, but not just any house, my dream house, nothing too special, just somewhere where I love. This is what this house looks like; It would be a tri-wing house. Son, daughter, and whoever follows us and I. The main center room would be a living room with a fire place and a kitchen with an island with stainless steel appliances, and off from the kitchen would be a sunken theatre living room, with a comfy couch for me to lay down if needed, a main bathroom, a spare bedroom, a den/office, with a laundry room for everyone in the mud room in from the backyard. With a type-of-spiral staircase leading upstairs to a games room, with a pool table, and air hockey. This is where probably em would be. My son would have his own entrance with a garage so he could work on his cars and bikes. His own games room with it loaded with games of his choice. His bedroom with his own bathroom, and a patio to outside. His own living room suite and daughter would have her own space; her bedroom with her own bathroom with a sunken in bathtub looking out to the backyard. She would have her own living room suite with a secret room, to have a just-for-us spot in her secret room, that has a door going out to the backyard. I'd want her to have her own photography studio attached to her side, with a black room loaded, with a patio outside. With an added upstairs with whatever she wants. My side would be with two levels with the upstairs as balcony looking down with my arts room where all my art and supplies would be and would be created. Down and around the corner would be a spare washroom. Down stairs would be my vaulted ceiling living room with a cream tile flooring with a fireplace. Off to the side would be my master bedroom, with a living room and a bathroom and walk-in closet and up the wrought iron spiral staircase beside my bed leading up to my writing space with my table/chair/desk, with a small library behind my back. On the main level would be my bed on a three-step platform surrounded with a double-brass handle so no one can fall from bed, with an open space at the corners of the bed, with a night stand with my stereo equipment, and lamps, with a round ceiling above me, with a hanging and billowy sheer curtains hanging from the ceiling covering my bed or just at the head. At the foot of my bed, would be Manna's bed. Across the room from my bedroom at the front of the room is my living room space, with a couch, coffee table, mounted TV, surround sound with a stereo. Beside about five feet to the left would be my master bathroom. A sunken-in jet bathtub, with a one-way-window looking out to the backyard. A stand-up shower with a glass door and brown tiled shower stall and a full counter. Attached to the side of my bathroom, I'd want my large walk-in closet. The living room space would have to be very large with the openness of the vaulted ceilings, with high curtains and an outside patio looking at our pool. I could access my half of the garage with a wall separator. I'd want to drop about two million for this dream house, nothing more. I want to buy some decent property in Maple Ridge and hire an architect friend that I know that I want to build this house. No one would ever have to move out. I pray that God will bless me with a better book after the next to make this dream happen and we can sustain this lyfestyle with humble servants at His feet in every step. That our house will be a strong Christian stance to the world, that we remain strong in Him, for everything we do. That we are good to each other and others. May our love be stronger and whole.

Your death made this, made all of this for me, and your death too and yours for all the generations and layers above me. My lyfe has purpose and I wouldn't have found it without you dying and His hands pushing me down my path to the next domino and blowing me where He wants me to go next. If you didn't die so many things couldn't have happened. So many things would have been, instead of what is. Even though, I would give anything to have you back, I know that it couldn't have been that way. This was the way it was supposed to go. With all of those nights in torture, to find who I am today, I wouldn't be who I'm supposed to be and I wouldn't have found it, and I would have been lost in another world reality that I don't know. You already knew, that choice for your life. You knew you needed something different than me and than I did. I'm not lost anymore. I found the Light hun. Over all of the prayers I've prayed, He's answered most of the prayers I've prayed for. You show me Yourself all the tyme. And after all those lost years I'm gaining new strength and new wisdom, and I'm gaining answers to some of my burning questions. But You've always known me, forYou built me and my lyfe that You constructed just for me, that I sometimes forget that, and now I'm building for a new lyfe, that I want so badly. It's my passion for lyfe and so I keep writing, letter after letter, until it's perfect/Perfect, and it's how it's supposed to be, and every word is in it's place. So you can keep reading and live my lyfe with me, so I can share with love and show you that I'm so messed up in some areas of my lyfe, that you can relate to, understand, to show us that we're not alone in our struggles, that you too, are coming out of a dark place, and learning and growing in yourself, like me. Loving you my love, has shown me great wisdom, and great power in myself that I could never have found otherwise. In the end, you were my freedom, through all that evil, slime and darkness, and a lyfe *not,* wanted. Struggled through everything, I had to follow where He wanted because I would have never found it otherwise my love, and what happened had to happen. I had to let it throw it out to gain it back again and you had made your choice, and I guess you knew something I didn't at the tyme. I whish to see you again, in my quiet moments when I'm writing like this, bring you to me, to my attention. For a life I could have only lived without you. A lot of people must suffer in blackness to reach Glory. I found my destiny hun. Even in my farthest thoughts of whishing you here, it's just not the same as it was, it's better, it's purer, and real. Like a grandma-loves-grandpa love, only in a very unique way, a very special way, that I whish upon others, that they find peace in the everafter. But I know I'm very special in that way. I may be able to, but it's okay, because it's my life and I'm supposed to live it in a certain way. Just like you and your life . . . does that make sense? I want you hun, to know all my secrets, my beloved husband. But if I tell you, they'd know too. Is it okay if I share? Yes, well, that's good, 'cause I already am. You can visit me anytime, I'll never tell you to go away. I love when you smile at me and show me your gap. I loved your gap and now she has it, with such intelligent. Beautiful. I know you hated being called beautiful, but you were babe. I loved your hair, with your blonde streak on your left side, where I thought it was dyed and it was really from the sun. Your smile was stiller. It was the silent whisper to my future. Makes words to let people know that this kind of love, is very rare and unique and Blessed from God, so I can tell our storyes. That now writes my heart.

"The End . . . ?"

January 25th, 2011

To not know, if or not, that I might have cancer. I'm scared. I'm scared enough to never smoke another cigarette ever again in my lifetime here. No matter how hard it will be, I will never smoke again. What's to happen to my children? Where is this going to leave them in their lives? If I were to find out that I have cancer, in the order standing would be the order I tell my family and friends. I would go to Andrew's grave first. Probably cry, a lot, and share my heart with him. Then, I would wait for my parents to be together, and then somehow tell them. Then I would tell my kids, then him, and have serious talks with all of them. Make amends with all of them. I don't know what I would say to the team that lead me to Christ again. I would tell them everything, and thank them, then I would tell the long haired goddess and that side of the family. I don't know what I would say to them all. I think it will happen naturally, I guess . . . not sure yet. I'm going through this alone, but this time, I know I'm *not* alone, it just feels like it. What would I say? To all of them? My kids. What's going to happen to them? She will be devastated, air . . . ? Entire lives will change, and maybe I need this scare, to set me straight with some things. Maybe that's what this book is for. To say good-bye to everyone. All I know, that that dream I had of the world ending, it makes sense now. Could it be the beginning of a new lyfe for me? This book will be very powerful in the process of now, finding out if I have cancer, to yes or no within days. Work day and night getting this book done, pay off as much loan as I can alive, so my mom won't have to deal with it when I die. But I may not have cancer and a new life will *start* for me. I'd never smoke another cigarette again. I'd want to go to Paris with her, and Ireland with him, and if those are the only trips I'll ever go on, that's totally okay with me. I'd write, all the time, since I might be on a tyme clock soon. To write about everything I've ever done, to sharing my experience of maybe living with cancer. Am I sealing my fate in these words? If I'm only talking to myself, I'd say a lot, and I'd probably write it all down, so listen up to all those who want to hear me, write the rest of my days explaining myself to many people. Use word power and the words I find out if it's yes or no. The impact of either answer will be pronounced. It will be clearly indicated in the following words and I hope you read on so to know the answer. I'd see everything I've been writing about. My pace is slowly approaching, and I have much to say, to say I love you, to all my loved ones, that my family, all my family, meaning all my friends, who have stood by me, when it really mattered. I'm going to make sure that everyone feels all the love I have for them. My thoughts go back to the team and how they would deal . . . the entire group of us originals, and how that's gonna go. LORD, know I'm scared. I pray for my salvation and I pray that I will have to make up everything before going Home. People will get very mad at me during this tyme, of saying my final farewells. Oh my God, this *could* be it for me. This could be *it*. It's intence. Deep seeded feelings about it. I just want to be done. Some will understand more than others on support. Well, my mother will be waking me up in the morning to go to the doctors about the lump I found, how ironic hey? I can not miss this appointment tomorrow, and it'll be a sad day when I have to explain that one to her. I want to end writing now. I know I only have a couple of lines left, so I'll just type gibberish. Why does the page sometimes look crooked on the screen? So, how did I do? Keep reading to know the answer.

"Playground"

So good news to tell you all, I don't have cancer. Holy water runs through my veins that makes me s/Strong. So, two lyfetime promises I promise. I'll never smoke again. I'll never buy cigarettes again in my life. Even if somehow/where starts again, I'll never do it again. Number two; I'll never stop spreading His word around the world. I'm not on a tyme clock anymore, in *this* way anyways. So, I'll start getting more creative again and I can pray with an open-mind again and not be cluttered, but it's gonna happen anyways. Stuff always clutters my brain. But sometimes, when I'm light in spirit, I'm more open, than like I am now, with stuff on my mind. And so now would be the tyme I call on the LORD to open me, to fill me with a blast of words that will continue to capture your eyes for a feastly read. I love feeling like this, I miss feeling like this . . . are you wondering what I'm talking about? I can plan again and not have to disappoint them again. I can come up with and create something of a dynasty. With characters and substances. Like this disco guy with an orange wigged out wig, big floppy shoes, flopping on a moving roadway with rainbows and disco balls echoing light elsewhere. See what I can do in your head? Are you picturing him running or walking slowly? I cee kind of fast, but not really, really colourful, black all around with disco music pumping on lights with floating fully-loaded music notes pass by me as the music is so loud, but it's awesome. Then at the end, there's a meadow with little flowers everywhere like in that famous garden. Then the flowers open and spread from the wind there, like a spring breeze gazing over your sleeveless arms and floating are the seeds from the loose ones. Then the sun is set on the beautiful lake that has the reflection from the mountains, with peaks so high, with a glow to them, they're perfect emerald green with such detail. Little girls and boys are chasing their dogs around, and they were laughing. Such happiness there I see behind that bush over there. It's another door to another place, so make sure you want to go there . . . you do? But what if it's a *bad* place? Do you *want* to read from a bad place? Where are you? I hear myself echo. I can't see you . . . where are you? I'm floating above and I hear people calling my name. It's fuzzy and blurry . . . I hear my name again. Fascinating sensation. So light, and I'm an echo, and I see solid below, but the face is so familiar, as I think about it, and just in a flash, I saw her, and them. They're all crying . . . I go to reach for her shoulder, but my hand swept right through her. Then I saw her crying at the funeral home, how I laid there, for so long, I'm tied to this place, but I keep seeing her crying, then in a flash, she was laying over my coffin. All the people I knew and didn't know were there tending to your side with comfort and support as you rain on top of my burial site . . . . where when I jump in, we go to another place. I jump in and I started sliding in a mixture with twists and turns falling in the down direction. There were slide tubes everywhere, and so many of us were crossing over and above and underneath and everyone was laughing. Some were changing colours as they'd pass sliding down, at one point, you were going so fast, you'd do a circle . . . WEEE! Then a top curved funnel down, but first, you have to go around-and-around until the hole in the middle, where it took a really long time before I fell through and fell into a pool with a tropical waterfall. A Voice from Above, in the light teal sky, says; This is dedicated to all the people who changes peoples lives on a daily basis. Be good to them, and be good to each other, because you never know who they are, a homeless or the rich.

. . . my childhood with my elder, and being his neto, being my portuguese side, and our relationship and how he came into my life, it was after tragic events to us, in our pasts, and because of him, I would eventually meet my other grandparents. I love my other side of the family. I have great memoryes that I've never shared with my new family members. Many wonderful moments in my lyfe. Everyone accepted us and we were instant family, and then came my new and different languages, but that never stopped him from getting up and grabbing me and kissed my forehead and gave me all but none, his famous and so beautiful smile he shocked us with every tyme, his voice in dialect I find fascinating, that I failed in trying to communicate with you, miserably I might add. I loved listening to you guys talk to each other in my second language to my ears of new normalcy. I need to let that part go, and love you, for all your smiles of love for your new granddaughter. I'm sorry I never knew you better, and for *our* tyme, I became a favourite, among the number of us on that side. But that wasn't *our* story, but the memoryes are very fond and I will cherish you forever, as my elder, who lived a mightily lyfe and was a warrior in his son's and daughter's lives. I admire you and love you. How I'm so sad among us all, to hear that he had forgotten how important he is to us and never let it go. You think about how tyme was lost. I will always honour him, in mirror to my dad, and showed him how to be the man he is today, and how he must have missed his far away heart pieces, how he had to let go, because that's what he knew he had to do. I felt love from him, every time he welcomed us back to our second home. How it takes something like this to dissolve old residue from a past moment. How he reached for me when he saw me and a kiss, always a kiss. I loved him, immediately and he become a favourite. I cry, you cry for a man we all respected in honour, and how he lyved a mighty life. Like a soldier in stance, stat. How God took precedence in his family. Always, it was his core to his soul. How the confused mind can rob you of a normal life. Nothing makes sense, always loosing your way to the beginning of sadness for us left behind, to your new beginning. As we leave, knowing how much you loved each one of us here today, of such sadness. As we leave our hands to the LORD, let Him show you how marvellous on how he was chosen for us, his family and friends. May we all lay our sadness with full of tears that flow in comfort knowing our loved one is with his soul mate, and how I will celebrate that fact that we all know. Tears will be shed for we have to, to show our sadness, because he deserved a few tears among us. But then wipe them up and live for the next domino. Lyfe will always disappoint you, at some tyme, but let Him show you mercy on the sickness that made us all sad for his loss. Let our hearts continue to lyve here and let you now love in a totally different way, and take your love for us with you, to show us once-and-a-while a laugh or a smile that you gave us and our memoryes of you. Let words be your comfort for this moment in our lyfe together and how it brought us together to remember all of our love for each other, in a great memory for his family or friends. We will never say good-bye to you, just, we're gonna lyve on until our tyme, and carry your love in us forever. How God loves you, He blessed you with a wife, who devoted herself to her family and three children, who will so grieve your loss and your grandchildren, and tell him one last time that we love him, always. And that you may be loved in your own special ways.

"Happy Birthday, Mom"

I'm being fixed LORD, through Your Hand. I'm being healed for my new love, it's new appreciation from being healthy, from all my brokenness. All my sadness, from childhood to now, has come to help me heal and become the woman I am today, and it's all from being *your* daughter. All my love from my innocents, has come back and I'm the child you loved so much, is coming out of me and I want to shower you with love from coming through so much darkness, that haunted me for over a decade, and now I'm a woman with stature and virtue and compassion. Because you were my mom, and dedicated every day of your entire lyfe, showing me your dedication, and how far I've watched you for, to understand. I'm changing, right in front of you, and you see me, once again, as a child who wants to love you for forever. In all my lyfe, no mother I want more, and if I had to pick a mom out of a lyne-up, I'd choose you, every tyme. Because of you, I'm able to write freely of my relationship with the LORD, and have a steadfast devotion to God. I owe my life to you, and may you know, one hundred percent, finally, know how much I love you and I'm not going to ever leave you, I may one day move on, but I'll always love you first and only, because I could never love another mother other than you. I've witnessed all the sacrifices you've made for me, the child who jumped on your bladder as I did all my cartwheels from one side, to the other side, to become someone strong, and someone I want you to know. A side to us, I never knew about, and I love it. Now I know how to do many things at once now, and I know when I need to be fixed, so I go away for a little while and I heal back up again, and I can come home and know how much I love you more today than I did yesterday. I have a strong new hold on something I want, and still be me, half of who I used to be. I'm loving the process of understanding who I am, has been unbelievable and I'm transformed into who I really am, as a person, a woman, a Christian, a mom. With some outside help sometimes when emergency arised again. To know a person like you. You are so special, to all your most truest family and friends, who've loved you for who you are, the person, the wife, the mother, the whole package, no matter what, and I've struggled sometimes remembering that, and I hope now, I can understand your love and commitments you've made for me and my children and your son. Who'd probably be dead by now under the watch of another person's neglect, that you raised him, and loved him, and became his only mother, his mommy. My mommy first though, and now I share an equal half of a child, when he came into my life, I learned I wasn't always the person he needed, and *you* did it. How you love your children and grandchildren and your whole family and all your friends that the LORD has given you, for them to be special enough that they get to know such a dedicated part of the church, and their schooling/education, and how I owe you so much for that, I'll never forget that mom. That when I'm away from you, you come with me in a way so I can grow in loving you in a way I didn't know existed. I never want you to think, that I don't know, one hundred percent, what you've done for me and how you've always loved me, my way, and in secret you pleaded with God for me to find my way through my darkness, to find You and live with her forever. Noteworthy and noted in this page of many other Love Letters that will be shown all over the place, and all mother's will lead in example of you, in loving your child, only as you can, is another person, but that's you. I love you mom, Happy Birthday, Mom . . . .

"To the Handicapped"

January 31st, 2011

I'm not angry with you, because I'd be cruel if I was. It was only a matter of tyme, right? It was just, *when* it happened. So, blaming me again hey? Fine. Do what you need to do. If you need to send me a poison-pen letter again, well, I can't stop you, can I? I'll never stop loving you, and I wish it never came to this, again, to bring out the side of you that needs so much love, from such a dark place, and I can't save you, from you. Your mind and thoughts must be cluttered with darkness and chaos, and you must feel that no one loves you when you spew in the only way you know how to. You must feel alone, a lot, but I can't help you in the way you need to be helped. *I was so happy*, when you came back into my life. You helped me with many things, and I love you for helping me and I thank you. I can beg and plead to you, to ask you to stop abusing mom in the way you do, with such anger, bitterness, so much hatred, so much darkness in your heart. I was there once too, but how I got healing will not save you from what you receive in return if you continue the way you are. I'm sorry for your sadness, and I was being me with you for as long as you gave me. I'm sorry, for your anger towards me now, and if you feel you need to be defensive towards me, in where I'm only continuing, to show my love for you, in a way you don't and will never understand. To when you said that I was the favourite, that's not fact. I'm just me. You need to know, that wyth what you're doing again, has nothing to do with us meaning here, in this house, it's where you are, in your spirit, your heart, your mind, your thoughts . . . that must be chaos. I know you don't know her like I do, and it's easy for you to hate her, but I don't. I will never make fun of someone, anyone, and never say it's okay to push anyone of a cliff. You took such joy when you said that, and I was so sad for you. With all of your emails to her, I know you'll take pleasure in sending them to her . . . I can only imagine how you must take delight in being and showing your bitterness towards her. I hope one day, when you are at peace in your lyfe and in your heart, you will rejoice where you're supposed to be, with the LORD. Just know, that any issues with me getting together with him, I will never, ever, stop seeing him. I love my bil, written in code, and he loves me. I can only hope you can support him, but I know you're not going to or even capable of doing so . . . no amount of poison-pen emails, will ever stop me from seeing him. And I know how you must feel reading this,.you must be fyred inside with fuelling anger and ready to blame me for something again. You're sinking fast, and I can only pray for peace for you, for you're in such turmoil. I can't imagine what you must feel and think every day, when you're alone, but know, that God will always love you, and always want goodness for you and for your lyfe here. I had to stop seeing you, because of your emails. I could no longer sit with you, or let you think, that I supported your funny efforts in regards. I will never support your meanness towards her. She has been my Christian warrior, and she's a special person, in many people's lives. She matters, to a lot of people, that you will probably, never understand. I wish we could have remained together forever, but it was only a matter of when and how it would end for us. You have this blockade around you, and even though I tryed to break in, to find you, to save you, it was swallowed up in your thoughts and the darkness that surrounds you. I'm not mad, angry, or bitter towards you, because you just won't understand my unconditional love or hers either. I pray that the LORD will ease your chaos, and ease your angry feelings towards anything & everything.

103

The urge is too great. I have to write . . . . to write, to have an impact on the world. I hope to shake everyone up and tell them to listen to the wise, and hear His voice calling out for you. To 'tear the whole world up' . . . . to shake you from your slumber and show you Him, in His Light as you wait to hear that Voice in your heart, then you must answer it. To show you Him from my perspective, and tell you about it, so it can uplift you, and rip you from the roots to plant your tree in a whole different place in your life, and then your life will become a blessing to everyone surrounding you to make a chain around the world, and hold hands and conquer the world as our own unity over the evil one. To let Him condemn hell to it's own mystery hell that affects even it's own fyre. It will fall into oblivion with shut eyes to never know when you're gonna stop, so drown, you bastard, you evil one, go away. With the LORD with me, He will wake up His children and show you The Way. To make everyone deaf with only Your love for us, to show us a story of this thing called lyfe, and sometimes people must dye for the world to continue and continue to make stuff, and make lots of money, for stuff that was a thought, so why not? I think, that if you're gonna lyve, lyve it awesomely, but don't forget the Main Ingredient. Don't be afraid of what's to come, because it's written already but you can still pray for a miracle, because they do happen. Yes, lyfe is going well, and yourself? What have *I* been up to? Not much and everything. Just doin' my stuff. Letting things take me away to another place, in the past where the tyme was much simpler. To remember how we all was strong, but we still did. To shape me, into a creative person. I never gave into it until last year a few months ago. To let me do what I needed to do, to get here. To belt out the tune and the words that will carry with me for my entire lyfe. To hear a story, I didn't know about, and to see you in a totally different light, to gain new respect for you, to listen with a full heart towards you, knowing things I didn't know before, and I think it's fascinating. To have you in my lyfe, and to know that I've missed out on so much of you from the past, as a child, who is now and adult and can appreciate your story, now, and be proud of you and our relationship. To know a stranger, who is no longer a stranger. How I've misjudged you, and today, was not only a blessing for my mom's birthday, I got to know you, for this was our special day as well as hers. To fill up my senses, with new knowledge and a new respect. You've watched me grow up, into the woman I am today, and you're very fond of me. You've watched me grow into my own, and now you get to see the real me, in words otherwise not spoken, that now shows you my love for my LORD, as I watch Him walk into the room with trumpets blowing and we all stand as He walks into the room, and we race to His feet and bathe them. To find who I am, in your lyfe that shows me a significant love, of purest form and you watched me pertaining to observations and love me in a special way. I love you back, in return, and how this day went down in history and is now recorded, so I will never forget this day. Everyone was busy with their own company, and God chose for us to be together today, to show me more love for someone I didn't know past yesterday. Where there used to be me, to express removal or separation, now is this wonderful gentlewoman, who's come from behind of what I now know. I give you a special piece of me, my special aunt, with a strong story, from both sides, and how we now stand for each other, of coming from a hard life, with strong devotions to serve our loyal God.

How my lyfe, just changed before my eyes. Tonight I was given a message. I was blessed so much today. I felt good in my spirit, and then I did my thing. As usual, I was listening to my favourite radio station, and heard a comment about foster parenting. Then, it came as a message which is how I'll take it. To get to love, everyday, and to help, and to save. I have to save now, with everything I have, to save them, and to love them, and who knows what's to come for the future now. Not in my professional life, well . . . I better take that back and say, that this will change everything at home lyfe. I'm so excited. I have to wait till afternoon to tell them, both of myn, about their new and crazy future with me as a lover of them. And who's to follow? Something that will change our lyves forever, with an open door, to the lost ones, and show them their ways back, with us being the humble servants of the LORD, and that we pray everyday to Him, and ask Him to bless us, as a whole family now, and love each other, and share God in some of our talks, and stuff like that. How lyfe was shuffled around and I didn't know what to do for you, because I didn't understand then what I now know of what will become of my future. I hope I saved you, like you saved me. Not in normal sence, but in our sence. How I just learned, how I can save you through our children, and to have an open-door, to save them, finally, from others causing them harm. To save myself in the triple forces telling me that this is meant to be LORD, in memory of those before me from my life, with the Trinity, showing me the ways to them, and to change the world, one at a tyme. Let them fall upon me and my soul. To save me too, to give me more purpose on surviving suicide. What a message to God and how He's blessed me and how the LORD saved my life, to show me this, a future that I'm so excited about, such a blessing for me. To carry on, in their strength, and to learn from each one, so I can love them even more than already. I'm hankering, hungry to save the world, in it's own special ways, as it shows through me. How to shine through Your noun, and to show me what's next for me and my children, and I know they'll be on for the ride. I hope they stand beside me every step of the way. Showing me how to do it right, the way I was taught with a twist, and a me-kind-of-love. To spread The Seed like bees do with pollen. Go ever where the wind blows you, and live in joy and tragedy and do it with gusts and shake you and blow you like sand, and you land there and plant *your* seed. For you to take root from your childhoods and remember Him in everything that you do for Him. Not saying it'll be a drill. But as yourself and yourselves, to be strong in being independent, and make up your own mind. I want to show you your confidence that's just waiting to come out, with gentle but stern motherly love, to point you like your compass will one day tell you. To remember where you come from since I've been in your lyves, and how I've loved you, but that is still to come in the future, but loving in knowing what's to come for me. As they surround me and tell me their here. How I can love them, like I was loved, and share my lyfe with me and be the best I can be. With strength in the LORD and pray to Jesus daily and ask for blessings that I will be humble for, and give me the words and love to break them down and open them to me, and heal their wounded souls, through knowing their darkness, as they see it and feel it. To give them another chance at lyfe, in another cycle in their lives, pinnacle to their lives of stance and substance.

I hope what's coming to him, he really thinks about messing with me and the power of the LORD, and what's coming to him, he deserves it, but I also feel sorry for him, that he has to resort to crime to have a lyfe. I can pray for him, and be a loving Christian woman, but when he said, don't mind me, and he was wearing gloves, so no proof, just a disaster in my space of privateness. I'm mad, sad, feeling lost within myself, searching for something that's lost now to me, and I'm just feeling so many things. This has happened to me three times now, even with a car alarm. He must have been a pro, because my alarm didn't go off, so now, it's a mess with stuff all over the place, and I'm waiting for the police, but since it's not an emergency, it'll be a while before they come. So now, I'm just feeling what I need to feel, and move to the next thing, the next domino to see where it may fall. I pray that God will keep me safe when I'm in my car at night tyme now. How night tyme brings out the dark side of lyfe, as it keeps and sits in the shadows of the night, and how it creeps and sneaks and waits till you're gone to do the crime. How today came crashing on me from nowhere, and everywhere. My head and car is a mess . . . . *that's what that dream last-night was about.* I had a dream of the devil last-night, and now I know what it meant. He was trying to sneak around, and he got what he wanted from an evil man, breaking into someone's property, and just non-shalontly, walks past my son, and says, don't mind me, and puts his hands up as if someone was to shoot him. And he just walks away from a crime that was committed, like he never did anything wrong. Just someone doing what he wanted to do, just 'cause. I pray for him, that he will paid for his crimes on you. He's the betrayer, while I'm holy in the LORD, so it was. I'm scattered all around right now, whether I feel angry or compassion towards the stranger that committed a crime against me, and I'm sure this won't be the last crime against me. I'm being taught lessons, but I just don't understand what feeling I'm supposed to be feeling right now. At one point, I felt unsafe, then I was mad and sad, and now I feel scattered and anxious about the police coming. I also have to tell them, the criminal was wearing gloves, so no finger prints. I pray for myself, that I remain strong during this time, and to feel whole again and safe in my own environment. I wonder who he is, who he is as a person, where he comes from and his background from just being someone who is a stranger to me, and I know he is evil due that my dream was of the devil. Was he the devil? Who loves him? Who is his family and friends, or is he so lost to the world, that he is faceless and does he just want to fit in? Why did he chose my car? Does he know something? What was his reason for not panicking when my son saw him, or why did things happen the way they did? So many questions that remain empty. He will be known as the criminal in my life, who has shaken me and made me remember how broken this world truly is, and how shattered the many souls are in this crooked world. So, this is what I have to say to him, where I want to be . . . after I've come back in from cleaning my car out, and that's after the police officer came and took a statement to the crime. I have no sympathy for this person. What he has coming, and all the other thieves and criminals in this world, I have absolutely no feelings for this man, who robbed me in the night. That sneaks under the carpet, and lifts it out and doesn't make a sound, as to get away with his crime. I can't believe, I have to lyve in such a corrupt world like this. Be watchful, over your shoulder, watch him, and put him in jail.

Andrew, I miss you, I need you. Where are you? You're supposed to save me when stuff happens, as I run the pages of my heart to you, to seek comfort in your arms tonight. I miss you. I run to you as you reach for me and grab me and wrap me around you, in your arms so tight as to not let me go. I'm scared. I don't know what to do. I have so much fear in my heart and soul right now, and I whish you were here, so I could talk to you and you could wipe my tears with the towels you thought were necessary. You could make me laugh, like you always did. Was he there that one time I kept hearing noises? I whish you could answer, but I feel a yes to that answer. I feel so unsafe in myself right now, and no one can make it better for me . . . I went seeking for comfort in many people tonight, but didn't find that peace from them, but they tried so hard for me, and I love them for it. It's now a shell of all comforts of home being ripped out and torn it from the pages of my life, and just torn them to shreds and they're lost forever in the abyss of the worlds evil. Andrew, why aren't you here? I'd call you first, to come and save me from the night predators, where you once lived. I felt that pull in my heart tonight, that I whish I was with you tonight, but sought comfort in my daughter and her prayers and her love and scared for me, and my son, who didn't know what to do either. But I felt a pull tonight to that lyfe, where no evil exists and can't harm me anymore. Can't touch me or anyone I love. I want to so badly, but I have a new fear in me, of the blackness, that can reach around my throat, and slit it with no excuses . . . as I fight for my breath and lyfe again, as blood spills from me and my wound, but that's the world we live in, minus you. So many dark secrets that come from someone of not knowing what's just happened to you. I miss things that used to belong to me, that someone now reads about me as a person and my thoughts from a long time ago, that I didn't protect very well. That entered my sacred place and destroyed it, and now it's hollow. Andrew, come into my dreams tonight and hold me in your arms and let me hear your voice, and whisper I love you, to me and stay alive the whole way through. Become the same man I saw before, actually come to me, and take me into you, instead of just standing there, looking at me, as if I'm supposed to know you. I want to be a heavy weight, as you carry me across the path to the quiet river where we can sit and have lunch, where no one can follow us and sneak or overhear our private conversation, and if they did, you could just think them away and they're gone. So, can I ask you some questions then? Can I do it? Am I strong enough? Since this is second, I'll watch things that make me happy or calm me from my turbulent heart right now. Silence my sadness, and lay and forget. My container that held my inspiration, is now gone to me, no longer is in my life. And I just want to lay and be quiet and still, and enjoy something that I totally forgot about. How both tymes, it's been a no. But this time, it was a sure sign, so what does that mean? Andrew, cee these are the questions I would ask you, but I can't see you, only in my dreams and the remnance of your life here, that you shared with me. Instead, you're not here in the physical ways that we used to feel around and forget who's that is. I feel solo, that I've done something wrong, to pay me back for my wrongs and showing me something else than what I want. LORD, I ask for Your protection, as I settle into my night, alone with me and my thoughts. Please settle my mind and heart towards darkness, and be my Light, showing and shining for me to find daylight with a new beginning and back to living lyfe, just different now.

Oh how you had to go. Even though I wouldn't whish it upon anyone, the way it happened, was written in the a kasha plane, and it has everything. How I whish many things from it, all of it. And if you stayed, I couldn't be affected by it. I know what would have happened. Just like them, in python positions, and venom that we would have shared as well, and you knew what the answer was to this problem. What happens here, is another reality from this one, in reality. How this song must play for me on much love that I have for you, but you had to go, didn't you? But if you were still here, you would have used, like you did . . . and I'm not going to pretend either way, through this spot you've never been in before, where we've both seen from past storyes . . . to use the brutality of your power as a man, and harm a woman, just because you could, and you could get away with it, and the superior sex bullshit is something you fed on, just like other abusive men, who doesn't care who the woman is. It's just a woman. Minus my LORD, my Jesus, who once upon a time, walked where we walk. He was the Only Perfect Man . . . . Once upon a time ago, we were equals, until you overstepped your superior sex bullshit, and thought it was okay to mark me from your anger and gave me an ultimatum. On the day I surrendered, I gave my life to you, and you knew you could have me and my loyalty forever, but I knew secretly I'd never feel like that. You took me, and took my soul and swallowed it and lived with what I was in love with. But how you shook me when you should have carried me. I wanted you to leave so badly as you continued to yell, in anger, and blamed me for your anger. So, one day in that future, I was to yell at you, and curse you, and how we were in killing each other, and the love died, that's when you died and I would live in sorrow and despair for over a decade of evil and blankness and unfocused on many things then. Now I am a very strong woman in Christ as I humbly pray, that my strength come from Him and Him only. In this cruel and compassionate world I live in, where the Truth is waiting to fall upon you, and affect your soul, in contentment, and surrender, to the Only Man who is entirely Perfect He is. Jesus would have never touched a woman in the way you do. So take your imperfectness and change your attitude towards the only sex in this world can have babyes to continue lyfe. So when your woman is trying to be stronger, which some of you won't, but if I know you, and you're in my lyfe, I know for a fact that not one of them, would lay a finger on a woman. But a lot of men, who's been given this name above all names, and whip her, punch her, and use your men to make us bleed and wound in silence, and fear. I'm so sick and tired of this mentality, that because he's a man, he can do it. How you show us your charm and slide your way under us and knock us off our feet, then you order, and show fort knocks, and you forget the LORD. But once upon a time ago, I got my black widow to come out and play, and how I showed my hand in your face, and know that I once was superior to you. How I am angered towards this, and if you're cruel, be punished. But if you're a good man, and know one hundred percent, that you would never hurt your partner in any form. LORD, bless these men and their fortunes as for all the goodness from all over the world that covers like it's blanket. Let it canopy and let the top crown support this statement. Stop making us beg for mercy as you beat her and to make your head level. What makes you so angry? Did you have no love? Pure Love, ask for Him. Make your life better and help the other people in need.

Please LORD, don't dry me up so I have nothing to say to them reading this page. How will I continue to write, if it dries up in me? I have to write and I have to do it now. So let's go somewhere together. Let's go to my dream living room in the main house, is a large/vaulted ceiling, and it's sunk-in, with two baby steps like in Cape Cod into the kitchen, like that. A fireplace, with fluffiness to the couch, with space to lay down and take a nap if needed. I'm not sure of the colour yet, maybe cream or very light beige. A big matching and comfy chair. Lots of floor pillows for in front of the fireplace, with openness to the kitchen and hallways, as not sure how the layout is yet, but I can imagine it. So that's what I want to write about, but do you want to read it? I want so much to happen for me, for us. Please pray for me, that I keep on writing new material so you can sit and wrap yourself in your soft and fuzzy blanket of your choice, and of the colour. I have a housecoat like that. Leopard print, like a furry cat, which I am, in case you didn't know. How I'd love to snap my fingers and let it be in an instant. I hate waiting. I wait for everything, and to the LORD's teasing me of my dreams and read my way to the top, to where He is, but not visible to the naked eye, unless in a picture of what He may look like. I want my house. I want to walk in and never to leave my sanctuary under His watchful Eyes and Care. He has His vastful of what needs to be here in my imagination, thirsty for anything that will make this happen, and let it be a blessing. As it enters me like an injection of hype of what could be for me and my lyfe, of all who surround me and them, to keep it going in me and the universe to show I do have a dream, and dreams, and it could happen, it may not happen, but please pray for me. Let me be contained with word entries to let you see and look into my head . . . oh maybe I shouldn't let you in, but if I don't let you in, you'll never see what could be for one day. I have to run on a full tank, that can conquer all the bumps on the way to this tyme in my future that I don't know yet. Only fractions I want to know LORD. I want it to let-it-be-known, that I ask for many more storyes to bore my readers, into a reading sleep, and let me fill their dreams with whishes for them. Let it be an non-invisible thing for them and let them lyve on. Let Him be your desk, your Table to hold your stuff so it won't fall . . . okay, I'm reaching and grasping at straws now, but you're still reading . . . I need to pray to God. Father, lead me along Your path of the directions of all the frays that You make for us to untwine and find the beginning and the start of the wire and untwine it, untwist it, but be careful, you may snap the wire in the middle and it become no good anymore. Be the One to minister to them to show them the high in knowing You, as once again . . . I must continue on to tell my story as to show you how I come up with stuff. I find words and make them make sence so you understand the words I inject into your eyes and brain . . . please, don't stop on my account, or should I say no? For some of my thoughts are forbidden for you to read and escape, and jump out of the page into another. Like bouncing from one tree to the next and make a fort to stay on, as in the childhood of playtime, and in some movies. Oh my gosh, I didn't tell you . . . did you know what manifold was keeping in it's secret, that it has identical devices? And those devices are this; that my stories are the same as His that He brings out in me and He can do anything. Create miracles, and sometimes He has to let go and let you lyve with free choices and makes you and helps you make the smart choices, and no matter where you go, there are no answers to this survey.

"Mixed Together"

I love you because of the way I can put you in a reading coma and lull you into another story like a soft song with beautiful lyrics that choke you up with oozing love. As you nod your head in tyme with the tune so I can produce more of this. I whish I could be those floating notes that you see in cartoons and out of them comes the chipmunks of their storys. So it's stuff like that you want? . . . well, okay, I'll try. I should make up a word and let it create it's own spot in the world. To be an inventor of words, well, I kind of all ready have/did. But you have to seek and find them, but be careful, I hide them very well. I want to become a maze for your brain, to start here, and then find your way through, with branches in the way, but you must make your way through . . . oh ya, I'm supposed to be writing about why I love you, and I love you because . . . do you want me to finish the maze story? . . . but I want to tease you, like sugar to the disorder, the fat you spit out, . . . okay, okay . . . so you're making your way through the maze with dead-ends and long pathways on emerald green grass, and cut trees to smooth the top, and we're running to find the way out. I think I want to stop and lay down and listen to the people calling for us to find our way through. This is lyfe, and this includes this moment in your lyfe, where you're reading another book, and that you have to figure out everything, like in my maze. You grab her hand and flew ahead in a running motions, and laughed in slow motion as she looks back at you . . . like her. Why I love you, is because you're awesome. You are the only you in the world. You are special, either to one or a hundred. You were built for His purpose for you lyfe, to change others lives as I have with you and them too. You have your own address to your soul, that you can invite others to join you and lyve right next to you, no matter where you are, that person will always have lived in your address of your person. Where you place them on your at home pedestals and place them on their trophy spot. Show them a life that can only be lived by you. Think of something that you can do, but only you can do. Someone who's searched for the path that lays before you. No one can think like you can, to hide behind words when that's the only thing I can do. And I choose my words very carefully, and place them in their proper place. There's an order, and I have a purpose to everything I do. But it's up to you to find that part of me. To discover what I really mean when I say this or that. What's the secret? But I celebrate in you trying. Why I love you, because there's something about me that attracts you to other people. I could say a jolt in my spirit and soul as I got to know you. Some I've had an affair with, some not. Like when I listen to him, and love him through it, and guide him on to that next place he needed to come to in his life, and to be his cheerleader and to minister to him and love him the similar to agape love. In a friend manner. To know that no matter what, I'll never leave you as my friend, because I cee to who you are and who you want to be. With the LORD focused from where before He wasn't. And to my loyal readers, and to my one, that announces himself on my account, and acknowledged me and my writings, where he says, write, write, write . . . you know who you are, the one tyme, we misunderstood, but even though you're far away, you still lyve in me, and I love you, and cherish our friendship. I must announce that, to show you that you are written in history, in our memoir, it is said. Why do I love you? Because each of you is a reason for you to come into my lyfe, to teach me how to love fully and to accept you as a sole, with creation to be you.

I feel all mixed up inside tonight. I'm not sure, but I know that she's feeling the same way today. As I feel her feelings and emotions, it's like were connected or something. Tonight is a very unique night for me, for I'm going to do something . . . whoever requires knowledge will lyve full lives vs. those who will not do anything for themselves and to better their life. I want knowledge, I thrive on it, like a lion killing and masochistically feast on it. So, what? . . . too much? Okay then, let's go here—Thank you for the invitation to lunch. As I laugh into the phone, feeding off the attention given to me. Please call me next week and we'll do tea, and read tea leaves, for fun, to see what they say. As it vanishes down the drain, and I can't reach it, and now it's gone. I can't believe it! Okay, now shake! Shake it like a salt shaker and shake out the salt to flavour your food to give it more flavour of savoury flavours. So then I was running down this rounded around the corner hallway, with swirls of colour leading you to the end to see it for the first time. So then, I went into the room, where it was quiet, and I laid down, but it was uncomfortable, and cold, but I did it anyways. So, now, let me ask you something, or let me tell you something, that all you should do it, the thing that calls out to you, when you question, should I do it? Or shouldn't I? Just do it! Because some of you will never want to come back to this kind and type of lyfe forms in the exisistinatly of the world and history, so stop thinking about it! If you know it's right, then it's right, and you'll know from the little voice from Him. Woah . . . stifle the potential, and you're robbing that person to know what they want to know. I get into position and cock the gun, and what happens next, happens next. Get lost in the noises that make you question things, and makes you get up and check what the repeated awful noise, but now I'm waiting, again, for the next time where I can't hold it in anymore. Does it make you wonder? To complete the story looking for it's way out and express itself and play itself in your ears to make something happen in your mind and brain. I can't find the highway. Can you help me? Take what street and what street? If they only understood how difficult it is to find my way. I whish it was easier on me. Wow, I never knew how easy it is for me to switch topics from something so important, that I must tell you! There's no doubt in my mind that I know that answer, one that I know because of my learning . . . am I being selfish again with it's just about me right now? But how can I make you understand? I need to be selfish, because you're in lockup. As I shake my hands back and forth and say, yes! The sun was shining and we were children and we were on the beach, and we were wriggling our fingers toward each other and we touched, and we screamed, and then we realized that it was only us banging into each other under the sand. As I take your hand in marriage as you flow me onto the dance floor and held me tight when you spun me around, to show our audience our dance steps together and we know what we're doing. We sway to the soft love song and you whisper something in my ear, that only we know. To go back to those days that you'd pull up to your speaker in the drive-in, and you pulled close together and make out. Oh my gosh! That looks so good! . . . as I reach for the waffles and put them in the toaster and smell the air and it is spreading it's aroma around the house. They pop up and you put marg or butter, so sorry, and spread it on as it melts into the bread, and you pour your choice of syrup, and eat. So, did you enjoy my story tonight? Will you let it sit in you and well up to be something to pollute you and infest?

"Never Forsaken" February 10th, 2011

If all I am is this . . . then You know that You are my everything, LORD, I love You. This love letter is dedicated to You LORD, for You, God, and You are my Everything and I can't do nothing without You. If I need to let go, then that's the way it is, and you can't do anything about it. My life doesn't exist if You're not with me, every step of the way and You are Beautiful, Father, of my lyfe, You are my reason. I won't capitalize it because half of it is me, but I'll always capitalized Your Name. I bow and worship you, Jesus, of the two pictures I saw of You today online. How You've come so far in this lyfe, how You never leave us, and people are even drawing You of what You could have looked like, and I loved both, because it's You. Some aren't the greatest, but You must love them all, minus in the bad in any ways. I could sing You this song, to dedicate it to You, and without You are my sun, and You shine on me and feed me, with Love, Never Forsaken, and I must believe that, or what is lyfe? I have a reason for everything, because that's how He made me. How You made me to know that only one person can understand me, the way I need it, and You gave me her. I love my friends, all my friends, and you know who you are. She explains to me what I'm feeling and she's right, every tyme. I feel people, but mostly hers. How she aches inside from pain withered from her innocents and childhood, the same with me, but we know. We were searching for our other half, and we suffered along the way and we felt alone, but then God made me find her, and it was a Gift, for being so devoted in finding her, and You blessed us. She knows me, she frees me in understanding like no other species. We are sole in each other. Only You could tell me and say to me to find him first, that was an announcement, and I followed instructions, and now we are together, we found our childhood again when we're together, and how we soar on each others words and feelings. 'Cause You are Beautiful LORD. And there's so much to say . . . how You saved me, when I needed to be saved. When I really knew I'd be okay in myself . . . to know what I know? I can't tell you because it's a secret, until it comes out. Am I knowing, and I'm in all of it for You. LORD, because of You, and I'm sorry for always doing that. I want to stop doing that, and I need Your help, and this is our moment, but I'm in there, that's why. But You know this already. I'm here, I'm listening . . . I want to continue my Love Letters to You, and keep saying I love You all over the place, and pray for a quick death, as I lay at Your feet, for You to pick me up and carry me. Do it LORD, make my heart sing for you and pray into You, for You to pick me, and choose me to do this, to light the world, in my own embrace of Him, you must find Him. He's worth it. If it's coming out of hell, He lightens me, and took me out of it. He literally, saved my life, and then when I survived suicide, when I went right down, when I didn't even care anymore . . . He saved me. You saved me LORD. The only ways I can share that is to share it, lyve it, breathe it, and You Reign my life. I wonder what You really look like? Him or Him? Either choice is fine with me. It's true in what he said, that a reminisce of You from that, to now. That You get millions to their feet and chanting and cheering, for You, all for You. As You sing through the choirs through this land, that continues to pass down the generations. To continue to live and possess some and make Yourself known, where others have troubles, but it's all for You, to love us, and to show us lessons to teach to the unwise and naive. All of this love coming from me to spread The Seed, for them to listen to me.

This is for you; the battered women, of husbands who doesn't even care if he kicks her when she walks in the door. Down, to the ground, where people walk, and you push my face into your dirty shoes and smears my blood over them, and pushes her head and she crashes her head, and he leaves her there, to die, with no concern and where's the remote? How I want to smear *your* blood, across *your* face, and laugh, and spit on *your* open wounds from the knife I used to slice *you*, and pour salt and vinegar on *your* bloody wound. Why should I care, if you don't? As he pushes me down the flight of stairs to our basement, and then he comes down and pushes me at ten-fold speed and corners are piercing me. You pick me up like a rag doll and throw me around, with your temper, why is she still alive? I want to grow muscles and whip him around and piss on him and make him catch my shit into his mouth and glued it together and make him die on his own shit-choke. Leave you there with your cut penis that I've shoved a screwdriver up your urethra and make you scream in agonistic pain, of untoldness. How I'd shove my foot and rip you open and then fuck *you* and see who's a wimp to pain. *I just want to be angry for these women, who lyve with abuse everyday.* And for the stupid men who don't know this, shame-on-you. You deserve to rot with leeches sucking your blood for yours shed when you beat your wife. And abuse is abuse; whether; sexual, mental/verbal, physical. I have no pity for your hurt feelings, but yet you'd shut me out of your area, but oh my gosh, I better not raise my tone . . . . NOTE; *I just want to be a voice.* I'm not threatening any kind of abuse towards any men. **Let's be clear on that**. I just want to have a voice *back*, to be equals in a relationship. Stop showing us bullies, we just want, love. Why would any father, show his little girl bad ? when he could show her her freedom one day ? for her independence to show the world that being *her* father, means something? How will we as parents, feel that because of abuse in the child's life, she has suffered, silently, screaming for her daddy to make this pain go away. A child. Innocent, pure, please don't hurt the child, that lyves within her, who makes her who she is today. Show pride, and show her what honour looks like. To look in the mirror, at her reflection and wonder why her daddy had sex with her, and told her it was their little secret. Or the daddy who burned her little hand, *her child hand, and he burnt them*. The father berates his wife's offspring and makes them scared of you and then makes them be embarrassed in shame and anger. Love him . . . he needs so much love from you, from a *real* man, who *defends* his family instead of looking to kick her when she just finished recovering from her bruises from the *last* time you struck her. To show you your anger, would be a cake walk with broken glass and don't feel pain as you have to walk your way over the coals. LORD, this world is so messed up, and we need attention down here, from the One Who made us, as we bow in humbleness and prayer that you remove our husband's hearts, and fix them, and sew up their saudered-frayed heart strands that can only heal from Your hand. That something trigger in his lyfe, that makes him cee You, for the first tyme. So angry for these silent wives, because of fear of a man. This world doesn't *know* peace. We wouldn't know what to do with ourselves, so we must have wars, for it's in the Bible, to make this world spin on all axels. We must hate, love, torment/torture, such compassion and so much broken love. Father, I apolore You, once and for all, show that it's okay to *not* fight with each other, but LORD, please grant us, one day. AMEN.

I know you're super busy now with a newborn and the most beautifulest little girl, I've have ever seen, . . . , so you don't have to reply . . . only if you have the spare tyme to actually sit and write with a newborn and a big sister. I remember those days, and I could barely keep my eyes open let-alone, write an email. So heaven's forbid, only if you have the time to respond, do. I hope you got my message from the other day? I left it on the answering machine? . . . I think? Did you get a new cell phone number ? or is it your house phone? Anyways, I left a message for you. Hope you got it. She's having a really tough tyme right now. She lyves a crazy lyfe . . . always going, and for the past year, I've had to learn her a lot. Like she had to do with me too. She's having a rough time, and I need to be here for her. She's very private with her lyfe and she doesn't handle other people other than her family very well, so me wanting her to meet you and her, and a couple of other of my friends. Only when she's prepared and ready, but in the past year we've had back with each other, it was God's doing, one hundred percent. I've practically taken on a whole second life and second family in the past year. Her home is my second home, where I help her. Clean, make supper, take care of the babys . . . but my other angels. I help with everything I can do for her. If anyone saw me do what I do here, they'd be shocked and bewildered in knowing, yes, I can cook for a whole family and be a second mom, who loves them as well. We have a great relationship. I'm so sorry that I seemed like I disappeared off the radar. Having two lyves can be a little crazy . . . . then, on top of all that, I'm full-on, head-speed, writing my first book. it's going well. I'm at a large number of pages now, a hundred and twenty-six. And then I have to make tyme for my own kids at home, and the struggles I'm facing with just lyfe. I apologize for pushing us to the way back burner, but I did promise you, I'd be your friend always and I'd always stay in touch. I'm so different from when you and you were taking care of me, and doing the best with what you had. I will never, EVER, forget what you have done for my lyfe. You've made it better, and I know *how*, to be a friend because of you and you. I will never forget your devotion, compassion, hard love, soft love, explaining things to me, for being my interpreter when I couldn't put two words together, and for holding me, so strongly, in your arms and didn't let me go. How you cryed and showed me that side, which I saw, but didn't get it, not for a long time . . . but I get it now, and how strong your love is for me and was. I regret many things in my lyfe and for so many years, I regret so much and the guilt I carry for loosing my children's childhood because of a fallen world's emotion, grief, pain, emotional torture, when you had to take care of me. I say that, and mean that. You and them *did* take care of me. Now, my children are teenagers and you have two unbelievable angels that were chosen just for you, to show another generations before you, Christian motherly-love, and there's nothing you can do about it. It just is, the way it is. It's very difficult to share me . . . 'cause when I'm not at home, I'm with her. But I want to, 1. talk to you, 2. talk to her, 3. make a secure date to get together when she is in town and tell myn that I can't make it that day, because I practically plan around her schedule, and it's complicated, 4. so plan ahead on the date, 5. go to church together, if we plan for a Sunday, 6. have lunch, hang, talk, catch up., 7. eat and be merry and take charge as we end to continue on in our daily lyves, and 8. embrace as we say good-bye, and always say I love you . . .

I want to travel the world with you and share dreams of a lyfetime of happiness, and riches that you're sure that you're home for forever, to never move around and spin around and around, and not to be able to enjoy coming home, every night, and know that you have your own space, where you get to do anything, whenever you want, with respect of other people late at night. Mr. me, is with the edge that will survive on, past the next person, with flashing bulbs in their eyes as you sparkle with your decorated studio, and I'd have my art room, where I'd build statues and sculpt and make original-unique sheen under the lamps that shine it's beauty and makes you numb in a coma, in searching for what it is and in your mind, and stroke paint on a canvas again . . . oh my mr. me, you could snap, and lights me out blinding edge, the edge of what? And my dreams are very large my love, who invented our uniquesole. Okay, there we go, one word from two entities to create one thing, in my mind, that is dreaming so huge, that we must work really hard to get to where we want to be. Hard work from my favourite pictures, to find the beauty in hard work. To make majic, to make my head shake and shake out all the nervousness in making something from a sentence into massive accomplishments. Do you want the dream? Then work, hard to make it happen, because that's what it takes to make dreams, real dreams, of good, and helping the world at the same time, ya know? To bring to lyfe what everyone wants, Paris. I want to see Paris so bad, so I'm gonna make it happen, and you look so beautiful tonight someone will say, in their French accent, and he takes my hand and bows down to kiss me, as you watch me light up and twinkle in my eyes. Roam around Rome, blessings from Israel and to see our tri next life, but to end. To learn to appreciate colours, all colours if I'm to feed myself with goodness and wholeness with such nutrition. As we sometimes go in separate ways as to be ourself, by ourself. To open my suitcase of first-class, to put on a hat, and shoes, and head out into the strange land I'm in and write down the address before I leave and then walk outside, smell the air, of wherever we are, I are, and start walking, and snap lots of shots of just me smiling into just me with everyone watching, as they laugh at the silly angle that my face is in the same positions when we thank God for His love and grace, and always make time for Him in your daily schedule. Even if it's just a thought all-of-a-sudden, to say, hey, I acknowledged You LORD. It's just an idea, just another idea put in your head for thought. From a healthy diet, with grains and rices and pastas and yummy food for enjoyment but healthy thought. Right? Eat of different cultures of different spices and flavours, and drink wine and laugh in your new short time home. To see the other part of yourself, the traveler. Someone asked me in mr. me time, how many places do you want to go? . . . everywhere. Of my dreams, of part of my of who I am, that makes me walk with style and grace upon myself to be me now and to build myself with only Him. Placing me with different people in my lyfe, who He knew could and would change me, with knowledge of Him as my Saviour, my KING, my LORD of LORD, my World. So come with me my two and build your storYes, to tell your children and grandchildren, and in recent. I love you mr. me. Let's grab our luggage tri of us, and let's fly to a place where this is no pain, no suffering, and when you cry, cry to the LORD and ask for Him. To just intervene and inject in your pain and travel with it and then when you're in a strange land, write a Love Letters, and place it in a bottle and it will be in the ocean to be discovered.

"Valentine's Day"

As I start another lett . . . . ahhhhhh! Weeee, this is fun! Around and around, I spin in dizziness and I'm laughing, with all my secrets that I can't share with you all. Not today, can I say this and mix, and that, and match, and criss-cross the ties that tie you all up into this unbelievable bundle, with ribbons and bows, with bows and arrows, with the love sign in your hearts . . . . clear throat, and say I want to hear. Tell me this story of when you were in a prison camp, in a certain situation in the lyfe process to get to today and tomorrow. Yay! Let's go play, and strum our guitars, and sing in awful tones and notes and have a blast laughing our asses off. Kissing each other in playdom. Sshhhh, I can't tell you, and you and to be quiet from her listening to us whisper in her ears. Oh my gosh, I'm so in and on and with it. It's great, and its mystic mystery, that I can't divulge to you, for the codes of bangin' with the lock. Wouldn't it be cool to seep into a door? To cee inside, with the grains and knots and the smell, is intoxicating to stupefy of the highness that needed to happen so the indicated could play with your glasses and your breaths. To make you gasp . . . Gasp! I love this, cee what I mean? To make you fall in love for the first time, by saying, Happy Valentine's Day baby. I love you, for coming down to my house to give me a single stemmed red rose, on our first Valentine's Day together. How we laughed and hugged and kissed and spent some time together doing things, and remembering our first Valentine's Day. We're so young, what will lyfe bring for us? Will you continue to surprise me? The man I want forever, as she says to her young teenage love. How could I say no? So now, I'd love to visit you sometime next week, back to my world but I needed to get it out, ya know? Where it says plan before you write, which is always a good idea, to think about what you have to write, because I know this, for I plan before I write too. I ask, God, what should I write about tonight? Then I start thinking of secrets I could tell you all without really telling you. God planned ahead too. So it makes sense. Good advice, here on the love day of the year, that has been celebrated since then, I read this history and it's when the birds chose to mate. How this day was shown since way-back-way. So come on! Lets splash the ocean water, as we press against the waves as I held your hand so tight. The waves crashed against us, and I wouldn't let you go, for it was a tornado under the surf on the shore. And you begged for me to let go and I yelled over the crash. No! And when you and your brother had that treasureable fight when you said, it's my life you know. And you were crying to him, begging him to accept you and your love . . . as I sat there, pushing my laughter of love that it was so pure and full of feelings, that me and others around you two just talk and say what you were feeling to each other. It was one of the most preciousest moment and memory of you two in your lyfes so far. It was so innocent and sincere moment together. I'll always treasure that heart-felt fight between brother and sister. How I sat, and I looked down at my womb and felt you move inside me, where you loved my voice, and when you showed me and played footzies with mommy. I tickled your fetal foot within my huge belly, where I tried to eat, but you didn't do anything but have your own rules with me. I will never forget that special moment of my entire life, to play tickle in my womb. I got lost for a few minutes . . . sorry. So do you know about your audience? The only thing I can hope for my intended audience can or is learning to read, and appreciate my unique way for writing, storyes and more storyes.

You let them flow, and let the pain out, cry, for hours, and keep a towel close by, because if your heart is broken, you need to let it bleed, until the end. It's tragedy that poets write, because of either we've lived it or we can ride up on imagination . . . . Let tragedy be a tragedy . . . . In response, this is what I have to say. You can't change it, you haven't gotten the power to remove it. It lives among us, and makes us remember how painful it is to say good-bye, whether it's because you're a ship in the night, or if you're human in love with your souls ghost, and how I can only imagine him here, just like all the military, all over the world, with different names, but the same meaning. And they miss each other, by a night. And the oceans a part of their view out their windows where they now sleep and serve their chosen country. Like the soldiers who stand at command and scream YES SIR! And you salute. When I say let tragedy be a tragedy, just stop always telling they can't cry or be unhappy or it's just being said. Cry. Wail to the LORD, cry on His Shoulder, and even though He's invisible, He's all around you, with His Seven arms Who's soothing you and calming you, and know it's okay to feel the way you do. No one else, in the entire world, lyves your lyfe. I can share that I bet that everyone one of you has a special and unique story, that's yours, and no one lyves your lyfe. No matter the tragedy, if they died, in some ways. I know that I was, but I to this day, understand how I survived tragedy. Two decades were dedicated to my late husband. Coming out of the first decade, trailing into becoming a wife, to a mother, to a widow. Which I didn't know how to do any of them. I don't know how I've survived jail, behind bars for the bad I've done. All the sins I have. And now I carry yours. Some days it's really heavy and some days it's nothing at all. It all depends on the day, and what happens during. I must now say I love you. Even though I know what I know and knowing it couldn't have been any other way. This was how we were going to lyve our lyves as husband and wife. I have the words of another poet and songs that have passed through my ears and filtered none of them, so it's a guess and find me the way. That shows you, that I'm listening to my heart and how it leads me. With blessings from the LORD, and I beg Him to lead me to where I'm supposed to go and where I'm supposed to be. At the right cross roads to meet up with the next avenue, of new flowers along the way and white picket fences, with the long grass being blown in the breeze. The mirror never leads you wrong, only when you don't feel well, with it fool you, but know, have options with subtitles so you understand the direction you're supposed to be on. Don't lead astray and won't change your route when asking for directions. I want to cee your aura true colours that show your own individual colour that only belongs to you. For clairvoyance's learn their own and be able to describe it, and have healing rocks and rocks with powers to those who need it most, and rocks are not of a cult, to the religious. Not to insult my own, but some are priceless gems from vitamins and they're beautiful and there's only one of each one as they serve the rich, with rings of glamour and royal stature. How if you insult something, at least know something about it, so when you boast, as I would, know your stuff, your informations from different things to gain knowledge and know the answer when someone asks you. Not everything, of course, if you don't know something, go to the Upper Hand in this game, and press the button to put your initials to the screen so when you go Upstairs, you'll know your door, to the only thing I want, is you.

As she's doing hers and I'm doing myn, the irony of that is not even worth it. As I sit and wait for messages from my heart that will lead me there, for me. To walk in my lyfe and owned it for once, as I cee a black sky with clouds of thunderstorms as I walk some more in that way. Lots of birthday's this month. The late winter that turns into spring, my favourite season. I'm a beautiful emerald. That one day I will wear my stone on my finger. Don't do that! Never do that! You'll loose what you're creating of separate meanings to the right ones. I look around and sigh for my next entry to entertain. If I was young again and I could go back to the east setting, I'd cee everyone who wants to cee me. As my prayer to You Father tonight is sad. When I grew up back there, it was the end of one lyfe to transform me into who I am today into another new lyfe, that I needed so make my way to my beloved and give birth and loose you and become a free butterfly. With my wings I'm colouring the world, in a sparkling and shimmering jewels in the lights and I'm shedding them all over you, with gifts of a rainbow. How can I think of stuff? Just keep writing and maybe look around again . . . How I've created a mess in my dwelling area. Where I come in and look at the beautiful masterpiece we've created, and try not to let just outside, another world that is my reality. So I must work so hard to recover so many new storyes. I'm almost half way there, where I'll proof read, and edit, and make sure it sounds all right and correct. And if I do make my way back there, I have to leave you behind, and I'd have to learn a new way and be some what of a bore to read, so you'd have to grin-and-bear it as I write to my kingdom, here, that I've worked so hard to give you all, my best work. That I've shown my loyalty to my readers, that I have succeeded in seeking and taking your attention. That I've opened up everything about me in these Love Letters, and just poured all of me, in writing, this writing, that I've created an award silence, that my fingers are prickling like someone's pricking them. How I can only keep going when something like that happens, and no looking back. No cheating to the next test. That you haven't studied for. That there is no answer. That you just have to do it, and hopefully survive yet another tragedy. I can do it in silence of the air you breathe that's right in front of you, and know I don't need tune to do this, but I do need the other art though. That I want to build, to sculpt in my art room, and display them in art shows, that I'd be able to do all four things. Write, sculpt, paint, travel with my work. To sit there and mold something into a form, that I've once again, created, and I'd show light on them and show their details and uniqueness And conform with everyone different and one-of-a-kind. And have people look at them and buy them, and how I'd have to learn separation and have the mentality and thought process of being able to sculpt it, and finish it, that's when I'd have to let go, where I'd never see it again. It would go to another someones home, but knowing I created it, just for them. And I'd love that. I'd own my own art studio. My own store, that I could afford to keep it open as I wait for the next person comes in to find 'their' piece, and to continue to bring new stock in as the old ones sell. Oh, I'm sorry, I was daydreaming again. Sometimes that happens to me. Where I share my dreams with the world, to wait for the next domino. I want that lyfe. I hunger for that life, I strive for that life, that you will support me and what I've been doing for the past months. I hope I'm your perfume that fills your wholebodyandsoul. That the names I'll call them, and title the next ones, achoo.

Fuck you! Throw your shit around ontop of me, because they can. Sorry, oops, I got six months. How you make me feel so shitty about myself, in complicating my head, from which they said she knows so. How I'm so angered, and digging in the dark stuff, so be careful, it's only threads. How I seek for comfort, but instead I sit and cry. Instead of just saying okay, now I sit here crying into my spilt writing. And just keep asking, why? Just pomble me, and I am. How I hide from shelter, but I didn't think I needed to shield my soul today, which I didn't take good care of myself today. I was hopeful, for yet another peaceful day in my head. That's why I had the black sky and grey clouds, I wasn't given any warning, well, okay I did. I must have been very restless in my sleep last-night. I'm glad they wasn't sleeping with me. I don't know what happened during my dreams last-night. It was, I was warning myself of the storm ahead. How I feel. Never an emptiness in that department. Always lots of feelings, to the tilt. Always intence. Fuck you, for not making yet another thing I want to talk about, easy for me, for always pointing out my errors of there ways. I always have to hide from you, you never see me. You think you do, and I'm very alone in my world. Well, *this* is my world. Of pretend, of who I show you. I need help, hang on. Well, at least I look good. Nice work clothes today. I love writing, and I know I've said that many tymes before, but that's how much it means to me, and show how much passion I have for it, my passion. I put everything into this part of me and I dedicated everything I have and can. Of course I deal with writer's block, and I hate when that happens, and everyone will know that we had yet another guilt fight, and I stand for your performance. No, I'm not mad. And he makes it impossible to throw his daggers from below, as he invaded my house today, and made this happen, and he has a tight grip on me, in his tormentant hands, you bastard. How I wasn't guarded from you today, which I'm sure you're glad at, you satanic evil spirit, that has nothing better to do, than to continue to try to fight for my soul, but I will NEVER give it to you . . . as I bring my LORD in now and take the reigns of my life and give me a spill of courage and fight. I needed to get through it with strength and determination, but still being sad for a fight that didn't need to happen. Thank You LORD, for showing Strength and not let this ruin the existing relationship, I have with him. To now have to show him love and that satan was having fun with us today, and that I prayed him away, this way. How your love got me through the door and how I just need, I don't know what I just need. How when we were younger, the songs we loved to sing, and how you got me through all my sickbays and fevers and my personality and how I was so ricochet anything given to me, and became a hard surface, under my cover. It's so delicate, like a flower, like a butterflies wings, if you touch it, I'll crumble and become sand and mixed in with the other earthly elements. That later on, I'll hear that sound again. How I have to bite my tongue to make a rough surface shiny again. How I have to bend, till I break, to give in and show my white flag. Will you come and knock? Or will I retreat there? Only time will tell, but for now, I'll stay down here and know that I'll be spoken bad against and anger will flare, more within my spirit and soul today. I should have just shut up, and to eat my words, again. But it was truth, my truth that was being knocked down again, like I don't have any. Well, I'll hide, just like I always do, from showing my face, the face that makes this place shake, to flare anger and tempers. It's always my fault. Didn't you know that?

I'm surrounded by addictions. And recovering addicts. And even still addicts. How lyfe is using me, for my affections towards them, and have placed these people in my lyfe. Most of it, has been around self-esteem, which is why you're an addict. I know how it runs your lyfe. How it sucks lyfe out of you, as you try to figure out the right way or answer, when all you're getting is the wrong one. How it causes you, physical pain, as you go through your day. How I need to scare the shit out of you, in showing you once again, how I will not allow violence in my home, ever again. I've watched the behaviour, and I won't stand for it. If I need to talk to him, then I will . . . as a Christian motherly figure. I whish I could just transform myself in my heavenly body, and get into a rocket ship, and go into space, and when we stop, and land on the moon, I unplug my air and just take my last breath and take seconds to breathe new life. But, since that'll probably never happen, never mind. But cee, that's how I think, as I continue to . . . . Yes, as I get picked up and placed in her mouth . . . yay! I'm going to take my final journey as that extra and needed vitamin, to get to where I need to go to help her be healthy, and try to forget how many errors I made today, just today. Like I did with you. How my day is carried by me, in some actual physical pain, and grieving you, and I carry guilt for most of everything today. I didn't do right a lot today. I used my anger. And it just should have stayed quiet. That's when you have hindsight and want to redo it and you listen to the quiet voice that says don't do it. But you do it anyways, then you regret it and you can't take it back. And take my heed advice. Take careful attention. But, it's gonna work out the way it's going to anyways. So, what you say matters, for it changes destinyes, and purpose. Hide, if you need to hide and come out. How God showed me two storyes of how He was needed elsewhere today for everyone else, who needs Him. Regarding everyone in your life. Someone's gotta go, and I'm trying to move to the next step going in the up direction, to race for my last breath and do what I need to here first, then enter my mystery, my imagination, my LORD's House, and sit with myn enemies. And tell storyes and forget . . . forget what? I never lyved on earth, I don't understand you. I lyve in another world that only has to send, and they receive. How I listened to the demand, to hear that, that makes me calm and sit in lulls of a voice. How I'm the mixture to an ingredient that doesn't mix oil and water. Where I'm to filter things, since I don't do it very well, that it starting to itch. How I long for that itch to belong to the person it's going to scratch. And be the sigh of relief. How I interrupted two lyves today and tonight and I need to faint as to not cause any more. Be the cancer that knocks you out to the ground and how I need peace and surrender right now. How the love song sooths such a stormy soul, that's been under thunder all day. Just please LORD, be my . . . flick, and it flyes to another place and now I have to go find it, and when I place it back to it's place, where will I go next? Will it be easier than today? Will I be at calm? How I'm not noticing anything today, and it's like everything I've learned, went out the window of your pane. So to carbon copy it as it smears down you. The news for today is this . . . someone took over, even though I fit into them and looked from another perspective today. Even in comfort can come strangulation of exhausted tryes to. So, I beg for forgiveness of the wrongs I've done wrong today, and plead for another pardon to walk away unscaved. Is it still okay to dream? Yes? No?

"Him vs. Her"

February 16th, 2011

Just lyke she would and must get along with her, I have to love Love. We must complete each other and not like and discomfort, will have to leave us at the door and I only have one night to prepare. So, let's talk it out. Okay, sigh . . . I have never, in my lyfe, appreciated this certain breed, until it came to a gull head, full on, situation. When we'd talk about him, I'd always pictured that dog, and that name, that was always attached when we'd engage in that conversation . . . but one again, I ignored it, just as it was a passing thought, in telling me now, that it was him. So now, sigh, I take a deep breath in and remember it's innocent. It doesn't deserve my anger from when I've had experiences with that one from a long time ago. That this one doesn't deserve that kind of attention and that I MUST, love him, Love. Just like myn would have to love her and she'd have to love it for me, like I did with him. We shake hands and say, deal. That no matter what, will I ever raise my voice with him minus extreme emergency and lyves were at stake, and that's how I want you to feel with my baby. She'll be the heaven I need. And that's just that. So, when I see him, I'll show him nothing but pure and wanted love for him, and so just what he deserves. He can't be the brunt of past bruises and whips and chains against my skin and soul, he's a new one and a whole another life, and not attached to then when I need to here. To play with him gently and always with tender care, never to do what I do with my other one. Play with gentleness. And that's the way it is. Treat him as I would treat her. Good and evil today, it's tow in tow tonight. To be weighed equally, but I know His Name above that, any day LORD. But we'll do it for love. The only language we know with each other. To play with him. I'm so excited to see him . . . his little face, like my fox. Maybe that'll be my nic-name for him, with her permission of course. To get to know what it's like to own a dog. From being a puppy, to a full-grown. To love each other and have special moments, to share our dogs, for bonding and welding. Just like her with her. Cee, I saw something like this in another one. That I will protect him from harm from an outside source. As if he was my own. Save his life when needed from me. Just like my own. It will brace me in danger, and I'm gonna love him. To show him goodness in when he shows me him. To have his own and dedicated Love Letters . . . doesn't that show you? . . . how important this new and fresh love, from something I hated and spit on, to a new love, for a new face that I'm callin' my little fox. How I want to play with him and for him to get to know me, fast, 'cause he's gonna get a shock from me tomorrow. He's going to bark at me, and I'm going to call his name, so he hears me, as though he was waiting to hear my voice, and he'll know it, for I've been thinking of him and calling for the right one. Now, you've been chosen. For over a decade, not only did you have a longing and yearning for you, and you've heard her voice and connected with her heart through my little innocent eyes. How it will only be through great test to get to carry him, if ever, and I must never ask. It must be given to me, like if he were myn. I will always respect their rules with him, and care for him as I would her. That that name wasn't meant for her, it was myn all the tyme, I was just waiting for you. I was waiting to be born, just for you. I can't wait for *my* turn. I need her. So bad, and I'm going to continue to pray for you, my young, baby, whose fuzziness will be my comfort, like he is with his mommy. So, now that I'm here, let's play, walk, fetch, learn, and no matter what, I will always love her unconditionally.

121

How I've forgotten that part of my lyfe, until I, or shall I say, He reminded me. Late in the bedtime hour of the night. How You are my focus of my lyfe and my lyfe's purpose, to spread Your Word throughout the world, this broken and in pain world. I say that with sadness, knowing that it may never recover from everyones, including myn sins. Of man, who makes most of the decisions, that will change your lyfe here, to show you another path that you didn't find until it was spoken to you, from the voice from within *you*. Find the LORD, for in Him, you'll find what you need to know, but always remember that He answers differently than what you want or expect. But know, that every single choice you make today, it will affect someone during your days. Yes, of course I'll pray for her, for she's my family, brought together, but a single decision. I'm so focused that I forget where I sit and listen to You speaking into a poetry Love Letters. I forgot what was behind me and what was in front of me, but then I had to look around, so not to get lost again. That she's so lost in a corrupt lyfe, that she didn't ask for, it was chosen for her, and for your half, that this was the reason. For he may not have been sober and we may have been lost to each other forever, and this was the way lyfe was supposed to happen. It's His Way. To kiss Your feet LORD and to beg for eternity, for it was said tonight, that to deny me, would deny You God. Don't forget I'm a holy person and I can say that, for I have deep compassion, and to maybe help fix you into a new you. The you *you* can be proud of. To make a difference in the world, when all it does, it starts in the mirror of your reflection, and I beg you, help us clean. I can't even imagine a life without You. You have chosen me. And I'm trying to obey Them. To carry out why I'm here, to find peace within my turbulent lyfe of inner struggles to be me, the *real* me, where I don't have to hide from, and to look at my reflection a little bit closely. To show myself close up and say, I've been chosen to do this. How can I show anything other? How we're all so messed up from human actions of abuse. For the innocent *and* the guilty. How I pray, that you find Him. Reach for the Good Words of Thee. To remember in the bad tymes, to go to the place I find myself and she fixes me with Him. Right beside her, and Feeds me what I need to hear to be me. She just doesn't know it yet. How do you think I can only love you as my most beautiful spirit, spilling me uplifting compliments, and tells me the way it is, but in her ways. That's why she was chosen from Him to counsel *me*, show *me* wisdom of advice. She is not of this world, for she has everything. Mercy, compassion, unconditional love, always giving one hundred and ten percent, acceptance. All she ever wanted, was me to be me. She wanted me . . . wants me, because I know how to be her best too. For she tells me everyday. How I love her. She doesn't pretend to be someone else either. And now I'm reminded tonight of what kind of potential you could have. If you just listen to His knocking. But only when it's the Right time, because if you do for anyone one else than for the right one, you, it won't mean the same as when you say, in your truest of hearts for Him, that, yes, I want this for my life, I want to accept Christ into my heart, and change me and my messed up lyfe. But hey, it's just a suggestion. This is my truth and whether you believe me, well, that's up to you, and everyone has rights of freedom of choice, well, in the common life, okay, depends totally on your situation. It should be a law, around the entire world, for every person to obey this law, that once a year, we reach for each other hands, and LORD, I pray.

How I love you thee, only throwds to you, my one and only. As I breathe into his neck, and how we have come alive for her, and she's been fed with brilliancy. I just want you. I wrap my legs around him as we lay on a red velvet pedestal bed, as we make love to our song again, like we do every night. I have such urges, you have no idea. I shake my head and it echoes behind me, and we just finished getting high. As our lighting was yellow with velvet all around us, on our round king size bed. As I sigh in pleasure as you eat me, up through those flared nostrils as I grab your head into my hands, and press. As we process our way through another session of making love, as man and wife, and of the LORD the Head of your house, as I want to get back to create a soft and romantic music in the background. And since He has blessed us, yesterday, our wedding day. As I say out loud, I love you. As you arch your back in your double eight, and they blended together, and as soon as you entered, it closes, so it's only yours now, for eternity, for that's how much I love you and trust you, he said yesterday, and how I want to pleasure him as my husband. How we met on set on one of my regular photo shoots. He was my photographer, and one look into the camera and we were instantly connected. How I posed for him, and made love through the lenses. We found a secret spot behind the black wall covers, and how we kissed, like we'd been waiting our entire lives for it, and how he just stole my heart, and we felt each other instantly. How he romanced me with gifts of of a rich taste, which God has blessed our home-based business, and worked with online ezines and work for a local TV station, and we were doing a shoot to promote literacy for the poor . . . that we made our own fund. To send them to local librarys and encourage one book at the end of each book, and learn to read. And when I found out he had the same Christian beliefs towards teenagers and the poor, we fell in love. We fell in love instantly. And the rest is history, and here we are, now that we waited sexually until we were married. That's how we wanted it for our marriage was very important to us. That I had to shake my head. We're married . . . finally, and thank You God for blessing our union on our honeymoon. Now on our together forever bed, together, entwined in each other where we didn't know who was who. Discovering our bodies together in our candlelit room. As our mouths cover each others in our passionate kissing and making love. LORD, thank you for my husband, that You've brought us together to make the world a better place and our devotion in You shows. And when I moved in and decorated with my best friend, she always had great ideas and I loved her style with my idea and we mix it and sometimes but most times, it was a show room. And she's been featured on local magazine covers. How we united as a team, and wanted to start our own business outside of our day jobs. I'm the head writer for the teasers and my own advice show in radio, My Truth. I'd write the promos and the letters printed in the TV magazines. And I'm hosting a live broadcast and taking it to the airwaves. How he found me as that organized photographer for this particular shoot I was on. He was new to me. He was drop-dead, head-to-toe, stylin' and gorgeous man. He oozed his way into my charm and he gave me his number and I gave him myn. I remember, I did great on that shoot. As we continue to roll around and laugh and play in each other, and then when it gets serious and we just need each other right now, and we sigh and breathe in each other, as he grabs my hair as I lay under him and I'm arching my back in agony for him.

To lure, entice me under Your vitamins like sand and the ocean The essence of tyme saying good-bye, maybe for forever. Waiting for you and if I'll ever see you again . . . open fields of undoubting love for you. Are you gone forever to me? Who started out as my friend, and became my lover, and then we ended and I'll never know when I'll cee you again. As you drove me on the back of your motorcycle, and we went so fast down the highways to our sea where we watched the daytime sky and saw the clouds and the rays of sun shining through and how I love you. How we stood toe-to-toe and declared our love and consecration. My thoughts are distracted and I am in an inlured to you. You are where my heart is, a million miles away and I'll never know when I'll see you again, if ever. I doubt the unknown in the future. To know where I've come from the second saddest tyme in my entire existence on earth, the saddest tyme of my lyfe. I cryed every day and I weep for the old past, to a brand new life and know I have to relieve it, to find my words to express. Oh how I need to grieve in these love songs. I'm left undone, and our storyes are all that's left and how we must live in a rare and sole experience for my lyfe depends on it. And now I'm on the right path and from my past thoughts in the music he used to listen to, to get that high and that relaxed state and how he got spiritual burnout, and I wonder what he did behind closed doors to the people when he was ruthless to a child's soul and affected our relationship since. In the head role under the LORD and how I've had to forgive you, for it was the first hardest tyme of my lyfe, both from where I even asked for more of Him, and now He's my entire existence. Other than when he left us here and joined the indivisible world, a world that only has one-way vision to us. How since then from when I lived alone and sorrowed into shedding many tears when the world was sleeping. I've been learning to be strong, for the first tyme in my life and learning how to be me in my future. But you must trust in me. For I give only but my purest love and explanation and you have to have an open-mind and try and trust in someone who has so much class and style. I need to open your mind, like myn has, and to give her the same treatment I did. Where I only think that my colour palette is empty, in print with my mind preoccupied for the future. What's to happen. To stayed focused for my goals, where I couldn't have experienced if I didn't know you. And how you turned your back to me when I needed you the most, but I've had to learn to forgive you, and lyve my lyfe the ways it was supposed to be lived, with strength in my LORD with a one way with luggage in hand, ticket Home. Knowing I had to give that up, for the most important part of me, and I belong to them, and my love for them was a sacrifice for my living lyfe. I couldn't leave them, so I had to let Home go, and to come to life again, after over a decade of suffering, and crying, silently, at night, where I'd sob to the frame that I held into my heart and sob to him, and I was so tragedy all in my own. How I had to suffer you, for me to wake up one day from my nightmare and it was sunny again, and now I don't have to cry everyday, maybe once every two weeks or so. My lyfe sometimes not that hard, to be able to leave and fix myself and find myself when I'm lost the rest of the tyme and being strong and being a good mom and being reminded every tyme I'm away I'm reminded of how I have to wait to have them back, to be patient, because when I get them back to myself? I'll be completely whole again, where I can only have vacant sign now, in my mind, for us, to be together, the three of us, for that's what it's all about.

Oh my goodness, this is going to be powerful, because it's a story of my LORD, my God, who gave me my LORD, my Reason. When I wanted to become a born again Christian, whose lyfe was such a disaster. And didn't know what was to come for me and the people that surrounded me. I'm here to say thank You, LORD, for blessing my lyfe with such good friends and a family and my children. Where You've been waiting to tell another story about You, in a commoner of little me. Where I've stood before the LORD and sang my love song for Him, around music and at the foot of The Cross, where I would have been bowed down by now I'm sure, as the woman who kissed Your feet, to get one Touch to take in Your trust. I plea, to shed my blood and beat in my viens and carrys a great significance. As Your song plays, and I'm just as I am, and I want to be more closely and finding themselves and struggling, just give them to Him. Fall upon your knees and beg for forgiveness, for the Light is at the end of the Tunnel. But for now, that door is closed, until I've lived my purpose and has spread the Word of God, and how I found Him in my darkness and giving all my pain to Him, and I've been born to a new woman. To never leave my LORD. I will never live any other lyfe or follow any other god. And I want to run to Him before He shuts the Door. See ya, and I grab your hand and we run together, as He stands at the entrance waiting for us, before a strangler makes their way in. How you'll belt out your song to Him, when He guides you through, to find your words and world as I find my words and His World. As I whish, for so much earthly and materials and stuff and I shouldn't be, because all I want is Him and I want Him to be Gracious to me and let me have riches to let me travel and have a home of my own . . . and I leave my lyfe to go into another of a woman who's walked in His tyme, and how I follow Him, as He walks beside a farm with an open field, and He sits down under a big willow tree at the side of the road with a river on the other side of the street. I watch from a distance whishing that I could sit with Him. Hello, daughter. Do you wish to sit with Me? Yes Jesus, I do. Then come over and sit with Me. As He starts to tell me a story of when He walked for a few hours Praying and a lamb was lost and He found his owner down the road. Then I woke up. As I groggy whished that was me in my dream, as I wake up slowly to start my day at work. To remember who I am today. To remember not to nail Him to another one of my sins. Now I understand, today, what my purpose is . . . to lyve His way in this sins lyfe. To remember The Son of God when you smile at that stranger today, because maybe their hurting inside and suffering, and pray they're not suicidal, and to remember where I come from. Watch for The Lamb today. Don't curse your distant relative on the streets today of your busy city of your town. How I had to cry out in a play for Him, and how I had to yell out to the audience, crucify Him, from a song, sung out from our choir. And to cry for You to another one in another play, and how I took that role seriously, and remembered to bow to Your feet and feel Your Cross hanging so when I go and reach for It, You are my Comfort, and how I want to, in my human ways to flush my heart to the Words. And swirl down their cheeks, into their palm and remember that The Father has forgiven you as soon as you let Him in. I can only be me here, and to live my Christian heart and soul and do my rightful and birthright duty in to share You with them. To live as though how we live and to be kind to the angered. Let You take us in Your arms, You say, children, watching for the Lamb.

As I sat and waited and the boom came into my ear and explode and the shock was awesome. And I wait for new for when I was a baby as my tears continue to fall into my cold hands, and I lost my blanket, so I have no cover for to protect me against the elements like snow and hail and such a cruel and poor lyfe, of how ordinary people pass by every day and drop in a penny, and I'm grateful. A shiny penny is my next meal, where I'll have to dig again in the trash for food, and how I feel as a human, knowing that this is my lyfe. How I shake in the cold and someone drops some pot into my roughed up paper cup. There's no God on the streets, no education, no love, . . . aloneness and emptiness. As I watch that man over there throw out half his sandwich and I run as for no of my homey's saw that too. My homey's of my enemy, and I gotta stay away from him. As I ask for some money in my normal spot and the same woman drops me a loonie, every day and says, God loves you. God loves me? I ask myself. How can a loving God, do this to me? And the answer is, it's not Him. It's of bad choices or economy, or something in your lyfe that brought you to this moment in your lyfe. Where I didn't do anything to ask for this kind of freekin' lyfe. Given away from my own mother and father. Left in the streets at fourteen and ten dollars, and they threatened me that if I ever go back there, they'd reject me. I had to find my way ever since. Oh, this sandwich is good, lettuce, tomato, yummy sauce, and white bread. I have to plead my case to that lady. She looks nice enough. Hey lady, do you have money so I can eat and buy my pot? As she snubs me with her nose up in the air, and looks at me like my mother did. Then I strick gold. That man is coming who always feeds me something, and I tell him twice my name is, Josh. I like this person. They ask if I'm hungry, like she does all the time, and I say, um, ya, a bit, thank you. She says, okay. I'm scared to ask for a blanket or a bathroom so I could shower and be warm for a while, but all I can do is say, thank you. As soon as she comes, I wait, and wonder what she's going to buy me tonight. As she comes from money so I can only dream of having her lyfe of getting in her car, and driving away and leaving me there, just like my parents did when I was a child. How I need to run to the next nights bed in an alleyway, behind a caved in wall, and pull my cardboard box, where it's going to be a long night. Well, she said it again. God loves you. Where she doesn't understand, I don't know a God. It's all about me out here, and stay away from that street and that street, where they beat me and took my loonie that that nice man gave me. They know I don't have money. They left me there, in a pile of my blood. I got up and struggled to get to a main street and stay safe for another day or two, where I'm going to have to heal and miss tonight's meal. Since I broke into that car, I can't go back there, for there's no innocence on the streets. When you rob, you make a mess, and take whatever you can get your hands on so I can sell it. As I run for cover and throw any evidence away. Another garbage pile to rummage through, and look at that . . . I found a blanket with holes in it like stretched out knit and warn with age. I found my new blanket and found a safe enough spot to sleep in the park where others lay under big trees with newspaper, and no one's getting this blanket. To never know what a bed feels like under me as I conform my body to the rocks beneath me. To each their own out here. How I need to get some sleep and wake up when it does, I have no clock to look at to say it's breakfast, lunch or dinner.

"Happy Forty-Secondth Birthday, Andrew"   February 21st, 2011

I can't help but full-well knowing, that it's your birthday today. And so now, today, I write to you, with a relaxed and broughten back to our tyme, when you were alive, 'cause cee, you died. And then I had to listen to our old dance songs where we'd dance for a long tyme in our first place when I moved in with you. We enjoyed being together. So, happy birthday, Andrew. I miss you but remember when you wanted to go out with him ? your friends that were the most important to him, he placed them first in his life and I know how he felt, but cee, I'm not him, 'cause I'd always choose family first. And we'd always fight about it too. We'd still be fighting about that, but then I remember when you surprised me at my grandparents' funeral, and how I was so happy to see you at the front door with your smile that stole me in the first place. Then I was later mad at you for not taking care of our first. What would you be doing if you were still alive? Normal work day, and then to your favourite persons. That took first place in front of me. How when you said the second to last message you left me. How you said, you never cared what anyone thought of me, you never did that. And how I know it verbatim. Word for word. Quote, quote. And that was your last words to me. How that is so heavy for my soul to carry, for knowing what I did. Haunting me, ripping my soul in agony of my flesh stretching and ripping it further while wide awake. With the devil liking me with his fyre tongue, and pouring salt and vinegar on the new rips. How none of it matters anymore without accepting what I did. Our fights, our words, our love, where we just had a fight a few days ago and now, you're gone. How can I live with this? How you gave and I didn't notice and now I see what you did for me, and how I'll regret never really thanking you, for all our memories, of all the great tymes we had, in our short but rushed relationship. Where I never even thought of you as only my boyfriend and fiancé. I always considered you my husband, from that first night, where we fell in love and shared breakfast conversation, of hey, I really love you. How it was so instant, of only two days. That's how sure we were that you and I were the one for you and me. And how we laughed sometimes and our road trips on one of your spontaneous intents. We'd just get in the car and you'd drive. For the week or two days weekend, and how you were so curious. And you'd beg me to let's do it, come on. As you laughed and turned to do it anyways. He wanted me to play with him and I was so closed-minded. Banged up vehicles, stuck in the sand, loosing our muffler in the sand of thousands of red ants and felt lyke we were in quicksand, and finally you got us out. I just shake my head as I remember, how you were on your own. How I didn't even offer to help us get out and have fun together in figuring our way out of the mess he got us in and not even care if we ever get out. And then one day from then, the only thing that could get your attention was your pending death. And it was knocking so loud that you finally answered. Would we have slayed our hearts by now? And hurting our spouse. Fighting like crazy, and you were planning and organizing the steps you had to do in prep for it. Little did I know. How I didn't understand your thoughts that last day. Where I didn't know. I whish I was me now, then, and save you and love you in a different way. That's when you ended our battles. And now our two are with me and I have to figure it out by myself and I sometimes don't know what to do with them. But that's up to me now, but I love you, wish you were here. Happy Birthday.

"Saved"

February 21st-22nd, 2011

Tonight, I sit with myself and self-appreciation day on your birthday, like you were giving me myself back as you sit in my reflection and tell me that I am beautiful and if I never date ever again, I'm okay with that. I've come through the darkest days in myself and in another's life and death, to take blame for that weighs heavy on a daily basis. It tired me. I was tortured, in nightmares, in my violent sleeps, that I'd thrash myself awake, and I'd be crying and I'd awaken and turn on the lights because I was terrified. It was horrible, and I call myself insane in those days where ghosts would taunt me and stare at me, and terrify me, and blood coming from the walls and giant spider webs, and I couldn't remember phone calls I'd make. I was so lost. I didn't know how to do anything. I'd want to pee in bed so I didn't have to get out of bed, because I couldn't face my family, for I cryed all night and I was a mess visibly. I had to be very strategic with timing and how long I had to wait for my eyes to become less puffy and lye and say I didn't understand the questions, can you ignore me and let me go? I didn't know how to be a mom. I didn't know anything, except that I needed to remember not to kill myself today. I lost so much memory from their childhood. I'll never get that time back with them. It's gone, and now they're teenagers, and their living their own lyves and I want them immediately, so let go, for me, who's fought for everything I've ever done in my life, sometimes with help and others, not so much. But I think that's normal right? And now this is where you've helped me get to and to dream and fight hard to get there and to achieve it. I've had much help along the way to today, your birthday, to show me in the mirror as I talk to myself for I'm all 1 have besides the LORD, but when I have to self-talk and self-appreciate myself and to feel good today. As I swagged my way around today. How far I've come from the tyme of my darkest days in my survival. How I had to grieve not being able to dye whenever I wanted and felt like it. Fuck you! Don't you dare judge me for who I am. Oh, I'm not talking to you, I'm talking to the people who judged me so harshly when no one knew my private world. Behind double doors. Where I've lived in the darkest and most sorrowful tyme of such a tragedy. A death that didn't have to happen . . . okay, I know, it did have to happen, for us to live the way we have. A good life of security and what matters the most in life itself, loving God and always putting Him first in anything and everything in your lyfe. But you had to dye, the way you did. And I needed to learn . . . a lot. To know what I know today that I didn't know back then, well, it was fatal information required and I failed, a lyfe that I was supposed to protect from the world, and I couldn't save him. I wasn't supposed to save him, but I knew something was so wrong with him. I felt it, I just knew it, but I didn't' know what. And how I had to find you dead, to show me my future lyfe and the lives that I touch in talking about loosing someone to suicide. And the horrors that no one understands . . . only those who have experienced, and I don't give a flying fuck, what you have to say about this, unlike when I said I was patronizing you, when you didn't live my lyfe. So to the hallucinations imagines, fuck you. How I gave you everything of me and what I had left to give away, and you stole me, and I can't even talk about it . . . The LORD has brought me out of this second most tragic tyme in my life. Two thousand nine, was the second hardest in my lyfe. Now I'm strong. I'm me now, and how I've opened my life. I know you had to go, I just whish it was so different than it was. I was tortured from your death, now, I write.

I'm just gonna start typing and cee what happens. You in? Okay, let's cee if I can do this with no intent story to tell. Other than, I'm glad he left me, as I sit and wait. For the next heart break from another man? If I never date again, I'm okay with that, because I have my kids and my arts. To paint again, and to paint with oils and on a huge canvas, with top notch oil brushes, and I'd buy my colours, the best brand, and to go home, my home and go into my arts room and after I've worked, I'd go there and paint. Put my music on and start doing my dream painting and finally put it to canvas instead of it just being a dream, it will be my reality. I wonder if this'll will happen for me? I want to draw too sometimes, I should have an art table with all my pencils and art supplies and to dedicate some tyme to drawing again too. Just think of what I could create and I'd get to shade and use ink, and that would be after I walked Manna, when we worked for a few hours, now we're going out for lunch and we walk for an hour and we play and run around with each other, and she works off the staying for a few hours that she wasn't mobile. Well . . . okay that's boring right? You're probably falling asleep wondering when I'll be good again and want to keep reading. I wonder lots about stuff with my book. What's gonna happen, for I want to become a best seller for many weeks and months. But am I good enough? What's to happen when I've completed all three hundred pages ? and I want to write more? Then I guess I'd sit myself down at my computer and start writing another book. And build and construct storyes, like he will build and construct my house one day, with all my dreams. And then in the next corner I'd want my clay and all the tools needed for sculpting and my kiln. So each wall would be one art. Drawing, painting, sculpting and then my kiln. To have a blockade at the entrance . . . not a proper door. It's a wall door with a maze entrance to my arts room. It's open to the other part of the house. Then when Manna and I come back, we'd have lunch and spend some tyme in the backyard playing. Then I'd listen to some music while I did one of my chosen arts that day and do that until I was done for the day. And then I don't know, but one day I'll know the answer to this burning questions. To find my mood for that day and of course work and spend time alone with Manna. To then write and continue to complete yet another book. I want it so bad. I'm aching with a delayed and differed reality for me. It's so far away yet I can reach out and touch the mirage of this huge dream for me. To be behind gates from the rest of the world. To watch my world change, from night to day. And not let anyone ruin me. Well, I can't stop them, can I? I would hope no one would want to harm others because of another one's lyfe. Which happens all the tyme unfortunately. I think of it like this, I don't bug you, don't bug me. I whish it were this simple, right? So, I was thinking . . . again. How my dream bed will sit on it's platform with three steps up. On the royal red carpet. How I want my balcony, that will look down to the main room with a spiral staircase beside my bed. Well, that's just me, you could have it anyways that you'd want. I want it so bad. And I hope they whish the same fortune for me. As I would love to hang my spare painting that I want just for myself instead of my store for sale. From my studio where I'd display all my art, and sculpting and even some pencil drawings. And I'd have a show once every three months and I'd even display Letters from my book, and I'd frame them and hang them for sale too. Something that's never been done before. So, whish me blesses as I'll do for you too.

If I get to live *my* dream, you get to lyve *yours*. I'm not going to the top alone, and by myself. You'll get that scholarship. The one you owned one day ago. I'm not gonna fly without my wings. This is the lyfe you so deserve my love. And one day, we could put on our own arts night to both buy our art and we'd have a blast doing it. Raising funds for whatever charity we sponsor or we sponsor our own charity fund, most likely, literacy. And we'd go on events night in Vancouver and announce ourselves, and show this city who's boss in the arts. Well, that's what I'd say if I were a rich snob. And I'm afraid that I probably wouldn't be able to resist being a bitch. But, I have to remember that I'm a Christian, but you can serve the LORD. Cee, could you imagine my Letters as purchase in my art shows nights, alone with her art? We'd support local artists and we could help one that we both loved, no matter what. Our partyes would be catered in black tye. Well at least I'm being honest with you here. For I create very well, with the shock waves from my behaviour tonight as a rich bitch, but it's true, and I'm so scared for that. You must know that. I'd wear designer jeans with always legging boots with wedged heels only. With a high collar suit. With the music of our choice is full blast and couples dancing, for this is our party. And to bring tree alive with us on this trip too. How she would shine in her brilliant and breath-taking beauty, she's so beautiful, undeniable. And to bring the angel alive in her stunning and paralyzing eyes with that gaze she gives you when she wants something. And me, big flare with boots and designer jeans and the fanciest blouses/tops. And I'll wear her jewellery everyday and myn too. And I'll have my sexy updo's. Walk around to my guests and my pairs guests as if I knew them too. Always say, God bless you when you say good-bye. To have a chauffeur from Vancouver to home. Of course my friend. Show my success in my dresswear. In my jewellery, in my rings. I love rings, and I'm going to have one for each finger and stacked, big and gaudy, but real gems and stones. Lots of chu-ching. Cee, I got you thinking about riches and metals that are precious and same with the stones and gems. Get our guests wine with caviar and dips with a bite food. Invite cameras and news and make them feel at home. And remember where I come from. Who I was to break into my new self. To be peak before each showing, so I'm at my best and peak. To smile to *you* from across the room and know we couldn't have gotten where we are now without each other, and to always remember that this is a Christian-based business. And can still throw an awesome party. Flirt with my male and female guests and show who've I've become, into my own. Invite everyone in my familys. The most important people in my lyfe. The one's who stood by me the entire way with me. And my new friends. I'm gonna look so good on opening nights. I've earned this lyfe. I've fought to get here, tooth and nail, blood, sweat and tears, many millions of tears that have flowed down my cheeks. Why shouldn't I have this dream of a life that is just that right now, a humungous dream, that's why should it only be a dream? So, here I am, sharing something that is only in my head, but now in print, this accomplishment that I want *so bad*. LORD, please Grant me, this prayer, to be rich, with gifts of what I want most in my entire lyfe, to travel. I'm going to travel all the tyme and bring both of them with me, when they can get away. And I dedicate my life to my LORD, for without Him, I wouldn't be alive, and who gave me my lyfe, my words.

Gggggggrrrrrrruuuuuhhhgggggggrrrr. I'm so frustrated! I just want to be in my own world right now. Put in my headphones and listen to my music. It helps me focus. I just don't know what to do anymore. But I have to keep going, and write, and write and more writing. Which is okay, because I love writing. I love putting and mixing different words in a phrase together. Now, you should ask yourself, do you believe me or not? Or is it just my imagination? You could speculate and wonder if that was me or a character. But. I wonder if Shakespeare ever used but in a sentence? So shuuu, go on, go, to the next sentence. Do I share another love story? I'm going to share everything, or do I need another lye? Oh, I'm sorry, did I say it wrong? Let me know what you want to hear and what I give you. Cee, you thought I was mad . . . but I'm so not, I love being creative. I can write anything, and you'd believe in it, and you should, because I'm one of the nicest people in the world, not the nicest all the time, and how words haunt me, so much. Not just any words, my words. Should I not tell you another love story? As to not fall in love with Andrew and Sandra. How you are sparkling through the gaps and shining down on me, or on me shall I say? What does it matter anyhow? It's not gonna matter in five years. So be the bigger person and live the rest of the day in knowing this is myn. Why is it? As I deep breath into his kisses on my neck and how I wrap his arms around me as he picks me up and . . . no? Can't do that either eh? So what do you want from me? I'm in the game. Did you know that a famous cartoon that was his favourite, is also my favourite besides another one . . . then what do you want from me? If I were an actress, I'd be running and stumbling on the ground in a Hollywood silent movie. But I'm not, so keep reading and I'll stumble you in that ways. I look back on that one time when I was so distant, I couldn't write, but now I do. I need to be random and quirky and total nonsense jumble of words, just put together like my secret puzzles. Okay, now onto the next . . . How I had to cry to her and tell her my woes and my distress. But to remember those less fortunate and how You show me Your Face when I'm alone when I needed You. And that You're the Only One who can calm me and You use her all the tyme. I want to leave for a year, and take my kids with me, and we'd travel with each other for a year, then we decide on a mortgage and who's gonna sign the papers with me. I want nothing more, in my entire lyfe, than being able to leave for a year, just the three of us. For this trip will be huge in their's and my lifes. Knowing her and I are very different and how we view life. I'd have to figure it out and how I have to get away. Be me in my kids and me in Christ my Saviour, and be your mom, the way I want to be, so much, and maybe God will bless us financially, so I can do that with my children before they leave to lyve their own lives in their own chosen part of the world they call home now. To bring us together in a way we've never experienced before. We'd decide on the three places we'd go to in the world. And for four months, we'd lyve there, get jobs and live in different cultures. I'd love nothing more. I'd open my children to trust me and believe in me and love me for who I am and be grateful to know of how many sacrifices of love that I've made for them because of the intence motherlove I have for you, that one day, if it's God's will, you will both, be blessed with healthy and blessed children that I was blessed with. Hiding behind my silence, in my aloneness. For so many years I was screaming inside and I went through the hole on the dream catcher, I wasn't caught until I was free.

Today, you found mommy, not in person yet, but in search for you for the next few months. Wait till we find each other, and know that we have that instant and final decision, when I look at your picture, and with my mirror by my side and know I'll find my little girl, that's going to find me and I'll find her. And then we come get you and bring you home to me, which includes; my best friend and my daughter and know *your* best friend was only a couple days away from seeing each other again, when we come together. And I'd encourage tyme with her and him, so angel won't feel replaced, or taken over feelings. We both want our own dogs so much and when I get you, she may feel that I've moved away from her, but I want them to spend tyme together, and there would be an everyday-spend-tyme with her later on, that kind of thing. No one will take the place of Carly. She'll always be my first baby. But I have to and want to move on and own another animal in surviving the rest of my tyme . . . or worse with the others. And you notice I'm not being very creative in my Letter tonight, but I hope to share my many and wonderful lyfe together as we finish our tyme here and when I travel, she'd stay with her, because of Lie bee. Wow. I can hardly believe it. Ya know God, bringing my best friend back into my lyfe, has shown me lyfe again in the short time span to just absolutely become small dogs bitches, and get lost in that world together and remember what these names mean in both and our lives. I'd bring Sete everywhere with me, and we'd probably get kicked out of every store because we have our little puppys with us wherever we go, I'd never leave her by herself for a long time and I'd have to figure out a new routine, total day transformations. Schedule change, big time! I'm going to hold her and she'd have to be on a new daily schedule. I'd finally have a purpose and a reason to get up in the mornings and we'd nap in the afternoon when it was tyme. Total lyfe transformation today when I discovered about Sete. Unbelievable and I can't believe it. *Me,* with a small breed. But! I'm still getting Manna. I *want my golden.* But in the meantime, get Sete and have a purpose again and the LORD is blessing me in becoming my own person and take my lyfe over. Into going for little walks with her, my girl, my new and sweet and adorable, and she's adorable, that my search will end immediately when I see you. I just shake my head, and I don't want them to know until I have her in my coat and I take her and show her to everyone and then bring her and this would be her home with me until . . . hang on, Sete . . . I'll be right back as it starts immediately, right now! . . . And the only thing I would do is pray. I put my extra with hers and now I'm saving for my Sete. That He recorded my voice and my prayer to Him for Sete. What a cool name. Sete Savage. That will be her name. Named after His Perfect Number. She means to me a new and total life change. In Him only, using *them* to show *me* what *I* needed to figure out. Think it out, get it out there, into God and The Universe. I know I'm going to love for her being her. Just like the rest of them and how their personalityes show. They were all so different from each other, so individuals they were. I'm going to buy her clothes . . . can you believe it? As I shake my head. What happened? My best friend. *She* happened. And then a year and two months later she gets Lie and a few months later, I would and will get my baby girl, Sete. Thank You LORD, for once again, for blessing me with another very different and personalityes from Carly to Sete. LORD, thank You, for showing me, Sete to me today. I must find her.

I'd be devastated if that were to be the case regarding it, unless it's not like that, I'd be so happy . . . as I straighten up in front of the mirror. I looked at my reflections and knew that I wasn't supposed to be a princess or a prince or anyone else, but I'm supposed to be me, and I have to stop wanting to be someone else and live someone elses lyfe, and lyve myn the way God would want me to. And love my jewels and diamonds, and the clothes that make me look good, and make me stronger for my destiny. To be just another person in the world living her lyfe when they pass me by too and know that I'm a stranger to them, that I'm not them, and to appreciate who've I've become as a woman in Christ, and know better. I know what's right and wrong. I may not have smarts in a lot of areas of lyfe, but I know some other stuff, and I use it to be wise in any advice I can so I can give it to you, so maybe you can learn from my mistakes, and let me tell you, I've made a lot. To sit in someone else's guilt, and wait it out. Cee what happens, right? As I say, back to the mirror talking to me. For the mirror to tell me what is to come for me. And figure out stuff and vent it to the world, to know that you're not alone in your struggles in lyfe, and that to you, another person is going through the same thing, but elsewhere in my world, in *our* world. As a round planet searching for the answers, and to be who they were meant to be, and if we all just lived our lives within our peace, we could calm down and just go for the ride and party but have rules and leaders in God. But I know, *this* is *my* purpose. To spread Hisness. I'm supposed to live *my* life and this is *my* destiny. That I sit and write in a small family room converted in half, and I sit at my tiny desk and create from then to now, and dig deep and went into . . . well, I could go on, but we all know what happened. I've layed it all out, so if you don't know what I'm talking about . . . or wait, am I trying to lay it out and I just talk in circles, right? How I sparkle in three different areas. How You hang from two places and come together in a pearl. Yes my love, how could I be lonely when I have you, my sweet and number one boy. Who blessed me by his presence and ruled half of his whole of my heart, and has now said to me, how could I be lonely when you have me? He said to me one day. How I have storyes upon storyes that either *are* my lyfe or the next half aren't myn and I'm creating a character, but it's upto you the reader to guess or imagine someone else's lyfe, me, and use your imagination to take an educated guess on whether it's fiction, or non-fiction. Discovering the undercover stuff out and learn me. Seek answers for burning questions. Travel amongst the rest of us, and discover secrets and betrayals, or nothing but joy and happiness. The LORD has yet again today, He has blessed me with inner strength and fight to an end, and then discovered a whole new world I want to cee. To a place where I would have never have found it without Him. To a new lyfe, of promise and mysteryes, traveling to another land and walk amoung my fellow man. And to cee another place that I only could find by finding her and them finding each other, and giving me hope with a new name that means something of a Holy nature. So, I want to go there and *not* get lost as I walk on new ground. So, pick your battles in lyfe, and let Him guide you if you follow the Dominos. Cee who you are. Find it . . . oh ya, I have mentioned this before haven't I? Well, that's okay, because I got lost in this world and forgot about what I have to discover and live out silently and then I can, ya know, go out with curiosity as us tri, and then separate and then do our own travelling to far away places that will change the world, *I*, change the world.

I hate being poor. No, I don't live on the streets, but I know what it's like to be poor. It sucks. You can't do anything, most of the time, the answer is no. I hate it. I worked my ass off today, proof-reading and editing my book so far. What an accomplishment I've come this far with this writing thing. That happened **one day**, to discover my passion, and the only thing I want for my lyfe. To come up with new storyes for you to read . . . okay, I know, I've said this many tymes before . . . okay, something new. Music. I haven't listened to music lately while I've been writing. I want to bring real lyfe, from real peoples storyes and make plays out of them, but changing names for them, but asking them to be guests in my audience. I want to share my lyfe as well as the people in my lyfe and other's lyfe's storyes. A new generation to theatre. Am I stupid enough to believe that I could dream a huge dream ? that I could become a famous playwright? For the theatre downtown Vancouver? I could work for them, bringing attention to the theatre bringing new jobs, bringing new talent to Vancouver, hiring student actors to be steady employees, that they'd have jobs, bring in media attention, new people/tourists to the theatre, new attention for international clients, charging a nice fee to get in the door. I'd do my best writing. I'd be the best, I could bring my lyfe, to the stage, and I'd get reviews, more money to be more elaborate with stage dressing and costumes, new or antique, depending on the time period, etc. This is what I could do with my writing. I'd be writing all day. I could hire people. This is my most recent dreams/ ideas my. I had a nightmare last-night. I buryed someone alive. They were trying to get out of the ground and they had such hate for me, they were coming after me from that. Build an entire play on this nightmare. On how; if I had committed suicide, look at the lyfe I would have missed . . . . God is rewarding me for staying strong and for the interruptions during my final decision in my lyfe. This is the biggest dream I've ever dreamed, more than anything that I can hardly bare. I could rotationally be the next famous playwright on Andrew and I together in our tiny room from when was living with us and we relyed on our room for privacy, and our making love scene, the one where we were in our room and we lit some candles and we talked and then we made love twice. It was my first favourite tyme I ever spent with him. During them making love, in a dark spot on the stage with soft romantic music playing in the background. I want soft lighting, and then after about 2 minutes, it fades to blackness, then another scene to take place after this . . . . next scene, we get out of the house and the actors sit on a bench and kiss and talk about something intimate. As I used to do to Andrew, that I don't even remember doing that with him. I would whisper in his ear something that only he could hear. I'd say to him, I'm so glad we're in love. And I'd always put my head in his chest, and he loved it when I did that. Then reenactment of the dates March 24th-April 8th, 1997 and when I was in the fetal position on April 9th, 1997, and then the play ends. So then I take over again from the LORD planning and executing this Love Letters and what I found and discovered in my own past into my now and future that I was told to go to, and I was to let Him guide me in where it was supposed to be told here tonight. LORD Jesus, how You just took my hands to work. Write what You said and as I gasped along The Way. See God, I'm listening and fulfilling my destiny and my humbleness and say it. Thank You LORD for helping me end a final end, and I was Lead by the LORD tonight, in His trust, I live.

I need to write. So last-night was so wicked. Since I didn't let it go, but what she said made me curious on how, you would hurt me . . . what are your thoughts? . . . should we talk about stuff? I don't know. How I achieved today and the manuvers I had to do to keep going, I'm on the clock now. So I don't have any spare tyme that I can give you, I'm sorry to be rude, but I must go. To her that I saw today on the way, I'm very sorry. But I said I was proud of her for changing the world. That's her purpose. She was very serious about it and it was intence on her speech to me, but I had to go. Cee, it's people like that, that change destinYes for another person. Because her effort mattered to another person and their lives depended on it. I want and have been becoming this own reason for my lyfe. LORD, bless this .com become world wide and spread out to the other branches in making us keep going onto the next hundred generations. Trifle information that will come in tyme, such an important impact that this will come into the world. A higher level of it. I must keep writing so it can happen then for me. How is it? Are you enjoying my thoughts? My twisted truths or fiction? I can't believe it. Not again. I hate this. Again. Come'on LORD, help me become a great writer of this tyme so it carryes to my next ones. I wonder what it does to him? It must be hard on him, not knowing how to fix me from way-back-when-stuff that you've heard before, when I confided in you. That must have been so hard to hear, and what could you do? Nothing. Just listen and don't deny my feelings. Ya know? Coins of worth to a lyfe to live is the same as that, um . . . I think so, but I go back to that question, of how would you have hurt me? To show importance to you and you and you, and him too. Don't buy anyone without knowing that it could . . . become boring to my reader. Mare, Came, Wild, Hope, Fail. So how many of you believe in aliens? So I ask you all, or I'll just say my opinion . . . ; why not? Why shouldn't I believe in them? When someone has proof, how can you deny them and the facts and documented . . . ? oops, am I putting my foot in my mouth by saying that? But hey, I can have an option too. But listen to the sound waves of space. To even think, that someone else is out there, or could be, why not believe in something out of your comfort zone ? for a few minutes and go back in time to your childhood and play martians with your friends, and you had an open-mind when children play. I came and went as someone is touching me and speaking their language and let me know I'm on the right track. I wan to get lost in Paris and drive with whomever is with me and get lost on the way to there. Isaiah 10;27 In that day their burden will be lifted from your shoulders, their yoke from your neck the yoke will be broken because you have grown so fat. Even though it's in the Bible NIV, I don't like the word fat. I know that unfortunately I might say it out loud one day, because I'm not perfect like my LORD is, so I won't want to. To lyve in that tyme of the distance past, to walk on the ground Jesus did, and how it was so awful. But hey, it's only my opinion. It's me, and my lyfe. But I'll never deny my LORD, but only in fear would I, for a split second because of others lives would be in danger here, and then you beg for forgiveness and hope I won't be compared to Peter, in denying Jesus three times, so I beg for forgiveness and trust in You and place Your words in perfect successions. And if I tell the truth, I will see Him one day and that's the most important part of my lyfe, and if you love Him, He'll always be number one, then thank Him for everyone around you.

Covenant and sacred words towards God, my LORD, in keeping my practice upto par. To never go back on my words of loyalty and commitment of my heart towards You God. To keep up on practicing all my dedication and trueness in You and for You.

To try and keep my promises to lift Your Name and to pray for all those who need it.

To bring together promise, and always keep my habit of my faith, under contract of Your Laws. LORD, this is my prayer to You, and to engage in daily prayer for Your words to flow from me, to Your Nations around the world and ask that You bless me, Your humble servant to refrain from human impulses to deny the Only LORD I know, and to always say yes, but I fear in human feelings, of steadfast intents. To know that my role in your life is to bring Him to you, show His face to you, to show you His love for you and your next door neighbour. To show my duty of utmost importance in His Laws, even though I'm not perfect, and I must admit that before moving on and afraid on fear taking over, but being Fed what I'm supposed to spread and say. To never interrupt myn, or your calling to serve Him from the podium. To listen to the trickle and crackle of what I have to make of It being said to me. So do you believe in me yet? Do you cee that I want to be the role model and consult for love and compassion? How I need to be filled by Him, so I'll be back in a while, when I'm better equipped with a better tongue-in-cheek, only in this situation, it's to be taken very seriously. So use caution when using phrases you don't understand. And make sure you check, and double-check and then maybe, use it for a discussion over coffee with Him in your heart and pocket. May He stand right next to you, beside you, so you can hear His songs made through human hands to reach out to everyone. To take my role seriously and to show you the meditations of my heart that can only bring You happiness through Him and hear my words for them to hear It. Where every hour is based upon Your Lyfe and Words. You are Holy and Marvellous and I'm honoured You're using me to say all this to them. Living the lyfe of a Christian, make sure it's real and I show all that He is my Rock and He lifts it up and He sees diamonds under the sparkling sand in the Heaven's. Here is my personal insight; to not apprehend and not grasp meaning of the constant itching over my body to know that this is what I'm supposed to share and say. To distract me and get in the way of telling them what they need to hear. Then, the Words you use to acquire possession of, leap from this page to another page to keep you going onto the alongside of the supposed-to-be. For in the beginning He gave us this and that because He knew we'd need it to get by here. There's proof in the pudding when He says He's the Truth the Way and the Life. If you long to worship with your fellow man, take a hold of a hand you know you can be secure with and make His power work in your home. This is based on the Truth as I know it as an individual in Christ Jesus. You're not to add or subtract from His Book, for He has many writers down here to scope and suffuse in different dialects from around the world. So, listen to me. Very closely. Listen to the Scriptures of God's chosen people, as this is His Will. I'm expected and required to do this. Under His Reigns and He gallops with His long White Hair blow in His power of the winds and storms and hail and snow and rain. Please, do it right. Make your free will to believe, make you another servants, joined together with me to jump ahead of the long line and live as He would want you to. Would want *us* too. I pray for you and hope you seek salvation and sew on furtherance.

"Carry My Love"

My son leaves for the missions trip in ten days. And then I have to say good-bye to the little boy that lives with me who's trying to become a man with everything comes with that. How your lyfe will change. If you let it to. Be wise when you step off that plane, be the man who was Created from God, for a purpose, to serve under Him, for this tyme in his life is the most important, for it's going to shape and mould him into Your Vision, in his innocent, until then, when he sees new and poor sisters and brothers-in-Christ. How I ache for them and I want to become a volunteer in this world when I become a famous. Travel to this poor place and give back to the people that needs me. To live among them and get to know them, then I come home, and live well. I want to help. So, then to come back from my thoughts. Where sometimes if it's not just right, I'll go insane with mental distractions that block my way and my views. I cryed about my son leaving tonight. I pray that he remains strong and be healthy and get lots of sleep. He let me hug him tonight. I love when he lets me hug him. I know he loves me and he's just as excited to move as us. I pray that he's strong and continues to have an open heart as he will share a special and one-of-a-kind loves for his new family. How there are rules that he doesn't even know about yet, but he'll know it all when he steps his foot off the plane. Some of it will make sense to him now and he'll be able to figure it out. I can guarantee that he'll come home with a new appreciation of the life that was given to him, and to see new ground and becoming a new man. I will welcome the new son that I can't wait to share with him. To finally be aloud to have a relationship that we need so badly for each other and for us all. I send you my love everyday and hold it tight okay, and let Him shine in your days when maybe, you may have a day when you really miss me. I'm with you, so far away. There was no way in saying no to this, one-of-a-kind moment in your lyfe. That you'll carry with you, forever. Take this experience and make it *yours*. This is *your* moment baby. I always knew you'd change the world. This will live within you and when you need to ever question anything, remember this tyme in your life. Leave your anger behind and put on your even-more-humble clothes and walk in poor. As your beautiful face and your beautiful smile, take a break for a while, where I have to say good-bye and I love you. And then try to let all of you go for Him to guide you, show you, help you, confuse you, and then it finds you. That all I can do at that moment, is try to be strong and never know until the end. Of both storyes. I can't stop your destiny, and in tyme, in His tyme, we'll be where we need to be, in trust, admiration, of a future that I can only write about and pray it out. Where I have to wait and wait and work my ass off to get there. And live there. To know that I have to live *this* part first, before I know what's to happen for us. To pray that you safely return and then to now have the new goals to look forward to, in maybe your plans for now, will change. And I'd except everyone and everything that happens to your lyfe. Where God calls you, is much more and more important for me to know I have to let you go, to wherever He calls you to serve Him. If you're home for good, let's go man. Know this, that I love you, my only son. You were my first born and your soul wasn't quite ready yet, is what he said to me in regards to you and letting me love you fresh and new. For then you found me and grew inside me, so you could be born. My new strength. How your gift of lyfe, saved me, on many days and you saved my lyfe. I love you. Find *you*, and carry *my* love, with you.

To show it that side. That's the way it is. It's by itself and stands in sole. It was underscope and it died. Not literally, but figure of speaking. So it happened again. When I said something stupid and there's nothing I can do about it . . . maybe there is . . . and who says it can't be real ? in certain terms of speaking, that even this code is near. Or is it? Not to know either way. Keep the lights on man, 'cause now I'm doin' it. So LORD, how's it goin'? Are You having a Wonderful night tonight? Can't tell what happened for fear of not believed me. Of fear of the nighttimes here too, like I'm haunted both. But I'm living within a shared half. Cause-and-effect, and speak in only notes I know, okay? To show you too, for the first tyme without knowing. Is it to him, it, but, her, and it's the questions right? I can't just reach for a book tonight, just above me, and look up. Am I making sense? To show me that more does exist. So I must exit. But before I do, I should go to another play-in-sessions. So, I haven't done a funny, and yet I try to go for it, but down on myself due to a mystery. To spill it in and know, but you won't ever, so keep reading. Let tonight be awesome and powerful. So LORD, thanks for keeping me safe the other day. You know. And that's all that's important, that one day, I may have problems decoding my own writing. Maybe that's a good thing, leave it in the past. That I've moved on and wonder what I'll be doing this when I'm looking back on fond and difficult tymes in my lyfe, but be so much stronger because of it. Be strong then and learn what I needed to. Kind of like tyme traveling I guess you could say or leaving a memory and a legacy for my children and their children as so on. Come on LORD, break me, not really, just create and let majic happen and my son leaves in eight days, and why shouldn't I record it? What a milestone in someone's lyfe, ya know? How could I not announce it to the world ? and for when you read this, that tyme will have ended in tyme and be Written as Ascquired in Taste, but if it ends badly, boy oh boy. Why live in an ordinary world and lyfe? This was scribed way before we were alive in tyme of existents, right? I'm asking a lot of questions tonight, does that bother you? Then well, I'll just keep going then if you insist. Grab me. How I got to look back in tyme tonight when at that tyme is now. So I'm glad you're back, because I was worried that I offended you terribly, and who are you to me? Do you know the answer to this question? Come on! Cee who you are. The three words in our song, when one day a long time ago, we let lyfe take over and it was the only number. Hey, I like the way you decorated. I've never seen one done like this before in this unique style, in your taste and *your* imagination. To make your world beautiful for you're in control of something of the pair of it. So, do you know the answers yet? Are you majic in the pixie dust latent on me? That makes me float. Don't make me get stern with you. Don't bite me lie bee. I love you though. I have your picture and you make me smile and makes me happy, when I cee. Don't you hate when I do that? To just end a sentence like that, so abruptly? So, ask yourself a questions about yourself and ask your reflection's mirror, that if you look in them, they go forever, and that's what I love about that. So thanks for tuning in again. So, if you're not watching that, then you're missing history yet to be written. So, yell to the page if you know the answer to who won this year. I love watching as it becomes my now. So, ya, thanks LORD for today. I learned that I only know. To stay coded for the future as I've forgotten and never brought up again, so thanks for the attentions.

So how much do you think I should charge for my pieces of seven around my studio and then copy and paste as to not loose it? I guess I would have to choose a price of the chosen priced item and get some feedback from my mirror, and let this help spread my name, and the other artist I choose to put in my studio. I mean come on, when you're picking artists, you have to know how good they are, and if I love their art, they get their wallkindof space. And I want to have shows and put my art up for sale. But I haven't even touched oil yet, and have my own large space to do that and have a large space for all my chosen fields of art. I'd invite all my past instructors, who were supportive in every way and without their help and knowing my limits of learning in an educated ways. So, all of you, who were my teachers and following instructors, you too, find your own page in history. To know that someone has actually written you a thank you Letter. And whoever comes in reply to my RSVP invitations, will get this Letter. From my little tyme in hairdressing, and then fashion school, so you know who you are now, so this Letter, of gratitude and recognition gets a page . . . so that's pretty cool. Only what matters to me, will be included as well, so you can too, read my stuff. And cee, now I have to say this, not to do what I did and do and will, that someone misses me tonight and my heart yearns for that side to me. Oh, I forgot to tell you that I'm a story teller and love telling storyes. Where does that come from? From my birthright and family history and write my legacy? I know, I know, my head just grew about ten feet around . . . and cee that's what I'm worried about. And I just want to forget and move on, and I had to say good-night with a huge hug from mirror. So do you ask yourself what I mean when I say mirror? You must wonder, and must know. But if I told you, there wouldn't be that mystery. Did I go too far? Thank you for your lyrics that inspire me and motivate me to be the best me I can be. So, I'm left on my own and I have to fly the coupe within hours after sleeping. Have I lost control of my trolls of cartoon ? and you know how they can fall from a plane with no parachute and then flatten and then pop out again, and they have the stars floating above their heads and there heads. Have you ever heard of the term; unitasker? Well, read it. Look it up online. It's exactly me. And if you're a curious person, you're gonna want to know what this means, or not so much if you couldn't really care and shrug it off and think I'm crazy. Well, that's me. Okay, now this is cool. There's a word and it's this; to be world known because the word I wanted was a famous persons name, who invented words. Can you believe it? I make and create made up words all the time, and maybe I'll be another him in the world of writing and how they'll be plastered all over walls of dedicated readers. I write for you, ya know. Have you ever had something that tasted so good, so good, like delicious good? Would you ever describe them as mouth orgasms? That you just can't stop going mmmmmm, mmmmmm, oh my gosh . . . this is so good, as you drool saliva because it's so good? . . . I know. And you eat chocolate, such strong cravings ya know? How it didn't break in the middle of the square of yumminess chocolate. Unless you are one of the people that in the world who doesn't love chocolate. I understand. Because everyone's taste buds are unique like their fingerprints. So, now, did we even talk about the cost? No, we didn't and I'm getting odeed on chocolate right now. But I never treat myself, hardly at all. But I just had to today. I love peanut butter chocolate bars and just the two together. So, I thank you for coming tonight, kisses . . . .

"Blessing My Prayer"

Welcome to my worlds of imaginations and enjoy all the strangers of my visions . . . .

Okay, to get to used to home again . . . sigh. I'd say; goodnight my love, over and over again, to calm him to bed. So if her bed tyme was at eleven every night, I spend half an hour calming her from the day, like watching TV together and just chill for an hour together, of mommy-her tyme, and to tell you my storyes and pick a new one every night and sooth her to learn to trust my voice and obey my voice, and to know I'll never get mad at her other than something dangerous and hoped she would know that voice if I've ever called her name that way. I want puppy tyme, but I know the day, for it was a gift. I trust you this much, to start and watch you as we start the hunting for Sete game later today for the next that number of months. Well, I can't tell you so as *she* finds out. A new beginning to both new to each other, starting in a new enviroment, clean, new smells of drying paint and getting to know a new room and they can sooth each other for each other when they're together. I'm going to share her with my daughter, and give her that gift of a puppy while we have to live here tyme. And don't forget to ask for vet papers for vaccines and shots. I want health first, but if I have to, I'll take her as soon as I can. Faithfully. Make sure she's updated on shots and save for spaying. To give her comfort of that type of thing. To continue to pray, that the LORD bless my credit card and to continue to help me and I know He's already blessed it, and has now given me an answer to take one and send for two instead of three, so I can do this right. She's so important to me, and I'm not going to stress over my book anymore. I prayed for Him to bless my credit, ya know? And now He's saying this is His gift. *I deserve* this in my lyfe and now I'm excited to save and dedication . . . I can't tell anyone, mirror. To trust her enough, to let her hunt through my personal papers and give her the only one, and we'll have to work that out, in my mind. I don't even have to question on the care baby-girl/boeboe, even though I've never really called her, but she does with him all the tyme . . . weird us connection again. Awwww, I'm so excited and now that I know the date, I'm gonna work my ass off getting this book done and publishing it, in which I have not a clue yet. Don't know. No idea. But, it'll happen, because I'm trusting Him and thanking Him for Sete. And to thank Him for blessing my prayers. And now I ask for You to bless the living conditions with a new puppy in my room. New rules for everyone and to let everyone in the house know that this puppy is not anyone's but myn and hers. That's just that on that subject. When I'm not in charge and appropriate hours, she is in charge of rules in regards to the puppy. I'm so happy. I know exactly what I want now. I know the exact date, at seven o'clock, around. But that's all I can think about right now. As if you couldn't tell. I have a new purpose and put into practice for her and get me into a new routine and get used to it *before* Sete. And that's not working at the moment, so I have to spell correctly. Into the next sentence, so you too, can start getting excited for her too. More storyes, more thoughts, more whishes and prayers waiting to be and be answered. Keep *you* surprised too, but to never *not* include you. You're *so* important to me, and I respect who can sit and read through my Love Letters, well, I feel honoured, and that's why I have to be so good, ya know? For you, for you to turn the page and get lost in everything I am, in everything I do and say and practise, live, to read into my head and my lyfe . . . well, don't you worry, 'cause I'll write about it and keep you all posted.

Oh how I must write and continue to write all the tyme, everyday. This book, these Love Letters are everything to me and those surrounding me, and this could help them not struggle so much anymore. To come to their aid financially and change their lives too. So my lyfe changes their lyfe. And that's what I want in lyfe. To help other people. So somehow, it'll happen for us. I just know it. And when it happens, it'll be amazing and I'll be blessed, and I must remain humble, everyday and thank Him everyday and ask Him to bless me and my books, for me to reach who I'm supposed to reach and find. I totally believe in that. That I'll find you and you find me, and we click. To welcome you into my growing familys. So, do you want to talk about Sete again? Well, it's my story, to shut you in my quietness to tell you, that I want to talk about Sete. She's gonna be my baby, and it's gonna be great. I have chosen a spot for her outside my house. And it's perfect. So I have many options around my house block, and safe spots for her to play, as to keep her on a leash at all times except if you train her in a big field to let her run safely without immediate danger, you have tyme still to catch her, and I know that that'll happen, but it makes me nervous, but I know I have to. To not have what I want, but I have to remain calm as to not anger the enviroment and to hear old songs of another choice I have in case of emergency. And today's an emergency. So back to Sete. So you can cee the way she'll look, I'll tell you the breed. She's a pomchi puppy. Dot com her, and that's what I'm getting. When I see her, I'll know, and she'll know me too. That when I see that face, I'll know it. I'll search on my computer, and when I find her, in my ways and terms, for the date I've set to get her, is very important to me, in how all this plays out in order for the final step needed to *get* Sete. Sete will be a female. And I have an idea of what she'll look like of the different options, and I know what I'm attracted to more than anything, but I can't tell you, because I was given a prediction of the final step and process to this set date. And I will continue to pray for her and that she be a healthy and happy puppy. And how now I have to keep ignoring him and shooing him away as to not him have a downstairs comfort zone. As my baby isn't feeling good, but excited to play the game I've started. Waiting is what I'm best at. I wait for everything in my lyfe. Always waiting, but in the meantime I'm working so hard for that waiting to be well-worked for and loyalty and learning my giftings. Sometimes his mood just turned direction, immediately, from wonderful and funny, to mean and cruel and ignored me. But it shouldn't matter anymore, ya know? Forgive for what happened on both sides, his side and my side, 'ause we both messed up what we had. So, I'm gonna let it go, and love you the way I do now and regret that I never told you how much I loved you and adored you. As I hang my head in regret sadness. But then, I just have to think it was supposed to happen the way it did for this tyme and growth and individual and strong and with my Loving LORD showing me the way. I am graced by the uplifting breeze that has blown beside me as a hollow swing and hugging me and loving me. So, what's up? What are you doing? Well, I guess that's a stupid question, 'cause obviously, you're reading. I know and whatever you do, be comfortable. Be warm, and in a blanket sitting on your couch. Or are you're one of those ones who sit in an arm chair with your legs crossed with just the quietness of your house in your spot. Well, don't stop on my account.

I feel like I've lost my edge in my Letters lately. I ask LORD, for more visions again, and revelation after revelations and after visions. Create something new. *a photo shoot idea* Look up . . . my calling and this is what I'd say to you my love if I was there before you died, or I'd ease you into your next phase of life of non-life, just like this is fiction-non-fiction, so let's juice it up again. So, what do I write about? A photo shoot idea or say good-bye to Andrew? Let me pray for the first one and the second one in order of how it's going to work out in this layout. Or you can sit there and imagine me scratching my head trying to make this decision, and who wants to keep reading my choices of ideas and just write something already, right? Okay then; people for centuryes people have been writing and storytelling about making the right decision. When conflicted in something, its not fun, and sometimes critical things depend on the right choice in that circumstance . . . okay now I should write about being on a beach, in the hot summer sun, drinking margaritas and have those types of guitars playing and singing under the cabana. People are playing with beach balls and the ocean wind is carrying it to you on a slant and you have to run after it and catch it, and run back in the sand, and then. Now I can roar LORD. For I must ask Him, LORD, for which is the next story I tell? To eat my way into their daily lyfe, in making the right decision, but for them only. I don't know the right one, or the wrong one. You must just decide. So do you want a photo shoot idea. Okay, the photo shoot will be placed on the side of the hiway, that you were in danger, but in the top designers clothing in fashion. And you'd be suffering and climbing your way to the camera, as if it's the hospital. And the hiway traffic is whizzing by you at top speed, with the wind and the horns honking for you to not be there and what are you thinking? Your hair would be matted and windblown, and the photographer would be snapping away as you lead the way on the side of a real hiway. And then this is when I write another Letter to Andrew. Since this will be for him, for I will show his death was not in vain. That I've forgiven myself for what happened. I've come very far so far in my lyfe, and I'll continue and pray that when it came down to it, I would choose my LORD first, in everything I do and think and choose and decide for myself in all this. To tell you that first you will grieve for a long time, if you don't start right away. Don't push it aside. If someone you loves dies, oh my gosh, don't let anyone, except yourself, tell yourself not to cry for a loss. If you've ever loved someone who doesn't love you back is the most horrible things to happen to someone in their lyfe. I've been on both sides of this unique situation. And no sides is not a possibility. I lost both of these friendships. And having to say good-bye to one, was no easier than the other one. So for someone to say to you for the choice is easy, well, I don't agree on that very well. It's not easy. And then you find out you have a fatal disease and you have to choose between burial or cremated. I mean, really? With that decision, now this is only regarding myself/me/ only me, I'd weigh the pros and cons of each one and the finality of it and this major end-of-lyfe-decision in total. No going forward or not making the final choice. For me? I have no clue, but I have a con on being buried. I'm claustrophobic. So, in that, knowing that, that my soul will be tormented forever always trying to not fear and suffering in my lingering spirit that ties to me to there for eternity, it almost makes that decision for me, I'd say. So, even though I'm afraid of fyre, I'd rather burn ashes to ashes, than eternity stolen.

What am I going to do if I have AIDS? I should have been more careful and now, today is my fate-day and today is the day I find out. I haven't been feeling well lately and feeling rundown. What am I going to tell my boyfriend? Um, will he understand? I was so angry with the fight we had and I took it too far. I watched other patients go in front of me. What's taking so long for them to call my name? I'm not feeling well and I just want to go home to him so we can get this over with. The nurse comes out and calls my name, Brian? I lifted my hand and got up and followed her to the office I'll find out if I'm dead or not. What a stupid mistake, and I wanted to know for sure. And now I'm about to find out. We walk to the doctor's office and she seats me and closes the door. What's going to happen? How could I have done this? The club was crowded, men were all over me as we got into the music on the dance floor. I could relive this over and over again ever since it happened. So many thoughts and I'm trying to focus, as my nerves took over. The music was so loud and I used my sexual side to flirt with other men and someone grabbed my hand and pulled me to the back door where all the action happens. As I've already thought about this, and so much guilt and now I'm here . . . as I heard the knock. Come in, I said. The doctor came in, sat down, opened my folder and looked concerned, and he cleared his throat. He said, I got the results back from your blood tests. He then looked up at me, and just looked at me, then he said, the news isn't good. I'm sorry to have to tell you, you have AIDS and it's well advanced. And it was also discovered that you have a fungi infection to your immune system is failing. I showed the doctor my rash that developed a while ago. I just thought it was something I ate, but the doctor said it was due to the AIDS. After he said that, I froze. I was like, what?! I asked him, are you SURE? Yes. What seemed like an eternity, I left the office and went to my car and when I sat down, I just sat there. In denial. Oh my gawd! I have AIDS. I have to tell Jackson. I started the engine and drove home and when I got there, I wondered how I got there. I sat in the driveway and looked into our home through the window. I shook out my head and just then, Jackson opened the door to leave for work. He took one look at me sitting in my car and he smiled at me, until he saw my face. He came to me and opened my door and leaned down to me and kissed me, and when I didn't kiss him with passion like usual, he stopped in his track. Brian, what's wrong? I looked at him as he knelt down to me. Brian! . . . what's going on? I couldn't barely hear him. I looked dazed and confused and I couldn't say anything. Then, my eyes started tearing and then I started crying and he reached out to me and took my hands. Jackson, I managed to say in my male-scratchy and crackled voice. I have something to tell you . . . um . . . there's something I haven't told you. I've been hiding something from you, and you need to know. About a year and a half ago, when you went to see your folks for that weekend? . . . do you remember that? He said, yes. I went out to the nightclub and was dancing and flirting and one thing led to another and I had sex with a guy that night, and today, I found out I have AIDS. And you may be affected, so you have to get tested. Jackson, I'm so sorry. Brian, he said, we'll discuss this when I come home tonight. And he left me. I sat there and cryed. I went inside and went to our tool room and grabbed our gun. I went to our bathroom, sat in the tub, and sobbed for forgiveness from God. I held the gun to my temple closed my eyes and pulled the trigger.

"What Do You Mean?"

Responsibility meaning what exactly? What does that mean to you? You left me today. You hurt me today. The reflection has disappeared. How can I be mad at you? But I am. Have you and are you, going back on your word about the babyes coming first, and you gave me silence and gave no praise, when you know I need it to be okay. Don't you know who I am? Am I everyone? Where I pour out my heart in my love for you, and you put down my choice of myn first like you were doing for yours today, and you question my responsibility? Am I a stranger to you today? How when I phoned you, how you slapped me across the face, with your words against my whole lyfe. Do I ever, show signs of that to yours? I regret phoning you today, but, it was written. Speaking to me, about responsibilities. What do I breathe, and the very reason I didn't commit suicide? For my children, and you question my responsibilityes? That when you gave me silence, waiting to dig deep and for me to cry when all when all I can think about, is if you're okay. So, then, there it is. So for today, am I everyone? How I know today, how crazy it is for you today, and in expectations I assume you'll say, I totally understand. But instead, well . . . I wonder that today. In knowing of your day, I must wait to share my hurt feelings inside and feel how my daughter feels right now, alone. The reason I'm here, for her, to not feel alone, and you QUESTION MY RESPONSIBILITY? You're the one who told me to rock the boat sometimes and have a voice. Well, here it is. So, in waiting till you call me, you're going to hear my silence like you showed me today. When it matters. When it mattered. Through everything you do, I support everything, and even when I have to shut my mouth regarding yours, but I support you and it's always them first, right? How I come to you, every tyme, the tyme away, for us and this is what I get from you today, even though I knew it, I wanted to make sure you were okay, because that's what I'm supposed to do for you, and we both know what's happening in our lives to each other. Am I everyone? When we dance and jump around, I'm there. But today, I'm not there, I'm with my daughter, when she really needed me, I cancelled immediately then I get a cold voice, when nothing else mattered in my lyfe. Isn't that first? But you gave me harshness and friendship one-sided. Responsibility, meaning what exactly? Haven't I proved that to you? How I work, till I can't think anymore and I can't say yes or no, tirelessly, mostly every single day, till my fingers are making too many errors and trying to be the best I can be, and you know that, that I work damn hard. To gain a new lyfe, with my children, to take *every, single, responsibility*. If you continue to bark towards the only reason I'm alive, then we'll have a problem. And I won't wait three years to tell you. Lots of feelings happening for me right now. I'm angry and instead of shoving it down, like I usually do. I hate feeling like this. It's robbing me. So now I have to pray. LORD, rescue me of the feelings I'm feeling today. My heart is angry LORD, and I ask that You take all the anger and replace it with understanding and compassion. But don't I deserve to be angry? I just want to feel what I feel. I'm always shoving myself aside for the people around me, and it's showing me my stronger side, but even You Jesus got angry, so doesn't that give me permission to get angry too LORD? So, now I have guilt, which I'm great at carrying, 'cause I carry it a lot. So, my mirror left me today and then I got mad and then asked for forgiveness and not showing my anger, because it takes lives, so I must calm in Him and shake it out.

"My New Beginning"

The day of my new beginning. My son, gave me the world. Gave me a new purpose to my lyfe. For his lyfe. For all three, four lives. How I whish to get on a, my plane, to travel. To all get on the same plane, heading for our lives, running. To be released, into the wonderful world. Where the only thing that could happen is we dye. Okay, well you knew I was going to say that . . . . come on. The whole world knows I'm a pessimist. But I'm a loving pessimist and want to be optimistic. To go to the farthest east in the world, to the French Polynesia. To write about somewhere where it's in the world, and how many people, do you know, that know things from the French Polynesia? Of course, Paris, France, is my number one destination. So who wants to know about something fascinating in lyfe? Who wants to know something new to their vocabulary and learn about a new place that has arrived in my lyfe? To have the new home being built while we're all away, and to come home together, as a family, who has the same memoryes as I do and know we travelled the world together, and alone. With God. I'd always walk with my LORD as I travel the world in His Presence. How You have given me my new beginning LORDGod. And none of this could happen without You. So thank You, for giving my son, the son who carryes me with him to spread His/his seed. How he has shown me a whole new world, new knowledge, and to know that your liye, once again, has changed the world. Wow, how you've taught me the world. How that joy, will continue to keep you safe, in His Hands, that I put my faith. To calm my mother-heart and know that He is with him, my chosen son, to change my lyfe, and to give him his freedom. Wherever he lands where his home is, if he choses the world, well, he gets the world. To let Him breathe His new lyfe into him, and quench his thirst daily, for everything he needs to sustain himself. To show him, the world he gave us this one day in time, to show me my faith and how strong I have to be, to start new one day, when it's suppose to happen for all four of us. Just to get on a plane, and go, to exotic places in the world and live, in this new lyfe, in this new journeys together. To love each other, in a whole different ways. To beg God, in His Tyme, as I will continue to pray, that in this tyme of waiting to travel the world, that God will bless me, with a great person who will become my new boss. I plan to beg, in a wowing different way, and it's going to touch their hearts, enough, to say yes to me and what I bring to the table. In my such uniqueness. But I can't say any more. It will change the world of me as a writer. That my future column was revealed to me tonight. But I can't tell you, as to ruin the big secret, the big reveal. To know that I'll be working as I travel, and I'm so excited for that part. That the power of one and three can only mean Condensed Strength. Why their world needs travel tyme, as we leave our worlds and head into a whole new lyfe, beginning with me as a whole of four. But yet, it must remain a secret until it's big reveal, when you'll know that because of faithfulness and love, this will be our new freedoms, into somewhere new and gain strength as one as we start new/together. For you all to find your destinys, and live as you were supposed to. To start asking readers to pay special attention to my writing, and always tell me the truth. Straight lines with me. And I'll be praying for strength for that too from Him. As I live alone with this new dream of mine, that one day, I will choose, with them, or maybe as a surprise all destinations and we'll get on a plane and tell them the plan. In all this I pray, AMEN.

I sit in the quietness of my room, listening to the noise in the outside world. Whishing I could be there. Out of my room. Into the night air, deep breathing the almost spring night in through my Taurus nostrils. And flair and run to my red flag waving at me, egging me on. I want to run and knock back on the door that's knocking, with no one on the other side. It's just me and the open door. What should I do? I already know the answer. Say good-bye to the constant inner warefare between them and me. I listen to noises before I listen to me, how I have to cover with the blanket on the ground. LORD, keep me safe, from showing. How do I make it? Till I can enter the empty room, to interrupt life again and introduce myself. How I have to learn all over again, to not think that this could go any other way. How my sleep is violated and violent in my wracked dreams of this and that with the end of the world, and loosing something important, all to show me whats to happen and come to me. Press the knife closer to the vitals that are jello in the ripple effect of this more of something I didn't ask for. Cee how far I fell? It's not a breakthrough. How water uses it's power to make someone's life become shit and try to cee the good in something that's supposed to give you lyfe, it also flushes to their deaths. Remind me again God, about this game that You've made for us, as I ask this in nothing but wondering and wandering to the future of what's to come. When will it end? Why, did you not ask for more than you're asking for? Because of fear? I completely understand, as I pretend I have nothing but smiles and warm bubbliness for the world would end for me if anything else happened. I hear my name being called from the farthest of east can get. Or must I fall again first? Must tears exit? Yes. God, I keep my aim down for that moment of when You say I may move forward to the next block on the board. Waiting for the next move by the Player of this day in tyme. Play the Move, then tell me so I know how to feel for this. And if tears ever come to an end. How the world could end in a . . . how I was angered against, and how much they don't know. To let it go into where it needs to go, inside to my blood and live with the residue of guilt. To shine in a world that is closing in and all I want, is to be a wandering writer, and write, and travel to the farthest places in and of the east. To shun myself in this lyfe till then, until then, when I can say and feel under the distant sky of the air that doesn't know me yet. Let it wonder who I am, as I whisper under my breath, hello and welcome to my lyfe. How I have to hide my slams under wraps until I have my own door. So, for now, I close my door and save it up and let it exit to that. How I have to love like a baby, from drawing their eyes with a lullaby to soothe them to sleep. How I'm not that baby. I'm fussing and stirring and not quite right. I'm looking, searching for that quite rightness of a lyfe I have to figure out, but wasn't asked if I want to be born, but it was written in the Scribes-of Lyfe and so whatever happens from me and my breathing, with a heart, who wants to find my plane and run away. To make up storyes and songs to stir you and make you realize how the world around you wants everything from you. So, I make a pitch to make you listen to me, and I bring you all of them with me, to show you them and their needs. To keep inventing, and playing good songs to make me go on, forwards. Where I want to be halted into the air and let me never rest until the wind places me in a surroundings of even I'm gonna dye in the end, as I run for that hill, that mountain, that place. Please bandage me up, I'm bleeding. As I try to rest.

How we're gonna bring new beginnings, that I just was told today. How the two of us, will bring our loved ones with us on the way up. Where the world is turning it's self against itself. How in me keeping faith and never leaving Jesus, my LORDGod. Watching us build to where it needed to reach, and maybe to partner with invention. Oh my God! LORD, that could be deadly awesome. And on it, I could freely write about You and my relationship with You. And not have to be down when I'm hurt. That we could pair up and finally get my dream of working with you and being business partners. A prayer, another prayer answered. It brings new hope, new dreams, updated faith. Get me out of here! Let's pair up, my darkened mane with your mermaid beauty, from a goddess from a fairytale that was perfect, but the only Perfect is God, but you know what I mean. Well, so, we need to communicate more so this can happen for us. As the world around us is crashing in on itself. Screw it! You and me, become our dreams. And how we've both worked so far to this date, and now, look where we are. Another somehow pairing. I think this is like our third tyme. Well, it doesn't surprise me, because it's the Trinity How I've heard Your Voice today. How this whole new world is opening up for me, for us, to help others. How her soul reaches for me in a subtle ways that we've always ignored it, until now. As the world is falling apart and whole citys are dying around us, let's go out in style and enjoy the angry world and become united in our part of the world, that God gave us each other. To help those in our lives, that only deserve rest, but have none. We're gonna get this right this tyme dude. Let's blood-sweat-tears together girlfriend. And I haven't even mentioned the invention yet, but now you are. I've been panicking for months over this, and now I'm going to share it with you. Not you, but her. Top secret, confidential information. How in this mess of a world, how He's still listening to our screams of defeat. Anger, so tired of crying, that I want an answer. And, this is His listening to us. To gain attention would be everything I've ever wanted. I want to bring God into the world, and what better way than to Blog It? With no comments to defeat me and Your purpose, that I just write what I write and I keep my strength through it all, and know NONE, of this could happen without God sending him to Costa Rica, that made all this happen for us. So he could help me find this partnership again and make our suffering stop. With the world collapsing in water, as we're sinking slowly, and with entire generations dead. If I'm gonna dye this way, I want to party and play on the way. Become an important name in history, have your purpose in print. That's important information. It's NEVER, to late to questions the idea of God. If you don't want to, to my readers, and anyone's looking for *their* meaning and purpose they live and lives of something that matters. And that's just my whole self. So, with my inner strength with my LORD, and blessing us again together, which is where I only want to be. To bond as friends, and women, of who we are. To come together and combine our wonderfuliest, the most creativeness's I've ever seen in my tyme. And to give them rest and joy and healing and moving on, it will be so healing. To share my lyfe, as my lyfe as a Christian woman. And to live our futures, and I say something magnificent and show her as a power force, that she can do anything and praise her as a partner should. And if we should start this, for our third time, and come out of our shells and be spotlight. So, I'm gonna stay with our Strength as we sort this out together and really talk.

Am I really that good? To write here and on a blog? So now, storyes and more storyes are gonna have to flow threw my tips to press down and to listen to my Calling. Where He raps through the glass and tips His hat and says, you can do it, with My help, anything can happen. Well, that's what I'd want Him to say anyways. To show me that He is listening and I pray LORD, that You bless my writing, in all directions. As a loyal reader, what I will say, is that you're going to get to read more of me. Starting tomorrow, I will have a professional blog site, and I'll be writing more that just a site. In having first knowledge because you've been loyal, and my readers are the most important people. Now I know why actors thank their audiences, because without them, they'd be no one I feel the same way. How I'll be asking You for more words and that I'm going to have to search more words for my updated new reason for living. To get what I want more than anything, to be famous. To be able to write freely, with yet another outlet. I'm so excited and I trust the Ocean, because You are Great. Do I really deserve this opportunity? I feel so unworthy of this, but I want to grab a hold of it, and go with the ride and the wind that blows through your hair and you feel the fresh and cool breeze and you're holding the reigns, and to make someone's day, but just telling them how my day is and was if in the past or present tense. To hear it one more tyme, the words with the song that followed with addicting music that keeps me writing, and writing and writing, as many people have asked me to. I'm someone meek and mild in showing myself, but it's only in private, that I show the other side to me. But you wanna hear other things, but this is what I'm talking about, so go with the flow. Showing reality here. To only imagine how it's gonna be for me and my mental health, in my thinking ways and feeling ways that I sometimes feel other than happyness and living in the non-dream world, where here I am, but what's to me? So, do you get it now? To be faithful and to be up even later and earlyer. So glad, as she said to me today, giving her a new dream and new hope. To not repeat myself. So what's going to happen? What am I going to written? As I'm going to poison myself with God and ask for literacy and knowledge of the Letters I have to type into another way of showing off. Why shouldn't I show off? I've worked so hard to finish and to keep being devoted, dedicated and extremely loyal and excitement to do this for myself and my lyfe. To show all my bullyes, how far I've come and to give them the gift of tyme of forgetting and moving on in lyfe, and to show you. I'm doing what I love. I have God in my lyfe and I don't want any other lyfe. I want to help people who are struggling and lend my unique gift of such a great way of writing, and combine it, and look, I've done a couple already. Do you know what I mean? So how can I help your imagination come to live? Why make sence of something that can't touch you? Reach but sink into the lull of the network of reading. Being excited for something when I'm not mad right now, where usually, I'd be pretty by now. To have a one way microphone into my insane head, oops, I shouldn't have said that. But I don't know where the delete stroke is for this, and I have no reason. So . . . . I want new and creative new inspirations, so I'm gonna look and search for you, so you'll never be bored. As I pray for the person reading this LORD, that even if they're not religious and don't believe, that maybe You through Yourself into them, and show and Shine a New Song and let them not be angry today or sad, but, just be there LORD. Say and repeat; Today, I am worth it Sandra.

Besides in being a devoted Christian, why shouldn't I be in this upcoming lyfestyle? I've dreamed of this my entire lyfe. Sandra! This way! And I look at the camera and smile. Sandra!—I can't wait for this to happen for me. I'm so excited. Emotionally, it's like a sugar high from eating all the cotton candy. This magazine wants me to look there and a teen screams my name like they do for her. To be recognized on the streets of my city and have an audience in only Love and not violent or angry. I'm soft-hearted. I like peace, and happiness, in thanking my LORD. To look good, every time I walked in public from my opening night of my art studio. Live my dream. A selling writer, art seller of my own work, of sculpts and paints. To lyve like the lady in the commercial where she's smiling while living a rich filled lyfe, I want her lyfe of going out to partyes and meeting people in both secular *and* Christian. Be invited to see movie premieres and meet stars and show my name as one of noble-blood. And be the best me that I can be and be on all the tyme, as I retreat back into my couch and fall against the pillows that catch me and welcome myself home. To a place where I can look at my art on the walls and see my statues of moulded clay. To lyve classy; red, black, white, grey. To have both locations in the house for an office. This is much and way more important than that. Focus on the number three today and given such a wonderful gift. That I believe in the invisible but visual proof to the eyes, and some hearts and some not, just to their heads, which leads to doubt. One day, I'll be gone and the only proof to my lyfe was this Letters, but it would prove I existed. Kinda reminds me of a certain Book, written way back then . . . . hmm . . . just saying. Don't hate me now, I'm just saying my opinion, but I'm gonna live how Jesus would want me to, and hopefully given privacy in my private tyme, to let me enjoy living in my dreams of dreaming for my entire lyfe. I just want you all to be clear when I say, that I live the way God has blessed me with and lots of prayers, but always with a humble heart attached as I bow and pin it to Him without looking as Light would Blind me. How I meditate in Your lyrics and lyve and always give to the less fortunate and start a literacy foundation of a case I came to love, maybe from the hospitals in my city. Helping, speaking in public, work at my local newspaper with my own column, writing my next book full-tyme writing, from home, helping with teens in crisis, in reality class. I don't want to just sit back and not get involved and be recognized in my city as a good person. I know. Some people won't like me so much *because* I'm a Christian. Already that's going to come my ways at some point. To have your constant attention, to drag you with my beat, so your nodding your head as with your favourite song. To create merry stoyies, to try to write like no other. And then you say this; No, you listen to me, I'm not lyin' man . . . or was too intence for my mellow reader who reads devoted everyday and I don't create new material, so now, I must read and be curious and be nosey. What does that mean? What does this mean? Intrigue your mind people. Don't be so lazy with it. Be crazy in who you are. Be happy in who you are. Not trying to bore you, just sayin' it like it is babe. I'm not the kind of person who will blow smoke up your ass, but with tenderness and Christian sternness. So all I'm tryin' to say is, be you, as I've mentioned in previous Love Letters. But I mean it. So go on. Go party with hats and noise makers like New Year's. When the camera clicks, smile. So lyve the lyfestyle. But always be ready for lights, camera, action, Sandra! This way!

I let my imagination go waaaayyy too far tonight. I believed for maybe a minute or some and thought, what a VERY and . . . I can't even say it. It's just so out there, but I can't even say it. I have to regain composure of a crazy imagination and just maybe. But it doesn't. Mask it away in your closet and make a curtain bow and close the door, please and thank you mamme. I can't imagine anything happening knowing what I know, and just enough to questions to the most important earth book. Ask it. Has in the forever of history, has this ever happened? In the span of a lyfetime, maybe, but knowing not enough to know. How I have to rebalance my lyfe, and when that tsunami hit and moved the earth's axis, it didn't only realine the earth, but all the people in the world and . . . ya. I'm just sayin'. I feel insane right now. Shucks, I hope you're reading on to see what I write next and if I ask you if its real or non-fiction. To ask if it's not real or fiction. I shake my head back and forth and say no, no, no. Wait for it. Oh it's comin' alright. A flood and we're all gonna drown slowly and that's it. Deep shit tonight man. This world is falling apart and turning itself on itself as I've said. Have you ever, seriously thought of your death? This world is falling apart. And I'm slowly loosing, and I'm gonna survive my death too. And it just gets worse from here. Have you ever read; Revelations, NIV from the Bible? And then, sit together and pray for mercy on your soul. Wow LORD . . . heavy stuff tonight. So I could write this Letters to whoevers listening. Tell me what I should do. Whish for what you want to happen, and cross your fingers for only good news. Do I go? Do I not go? Does she want me? Does she really and actually want to be alone? What would Jesus do? Of course He'd go, so I should take responsibility for my part of the friendship, and stand by her as she goes through this, and by the tyme you read this, I'll probably forget to tell you that its already happened and I forgot everything. So, I'm gonna step up. Go to her, but then again I don't want her stressed for yet *another* person in her lyfe. So, I'm not sure, but I don't want her thinking I just forgot about her, on her birthday, and you're probably wondering if I go or not. Well, you'll find out sooner or later, since . . . . To know that I own my name. And the blog is going to be wonderful, and I'm excited to start The Savage Novelist. But to always lyve in the Honour, and be humble as I ask for my imagination to go places that will make a testament of what I say is truth. But hey, it's just my opinion. I stand on the Name of the LORD and ask that I have peace for the people around me and for me to show my love, to reach you and show you there's another way but violence in shaking myself to remain strong in Him and write my hearts notes. And now how I can add and subtract whatever I want, whenever I want, on my blog, where I'll combine things to make, yet another one. Yet another idea. To never tell the secret outloud as the air will carry it to the next ear and it spreads like fyre-of-destruction. So, only in my head and maybe on my blog. But how do I know you want to know? That's where I'll question things and try to make sence as I spill it. Not to fight or anything, just because you're really loving m . . . To mix that and the other one? Nope. Like fish and water. So now I can do anything and have complete control, meaning my writing. I can write this, as I cough up blood and I pass out . . . no, but creative right? Did I have your complete atten??. Wait, I've asked you that before, so it's been a rough day in my lyfe with three, so I have to keep doing what I'm doing, so this, can save lives.

Once upon a time there was a small animal, named Liebe, and Belie was quite retarded. When Lie Bee was told to sit, he instead laid down. And when he was told to lay down, he instead, sat. Now like every retard there were some perks. He got free candy, like a boss. Then one day, and this fateful day would be remembered, Lee Ba killed his retardism. When the retardism was dead, there was no retardation anymore, so essentially he killed every child, woman, and grown man that had any type of retardation. This maddened the high politics, so he sent out the swat team to kill this dog, that killed almost the whole of a country. Including himself. So really this story is impossible. However it happened, with the power of imagination.—by someone else whom I love and consider family, but I can't tell you who it is, because then I'd have to . . . well, you know. Intricacy, the lace effect of something so beautiful that heals and will guide me with my connection, but it's beautiful. It's purple and royal. Blessing my fellow mans. I'm sorry for the delay in reply to you, but the world changed. I suck in like it's a tasty treat and I love my treat. The need is much to great to reserve what I must do to be busy. Make it end, please. Your reflection in the mirror and your beautiful blonde mane that makes your splendor more the fantastic in anything. As she uses one hand to work for the hands of seven and three. You're inspiring me you know. And how that might be? How am I inspiring? As we quietly go amongst ourselves. Don't make a sound, we have to quiet. Then we yell! As loud as possible! I must commemorate. Your commitment to make it perfect. It lives in you my mirror of the reflection I saw later then. How you'll always be like that in your picture and frozen in time to match the rest of the world. Your smiles of committed for love. I'm just trying to be me, with your all wonderfulness, in this critical, so now I must go for now . . . . good-bye. And now I say this; tonight was great. The flavours, textures, smells. The heat from elements for it cook and make us full, and to do our own things. Which, I'm okay with, so over display your soul into your dreams of visions and lay it down and drink some red wine and unwind. So I'm sorry to have been away for so long, as imagination has been called to another calling. For an incline to give the information that was required, which is lyfe of and show me the man to signify then anyway. And the wood is stuck in the centre of your voice, and you're choking on it and you can't breathe, can you help? LORD, help me with things. Don't leave me when I need it most of all. Don't keep me up at night because I suffer from insomnia and I sleep with a fiction-non-fiction mind with all that comes with it, and I beg the pardon. OW! Don't bite me, I'm bleeding out with warfare of heartbreak of more love needed. These are sufferings and I'm reaching for straws to complete the session with my clients. Do you want to see it go? LORD, heal me and I don't want to sleep, let's deal with it now and I cheat my way through more. How he slashed and played with my hands as he bit his toys. The little yelp that turns my attention to him, because he needs me. Do you feel the same? And then the game ends and all the answers are answered. So, lay beside his bed and whisper lullaby noises to sooth him and his rushed heartbeat. How it's so quiet here, and sleeping in peace, 'cause she's so tired. How three plays a major role and used as a model to copy carbon. So its balanced in my eyes. But use the flashlight to find your way in the dark, like chocolate waxed over the surface. To read. Unlike that used to indicate that bright light over there. So go easy on the slippery ice. Don't fall.

I miss making love. I feel a man's presence around me right now. It's been happening over the past little while, one or two months. I feel a wiggle in me and want to hunt down for him. Who is he? Is he finding me, and I'm receiving the message to get ready? How will I prepare? Will he love me? Or am I just imagining him? And he's no one. Just a figment of my imaginations of is it longing? Am I longing for something I never thought I'd want ever again? When will it be? It's no one in particular, no features minus he's gorgeous. Maybe it's Andrew, being near me and him just letting me know he's not far away. The same thing happened before I met Andrew. I'd have dreams of a faceless man, and we'd be making love on a fir rug in front of a fireplace. I have that feeling, like I did as a child, where I wanted to get into some stuff and how it was setting me on a hunt for something to do. Get into things and go off in my own worlds when I was alone, in the quietness of napping tyme. So then I return to my first sentence, about missing having a man in my life now. Sometimes I feel like I'm okay to date on a serious level, and sometimes, I just don't want to. Hard to navigate sometimes with that one. But to kiss a man, to hug a man, to have his comfort, to hear the voice I'm craving, so badly. To hold his hands in miyn and whisper something in his ear to make him crave me and take me in his arms and kiss my neck, to gently bit it, to hear his whispery breathe, to feel each others bodys and entwine like branches growing from a tree. To feel his chest under my palms and to feel a man, to brush his hair through my fingers that write his Love Letters, from tips given by God. I want to become his dictionary of knowing what and what not like that, like this. To stare into his eyes with passion and lust and let go, and just be in each others. To caress you, to hold you and hope. Are you him? Or is it yet another, no? Please one day hear me, and I hear you. But you're still so far away from me, I don't know who you are. What's your name? How tall are you? Do you wear glasses? Do you have blue eyes, grey eyes, brown eyes? What do you do for a living? Are you feeling a woman's presence too? My name is, Sandra. One day, if you want to, we can meet, but only through Him can we meet. But until then, I can only hope when you find me, you'll love me in return and appreciate what all I've come through. To understand the fight I've had to put in, to save me, from me, and for others to help me along the way for I've been silently living by myself and work everyday at things to help my upcoming and new life. To sing to songs and match to notes to that I hope you like my voice and say it's beautiful. To come home to me and be welcomed with open arms and tight and secure hugs. To have the feeling of comfort, feelings of safety and loyalty, to hear your voice when you call me the grizlient times, just to hear me say, I love you baby. To write so many more Love Letters and they have yet to be born. Yet to be discovered and unsecreted in the next love. So, God, in You I trust, that You have a chosen man, to come and find me and my lyfe. That I will one day finally know who you are to me and how you've come into my lyfe. Is it this way? Through gravitation from my fiction-non-fiction? An accident, an author, an agent, crossing the street, in an art museum? Well, it will be answered one day. Or, will I remain single and focus only on children, career, what needs to be done? Will you be him, right there? Or him, over there? So, then will happen and I'll gladly wait, because I know that when I meet you, I want to have the same connection as with my first love. I will wait for you. I'll be faithful in all my prayers.

"The Last Tyme"

I would have written you a Love Letters for you to carry it in your pocket as you breathed for the last tyme of this earthly world, and you showed me a great tyme. Living to meet you, to just go out of this world in what we shared and had with each other. I know what day it is today. Do you remember, Andrew? This was the very last day I saw you. If I knew that that was the last tyme I saw you? I would have told everyone to leave, for my mom to take our children home with her. I would have cryed my soul and sobbed in begging you not to leave me, and show him how much I loved him. I would have locked the door and ran to you, and you pick me up and take me to the living room in front of my fireplace and kissed me like the first one, and I would have repeated; I love you, I love you, I love you. I would have shed my tears all over you, and beg you for forgiveness for all I did wrong. I know what day it is. The last tyme I'd hear your voice and to never hear your laughter again, to break my heart in front of you to show you how you're the only one for me. I would smear my tears all over your body to take a part of me with you, to cry and sob during our last tyme together. To sob out our mistakes with each other and not pushed them under the rug. To show you my wretched in pain in your eyes and heart for you to remember me as you go to sleep and start dreaming, as you take your next journey without me. I would do anything for you to know that I know that that was the only answer in your eyes. To know, that there was nothing I could do or say. I know that. You know I needed many things, but after a decade of our souls being tortured in our own planes, and by now it has to be forgiven and made it into something wonderful, through my own journey to reach the peace sometimes. Today was the day I saw you for the last tyme. You wore your cowboy hat and you stood not even a foot in front of me, and knew the whole new plan. But I wouldn't have told me either. I was stupid and naive. I wonder what you were thinking? I'll show her, she has no idea. I had no idea. That you maybe laughing at me as now I'm suffered and conditioned to love you in a new and whole different way. I was interrupted in the good and cleaned my lenses so I could see you a bit better. I would have let you say good-bye to your children in private, with me right beside you, holding you like the day you came home and you wanted a Sandra hug and the way you held me, we would have said good-bye as a family with you holding your children and saying good-bye the right way, and know, we couldn't hold on anymore. To go through his own lyfes journey and death journey, alone with God, and His Hands pulling him through the silver lining and Lift his soul to the next breathe. That was his destiny, like this is my destiny and that's your destiny. To show us our next path enterway. To lead me in the posting of beginning to mourning and to get lost for over a decade to find. Finding my LORD-heart, and but living my guilt-heart. That one day along the ways, I'll need to find me and Andrew but on a different level needed to become someone of a great love story. In a way that hasn't been told before. And oh, I'm sorry our last couple of days weren't so great and I whish so much I could go to you, and know, I only have one option. To live. And you had only one option too. To dye. And now to live without each other, and to grief in our own worlds and lyfe was an illusion of darkness and vines strangling me, and for you to be stuck until your watching me grieve you and to reach me. Only now, can I find peace in your death and why I needed to live and why you needed to say good-bye to us the way you did. I'm so sorry.

Please LORD, don't take it away! As I beg You, to flood me with thousands of storyes, waiting to be born and spread. I need this as soft delicate music floods my ears and it always goes back. Is it just a daydream? Just take over and write LORD. Go to talk about insecurityes of not being good enough. I'm stale for romance or anything that could be fiction-non-fiction. And let Him in and tell my storyes of my lyfe and their lyfe, and I'm reminded of Him, the Holy and Anointing One. Please give me peace of my book being published. That all my hard work will be not of nothing, and know, one hundred percent that it will happen. Whew, what a relief. I trusted that instinct and closed up. In starting to listen and go. To have a private love affair. To never tell anyone. Impossibly. An non-extinct private life where the vultures come in and start pecking. But it's expected, so I'll just say that, can you? So who are you? The presence I've been feeling in the other ones. You're so close. Please LORD, build me up again, Breathe in me the Words carefully chosen and dropped and typed here and next. I have to remain focused and struggle. But if I talk it out maybe I'll feel better. Dollars and cents man. Notice I write them? And not number them? I can not have any divided attention, but it's what I'm about now, a new storyes to tell. As I go and welcome my son back home, and wonder if he missed me, in any incriments? Is he going to hug me back? Will he show me any love? Will he really hug me? I won't go with any expectations like Andrew taught me. All I want is him, to love me. To believe in me, for even a second. To apologize for us being so far apart, because of not able to feel love towards his mother. Does he know? Does he know the pain? How will he return to me? Will I be included? Just wondering. I want to hear all about Costa Rica and get what I get, and remember it's about him after all. Should I not be telling you this? I'm just thinking out loud. To show Letters vs. blogs with my red, black and white words, which one is most important from both of the choices. As I remembered that all my friends were in trouble, and now some are okay and back to normal. Living their lyfe as supposed to. How I have to have both ones and dedicate and pray daily for more a unit for language, and to try to bring this forth. I'm really searching, trying. I'm grasping to find my voice. As I sigh and beg Him for more. Am I spreading myself too thin? With this *and* that. Is it fading within? No . . . please! I beg You God, please don't take this passion away! This is it for me, my lyfe ends in my writing. Should I write a story? One day, a long time ago, was a man who looked at peoples' handwriting in a curious way. He paid attention to the angles, pressures and the rest of his interest. And study the formation of structures of letterings from handwriting. To slow mental minds and carefully said. Comes from once someone said I was wise, so I speak with wisdom. So the story ends. To feel my heart beating, for bleeding. Please LORD, drum in the words, type the words, whisper the words. As I stumble to the upper stair and pull myself up with my hands and I'm sweating and bleeding, trying to reach my typewriter to just bleed out the pushed words through pours and blood is running into the crevasses. I push down with agony of pinned was pushed in and scraped up tips and so painful. But like a person learning to play the guitar with pained tips to make calluses to make stronger. Please LORD, reverse the bloody hands and plant seeds to make pretty flowers, that smell wonderful. I take my bow and fall to the ground and fall asleep.

"Dear LORD"

I must have done something *really* bad to You God, my LORD. I beg for Your Forgiveness, unless I am unworthy of forgiveness? Have I done wrongly horrible? Was it that, when I said that? To bring from me my unworthy hands as I write Your Name, in Your Frustrated Mynd with me. Have I forsaken You LORD? Did I write wrong? Did I teach my children wrong? Have I betrayed my best friend? I shake my head at myself and know I ruin everything I touch. I say things that don't have a filter, and I slice their hearts in failure. Sigh. Will I have to survive another suicide? What am I going to do? I think the LORD is Frustrated with me and showing me a lesson. Of what it's like without Him in my lyfe. To judge myself, once again and check off another one who left me when I stumbled and whined once to many. I'm so sorry LORD, for failing You and I'm soon to find out the reason for this month, for the way it's turning out and going into April. The worst month of my lyfe. With knowledge of what has happened, but there I go again, right? So now, I have to suck it up and be reminded of how I ruin everything I touch. Has my imagination taken me way too far with limits of and from the LORD? Have I betrayed Him in any way? How? I'm so sorry God, if its just the way. The days remind me of a time that ripped with shredded freys of wire string made up of heart. To be sad and alone on the following days to come through to the next month, then I'm fine again. So, should I become isolated again? To have no one again ? to take care of me? But I may have endangered it and over stayed my last welcomed. To imagine my lyfe without a best friend again, but maybe I don't deserve her? It all came to head when I started blog. About some of my storyes. Have I taken some too far into the make-believe? To have my powers taken away, and what do I have to do to regain them LORD? I have gone stale, haven't I? Will I ever be aloud to be creative again? To write in poetry again? I'm so disappointed in myself. LORDGod, I humbly bow to You when I struggle, humbly. But there's always that. Is that why LORD? Am I exhausting myself emotionally? As anyone prayed to You this way LORDGod. As someone else crumble from Him to me and myself to show me I don't deserve love, and I know about their feelings for me. Do I suck the lyfe out of them too? I'm sure I do, and I don't know how to be normal and who they need me to be. I bow for forgiveness and plead for mercy upon my soul. To relive the worst days of my entire existence of how I bled out and couldn't do anything, and thrashed myself with guilt and be reminded of the promise I made my son so long ago and I promise my daughter everyday I won't leave her, and I survive suicide because of them. What a and such a big burden she carryes when it comes to me, and how he loves me, and to know I'm sometimes unloved from unresolved. Did I take my creative gift for granted? I have to save myself from myself, somehow LORDGod. How I can't do it. How I know how he felt and was alone in debt. And the failure of your children and show me. Maybe I deserve it. Eat my own shit. To have nothing again and hope I have one more option, just one more and that's it for me for months. I was greedy for material things and maybe I put Him last in a situation I'm unaware of right now. LORD, I feel horrible. I have to be put together for her, and fake every breath. Please give me Mercy for the poor and thought bad of them once in a passing thought. For all my thoughts that haunt me everyday of my lyfe. Please forgive me LORDGod, for I've sinned.

"Dying World"

The world is dying. A slow and painful death. Do you not see that? Am I writing for nothing? How can I be happy ? when everyone is fighting against each other? And I'm one of them. I always thought and questioned why child turns against parent, sister going against their fathers? Because it's in The Bible, in Revelations. For it is Written that satan was bound and locked for a thousand years then released for a short tyme. Maybe this is the short tyme. That satan will knock everyone down and lick us with his jagged tongue and hear us scream for the pain to end. To maybe show another perspective and another tongue lashing. Shall I mention how everyone seems to be stressing and worrying and writing about how the world is falling apart and turning against one another? The parent with the child, the child with the parent, siblings against siblings. But how I'm not angry at Him for this happening. It's mans choice. I'm sure that God is frustrated at some of us, me included. Tell it like it is LORD. To exclude me is not a piece of the puzzle, 'cause I'm included in all this mess. I'm just as guilty for this world corrupting as the next person in a war zone. And sometimes you don't want blanks. I'm just stating my opinion. That's all. Whether I'm being absolutely selfish in complaining. I whish I had my poetry, but for right now, I need to be in my own world, spilling my own problems and thoughts that make up the world. My part in all this. How I changed the world with my angry words, that ended life. How that has changed two lives that will change future lives, because of my anger and my venomness words. But I can't go back there. Not ever, to change the world in reverse, to back up and do it right this tyme, with only one way out, one option. And now, here I am. Living. Where I'm supposed to be, here. Where they're not. This world is a cruel joke, with some magnificent views of mountains, ocean, beaches, ribbons, pies, tea, coffee, chocolate, and art, with crime, violence, beating, jails, ghettos, guns and knifes and blood. Whether you're a man criminal or a woman criminal. Equal on feelings of hating the opposite sex. Control is the story of today, whether you accept it or not, and money. But don't they go together? Should I not be saying anything like this? I'm not an optimist, on most occasions. I see hate and love. God and satan, and I will not type a capital s for him. he's the reason for all this mess. Creeping into people's lives and messing with their thoughts that make some of us insane full-time. How our secret warfare's in our minds, that fight back and forth, sawing back and forth, torturing us, up and down on slades of glass. To see our thoughts is showing us as an expression of releasing it. And some of us can't express because we're in catatonic zombies. So, most of this mess down here is invisible with maximum vision. So, I'm just as angry as you are. I have, like you, a view on life, and I have every right, as some people don't have rights in this screwed up world. Rights are taken away and put you in prison and starve you and beat you till your death and left to rot under someone else's nose. Because of them, of free choice of power and control. How bout you get beaten and dragged threw freezing rain and frozen to death or let you bake in the boiling sun to starve and rape? I'm just as bad, because I'm human. I make very bad decisions. Ask anyone who knows me. How anger from lyfe has leeched on me and I play my part well. So, now, I must pray, for this is an agitated feelings to it. LORD, please heal us. As a nation and international of two hemispheres, with islands and below the equator and as a land who needs to bond, and know, it'll never happen.

156

"Public Announcement"
March 31st, 2011

I need out of this. Such blame and consult in my heart and head. And what about you? Putting it all on me in announcement. What about you? How it comes down to my fault, right? Ignorance is something you don't know about me, in how you think I'm so irresponsible and don't know better, right? Isn't that right? Your lack of knowledge of me. Thinking that I can't do anything. Well, you're wrong about me and you have no inkling to get to know who I am. Give me some of your suggestions. How you don't whish me well, well, that's how I feel pretty much all of it. How when I read it, it held me back from accomplishing my goals and don't care how I feel after your words are said, as I hang off every words of blame and pointing in my directions of ways I have to go. How barely words can effect me and make me go in another point of your compass. To leave. As I take *my* compass and let it led me in it's way. How my world, how my thoughts can led me wrongly towards the path of which it is, not how I think. How I deleted it due that it made me feel bad about myself, which is what it's great at. Instead of making me well, it mades me have another heavy load. It's a question of, do you really love me? I show what I want and it seems I'm not understood in the eyes of your windows. To stand sole under it and as is. As I whish to take all my possessions and run to another land and I can no longer hide under masks of pretending to be someone I'm not. Let me find a new way and don't touch it. Has the line stopped so it stops? Erupted from the inner soul of my being. My thoughts are complex and innocents is lost in my mynd that makes it guilty in pleads. I might still have my fever and not dressed to perfection today, for my way is the way it is until the end. How I communicate differently, in most every way. And I wonder where you've gone to, who has your heart, because I don't. How deceit is on the menu and eat soul and not like it. How the distortion of the truth is the way he goes by. To never understand his ways and to never know the realness of a story being told in a book. To hide who I really am under codes that must be broken in a way where I can't be found. Why would I want it ? when it's tainted with nasty bitterness to the tongue when all I want is sweet. How my mynd is cluttered with questions of what's real and what's not. Tainted, perfected aim, is what he lives on to make sure it goes sour . . . gives it contaminations to hear every words the instructions say. To always question how they really feel about it. To play hide-and-seek and to never come out and never be found. You are some of my inspirations and you wanna play? I'll go this way, you go that way, and we won't meet in the middle, because of new rules for the game. Yesterday is gone and to now live in today with everything that follows. No support. No hope in knowing what's the purpose? What's the secret? Or are you keeping it to yourself? How public displays of affection is gone, for it's not right and it's not it. To watch the screen and see what happens from simple words from it/him. I will never be whole, comes from a story from a long time ago, decades now, of not following protocol. To unleash etiquette, to unmask that's one, and to show no grace with no grave. Do you even love me? Am I in this for nothing? Or for anything? I am dust on your shelf, building your allergies to show you what is shown? To always second guess myself, on every situations, with unknown trust and faithfulness. With the slate slicing the pieces to chew and to make fun of it getting killed because it was stupid and couldn't escape the capture. This, from announcement.

How many diary entryes do you get to read? How many of us, want our work published? Well, I'm one of those people who want you to read about my lyfe. This is how it is. I have no props, I have no lines of bullshit, just the way it was said and told for here. What do you think about this? Am I going to cough up bad words and wrongly put together sentences? Keep in mind, this is for us. Get through it, with swords cutting the edge. As I put together another Letters, to be the best I can, to deliver something long and makes sense. That's more like it dude. Ya, break it, break the bank to make it happen. Is there any real eats here? I guess I'll be a little creature with a bit of trouble learning where the food is. Will I be another story that's waiting to be told? To royalty and the commoner and I'm starving. For something to happen, to see in your world, so I can live myn. Am I going too far? No, I'm not, but with no laws there's no abuse, to the Master who created it for you. Damn, I missed it again. Is it less than what you had before? So come in, enjoy your stay. Incorporate a new society with a couple of things and it fell off. To hear foot steps where you must go back stage in your show starting with cheering and clapping. Will I deliver what you're looking for? Are you together? Are you separate? On behalf of me, I thank you, as I shove my cape behind me and fly off to another one, with the crowd going wild, it's so cool. How do we put all the pieces together in such a small space? Carefully I'd say my friend. Do you know me now? Awww, thank you for making such a sweet treat. Do I get it? Or will I starve? Get out there, live and cough it up so it doesn't choke you, so you're breathing under water with nothing to save you. How's it going? Good. I'm glad you're good. Sigh. I started a new one and I only have one to go for the night is closing quickly, and who's going to be my goalie to save the shot? That may be hot, so . . . . oooo ya. Melted chocolate icing and only a few more to go. As I listen to the background, and this is my production. That's cool and I'm glad I got a chance to do this and it was worth it. As some people crack eggs and whip up some cupcakes, and I whip this and make it fill you and make you rock and roll, my way. Let's do it man! Make it bigger, make it awesome and laugh with a jolly laugh. Everyone is so dressed up, with suits and shimmering gowns and what are you talking about? Do you guys remember when you were one? What was invited, was flips of the fins, like the fish just out of water. Look out! Screech! Oops, I'm sorry, I almost hit you. I put it in the heavy containers of coolers with ice and smell of fresh fish. Get your hands on it and squish it under and get it to work. Do you live in days savings time? Oh, right, we all do as you are somewhere in the universe with plenty of gory credits. When I was little, I lyed and my mouth was washed out with soap and I played with Barbie Dolls and would yell out my pretending conversations and she would yell my name and wonder what I was doing. I'm just playing, I would yell upstairs. Well, okay then. Please let me finish up creating the one that I love. Coming up; riches, jewels, red carpet events and eat the menu of impossible crowds, shooting their camera and lights. My happiness is you. Joining me and reading a new idea. A spectacular story to wake you up and pre get you ready for a showstopper. I encourage you to eat, sweat, and bulge out your stomach in private, so no one watches you spit out seeds of the different fruits. On the beach with your childhood dreams of climbing with no rope to hold you in place. When I was so far up and I was stunned in positions, and was shaped in portions; here and here and there.

I just can't think about it. It's going to drive me mental from now to then again I have to say it. They want to see me. I bet they were wondering when I'd contact them to talk about it. I've been invited for dinner. And then gathering with others to end the evening and then leave the hotel. What have I done now? I always ruin what I touch. Who told on me now? What did I say as I haven't talked to them in the last couple of years. Did I say hi wrong? To her when we were congregation together? Probably gonna surprise me with something I didn't think about yet. And it's going to drive me crazy! What mistake did I make that I will never do again, again and again. How was I inappropriate? How I've been shunned. And that don't come please. You're not invited. I bet that's it. No longer known as a friend. I'm ungoing to something I wasn't invited to in the first place. That I'm being asked to leave it. To be shunned by own people. Right? Does that make sense? Hmmmm, I'm just thinking. What is it? As I paused and got right back to work, as I hope this world will change one day, and let me free of this place of thought you were my friend and then tell them I understand and nod my head, as I can't believe this is where we are now. To be unloved by another. I must be a bad person. Not to be selfish again. How I'll have to only imagine the worst, never good. How I'm hypnotized in my printing. And whished I was back in the seventys and lived in bellbottoms. The hair, the big glasses, big everything. It was such a simple time, even though I still fought everyday, but blinded by the colours of orange, brown, and the big wavy lines of flowers and bizarre circular patterns. Uhmmm, it sounds serious. The music, the beats, and all the jungle animals. Glue me to the keys and keep pounding them into succession. To sigh and just breathe and not to look in the mirror and see fat and ugliness that is non-lovable to used-to-be best. And now, it's no longer in the world and doesn't get any where near me. So, I must have done something horrible, and cee . . . am I real ? am I writing you a true story? Or am I writing fiction-non-fiction? Is it just another page in the book I'm reading? Is guessing like a drug? Is she telling us the truth? Shaking my head in disbelief, and asked something or told me. Let me know soon, okay? As they'll have to hold me down again and given tough love and . . . are they worried about me? Is it about him? I hope not. Can I or could I handle it? With my plum lipstick waiting to be smeared off in humiliation and let me run, run and don't ever come back. Leave. When I can. Sell all my possessions and get on a plane to Paris, and never come back. To become invisible to strangers busily living their lives with another English person in their city. Write books on my lyfe in Paris and to find work in writing. And to live my lyfe, as a complete stranger to you everyday. And that's what I just might do you know. When it's finally over, and I'm ready, in every way, and fly. To finally find home. To walk the streets of my fantacy. To live my dream lyfe. To let them go and don't forget my lyfe too. So, I'll say good-bye and hug them, if they want to come, I'd say come with me. Find your home from here. Lyfe would be different. Everything would be different. But, if you want to, come with me, to Paris, France. Seek and find you with me and seek me as wise in your lyfes. So, in the worst case scenario, this is the new plan. To know that this is no longer my land. And why shouldn't it be that way? To live the way you do. To find my place as a free writer. Is my home beckoning me? Telling me my future? So this is the new plans guys, as I tell you another fictionsnonficitons.

What? I don't want to look at nothing but a blank screen page of paper. So, to you. I say that parts of your lyfe is only for a short time. And because you love them, you want the vision of forever to be true. But sometimes we meet people and we don't work out well together for more than His Calculator. I can only assume it's about this way and to not go would be okay. It's either this jewel or this jewel, which means both of almost equal balance board. You'd win, everytyme. That was hard to swallow into the bird of in the future. To sigh and know I have to wait a year. But! Work from home and on my hours of work. ? And write another book of some kind. In the second half of my day. To write in my room area and work in my office with my twin soul. To also allow a new photographer for my column every week. So you'd be giving two people, employment and new opportunitys for career possibilitys. So then, I'd have to come up with their own"Love Letters" for people to read and hope, and maybe some others will whish me poor and bad, but I only want love. It's the answer to everything, but hey, that's just my opinion. To let her express herself through her work, with new locations, and such. So, maybe you'll be my next employer and have read me and my storys . . . well, that's just me being selfish again. How we'd go in together and show him our portfolio and all my diplomas and say, yes, come work for us. You get probation for three months at regular pay and prove yourselfs. To hire me so I can create. To bring to lyfe, people who thought writing is only one-multi level writing. To bring the new generation of my mynd of like Shakespeare. To read out loud, my words. In my play and give me a grand lyfe, for which I beg for. To bring to lyfe, new art. New actors in a strange style of interpretation. To bring some stuff with us to be the first out-of-closet Christians and people get to know us and a mother-daughter team but as individuals to express ourselves separately. To bring new readers, more everything and a new meaning to your jobs of everyday lyfe. But that's my thoughts on that. If I had the chance to hire someone like me, and they showed me proof of their hard work over their years of lyfe, and show the employer how hard I've been working for this kind of break. To know you made a difference in someones life. Two lives and the beginning of thousands of hundreds. To change the newspaper in history. To know that I'll be in the job that I long for. That I'll have employment with a publisher and paper, or, if a publisher finds me and needs me! To work at home, together yet separate. To live my lyfe the way God made it to be, and to follow His Voice and hear His Words to the general people that want to listen. To want to be someone of importance to the world like your familys. Don't you want to make a difference in this world for someone like me? I change lives, in writing, not verbal. I purse my lips together and keep on doing this. Okay, verbally too. But in the long run, wasn't it worth it? To finally know my meaning in lyfe. To finally know that all the people that stayed with me through the duration of the last over a decade with me, and never left me, and who's found me, to help change my lyfe, then to have found my reason for living, along came a long road of aloneness as not a mommy, who couldn't do anything, and now to show them, I'm worth it. I hope I get to meet you one day, and may you be blessed through Him, when you read it and pray upon it and you make a phonecall, and give me the answer I've been waiting years to hear; Yes, I'll hire you. Will I hear those words? Only keep reading if you enjoy and whish for the answer.

Something is happening. It's creeping in my thoughts. What kind of life would it be? It's make-believe day today and all is made from the fairytales you hear about. Into that cartoon, make-believe story to tell a story, just in the mind of a creative one. So think of all the cartoon colouring. And imagine this story. Oh my gawd, hello. I'm glad to finally be able to reach you. I've been thinking about you for ages now. Not cursing and waiting to hear from you. Is what I want to say to you, but can't until I know for sure, as I hang up my ten times bigger fone and everyone laughs. As my eyes bug out of my head and dangle inches from the floor. The first tyme, ever, in history, has this, ever happened. As stars are above my head 'cause I was knocked over the head with a swollen hammer head. I can't tell you. I'm sorry. It's confidential information and I'll announce that to everyone . . . as I sit up and spin on my fluffy tail, and wonder if you'll ever get it. Laughing behind me and I turn around and fall forwards into the puddle and my tail covers me. To even consider to mix the two, scares me, but . . . what and maybe in this day and age, as voices in my head are spinning me down stairs and poing music as I tumble each step and laughing from behind the screen in front of me. To ask for it to make sence in this peeppeek and it can let go later when allowed. We tried so many different ways of trying to connect with you today, as I accidentally drive off the cliff and wait as I look in the fake camera and start falling. Am flattened at the bottom and start running. To ask for proof that this is real, meet you, sit with you, look at you and wonder the entire tyme, if you're reading my thoughts and knowing what I'm thinking?, like in the movies. As I race down the street with the big white truck chasing me down and runs over me and when he goes on by, my head pops up and just thinking about it makes it explode and we're so different as I hear your noise from your upper room, and how you're wasting your lyfe away, but that's off topic. To even consider to let you open me the first tyme, I'm gonna look smoken hot. Make-up done to the tens and straighten my hair and look excellent with my plum colouring and as they play, I play. Okay, I can't spend anything this month, because I have no money to play and maybe. But no. I wonder about him, and I wonder if he's gonna look hot too? As I lean myself out the window and jump and the boingy thing at the bottom makes me spring back into the ayr and I keep falling and bouncing and rushing music as I finally fall to the ground and music surrounds me. To continue to live in the make-believe as I'm being drawn on a page and I come to lyfe as they flip me to watch me move forward to run. That I'll hide it from you, I can't tell you. Are you going to think I'm beautiful? And I can't mix both worlds as one because it's against the law for I need to protect you in this, as to be true, and know I'm not committing suicide in your eyes. I will be diligent and ask for guidance from them. I have to deal with it, as soon as possible so it doesn't get worse. It may be an infection inside, as they open the top of my head and out comes springs of trees and balls and tables and roads and bushes. To unbreak the secret code is locked in a safe and no one knows how to break into it. And I made it small. To maybe fall in love again and marry the one this tyme so not for a third. Forever this tyme, with love making and falling in love until it goes threw. But I can only imagine it would be amazing but I couldn't loose who I am. To do it more, to fight the knowledge so I know the information needed to take the next step, in this crazy worlds of all sorts of stuff from the imagination.

"Artist of Expression"

April 3rd, 2011

Of all the great storys of untoldness and guessing if it's real or is it not? LORD, I humbly beg for Your forgiveness for anything I've done wrong towards You in the ways of my humanness. I pray for my daughter tonight LORD. She's in pain, and she needs Your Relief from sickness and pain and lack of sleep due to showers. I just feel horrible for her right now. I feel as I've failed her as a mother and can't give her relief from her troubles. That this was the package deal if you were to be my child. Which could be either one. So that needed to number one on my list tonight, a prayer without my transgressions as a dog tag around her neck. And all that I come with that's involved. I beg for my soul not to be nothing. To live on, in Heaven, as it says in the Bible, in I do presume, all versions. So take me there LORD, don't forget me, as I call out to You up There. Let me live on and live the lyfe I've always written about, in my imagination of words made into picture in your mynd, so I sweep you away for a while, and cee, gotcha . . . laughing . . . no, but seriously. I won't be able to live that lyfe until I stop living in human form and hope that God thinks I'm worthy enough to save in His Name and hope I lived a good Christian life and did my purpose of spreading Your/His Word to the world and be me in Him and who He made me to be in Him. And hope my lyfe has had meaning to it and that He blesses the people who've helped me and who I've helped and never looking for recognition for it obviously, but I want to help my friends, because they're good people and I've been blessed to know them and want to help them when I'm getting the break I deserve for this book, that I'm working so hard on . . . to make a difference in all of our lives to change the world, like famous who've passed away to let others take over, to continue to spin the earth until He says; Stop! But until then, I want to live. To keep doing my art. To continue to live my Christian and my lyfe. And to live my lyfe, whatever may come. And to adjust quickly. But in a humble bow. Always in fear of God, and in love with my LORD, Jesus Christ and I shouldn't even say His Name. I'm just a human, who makes horrible mistakes that make other people suffer around me, and I suffer in guilt pangs of agony as the guilty mother, of leaving all the tyme for my healing tyme to be able to come back fresh and new again. But to never talk about it. Confidential information. And what did I just ask you? I'm just pulling your leg, have a seat and listen up. I have something to tell you; Should I let my imagination play with reality? To be guessreal? And unmade up? Like in a costume on Halloween night as ghosts and goblins, witches and bunnies. To say, with no reason at all this; guess, the what. As I say thank You LORD, for blessing me and my lyfe with all that we've had over the decade of tyme spent as a unit, and for giving it an ending to start something new and exciting, with new storys and things to write about and make a stage play about, to bring to lyfe, my mynd, and make them my human puppets and make them talk and stuff and lyfe-the-lyfe of an artist of expression. And spread things around the world and make important things happen in the world, to have helped in some way to help another person and spread the Holy Word through just my belief, the belief of a lot of people in this world, so I'm glad I'm not alone in this fight to do our calling for Him. But to also live lyfe, and to make up stuff, for others to believe in, to forget about the world at war and hatred is one of the main words down here, so continue to bless me with Your Word, as You Sprinkle Your Words through this venue with Love to us. AMEN.

Dear LORD . . . . It's me, I need to ask You something regarding my lyfe. Is it just a guess what? Will You understand it and why I think it would be so great? To know that I'm the only one, as far as I know throughout the tymes of myths and poems and songs and movies and books and authors that make it up to captivate your attention to make it real. But You LORD, You Are Real, I feel Your Presence and I bow my head in prayer when I'm desperate and in need and I pray in knowing You've Heard me. Just a picture can put a damning scent on it and mynds become one in secret. That's all my lyfe has been; pictures. Of this place; Paris, France, and where the beaches are with sun and heat and tan and write later on in the sunset from the place I'm in at that moment, living a rich lyfestyle. With a beautiful man and with the LORD's blessing I even get to live this lyfestyle, that I've been praying for and working my ass off . . . oops, sorry LORD. To long for it, to jump and reach for it and for it to be still to high to reach it and my heart aches for it, and I rush my heart to see him. To finish what I need to finish quickly, get all the necessary papers to say yes I am. To continue to serve my LORDGod and to work for Him, because that's the only reason I'm still here and that He saved me. I'll never forget that. And everything that's followed and the days that have given to me with such blessings and I wouldn't be here if it weren't. And I owe You in serving back Christian love in me and what I can do to make a difference in the world. Just to be doing it in riches and styles of different jewels and diamonds and having the best working on me and photo shoots and smile through all the flashes with him beside me with his style. To be called by name as he holds my hand and smiles right next to me. In my skin tight fancy jeans and beautiful top and hairstyles and make-up. To go sit in our seats and meet and greet our famous friends and fashion people. And get ready for the fashion show, then go the Eiffel Tower for a romantic night with red wine and the summer night ayr. To wrap my arms around your neck and to bring you to kiss me and make me filled with delight and happiness and on our tyme in the world. I want to be in love *with* you, for a long tyme. I want it to be about us and no one else in our private tyme together. Thank You LORD, for giving us all all this. And for even the imagination to maybe create a make-believe world in my own head to make storys come to lyfe in you, and I love to do this for you. As I once again thank Him. To find him and share a lyfe of happiness together the way I imagine it, to have a secrets about child. Anything could mean that. To confuse you and to tell you tales of a tyme a long time ago. To be real and not real to be my famous saying lately. To push you forwards to undiscover or discover. I'll leave that up to you. To live the impossible together and maybe it should be a Hollywood movie babe? As I can only think about you in this way at this tyme due that the director yelled; cut! And to cee you in the wings of fame I'm walking to you. Do you know my thoughts yet? Can you read me? For my God gave me this and I pray for it to be blessed with an edgy spin on it, just for us. To open my new joy in my lyfe and to be seen as good. To tell him who and what I have am. That's going to be interesting. How will he react? Will he be surprised or not surprised? I ask for Him to cover me with His blessings and gifts that He feels I do possess in me, that He can use me and I'll be faithful and believe in Him always. To live with something that no one has ever had before, so that's just so awesome.

That I wonder if something like that happening, but in understanding my importance to others, and to him. That whishing you in my head, I found you again. I'm insane right now and I don't think I have anything to write about tonight . . . okay, fine . . . I always have something to write about. So what do you want to talk about? Let's have a conversation, my way. So, what are you doing? Well, I'm writing a book at the moment. And you are reading, that's probably what you're doing. But where are you?, that's the question. Are you in a library ? in a book store ? online/eBook? How did you obtain this book ? and how did you find me? Well, I found you all through words that were meant for me to hear and I did something about it, and now you're reading the next following words. So, the next questions are, are you going to just buy it ? and by chance, love it enough to buy it or obtain it somehow? so then the next question would be, where in the world did you buy it? Asia, Russia, United Kingdom and all over international ways of purchasing an item? Or are you from my Native Land, Canada? Or my next door neighbours ? from the USA? Okay, enough with social studies, right? Let's get back to story-telling. Or do you want to travel with me and for me to tell you all what the world looks like through my perspective to share more of someone unique soleity. Do you want me to tell you in my eyes what Ireland's green looks like ? in a magnifying glass with the purest of green pastures all over there and here, where you may be? So tell me, through *your* words what *your* world looks like, and send them to me via thought and I'll catch it and mash it into my page and make it so. Make it real. For you, for it's my career to make your mynd wander under my control. Come and I sweep my arms to come into the large room and as butlers pass me by and make me unbalanced, but he caught me and led me into the room. There were black tie events, carrying trays of tall champagne glasses filled with champagne and wine choices, and bite size appeez and waltz to the next laughing conversations, with horn instruments and strings blaring in the stage and people dancing to the music. As it slows to the next song, I grabbed her, and flung her on the dance floor, and whizzed her around and looked in her eyes as the floor was circling us and laughing and clapping, and talking loudly as they can't hear next to them. So I had to itch my head as to what to say now. It's just a mirage. It only looks close, but the horizon is so far away from me, do please. Totally changed songs to the one You wanted me to hear, so I'm listening LORD. That You Love me. So let's go back to creating LORDGod. You're going a million miles a second, down this tube slide with whizzing stars, twinkles speeding past me as I hold my arms close to my chest as I'm going down fast. Where am I going? I hear A Voice. It's calling for me to hurry and He can't wait to see you. You see the bright Light and A Man standing there, waiting for me. I arrived and He helped me off the slide at the end, and picked me up and led me to the rest who've been waiting for me. Is that what happens? I whish I knew the answer. And I'm reminded me of the male presence around me in the corner of my mynd/eye. Thank You for the flavours for making my mouth water and run off with saliva, salivating for more of Your Words through/threw the holes. When I'm with You, nothing else matters, to feel That Special Love threw worshiping and singing along with them to sit in my own church of the LORD and praising Him under solebriety. And tapping my fingers in tyme. Let's thank all of this for without Him, I could not love rightfully and wholey. The End.

"Style of Man"

April 4th, 2011

Are you reading them? I'm so excited! I feel like such a kid in a candy story. I hope you're reading them, 'cause they're really good! Like tasty treats. Go read into my mynd, and listen for the majic. Hhhhhh, your eyes. Breath taking and gaspingly beautiful. How I want it to be real and are we in real lyfe right now? Or are we in a mythical book looking for our way out for expressions of hights and peeks? I saw her today, she wanted another to remove a gift sometimes to another person in sickness, and so I took her, but I was there for her this tyme. I was able to ease her day a little bit and to cheer her on. I was the first to cee it, and is she just part in the play? Is this a vision, for a message to say to show you another way out of your maze of makeup stuff and make up stuff? How one day, I'll be on stage introducing my play to the audience and see what the producer does to it. And know when she looks in the mirror, she can envision me in her head smiling at her and giving her a boost from me, or whatever she needed from me today. I tried to deliver and I think I did good by her today? And show me his eyes again and his mouth, how it sits like that, pouty and sexy as hell. Perfect nose, not a flaw in site. Your eyebrowns are sitting almost perfectly on your bone, and your rounded jaw that leads us to your fyre. How it swirls over like that and curls and spiked it into place, and your arms with tattoos. To even think of you. Makes me crazy knowing I can't even know if you're even real. You're my make-believe mynd. You're sexy as hell, and I want to take you. Please remain in my head for more crazy head takes over. To look good all the tyme, just in case you can read my thoughts and you just show up at my door one day and know everything about me and understand why I am the way I am. To have an old soul for wisdom and comfort. But that only happens in fairytales, right? Not real lyfe or normal. How my raised gem sits in it's crown and shows me. He doesn't exist, he's just a figment of my imagination? Too gorgeous to be real? Just a guy? Some random picture to catch my eyes? I'm thinking of him again. And the end of next week, is gonna drive my crazy. Am I just pretending? Is this real lyfe? Maybe it's all a myth, and I'm seeking it out in this lyfetime, to find him. Maybe he'll meet me when he reads my book and he does exist not only in picture. Will it be your voice? Will I see in real and reject you because you're not perfect in every ways to me and in my style of man? Will I have inches of mass brown hair in my hands when we make love later tonight? Will I be pretty enough for you? Him, in my head and not in my reality world, but so whish it. To find him, to see him, waiting for *me* because I'm running behind. Which is why *I'll* be seated and I'll watch *you* come in and matching every inch of your picture in my head. Will you be the reason for so many "Love Letters"? To become real in words and mental pictures, as you slide next to me and whisper in my ears that you want to. To be the picture you have your head *for me*. That you say I'm even more beautiful than my picture and you behave exactly in etiquette of old times of respecting a woman. I know what I want, and I know who I am as a person, and I can post it. For you to know answers to me. If I give you permission to take some sneek peeks. So now, once again in my lyfetime of waiting! I'm always waiting for something, and this will be no different. So, I must wait to hear if he's real or not, to guess the what in guess what? Will he match his picture? Another illusion I've made created? Will he capture my breath again ? one day? Will God let me know whether I'm in a fiction book or non-fiction ? but I couldn't.

Gotta love the imagination, to create majical storys of curious species of male or female. You're just fictionous. You don't live in real lyfe to me, and I have to let that live in it's own world and put together my puzzles of here lyfe. And I'm glad I can make storys wake up in me and inject into your vision tunnels, how I'm never at a lost for words. This is what happens now. Climb to reach the peek where the snow lies and coolish ayr that fills your nostrils. How he stirs me up with adrenaline and then closes the door and I watch him leave all over again, with his blonde hair and killer smile. How he races my blood in excitement to see him, and then, just turns on his heels and just walks away from my arena of burrowing. How now, I must enter my produce and sprout new ones out to you. Be back soon. And from now on, to imagine him, is just that, to imagine. Oh you're just a picture. To know that I'll never meet you or know you . . . but, are you made up from start to finish? I know for sure *he's* real, but what about him? Yup, I like pretending you. I love imagination world; anything can happen. So close to the fingertips, guess the what again—yes—no? You're never quite sure, never quite know. Attention; about the royal wedding coming up . . . so excited. I'm so watching their wedding! Could you imagine? Being royalty? I can imagine, 'cause that's what I do best. If I cover up, will something punch me again? Are you reading? Okay then imagination, let's go lock up for this evening. No more storytelling . . . tyme for bed now sweetheart. Okay mommy! Wouldn't you want me to crawl under my blankets ? and turn my flashlight on ? and start writing about being under the covers? Do you remember that from your childhood? Cozzing up for the night when your mom closed your bedroom light off, and you'd play soldiers and war or you'd read a comforting story that haunted you asleep. I can't even write about that tyme and experience. Don't do it! Don't worry, I won't but and as I *would* bow, out of respect of your title, but in my heart of who I am, I only bow to my LORDGod, you will never be equals, but close in the earths atmosphere. Well, I will write love storys of your love, like Hollywood. Only in *my* style. To be chosen to live such prominent lives. God *chose you*, to be these people to the world. No one else could live your lives. This is your lyfes, that God's chosen ones to be His Earthly Royals. So, why wouldn't I bow for these people? To pray for these chosen ones. To ask for loyalty in the marriage and for *real love* that they have towards each other, like in the Hollywood movies, of when it was of true love times in some of the renaissance people. When in the movie they'd be making love madly and loudly with dominant love music, and that's what I imagine for the prince and the princess. I mean, come on? Have you seen them? Both drop dead gorgeous and their attracted to each other obviously, and they obviously love each other in the way you do if it was you. When you're in love. I would only *hope* it's that way. To take her on her wedding night and sweep her off her feet and run to your bedroom and drop her on your double king size bed and smear yourself, and well, that's all I should say about that. Laugh. Are they going to kiss at the alter? Nope. Or just on the balcony? And it's a double one. I'm so excited for the wedding. I just know I'm gonna write about it. Can't wait. And because I've done it all my lyfe, I have and will imagine it true for me, and have the lyfe I want, more than anything, to be loved around the world for my storys. So are you waiting ? for all the answers to your questions about your lyfe? Wait for it.

You *are just* my imagination. You're a *fictional* character in my book, that leaps and jumps and who doesn't cee you? Let's go out and play, like children, as our mynds take us to another imaginary place, where your childhood friend says; let's play and come up with brilliant ideas for who you can be, and for me to be. You're just fiction. You don't really exist. So sorry to call you on it, but I can't play anymore with; what if this is true? Somebody made up this story to make some picture guy, real, but I just can't cee it anymore, where does he, doesn't he? To know that *God* does, but a human man, not. I *will* believe in the invisible, but *only* what makes sense and sence. I whish to sneeze you out, and release you from my brain and you become something of discard rather than a mixture of a beverage to drink. To cough you up and let the ayr filter you and make you dust in the ayr. I can't talk about it with you. I whished for you and now, you're just a picture. So that gives me an hour to do something, and say what needs to be said and then I'll press send. As to your compliment, as the only place where I am going is to heaven? Only God knows that answer. But thank you for saying such a sweet thing to me, so I read it and appreciate it and wonder. For sure, one hundred percent. As I stand in front of you and push you over onto the ground and say I love you. Your fyre is just that, fyre, to make into ash. What if you actually walked in and were? What would I do? I would wait for you to show up, and you'd never walk through the doors. You're just someone *else's* story. What do I say to that? Oh, hello made up person, as I sit across from just an image of your face that was haunting me and you're piercing threw me. And how your imaginary life is created from a girl who's looking for love and I love her anyways, even if it's not in sanction with real facts. Looking for approval. From an oath. Aww, out of the mouths of babes, right? So, I just play with a five year old, play along for the ride and let her think I know it's real and let her keep sharing who she wants to be and a lyfe of profane expression to a figure of a role model. And it doesn't belong to you! It belongs to me and I want it back, *now! No, you can't have it!* I'm so angry that you have something of myn that you shouldn't have in the first place! Just curl up in a blanket and let the wind breeze past you and breathe ice into the ayr. I can't tell you that you shouldn't have gone out with him, but you needed to cee that part of them to know for yourself to know the next tyme. Like it never should have happened, that I believe in you, and I have no idea of knowing the truth. It's always guessing. Will I? Will I cee you in the future? To hold the note and to not shake and shiver under your spell of your eyes and your face. So, I ask again . . . I know, you're *not* real. To bad. 'Cause you're gorgeous. And I would have dated you, in all the wrongness it is surrounding my whole lyfe, and I can't be wrong in such an important decision of saying yes or no, and not in the future. Were you styled to made you look like that? Were you in wardrobe and make-up? Was the tattoo drawn on in make-up? To make you look real? Just like the whole world to me, is just a picture. Does the world even exist? 'Cause *it's* a picture too. I know there's a world out there, on the two hemispheres of the globe, and I hear storys of this place and that place, and I've only been there and there and used to live there and there, and I've driven to there and we've seen the Statue of Liberty and the mountains and the tower and touched a cave with them to show them once upon a go, we were there. I ask you again, are you real? Will you come meet me, or won't you show?

"Yelloe Brickk Rode"

You're just questions, unanswered. You're an unknown with a side to you that's someone's thoughts and thinks. Should I believe you? Or shouldn't I believe in you? You're my confusion thoughts now and I'm confused in who you are to me. Show yourself so it's no longer a guessing war. Your truth is but, what if? Bits from here and here . . . etc. I'm starving/craving the truth in you, in your picture and I might just whish it real. So go on, tell me more. Tell my *your* wars between the good world and the bad worlds here and show me, someone like me, the world behind the back closet door, into this majical, mythical worlds we have here and as the tree trunks wrap it'self around you and pushes you ahead as the upright position character from a book or something. Tell me your truths, that I must believe in. That your words that you print with that face and you're real, ya, you're right when you say I have lots to cee. Things you only read about. So, since I'm so good at what I do, I can never show your face or tell them if I've ever heard your voice. But, hey, hey, hey . . . no buts here pal. Leave them at the door on the way in. I myn as well just get high into it and just get high and have no control. Because in *this* world, you can do *anything*. So, I'm high and this is my storytelling of this night; Ow! A blinding pain in the corner of my eye again, and then some weird character was watching us as we walked down the yelloe brickk rode. Ever wonder what it looks like? I soak in your ice, and you want to freeze me. It's a pass. When you've gone to the Portz of Sinn, you're almost there. When it says Onna, get the Foyl and to go back to the yelloe brickk rode, turn the twist and you're almost there. So, lead me, the way to your way, your truth, that since you have me following, lead the way. Show me your storys, so I can write about them, and breake you out of here. Get me drunk on your venom. Well, I won't be that famous, just enough. To get me there, to find you, and whew . . . I finally found you. I'll belch out your truth as I have nothing to offer you, with sourness to swallow, to digest this information. To defeat in truth. To have two pairs of eyes in my room, three, four, how high to you want to count? You should be ashamed of yourself!! How dare you . . . ?! Just kidding. Ya know he used to be a church pastor, and now he serves other people, through where You have called him, and that's the Way. And Your Forces to Ward off evil spirits and just how You Are. So how many Names do You Have now? This is me getting mad for you, as I breathe from my mouth and whisper it into your heart as I plead His case and How He Loves you. In regards to him in my lyfe as one of the best parts, as I find it again and give you a message from a voice in my head, and for believing in Him, your story will be read down in history. So my message is to find Him again, to lean on His Hush. And to find your purpose again. Just saying. Things I do say, have meaning. It's like they're telling their own storys through me, the characters that you forgot about because of what just happened. Okay, I'm not gonna put pressure on myself to other to you to confuse you and it's back. To vision you as I write and then to find it's a message about you/for you. You're to find your Path again. And when you ask if you can stay, I'll have to say no on that, I'm sorry. The doors close soon and just like in Paris, I'll have to escort you out. So I must finish telling you the story. I'll have to file them right down, make them almost perfect for the next visit, as I not live you, only in secret, can I tell you about it, or not. Do you have any final questions? Please escort by this exit on your way out, night.

"Doors"

April 7th, 2011

Okay, let me get this right . . . *I* opened a door? To a majical place, I can only imagine, and is it through *my storys,* that this happened? I mean, that's pretty cool. So then, who *am* I to you? Am I supposed to tell your storys, in my way? So, tell me how this works, please, when and where do I sign up? So I must be pretty important then uh? So how do I help you, do I hale you a story ride to home, not making fun . . . promise, just gotta know this, so however I got you here, I can get you back, or is it the other way around? So how did you find me? Or, how did I choose you? I just wanna get this straight, due that's it's now, an important part of my lyfe. I should know about stuff like that/this. Am I right? Well, this will definitely open me. And gain more wisdom and knowledge of a hidden worlds. Are you supposed to *tell* me the story subject? . . . and then I write about it? Are you someone of importance? How are you able and allowed to talk to me? Like, tell me who I am. I am full of wonder and child-like curiosity. Is this top confidential information? I mean, this is huge man. This isn't just a lovely picnic on a Sunday afternoon. Do I have powers I don't know about yet? You did say, if I had any further questions, to ask you . . . sooo, . . . this is me asking you. You live in a majical place, where storytellers live. To have both worlds, day and night, in the next lyfe too, right? I unleashed something, so was it trying to find me? . . . and did? How long have you been stuck here? I'm sorry to keep you waiting. Well, you found me, so tell me what I have to know, and I want to know EVERYTHING. I want all the answers, to every questions, so I can mentally prepare my imaginations. Wow. What made this happen? To erase real life, to add something new, a new flavour to the normal ingredients. How many of you are there? How many of *me* are there *here*? Do you follow me where I go outside of this worlds? *Do I have visions* of something yet to happen? LORD, this is where You come in, to Put Your Light around me, and I fight with Your Cross around my neck, and I can feel so much right now. Sigh. Okay, so now what? So, I just start telling a story of when he followed me there, and stood in my living room and he was in the corner of my eye, which is probably the second tyme. The first was we were in the kitchen and we both said at the same time, the same thing, meaning the same person, and we both turned to look, at the same time, then he was gone, and we looked at each other, and then I carryed on to tie your shoes. Both tymes he wore the same clothes. The clothes I buried him in. So like that? Like those kind of storys I have to tell? Without writing without the LORD, I can write about stuff I want to. Can I say about how he looked? Or is that too far? But why not say it and share it? It's a part of lyfe that we all live with, if not once in our lifetimes. Suicide. If you've ever been touched by suicide, it changes everything and everyone around you. But I'm getting off topic and things keep touching me, in the darkness from where I write from. You probably think I'm insane. That's okay, I'm sure at one point in everyone's lyfe, someone has thought they were insane too. So are you ? the reader ? good at telling storys? I've always been good at telling storys. No one could trust me, because I lyed all the time. So who's to say I'm not lying now? Am I telling you the truth? You'll never know. (*; Well, I have to continue on with my story, so please remain seated as the attendant will show you the airplane doors in case you have to jump. You never know, ANYTHING, can happen. So, now, try to process all of what I've said here tonight. Ask yourself the same questions of something for importance.

Dear You—I have something to tell you, in a way that I can put into a storytelling note. How much do you believe in me? How much do you trust me? Umm, I have something to tell you about me. This is important to me and my lyfe away from you. Can I trust *you* ? enough? Can I share such an important secret? You must trust me. To know, such a story, but I'm gonna wait to tell her. I have to prepare myself to tell her. I'm developing a new gift, and I'm excited for this new venture in my lyfe, because Today is just another day in my lyfe, that doesn't show me the future back then and I was stupid. What did I know? I was living my lyfe and nothing bad could happen. I didn't know you were sleeping alone and sitting in your stuff. How I would run to you and pray that I can breathe lyfe into you again. As you had already taken your last breathe. But that could be for tomorrow, but I must go on, and live my lyfe for I'm chosen to do stuff. Something of importance and meaning. I should have done what you needed from me as your wife, and I fucked up. Big-time. I didn't know how to be a wife to you. You didn't come with instructions and I'm sorry, for the billionth tyme. I said somethings that were wrong. And I know I've covered this before, but just bare with me, as I figure out what to say on the eve-day of the eighth. The day that changed my life forever, and took me on a long journey of repair and living with what I had done to your. My first love that I take, and whished you back, but I know what lyfe we would have had, and I know that was your only answer. So then I'm drawn back to my lyfe now, as word then. And to know, I'm the only one who can do this for me. And I can't go back and reread what I've written as I'll break what I do best. To make you believe in the make-believe world that others only fantasize about or write down so you can cee it in print, but it's what you believe. You can't believe if you don't open your mynd and let the others in there worlds, come into your mynd and make a stand for what they believe in. Is it majic? Is it magic? Maybe, yes? Maybe? No? It's what's in your heart and eyes. I have a majical world that I will create and let your mynd deliver what it's going to. So, it was sunny today, as it was way back then, when I open my sences and knew something was wrong in the ayr. It was coloured grey. So the day went not well. I can't cee my peek, so I must do it under my peek. And tell you what I can. So how are you today? Did you do everything you had to do? Hey sexy, wanna ride? Hop on and let's go out on the town and be romantic and hand-in-hand. Can you read my mynd gorgeous? I'd wear my best jeans and blouse and show off, and go to partyes and open my studio. And dress to the nines/tens and look hot all the tyme. And hopefully have my man on my arm, smiling right next to me. To be writing in my own house and working from home and my studio. To never forget my other in all of this . . . this couldn't/wouldn't be happening if it weren't for her. She plays a huge part in all this and she needs to come to the top with me. I'd own half the studio or have her own with me and she'd be the other partner. She'd have to come with me. OH YA! I haven't told you yet, that in the last month, at certain tymes, I'd sence a male presence around me, like he was right there beside me, but he wasn't there. He's captivating/ed my attention for a long tyme now. His face, his lips, his eyes, his chin, his nose, his fyre brownnut brown with swirls, and I just love them, and his hands and the way they sit on top of his knee, and the turns in the corner of his mouth, his brow bone, his cheek bones, his arms with the tattoos. I just am so attracted to everything about him, and what we could have together? Only, once in a lifetime for this special event. I haven't heard his voice yet, and I'm scared I won't be attracted to his voice, 'cause that's how I'm gonna know. It's a special voice, unique voice that's going to captivate me and put me in a tranz. Just like his picture did. This man is important to me somehow. I don't know yet. 'Cause I haven't met him yet. I've only written him in the most romantic way I know how, through my words. Expressing my real feelings about things. Cee, I'm doing it again, going into la la land. His words; you have to believe in something . . . .

So, this is my lyfe. So, I'm gonna live my lyfe and accept whatever comes and happens, that I'll continue to pray that my LORDGod will be protecting us. To develop my new gift of ceeing, who is who and like I said a couple days ago and I'm so glad this is my lyfe and maybe live my visions and you could never doubt me, ever. I just loving creating storys. It's sounds so real, don't they? Like it could happen, but only in movies and books and the about the male presence was you, I believe? Someone recently said they wanted to come into my head, and that I'm her idol, her earthly idol, not subtracting God in any ways. That my writing has opened the distance plain. People who get me the best I can be will be this being it. So I went to bed some tyme ago now, and it was just a normal night, and I wasn't sensitive back then to where I am now and where I want to do later on in the coming months. And that I'd be someone in Canada Hollywood. But, first things first. Meet. Talk. Cee if he can read my mynd. I'd ask him, can you read my thoughts? You asked me if you could fall in love with me, well, from the beginning of communication for us was just a fairytail and none of this existed in anyone's lyfe. That I am a very important person in all this. I shake my head and say; I wonder if they believe me? I hope not. I hope so. Do what I'm best at and write future things of importance with the power of You/you/Him/him with me and for me to develop my new gift. It's all I want right now. To join forces for wherever they come from that I stand strong in Jesus Christ and pray for Him to watch over us and that I pray for it, in Your Name. And then I could enjoy today more too and to enjoy lyfe more and to believe in everything and anything. Never say never again. Because you *never know*. Especially in my future storys to tell you, if you want to keep reading that is? Love is my lyfe. In the passion I put in things. To sit in my chair and sway to the love songs that float in my ears. And just escape to another worlds that I come up with. That he's Jordan. And that story will be out someday too. That I continue to create my other books that I've put on hold to write "Love Letters." What a journey I've been on in writing this book. What a trip man . . . holy smokes. The stuff that's happened in the last couple of years? How I've evolved as a storyteller, a writer. But back then I wasn't as gifted as I am now and I'll say that I'm better now, more sensitive. To receive truths that no one can tell it just like me, but cee now, I'm boasting and I never want to do that. I'm grateful for what I have and to live my lyfe as only I can, like you guys. So I want to finish and get yet another diploma, but this is kind of like my final exam. Of all of what I've done in my lyfe, in this form of life. And to never forget LORDGod in all this, because without Him interceding in my lyfe with 'him' and his lyfe and his choices, that he was going to change two peoples lives to me and her, that we found each other, to live this crazy and insane world, together. But, this "Love Letters" is dedicated to his voiceless and intence eyes. My captivator. Who will one day come back and relive surviving suicide has benefits and I hope you can remain strong in the LORD when you feel suicidal when you've called 911.

"Understanding Suicide" April 8th, 2011

Sad day, and soon, soon. Then he says hello to me. I picture small size, he's probably half of me. That sucks for me to be like I am. I'm going to work like hell, to loose more weight, so I'm not three of him and one of me. Ya know? Today was the anniversary of the day I found Andrew dead. To live with that, was mental anguish in remembering where you are. To not know the reason, why you committed suicide, so one day, a long tyme into the future . . . what you just said? You said, I love you, to your son. I want so badly to say good for you. But I'm scared to, not being this day, of all of the days in my lyfe, the most tragic day in my history of tyme, that I understand. And I'm here to tell you all messages, and to pass it along with Love from Him. So how's my story so far? Is it boring? Am I putting out a good vibe on the story lines? Of experiences and all the lives I've lived here? The beauty industry was my main focus for many years, but there I go again . . . but I'm so proud of my many accomplishments and diplomas and certificates. In the fight I've had to reach this point in my lyfe. As I tuck my chair in further, and nicely done. She was with me all day in her heart with this day for me. If anyone knows, it's hershe. To just come up with that? . . . that's her new nickname; hershe. She's been there for me every ways. And she knows this day and now I met and was introduced me. And so now this day has two meanings, both unbelievably difficult. But I need to come out of that now, into the sunshine and bask in it all in and this is my last tyme here, I'm not coming back. The pain here, is just crushing, and sometimes such a catastrophic events that happens to people here. So, in the beauty that is here, I'm gonna enjoy it and live my lyfe, and my fantacy lyfe. If this is the lyfe God has given us, then why not? We'll be the only 'ones' like it and us. But, step-by-step, because here, we have boundarys with somethings in our lives here and you must be polite in someone else's home, right? At one point today, I thought my head was going to explode if I didn't get to my computer tonight as it's the anniversary. I'll be back soon enough, hang on. You're glittering love from me to you. Do you like your new nickname? It's cute, as you're so tired from the long day you had with just about everything that could happen, did. So I'm going to get back to writing and saying that today was the day. When I understood suicide. And many other life catastrophic explosion for the rest of the lifetime because of attachments we all have here. you have here. My heart breaks everyday over loss and love and passion and fight. I have the fight. I have the passion and love and loss. As this day where I had to start a completely new lyfe. As when we fled west from the east and we've settled here, and this is where my lyfe is, and I'll only leave the city not where I am. To live a lyfe that no one would know about. Only we would know the full details. I'll come up with storys that'll blow your mind and open up to a whole new reality. If this is Chosen for us, then who are we to say no? I want to be able to communicate with that girl and feel them touching me and reading signals and hear them and talk to them. To telecommunicate with the distant plain. So the story goes on to say this; in knowing Andrew, I know *you*. in knowing hershe, I know *you*. So you have to accept both lives, all the lives. It's okay 'cause she's hershe. So, I say another year has pasts and now something new and wonderful is happening, so I must say, come back anytime, Andrew. You're the reason to my lyfe, in knowing, loving, and spiritually, you've helped me shape my lyfe now in knowing about the LORD. See you soon.

"My Little Sparkle"

April 9th, 2011

To my precious Sparkle; I just want to tell you how much he and I love you and your mommy and daddy. How much He Loves you and He wants me to tell you some storys of how much I love you and your mommy and daddy. I remember one time, I was really mad. And I was with your mommy and auntie. You know how sometimes you get angry at something? Well, that was me, and I point to me, and I had my foot leaving the room, and your strong mommy, came to hug me really tight, with all her love-power and she didn't want me to leave, and she said to come and stay with them and help me because I was really sad. That will always be the tightest hug I'll ever get, and that was of my lifetime of hugs, number one in many pasts. She hugged me so hard because she was showing me, the same kind of love she has for you and your brother and your daddy, and the rest of the people she loves. And I can tell you, that your mommy and daddy were and are who you are and become as you grow up into a strong, devoted, adoring and compassionate woman. I'm going to continue on how much I love you and how much Jesus loves you, because He chose you. You have a great future and know that every tyme you look in your mommy's eyes, when you look to your daddy for comfort and to carry you when you're weak and sick. Somebody I loved went to Jesus, in Heaven. It made me very sad. I was very sad and lost somewhere. And when I needed someone to hold my hand, and hug me, I always want your mommy *first*, and for many years, and now her daughter, will be my Sparkle and shine in God's Name. Well, this Love Letters is directed in love to my little Sparkle. I'm very special in God's Eyes and I cee things with the help and his pictures and videos He shows me in my mind, like when you look at a picture together when you and your mommy or daddy read a book together, and they read you the story? Well, I can read you the story. And because I love your mommy, so much, He gave me your mommy as a friend. We met through Jesus, and so now, I can tell you some storys. He Loves you, and now Jesus gave you a blessed little brother, who you love so much and he was chosen, just for *you*, to be *his* big sister, so you can love him like your mommy and daddy do. You are my sparkle. I'm very special and I've been blessed with you in it. So you know, all the time, how much I love you. I want you to know how important your mommy has been to my lyfe. She's been the best friend to me. *So* dedicated, *so* unconditional, *so* loving and tender and *so* strong, like Hercules and Popeye, and your daddy. And I get to be a mommy too, and I know how much I love *my* children, so I know how much they love *you* and your little brother. And that's pretty much as big as the world and lots more. So whenever you need your mommy's strength when it's just you and her, hug her tight, really tight, like when she held me, and tell her and kiss her and say what only you two know of. And God too, because He made you. And tell Him to remember them in your heart when you're away from each other. My love for your mommy is beyond this whole world. Can you tell her for me? Thank you darling, sparkle. I remember a tyme when I was with your mommy and auntie, and we were playing and laughing with each other, and I was telling your mommy *her* story. That she would marry your daddy, because your daddy's loving face appeared in the corner of my left eye, and your daddy laughed and shook me, and I told your mommy, and now, they get to love you and your brother because they both loved Jesus. Take a piece of me of my love/His Love for you. I love you Sparkle.

"Very Special Man"

Oh my God, He did Well, when He made you. Thank You LORDGod, for creating such a special creature of another world, that I'm going to love telling storys about to you, that my imagination is so great, that you won't know if they're real, or fiction. Is it real? Is it a story? Let's see if you can guess; Dear John; About two years ago, I ran from church because of a situation that tore me apart, and ruined me for two years. When I left church, I left everything. Even myself. I was suffocated in sobs for a whole-day-basis and I was alone, in my shut in isolation and that's when I found myself. That's when I found my LORD, my Calling-me God. To shed myself in front of Him, to be weak and helpless and alone. I cryed everyday. Everyday, I begged to God to let me die in my sleep, to come and take my lyfe. Life was so painful for me, and I was so broken. I shut my door and I became invisible. I hid in my cave, in the room that has seen all my weakness and my new strength. A new love came to me last part of 2009, late 2009. I was lost in pain and grief and silents. In my coughing and suffocating breath to breathe. I knew that the next tyme I would find love, that he had to be a very special man. A man, who would love my Christian love, for my LORDGod, for my God, who gave me an answered prayers. Because you are, a very special man. To know who I am and know all of my lyfe, and lay it all down for him, to cee me. Whether the distant shore, or wherever you came from, I don't care. How could God damn this unique soul He created, and given him breath, to live to find what you needed to? Us. I think? Still trying to figure that out. How can He not give you to me if I all I had were prayers in agony of picturing my future alone and accepted that. And I was okay with that decision. I'd have my lyfe with my children and be a single mom, who has an edge. With the power of God in her home. How you have future pain for me if I ever lost you. Yes, I just would probably loose happiness again, but this is the last chance for something like this. The LORD has blessed me three times in the last little while. My lifes dreams and fantasy. Prayers to God, to show me peace in being me. Thank You God, for him and his love for what *he* does. So, LORDGod, I now pray for a damned soul, of human as we can feel damned from You, I pray, for a soul that may be damned. I ask that you bless the lyfe that You gave him. May I remain strong in You, to love him, in such a special and unique and sole way, that you gave him to me, to believe in something other than what I've been living and repairing from a catastrophic shotgun, putting a bullet through my heart and shot me to the ground and crashed my head open. I pray for continued words to create these majical storys, that you think I'm saying something, when I'm in fact saying that. How you capture my eyes and heart that tugs me. But, I want to be careful, as to show a new type of love, to a new type of man style. And that's why. I picture you the way I am, but gorgeous to me and my eyes. My urge for you, to want to see you walk to me. How I walk to you. When I'm myself, I climb as I high as I can. To reach for Perfection. And for it to write it's way down, I must get up and walk towards my mental Light and become One/one. And when I come Here, it's essential that you believe in me and my abilitys. And I trust in you and your abilities. I never want us to change ourselves to be us. Trust each other, and when we go places, read my mind, of my thoughts, so I can whisper to you and you'll look as we walk hand-in-hand. So how's the story so far? Enjoying yourself? Have you guessed yet? If it's true of false?

"Instant Love"

April 11th, 2011

I believe God will keep you here, because I need you, for my book, to live, in this lyfe. You still don't know who you are do you? I do believe that you may not change to stay here after all. One moment turned into a long lyfe. Please don't leave. I have so much to tell you, to show you, in who I am now. Love, is involved now. Love is stronger than anything. I will fight, 'cause that's what I do. Fight. I fall on my knees, and I can't believe that God would let us find each other, and then take you away from me. I'll continue to do what I'm doing. Write, to keep you here, in my world, until we leave together. *There's a lining attaching you to me and me to you.* So, this is my story tonight, to hide my secrets, far away from light, for I may go blind looking for you. To keep looking through the parachutes with the light shining through the light behind you, and you grab me, and pull me into you and you heat in me. To spin me around the fabric and we fall to the ground and you wrap your arms around me. Please don't leave me. I've never touched one before, and I don't think it was bad. I didn't really know what to do, when I found out what it was. I think it was okay to touch the wolf of the day. You can't leave me. You have something of myn, two things actually. But you have to cee me. Up front and I need things from him, immediate thoughts when I cee him. So then she looked in the mirror, flicked her hair, brushed her long brunette hair and looked like a beauty, that I never recognized before. And now I know, I had a girl, and now. I go to my car, and try to think of her as I walked away from the abortion clinic. Confusion is a mess, isn't it? It rattles your brain. As I placed her there instead of in the past. And now, I have a barrier up, to hold off to the end of my arm and afraid to touch the screen where you sit, staring at me. Urge. To feel you as you impel with force. Through the screen, on the screen. But I won't touch you. I just stare. Then when I'm away from you, things happen to me now. But I love it. Is it too simple? You stare at me, from a distant plain, a door painted white, with flowers all around and popping out of there, is that strange creature, that touches you and turns you into a feary. And your hollow body shape allows for your size and there's no ayr, so it just, floats to make sure the door closes tightly as to not let anyone out. Then, we run as a free black horse and white wolf when we ran from the door to our own worlds. Leave them behind, I'm there with you. Galloping as fast as I can, at elevens speed and you're right next to me to our next world. If I have to know every detail to keep you hear, I'll write for twelve hours, everyday, to be beside you for forever here, you can stay. You can't ever leave me. Please, you can't ever say that to me, ever. As she said. If I have to create like this?, . . . to keep you hear, I will. Please don't leave me. You have something of myn and I want it back. Three things actually, but I'm going to forget, for my secret to never come out for anyone. Three main things to make a lyfe whole. For an ayr lyfe? I'd get on the plane every tyme. As we run to each other, like we missed each other for so long, and I run to him after I excuse myself from the public, and praise the LORDGod the entire run. Gallop to him. Run into his arms, like I haven't seen him in years. Instant Love. A couple. Missing each other. And run to each other. Ohh, the tug is back, the urge to push threw my skin and break out and find you, and to not have to wait one more second. You're so beautiful and squish our faces and lips together for a pressed kiss. Something we've been wanting for, since you came to me that one day to say good-bye, now it's hello. Thank You God.

"Sexy As Hell"

Where *are* you? Are you just a note ? and an email away ? but not real? Are you just cyber? Where *are* you? Are you just a figment? Are you my mental invention? Breathe the same ayr as I do. It's the cough that forces you to cough by so much pressure that you'll explode. I can't hold it in . . . cough, cough, cough. As I lay my head on your lap and fall asleep to your heartbeat. To *never* leave you. This is to you. To hold your hand and we lift off with our three. And we leave here. As I shake myself out. Okay, pull yourself together. I walk across my bedroom, to my spiral staircase to my upper balcony. To have my stereo on as I write. Where are you? Can't you hear me calling for you? They ask who you are to me all the tyme. He's my eye candy, and he's myn. I would never say that of course, but I may have to once and a while. Then it might end. Because of the law of tics. I have something to you. She's raes. And I want to watch, don' t you? God, has now blessed me twice in this way. Some kind of prayer I think. I scratch my chin and look up. Nope, no answers. I have to tell you. Stay in my sights for more than seven. I can never quite finish a sentence, can I? It's always a cliff-hanger of what's next, at least that's what I hope. You come up to me on our balcony, and put your hands on my neck and message my shoulders and went to your knees to get my attention, and I try to give in, all my will and let my man control my body convulsions when he touches me. I fall out of my chair into his arms, and do you know who it is? You cee me in your passion of lust for me, as you've repeated in my ears I'm beautiful. And so I might let in fully this tyme instead of letting my insecurityes of my body to him, and just love him, the way he loves me. He slides his hands and arms to push my hands above my head. His heavy breath on my face, in intence, more love than anything ever existed. I grab your fyre in my hands and pull your head towards myn and ravish your lips, and wrap my legs around you and swallow you, but you never let me. You slide my blouse over my head and threw it downstairs. He rises to his knees. He's so sexy, sexy as hell. He's moving to the beat of music and unbuttoned my jeans to see my sexy understuff. You lift my legs to slide them off me, and you kiss down my legs. When you reached my stomach, you slid your hands to my wetness and rubbed and massaged me, and whenever you touch me, I have no control and I reached for you, under your tight jeans, and did what you liked best. I had to do crunches for you to kiss me, heavily, intence passion, making love-sex. You teased me, and he still had his jeans on. What a tease. He slipped away and he took his hand away from me. I arched my back, for he made me quiver in shakes. He took my breasts in his grabbing hands. Give me that. The music was going on in the background, and the next song was great song for what's happening to me right now. He's so beautiful and I sat up and pushed him to the ground. It's my turn to tease your myn. My long hair fell in his face, and I kissed him, but teasing him with my tongue and slid my grabbing hands and I race to take his jeans off, but kissing and biting him and grabbing him and biting him, rough but not too rough. (*; I slid to his waist and I ripped his button undone and went to the music and we had that look we have for each other in longing wanting each other. I couldn't wait today. I wanted him so badly. I was so happy the second I saw him. He had powers of seduction with me, and he makes me feel beautiful. And wanted, so I show him, how so much I'm in love with him. So tell him. I'm so in love with you. As I bow in gratefulness to God to bring us such passion.

You must tell them about me, and my powers and visions and revelations. I had another one tonight. I found my purpose. You're my purpose. To find you, through the mess of lyfe, and my skin home is driving me mental. I want to communicate so badly. Do you understand me? I can feel you touching me, a cold touch on my left knee. Hello? You must make the others know about my relationship with, The LORD, and how He, alone, is my Number One. Then, comes my husband, then my children, then my parents, then my best friend, then everyone else. So you can know where I stand immediately. With God, and to listen to Him, when He Speaks to me. He says . . . . Ya, right, like I know what He says. I whish I did though. That my light flickered so I know I'm doing the right thing right now. And to never doubt me, when it comes to my relationship with God—Jesus—LORD/ Father—Son—the Holy Spirit. For this, you finding me was the purpose I was calling for, in pleads of, the LORD, He heard me. And I do believe I am the first one to experiencing, and I'm sure this has happened before, but, when? Not just one, but two?! Who gets blessed like *That?* To tell you that I want you to know how precious life is here to others and when you're feeding can only as a deer and the enemy of you. Choose them, instead. And, to let you know, that since you have to change in front of me, I have to change too, for you. For you to witness my devotion to, the LORD. And what happens to me when He Talks to me, in my silents with my music and my strange thoughts of when I climb as high as possible to say what I have to say. That I have found my purpose, and how I have to touch every single one of you, to give you a soul. To stay in my world, for my lyfe to continue on, to the next step in the faith directions. And to hear the calling in another flicker in my light. My single standing light when I work. Soft, delicate lighting, in my solitude into knowing what to say from Him. To pray for you, for you're one of His creatures, in His way, in all our humanness. He created, and I have to pray for you all. I have to protect you. So, now do you know the 'purpose' now? To be here in our bodys, until He takes us Home again. I'm not coming back, LORD. Don't do this, one more time! As I slap my face for even saying that. For His will comes first for/ with me. Just know that.

Paris is so beautiful in the springtime. The smells of the ayr, with people buzzing by me, and I'm just holding my head up high and blending in with the rest of the people of the city. The buildings of stone, with steeples and rocks in the roads. People smoking everywhere. But that's just the part, because I was lighting up myn too. I wondered where everyone was going. To work? To have a massive love affair? To the hospital to cee a loved one, sick and dying? To home? Who knew? I was going to work. To be in charge of my professional photo shoots, as Head Coordinator. Big shoot today, so I better hussle my ass to my office, where I could see the Eiffel Tower, in my view. I had to make last minute phone calls, make sure everyone had the clothes and accessories and props for the shoot. I got to my office and hung up my suede jacket and put my laptop on my office desk, with people coming and going. Giving me last minute important information about names and who I met at the last party. Yes! Yes!, I know. My phone started ringing, and my day started. As I looked in my appointment book to call back Franck, to let him know every detail of my day and what tyme the shoot would begin.

"When You Come Home" April 13th, 2011

When I cee you, you walk fast and I walk fast, to make up for all the tyme we've missed with each other. You look straight into my eyes and my soul and my heart. You're home. You've found *us*. I hold you so tight, like I'll never let you go again. I look at your face, like I haven't seen it in forever. Oh my God, you're so beautiful. You've come back to me. Being away from you, when I don't know you. Such anticipation to cee you. I cee you both. As them. You look like you're sad. Are you sad? Have you been searching for something? Have you found it? Are you home? What will it be like? When you and I cee each other for the first tyme, what will happen? Will you know me instantly? Will I recognize you when you look into my eyes? Will I be pretty to you? Will you make me squirm in the first glance? Will your touch be my home? Will your voice send shivers down my body? Will we make love with our touches as we hold onto each other? Will we escape the group and go and hug and kiss and finally say, welcome home? You're all I can think about. I haven't seen you, for a really long time, what if I don't recognize you? Even though I've studied your picture, and know what I cee. Like you grabbed me with your deep eyes and your soul. What will your first words be to me? I miss you, so much. Am I sending this to space? Are you listening to my words of longing? The stranger in front of me, who came a long way, far away to see me, to find me and live a long time with me and us together. Him and Sandra. Whenever I write this, amazing things happen to me, so I should write it a lot. Will we go away and make love all night for when it's time to sleep in your arms? From the first time I saw your face, till now, what do you say? You say you're in love with me. I hold you at arms lengths to protect me and my delicate spirit. But what I want to say, lyfe would be over in a second. My fantasy is you. It's all about you. It's always been you. No one else has ripped my soul and lived within me and invade my thoughts about who you are. Your eyes were pulling me. There was always something about you, but I ignored it, so as to not believe in your worlds. You're so far away and you can't help me with my eagerness to cee you, to cee you, to look at you and cee what I recognize. You're so gorgeous and I'm yours. And I just want to ask, are they out looking for her? Is she safe now? I've been praying for her safety. And they have to find her, and she must come home. I pray against evil, for her to regain herself in who she is. I'll stand next to her to protect her as she's *our* child. Does this makes sence to you? Do you know who you are yet? Are you still trying to figure it out? When we cee each other, and if I get that feeling when I cee your face and look into your deep eyes, I'll take you away and tell you who you are and tell you who she is. Just hang on to what you believe *now*, and when you come home, and you find her, all secrets will be told. I wonder what the cards will tell me tonight? Will they tell the secrets I haven't said yet? Will my answers be questioned? Will the future be revealed more to me tonight? Will they answer who you are, in facts? Her too? I'm going in the right direction to figure all this out and it's symmetrical again. Not for long, but I need to be balanced for I can't be knocked down, when I need to remain erect in position, for on to carry responsibility for the day to continue on and bring me what I need to know. So, now I say, listen to my heart, and hear me and my wishes and dreams of the future, for it speaks loudly to me, and you're all involved. I pray that the LORD will keep you all safe and . . . . Come home.

"Playing Love"

So you think I'm a terrible person eh? Well, here's your slap across the face, from me. This, IS!, the last time you'll ever hear from me. You showed me no mercy tonight. I am no longer your aim. I will never reach for you ever again. You are worthy of my love, but I no longer love you the way I have been. The walking alive, dead shell. It's a shell of a fantasy. All lies and deceit. Pretending to be someone you're not. Go away. Never come back into my world. The light switch is turned off and never to be turned on again. This was/is the series finale. No continuations. Poof, gone. Are you laughing at me generation? Showing me, revenge on my tortured soul? To pain me even more, as you laugh at me, and say, good, she deserves it. A little wake up call for me tonight. To show me how love is always conditional and there are always blue-prints to work my soul into a frenzy. How she loves, it doesn't exist. How I shovel dirt and show no love when I'm devastated in my character as a person. Go away, don't love me. Your love is my poison-pen. You choke me up and stick your thorns into my bleeding corpse. And you rape me with your wrongness about me, and how you slide your dagger in and twist it and make me gasp for breath, as you look in my dying eyes and laugh and spit in my face. Leave me alone, in your pool of poison-pen, as you cee me suffer and you stand over me, laughing at me, pushing me down with your fingers. I can no longer love you. If I cee you walk down the street, you are just another stranger passing me by. You are not myn anymore. You killed me with you and I'll never see you again. I'm so stupid. For believing in it. For even considering that we could *ever*, have a normal ter-ter relationship. Showing me, how you *really* feel, was your projectile poison-pen and spit, went into my lungs and I can't breathe, and you watch as I lay down and take my last breath. Always killing me, when it's you're living half. Here *and* there. I'm finally awake to it. And know, that you'll never be you, the way we were when they were friends, and how when you protected me, and now, you're my abuser. At least I didn't leave, like you did yours. You abandoned them and left them. And now, she doesn't love, and now, I don't. He's *NOT*, **NOT**!, *yours*. I have to be angry when I write this or else it won't be authentic. You know me as selfish and cold and a user, so that's what you want? That's what you'll get. But, and and, there's the flip side of being so angry that I walked out of your house due to that you know *nothing* about me. Or you just didn't give a shit. Hurt the ones you love, right? So here I write you, this angered Love Letters, of how deep you cut into peoples souls and rip their flesh like a cannon besieging their captives. You surround me with play love, then you go for blood and tears. So many words to ploy with, right? How when you said I was empty with no love, and that you don't believe in me for who I am to you. I think my words are okay, with you gaining momentum as going on a merry-go-round with; ready, set, go, and shoot me in the heart, many tymes, and yet I stood there, professing my love for you and your half. But it's the wrong half I'm fighting for. The half I knew and loved, is already in His Arms already, but I try so hard to love the shell that you left so many years ago. I must, love you from a distance and distants. I will no longer be your shooting range at close call. You live your lyfe, and I'll live myn. I can't be with this part of you anymore, for this can no longer be okay to abuse me with your violent thoughts of who you think I am and who you think I'm not. I'll never reach for you or for the person I wanted you to be.

Don't you worry. I love him. I will do my very best to love him, like he's never been loved before. I can't even imagine, the things he's going through right now. I feel that I failed him, and I'm so sorry. If he really loves me, then I won't make the same mistake twice. I'm going to love him, so much. Thank you for saying that. Because I need to hear your side. When he comes back, and I cee him for the first time, I'm going to hold him and never let him go. But, remember, I've never met him before. But knowing what I do know, there won't be a problem. Don't worry. If he loves me, for real, this is *it* for me. I'm done searching. I love him. I'm so sorry about what happened to him. I was devastated when he left. And I felt like a failed try, in saving him from a snake. I will love him. We got him. Well we almost have him. Don't worry we got him back, ok, not quite we have him, but we don't have him. I know that's confusing but you are gonna have to trust me. We don't have him but he can communicate with you. I love you! You won't believe what happened! This is truly amazing! Never thought it would happen at all. I think about you, all the tyme. I'm questioning myself and trying to make sure that I'm who I am, is who I am and not trying to be something I'm not. I'm waiting for you. So many questions left unanswered. Questioning am I really what I proclaim myself to be, is it real? I really don't feel worthy to be a role model, and am I? I want to tell you that, I'm always thinking of you. I miss you, like crazy. And I must say; I love you. So much on my mynd. You stay strong too, baby. I can't wait for the day when I can run to you and run into your arms. If that can even happen. I'm still praying for you, and for you to be released from where you are. Do you like lyfe here? Where is hell and what is it like there? Where is *your* world in comparison to each place? Is it up and down as the ratio of the world of up and down? How did you try or did you even want to come here? In you finding me. As I sit and think about all this. From an unknown kingdoms. So then, have you spoken to my late? Has he heard all my prayers? All my guilt I carried for over a decade and continuation? All my pain? All my personal anguish I still carry? . . . . So what made you come and look for me? Are you still in love with me? As I show you a side that I usually hide? I let you both down. I sent you there. Should I tell you that I had a flash of you in form? I saw your colour. That God has put something so random and centurys old traditions to aging. It's come to my attention, and now I get to write about it, and show you, yet another way or perspective to live as living proof it's real. I mean that would be pretty cool. As I bow in worship to the LORD, and write my heart. To love a new lyfe. To fall in love with my, myn. How did you even want to come here? In reference to finding me? How long were you were wandering here? What's it like to be that old? To be passed through the next ones to live this lyfe and to roam and visit and live in Paris. I live in my own imagination, and things come real. And none of this is true. But! So, you tell me, is it? I'm sorry, but I just can't tell you. But I have the willingness to learn everything and know everything in knowledge and to predict the future and be psychic and to know events through Christian visions, so I can let them know. Will You let me? So what happened back then? To make up sorts of things of curiosity? I mean did you ever dream of something so out there? That you just can't believe it, when someone says to you, you have to believe in something. So, then that's what I need to do. Meet me in my thoughts myn.

Thank you. Sometimes, most days, I feel pretty worthless and non-love-worthy. I hope that you know, that if this is meant to be, then I'm going to love him, with every beat. I will accept him for who he is and what he comes with. Friends, family and the like. I miss you so much . . . I miss you and I've never even met you. How is this come to pass? Today was the day I buried my late husband, fourteen years ago. And my thoughts go towards you now, but I try to remember every detail in his funeral. My perspective. I only remember bits and pieces of the day as a whole. And I must tell my story. Please let me express my sorrow on this day, so long ago. I don't remember waking up and dressing and going to the funeral home. I remember standing outside and smoking as people arrived. I only remember fragments of that. I was lost. I lost my way, my reason for living on without him. The love of my lyfe. Even despite on his temperous moods sometimes, and him crossing boundarys and hurting me. I know, I say to one of my best friends. That's why I wrote it. So I recognized that he is your dislike. So, go to the next Letters, because I have to write. I was seated in against the wall, with the isle opposite, with his casket up front, because I kept getting up to stand against your coffin. But I didn't cry. It was a closed casket funeral. He looked too bad for an open coffin. Now, I'm terrified by dead bodys and coffins. More than snakes. His pictures sat on the closed lid. People were talking, but I don't know what they said. I didn't understand. What just happened here? My heart bled onto the spot I stood. Draining, like he did. I was no longer alive. I crawled into a ball and sank in blackness for over a decade, of pain, sobbing uncontrollable, couldn't breathe crying. The guilt I still carry. And there's nothing I can do about it. Then songs would come on and I wouldn't know what to do. I wanted to scream you alive. No one could console me. Don't touch me! Get away from me! I spoke at your funeral and I told an infamous story. When we went canoeing and I tipped it over and we fell in the freezing water, where it was so cold that I couldn't breathe. And that's what happened to me. The death whipped me with poison in my dreams, my nightmares, of death and murky green and dark-dreary greys. My body whipped my bed. In the continuation of this story. And so now, fast forward fourteen years. Then I meet this total stranger, this gorgeous, captivating eyes in his sitted position. That you've given me a new beginning to a lyfe of impossibles and now, I'm ready. I'm ready for this new lyfe, with you. So going back to his funeral for another minute. Then I stood there, looking at all your pictures and not prepared for what came next. The service ended and I accidentally started collecting all his pictures, but then my mom took me in her arms and told me that it wasn't tyme to take his pictures off his casket yet. So I went to the wall and rolled into the wall and my mom comforted me. Then the Directors came down the isle and both stopped and bowed at him and then took you away to the Hurst car, and we were the last ones to arrive when the pallbearers were placing him on his burial spot. The hole under him, lays his final resting place. Where I would go as much as I could. When the graveside service was happening, I only remember fragments. Where they were laying their sand on his casket after I just dumped it into a pile and others following me did a Cross. I couldn't take that moment back, then you were in the ground and people were leaving and my dad carried me up the hill and was my wheelchair. Then, this is the day I started living my own lyfe. Without you.

Dear LORD; Father God, I live for You and Your Calling upon my lyfe. New and marvellous things are coming real. Can You continue to bless me and my writings ? and creating new and wonderful, fiction-non-fiction books? Can You tell him to tell me the secrets regarding the universe/galaxy? I know I won't know everything, but can You show me? Will You let me come to lyfe, my unlocking? LORD, I pray for him right now to give him strength, in Your Mighty Hands and show him mercy, and this is his lifes journey and he must experience it. Why shouldn't I believe it? Can you only imagine me not showing you anothers mynd? LORD, I pray for letting my creativity and imaginations be real. Make all my storys bring new lyfe to here. So I bow my head in sombre prayers and beg for more. That I get more into that headspace. And share more of my imaginations. Father God, thank You for him, for S. Nhojanders. I pray for his soul, that You go down there to hold him and tell him it's almost over. For You to show him his lyfe, he must be there to be a part of this. Make all my storys come to lyfe, in all their forms and coats and firs of expensive tastes. LORD, let the unknown kingdoms out to cee if we could keep habitat. Like in Paris. So getting back to the kingdoms that is open to the person who's being transported from one lyfe to another lyfe to live your lyfe. What does/do it/they look like? Can you see heaven ? in broad day light ? with everyone waving at you from your travel into space ? where if it was me, I'd open the sealed lid to the space place where it was and I'd stay. So in the galaxy, there *must* be other planets, with suns and moons but just in different parts of the universe. And so, what if I made the transformation into my next body and travel throughout space and tyme with the freed creature from another worlds in it's own. It goes farther than this page of silly words put together by just another perspective. LORD, how many are there? Am I, worthy of telling the storys of beyond here? Can I be creative enough? Do I have the correct information to pass it along? So, I open up your mynd, so you can look upon yours and do some thinking. And when I take you upon this journey, I put you in a lull. And show you another lyfe, that you didn't even knew lived. That's what this lyfe does. It closes off who you really are, and where you come from. To find your destiny and walk the Path Given. But some of you have forgotten, but that's okay, because this lyfe can sometimes be a bit fuzzy in your memory and because it's too confusing in this world. So, Father God, tell me about all Your Creatures. What do they look like? Are they beyond our knowledge? Do they have horns and popping out veins and claws that grab at things with seven arms that grab people and place them on earth, then stretch their arms back to their homes? Are they a cats who can't decide on their forms so they change right in front of you? To become anything they think about, like a blinking light. Do they fall in love like we do here? Tell me about the way they love there. Have they lived the human lyfe yet? Where there is pain and suffering and loss and death, and the happiest days in your entire lyfe cycles? I can only imagine love, everywhere else beyond earth. A whole lyfe, with no interruptions beside the LORD. Always listen when He calls out into His galaxies! Never speak over Him! Can the breeds mix together? And make new Creations? Hmmm, I wonder if there's another planet like this one on the opposite sides of the universe, and there's more planets. *Make* someone travel beyond the farthest point so far. To see Heaven and all the people there that you loved. Look, Heaven is right their!

I love the nighttime. It's my favourite tyme of the day. And I'm so happy. You're coming to cee me, you're both coming to visit now. I'm so happy for you both, I really am. I'm so glad we're good friends. Your friendship is one of my best friendships that have lasted a long tyme. The night brings new storys of what can you prove to me? Of you unmasking yourself to me, of this invisible cloak you're wearing. You're there, but you're not there. You're my ghost love affair. Shared as the same person who's never left me and stayed by my side as I grieved. That you're so close to me. You pushed through me and got my attention. And the almost spelt wrong word, but how? You're a fictional character. A white wolf. Who captivated me and followed me to my carlot there. Where he came to cee me and for me to cee him and rocked me and settled in me. Can you hear me? Can you hear my heart? Can I send this to you via mynd control? To feel a jolt of a bolt of surge bass threw my body into attention. Yes, hello. I am to wear my pink blush as one of my trade marks of my face and my black cornered eyes. And the puff too. I'm sorry, my attention has diverted away from constants. I live my secret worlds, and I love it there. Do please tell me about that worlds. To ask more questions and invent new writings, with Holy Water protecting me from outside the doors. And you must be wondering why the recent strange worlds entries/postings? With this being his presents now, about him, yes, of course. So come on, as I tug on your sleeve to pull you into my private room in my head, that is every shape and size. Let's hang out and talk about future worlds of lyfe and more lives as you howl at the moon. The peach moon tonight, was exquisite LORD. I've seen a lot of moons, but nothing like this in a really long tyme, months. I bow my head in prayer and I pray begins. LORD, I hope I'm writing what I'm supposed to be writing about? Standing under the peach moon. Let my mynds flow out of my human body and step onto the path to the moons and suns that can't hurt us. But I can't tell you what you'll look like. Another secrets that may never be unsaid. What does that even mean? As I pardon myself from chit-chat, for I'm focused on this, telling you about the mystic events that are to follow. To never wake me from my dreams, to let me live in unconsciousness and to rush good-bye as I want to go. I can't feel closed in or laws of locked doors of not being able to leave whenever I need to, for I'm claustrophobic of space needed to grow up on earth, due it's who I am. My mynd needs space. As it could be my poison. To show on my resume for my next lyfe that this is who I'm supposed to be. A free spirit, walking to my next step. Where I can close the gates to my privateness that I have for this lyfe. Where I can enter with ease, every time, and walk in my own living room going into more rooms of large size. To let me escape into all of the corners and cracks, to know every part of my house. Cee, future happening here people. I walk threw it with grace and me. To look outside to see the midnight sun, shining down on me in the darkness of my daytime. When everyone leaves the door open and they creep in. Under my will of course. LORD, keep Your watch over my home tonight, as my future says to me now. To live only as He wants me to, with style of me. Where I'll look through my dome at the sky, and try to imagine every planet, every star, every moon. To head-bang in fun, in nods of well done. Well, my ghosts are calling me . . . . I'm just kidding. But you wanted to believe me? To think something else that what it's written about. Come on, come sit next to me.

You've stolen me into your world. A look, into your windows at your pane. You're an invisible love force. You have fed me grains and now I am healthy. To be the last one on the shelf, needed to find it's home, for something necessary. For a little girl to use it's as it's purpose for you. Will it do it's job ? for its intended needs? I'll find out soon enough. Well, hopefully. I'm sorry, I have to cee your face again . . . one moment please. Am I sure about this? Hell ya! I want him so bad. My heart *aches* for him, for I haven't even seen his face, or height yet. Or heard his voice yet. Is it dark and horsey with a rasp? Is it highish? Is it downish? Is it monotone? Is he tall? Is he normal? Since he was different in his childhood. Will you be myn forever? There he is. The face that stole my eyes, that encircled my heart and made yourself at home. Another one. Lucky you. To sink you into my thoughts, to try to rationalize this and to make sence of it all. To look in from an actual form, instead of being in visible. Which I *am,* and that's why people leave me. I become nothing in my eyes, when I question their length of our relationship. Will you let me run my fingers through your fyre? I don't know the reason why I love you so. How I say your name when I miss you into the air around me and that I breathe alone. To leave and find you in this big world of circles, and stops and ends. To collapse in your arms due that I can't stand without shivering. To know, with no doubt that you love me for who I am and things I don't want to bring with us. Such a struggle with sugar, the addictingness of it and how it's my main diet. So do you believe me? Or is this another tail? A deceit under duress? Will you come with me please? I want to take you to a place far away. I open the next door and we arrive on a platform and the water in front of us. It's sunset and a flying sailboat with full sails flys by us, and we hop on. You take my hand and you say you're so happy to be with me, and then we count as we exit the boat and go on on our own. Stranger, to my new love for you, show your features to my features and mix and match the ones to follow us, in their own lifes to *their* stranger of acquaintances that grow into love by only words and different worlds of my mynd of upbelieve. So take a sip of the drink, and go where it's supposed to go, down into your body, to refresh your energy. As the flavour only lasts so long until it must go down to give you excess digestion to recycle into the ground to keep a green Ireland world. That eagerness and urge of grabbing you, inside your picture and show you how I miss you. But I only get one surface. As the bass strums to the beat of the voices singing, loudly. Everyone is dancing and rhythm and dance. Are you there? I scream in your ear and breathe on your mystery fyre. And then when we get home, we madly make love. But it's only a thought, only an image in my mynd. What does eight . . . . zero mean? Something I'll know one day? Is it a combination to the other secret door I must open? Well, I'm an idiot to it now, but when I find out, it'll be as important to me as to you. So I go back to the face that I looked at months ago and lived as I had to in protection, but then, one day, I changed my mynd. I needed to know this face, this man. I wanted to make him go away, so it was just a face of a picture of a model posing. Then it came to me that this was an actual person wanting to protect me. Okay so, he came back after I had him, and now, he's an in visible field in my eyes and hold him. The only way I know how to right now, through my words. My silly words that invent words and storys, to make *you* come alive in me.

I'm going *crazy* sitting still, waiting. I'm *just desperate*, like a normal insane person would think and rely on myself to get through yet, *another* love cycle. In my own film that *I've* created for *myself*. As like writing on the walls, writing on my jeans, toilet paper, anything, that will take my pen marks from the tips. *So many writings*. What do they all mean? Can *you* tell me? Out come the thoughts of a pink room, with padded walls and my arms are sewn in the back of me. I yell, from the inside of the doors, and scream, HELP! *Untie me,* so I can write and not have a heart failure in my mynds, of pages and pages of untold truths/lyes/storys/lyfe! My head feels like it's going to explode. Please! Someone help me! As I loose energy and fall to the ground, with the cell door locked with no exit signs near. I need out of here. Mental heads, I need out. Make me fly. Through *that* window, with the bars sealed for my safety. *My safety*? They're keeping me *prisoner* here, *locked up*. Can *you* help me? I wriggle in my hugging position. Tears flow down my cheeks and I'm unable to wipe them up off the ground and rewind them back into my eyes, from a situation that did *not* happen. I was crazy. I was out of my mynd. What could I do, but in glory? I start screaming. My adrenaline is upto par again. I scream, and scream, and wriggle out of my straight-jacket. Where the buckles do up in the back. LET ME OUT OF HERE, MAY I SHOW YOU MY STRENGTH!! Ya, right. The strength of how long they won't come to show me my way out. That's what *that* means! I crumble to the ground, into a little huddle of my many persons who make things up and make stupid faces to the strangers on my street. The water started overflowing and the people downstairs put their broom through my basement floor. I write messages all over them, and I repeat; I will not suffer, for I am in God's worlds. He makes me love Him, by sacrificing myself. I picture them, all of them, in my head, as my dolls and I was playing dressup. AND, AND, AND!!! I'm a triple threat. I can tie, punch, *and* bleed. I come back into my reality, and stand up and look out to the hallway and scream for someone to hear me. Tear out of me! Save me! I know my mynds are entwined like picket wire with sharp pointy things that cut you when you escape. I turn my lights on and find my way in the darkness. It's a game of my mynd and I'm up against myself. Will he love me again? *Will he*? After knowing what I have done? I'm not normal but as normal as they are too, but in my mynds. There are against me. Did I say that right? What did I say? There are against me? Oh yes. That's right. I bang my head on the door glass, and my head starts hurting. HELP me . . . . I was distracted and now I can't think anymore. Look what you made me do! This is wrong! I can't run my fingers through my matted and bloody hair. AAAAAAAAAHH!! I pound my head on the door. I went all around my room to shed my blood everywhere and then, finally, I heard someone unlock the first door. I scrambled to my feet. Blood poured down my face and I smiled for someone was finding me. The nurse opened my door, and saw all the blood I rubbed all over the padded walls, over my bed, the door. There were two men. They said some things like; it's okay, calm down. What's wrong? They looked around at all the blood, and took out a long needle. One of the men had me and the other one gave me a shot of something. NOOO! Please, I'm not crazy! As I'm being shaken and I open my eyes and realized it's a dream. I sit up and cry into my palms for I know something bad is going to happen. I'm not ready to handle anything right now.

LORD, I plead for mercy on my soul. For mixing up good and stuff, and trying to do the right thing by You. For shaking up downstairs a little, and now it's on the run. I beg for forgiveness for my sins upon this situation and pray for grace, forgiveness, and running really fast away from him. To delete all messages to lead to no proof of communications from one to the other. To hide from the wicked. Sad that all of its gone now, just like last year on this day. To remember the loved ones that have gone away to another place and only memorys and cherished photos live on. LORD, intervene into this situation and take control of the surroundingness of everything now and protect the innocent. For You answered prayers and took one of Your Chosen ones back. How my blind faith, must be overshadowed by fear and others distastering our lives as we have to live them. For others to medal in our business is not cool. How now, stop communication with her, due to it, its tragic. And to know who she is to me now, I can't wait till the day when I get all three, with just me and my future. All for loves sake could all of this happen, and destroy what they all have worked so hard for to NOT happen, happened. To live the proof that God does exist, and He *is* Listening, but. But, so now, I just have to keep praying for evil to disperse and leave them and for them to make a pack of four, to make the power of one, and stir up the else in tyme for saving your souls, and bringing lyfe, to lyfe. And how I wonder if you've found your fourth member yet? Have you begun? Have you started chanting at the moon? Make smoke surround you in warding off evil spirits? For through words I will be yours. I must go and climb to reach up and grab A Hand for rescuing, so the next step is to follow. To feel sad on this day for all around. To remember my losses of their importance to me, of only three days difference. To continue to fight it and come back to and for resolution. To have the words that we spoke back and forth, just gone, just by a click of a button. To never have those words back, and the attachment and I must unattach and not let important words of love and devotions, just disappear and never to be seen again. For what an answered prayer many days ago. Of keeping notes, and placing them in plain view, so those words have been kept in my sacred hearts. To live those moments, I'd never say; what a waste. I'm sad today, for the loss of so much. From what I thought was good one day a long ago, is now at pass. And now it's to live through which is and will build you. It makes you stronger. How I was given no warning, of the consequences of our actions, as us trying to live, to live on. Bring out the wrecking ball and say what you're going to say, and just bring it. I can handle it as I say it with ongoing caution. How your determination must play out in this. Become great! Leave your legacy, in whatever you do. Give your gift of your property, be worth it. Why you shouldn't you live anywhere? And I'm not talking about the people who can't. Because there *are* people who are less fortunate than I am. I want to change the world. I want to share *my* storys. To build and keep building my lyfe to the top of the mountains I've been climbing for so long, to reach for this day in tyme. How remaining strong, has changed my lyfe, but sometimes shadows come and knock me down sometimes, but all my Strength, hasn't always been flowery and paisley. I've had to make some pretty important decisions to get me to today, to remind the world to open the curtains and bow in your play, where Strength is *your* story too. Hear them, and Sit Right Next to them, and say, Yes, My child, I hear you . . . . LORD! . . . . I pray.

"Royal Rooms"

April 23rd, 2011

As I escape into my heightened scences, I want to keep my promise when I say I'll never leave you my angel. I will never leave you for if you came with me, we'd never leave each other, but is that the way it's supposed to be? To know what I know and the secrets that make me me. Hello gorgeous. What are you waiting for? Carve me into your eyes and keep me in your thoughts everyday. And everything that follows these words comes my power. My Power. This is where I'm strong my love, did you know that? Growl at me and roar me awake and shake me alive in my senses. To know that one day in years to come, we'll go through the black holes and jump from one lifetime to the next, and show you, finally what they're meant for. And where they go, from one lifetime to another, and another planets for you to live yet. Where we find each other, every time during our human lifetimes on these different planets. How in one lifetime, I will be your mermaid and you can be my reason for coming into a different form for you, to share with you our lifetimes. And you keep saving me from traumas of a rector scale of nine point nine rector disasters. You take us through many passage ways to live a lifetime ago and how we just happen to say, hello. Where I can't not think of you every time I breathe. You know? To love this much? Only good things can come from it. Where I'll continue to open the doors and ask that He, my LORD, Protect it and whatever happens, happens. I'm human this round. And may I might ask ? how she found us ? from another lifetime and she brought us back together. Well? How's my story so far? Am I showing how much faith I have? To create in you, a story, to tell you of a great love affair, and when you find the reason to your, to being. For thanking God for creating my majic that I write with to make a story come real. And you're not, but I accept you for everything. When I'm waiting for you? And one day, I'll see you again and we'll know. To live for our love for each other. For God to hear our begs for death to come into contact with this person again. The battles I've had with good and evil and if. That's all I can say; is if. My world must remain private in my public speech. In my invitation to take a seat in my royal rooms. Let me once again, hypnotize you and take you to what love should be in your lifes too. And it's all been for you my beloved. To take the shadows away from my blockaid of dust and clutter; when I say. For my power with a love like this. For our sole situations that have us together again, for more love. May my heart speak to you, to make, you real. For you to just appear, from nowhere, into my lyfe and capture me and put me under catatonic mynd-blowing, in having to be patient. So, I took a moment to let it all soak in and remember that this has to be. I know, I know, what I want and what's really *gonna* happen, are two totally different things. Don't I know *that*? To share the only connection like ours in a world like this . . . maybe? And you must always know that Jesus, was born in Bethlehem. The City of David. All I have is; if and my faith in the LORD. To remind you, of who I am, someone to tell you storys of unknown kingdoms. To press open in a digital world. To remind you, that He gave you them. So He wants you to enjoy them. Remember Him everyday, thank Him for your lyfe and the lives that surrounds you, to party, to have fun, to suffer loss and tragedy. He made this for you. For you to remember where you come from. Somewhere else. From far away, brought everything I know that's real and not real. For it's for You. For You to come and wrap me in Your Loving Arms right now, as I am sad in everyway until I know for sure.

We're all trying to put the lyfe puzzle together LORD. Like You're the Chessmaster and we're all trying to play the game and figure it all out. Even legends are struggling. How on earth, would I even know, that this would happen for me? For all of us? It's like we have to move around pieces to fit the pieces together to make our lyfe filled with purpose. How we're colliding all together and maybe lyfe can't work like this. With the earth, and the supernatural worlds banging together, is it supposed to be like that? As I pray for solitude and letting both, and all worlds, live as one. And this is because of me? I love telling storys of legends and supernatural, and think of all the scopes of my imagination, in telling these tails. Let the *illusion*, of these worlds be real. Why not? Find out who the Creator is of such an important part of the history of an important piece to make who wears it. I need to bring wind, fyre, ayr, and earth together, in one, and fight the battles for innocent lives and now and understand all the fragileness of it all. To write, about how everything works, and to be cautious. Praying all the tyme, to the Father, who made all of this for us. To make our lives interesting with lessons and curves with turns and corners with rocks and hills and blockades to knock you over so you can get back up again, to knock the next stick down. To have control of your lyfe from any others who want bad things for you. To be open, and to bring in spirits, that relax you and calm you in a turbulent situation. To be who you are to the world, to God, to people around you who love you and will protect you. To make any contact viable. To develop a language that only you know with God. So, with the ayr that passes me, send my prayer to Him, to Him who Hears me, and bring to lyfe a lyfe that is forgotten about, and one day, someone wrote about it, and the wind and ayr heard and made it so. To maybe piece back the worlds together, who's made it hard to know the right things to do. Now, close your eyes. Concentrate on your breathing. Listen to my voice. The words of a world only in others dreams. I keep waiting for the knock, to ask a wanna-be-shaman, a wanna-be supernatural, wanna-be, something of diligent purposes, to help, to come to aid and to rescue. To be offered something with thank you that follows the kind gesture. To continue to grow into who I am and what I want to be and become, who's closer to the unknown worlds that are clashing and crashing together. What good tyme is for this to happen? She does that, he does this, and I do this and that. Into one ball, that bounces on the fingertips to the next person in line. The ball keeps going to the next one, and then the next one, for the right person to take the ball in their hands and carry it with care where only that person knows and has the answers. To finish what they started in the first place. Be proud in taking charge of your lyfe. Don't let the evil one take your hand and let him show you the way, because that's not it. That's not the answer. Be smart. Take a bite in lyfe, let the bite be filled with answers, and know what questions to ask, as the fruit will fill you, and as you put the Armour of God on. Stand in truth, justice, with the power of God. So when the forces of evil come calling to you, you can stand with God, right there. He says; Therefore put on the full armor of God. So that when the day of evil comes, you may be able to stand your ground, and after you have done everything, to stand. Stand firm then, with the belt of truth buckled around your waist, with the breastplate of righteousness in place, and with your feet fitted with the readiness that comes, wear the helmet of salvation and fight with God.

The object of such devotion. Everything I love, within my private lyfe, is learning everything, loving everything and everybody. I want peace and unity, and God, is my Number One. I've always believed in my dreams and that when I'd have very real, lucid dreams, I always knew they all meant something. So to do this, would be everything and completion for me and my lyfe. Complete healing, with lyfe my way. With Him guiding me, in every directions. I want White. I want to find my others. To know everything needed to know about everything, and how now, have reasons for why I agree to everything. I mean EVERYTHING. There's VERY few things, that I don't agree on. So now it makes scense. So then, the next door opened, so I can help *you* find who *you're* looking for, but only for good. No brats or trouble makers. No bullies allowed. Has to be a safe environment. For *all* worlds. No sonic lazar shooter to create mass destruction, because I won't let you in if that's the case. Like at a bar or a club, members only. To do this, . . . I have to talk to her about it. I wonder what they're both going to say about it. And to pretend that's the next secret to hide is all the knowledge. One might be called. He or a person will become seriously ill mentally or physically during this calling. So then I started thinking about learning, again, but this tyme, have a title I deserve. To listen to my Calling, and they will then realize, or be informed of their calling. Once the person begins their training and accepts their calling, they will be freed of theirs. This calling is not a request, but rather a divine command. Always listen to God. He's the One Who Created you. The Creator. As like myself, may be raised in a Christian family which rejects the path. But to ignore the call would not be acceptable. Most cultures believe that rejecting a call is a fatal mistake. I've been praying, searching, listening, and being a survivor, and surviving the call is what gives the experience needed to begin helping others. And then I closed the book. It was infuriating me. I was screaming at it, don't go in the room! Don't do it! And I couldn't put it down. I slammed my hand over my mouth and eyes popped out of my head. I knock my fists together. I have to tell her, and adopted into my own, smile. I want this, so bad, to finally know where my faith is taking me, to end the searching and finding, and finally know, what I've known all along, but waiting to catch up to my lyfe being me, in all my strength, in all my fight, in all the knowledge I have and will continue to, grow in know. To find my power once again. To trust in It. To follow my hearts desires in the others and next worlds. To become a leader in knowing how powerful my prayers are to Him. Everything that comes out is truth, and I will continue to wear and carry my Armor, and stand up and float into knowing farther than my gravity here. To understand why I'm here. To practice who I am. To never stop learning, what I so desperately want to know. I always look up in my private tyme. To not think that all this is for nothing. That the claw marks on the mountain side show the bottom feet footprints for me when I jumped up to the peek and sat down and never stop praying and talking to God. That's what I want. To jump to my peek, as you should jump to your peeks, and sit, and wait, and listen, and cry, and laugh, and think about all the people you love and know that what really matters, is love. Love someone who you loath. Pray for inner strength to ask yourself about *their* lives, and what *they* go through in having to be a bully or why you clash. Then get rid of them, but from your thoughts, not your soul or heart, because without them, you couldn't change the future.

As a young child, I had many high fevers from illness and sickness. I spent a lot of my tyme sleeping. But I don't remember my dreams, but I had many dreams. I became ill when he died and I suffered, in every ways. So, cer, with no name for your privacy. So to be *this* calling, doesn't really surprise me. I love dreaming and getting the messages and I love visions and their revelations. I take them very seriously actually. With combinations of both illnesses and fevers developed that membrane juice needed to swallow up what I know I am now. I want to go into trance. I want beat so I can go to the Middle, Upper and Lower, to know what I need to do what I want to and progress in who I am and what I can do with my power of God and with humbleness I take this path and hear it as my Calling. To practise and to heal. I've had many visions that have come true. Hot Pink. The room was filled with hot pink and white filled up to the top balloons. And cee how I can change within a moment? And people were getting ready to yell, surprise! On Holy Groundings. I want to share with you something that's unknown. So, just trust in the majic and use the fungi to feed the ground it's medicine and it catches fyre and carrys to right here, in me. So, Cer, please except me as one of many who call on your services. For the purpose why I'm here and I've survived death and being very ill. Ahhahhahh! That's so funny! As I slap my hand on my knees, and laugh my ass off. Ohh . . . that's funny . . . To tell you what I am inside my private lyfe with my intence faith in God. And He's Called me to *right now*, to make me figure out another piece to my future on my own. I will hold this with me, like the private lives of the royals, so I can serve my purpose in helping people. I will be a touch partner. Can you hear me? Are you understanding? This is for you, Cer. To get to know me, and what I can do with my power of my Deity and my supernatural worlds to lyfe and open doors. To search for my guides *now*, so when I join this next lyfe step, I'll be prepared. I have no lineage, this is a Calling. To be a healer of the soul, to help cross into their next lifetimes and show them the next door and whish them well and see them again, when they live that lifetime. I want to know everything and I found the book of life very interesting or the a kash a. And I have to show you the secret passages to my next story. So you can read my application in code, cer. The esoteric of it all, if you can understand. That there are so many worlds that live in my imaginations of ways of criss-cross and under and over where they pass by so fast. With God blowing in the wind of stillness and blow you to your next door. He blows you a kiss and says something like, I Love you, My child. I won't forget You Father. I love You Too. I reach a dence forest with many emerald trees with blades of grass blowing in God's breath of tranquility. How I take comfort in this prayer tonight LORDGod. As we go back into the forest, where all the creatures lived with sorceress protecting their home as special creatures you find only when you've been accepted to join you Cer. I want to ride on a Nova's belly and spin and twirl in the space wind for where I won't be chilled. So, take me on as a soul reaching for wholeness, so I can extract, and meet my animal, so I can ride on the back with just the mane, no saddle, ride fast to catch up with my soul mate. To transform into another, in astral and in the many panes of my cave, where I called it this before I even knew about this just a little while ago. Where my soul lifts out and jumps in lineup for the next door. Jump in and thank you for letting me your shaman.

I want to go to the under and upper terrene. Escape into ecstasy of a Perfect Place, and Perfected Colours. I will not enter middle worlds. Not yet. I'm not ready yet, not even close. So, I tell you, I want to heal souls and get them back to happyness in the lyfe before the afterlife and different worlds of the supernatural worlds. I want to help, heal lost souls. Do you *really* love me? Like *full-heartedly*? That you *trust* me, more than *anyone* on this earth? Answer these questions carefully, because everything is in your court now, whether you want to or not, know. What I am, who I am, what I can do, and all my now and coming future gifts? To share with you, my deepest secret from everyone, for a long time to come. Because I'm not who you think I am, You may *never* love me again. You'll throw me as far away from you as possible. Remember, you have been *chosen*, to be my friend. That *wasn't* an accident. You have to do this with some selfishness to taking on such an important role in this and in my lyfe. I have a secret lyfe that you don't know about, and it could be anything. It could be the worst thing that you could come in contact with. Quality tyme is sometimes better than quality. They're so beautiful today, we're beautiful today. All of us. Okay, I've made peace with my heart. Like you and me, so I go back to the secret I have to share with you. I go and take souls home, and to build a good name in world. If you want me to tell you, you must believe EVERY *single* words. If you don't absolutely, then I can't tell you. I spent/d most of my time asleep and most of my lyfe has been at and in sleep. So I dream, a lot. I'm connected to that world, and now, I'm going to be able to journey through tyme and space, and when I come back, I'll tell you all about it. You've already read it. It's a secret message and secret codes in my head that only I know about it and keep it wrapped up with nice pretty bows and ribbons. I have new gifts. I have newness with hands lifted to God and my belief in Him and His Power with a twist to an ancient cereromonys of a sole to make a new spin. I love you, my mirror, and I'm referring to earthly friends and the ordinary world, not the no ordinary world. S. This is my lyfe and I can't say no. This is where God and I are teamed up with His beings in every universe, and without Him, I would not exist, and so, this is where everything has led to. I have and want purpose for my lyfe, and if I can help lost souls and be the best one in the world with a new gust of wind behind me, pushing me forwards to take the next step. I know the order and when this will happen, for I'm in on the secret. I must say, listen to the plant. Let it talk and connect. It's doing it's job and the grass will grow, the soil will be moist and the flowers will grow. Trust in me like you trust in your garden. It will grow to feed you, nourish you, and you know that you'll get fruit and vegetables, so, I'm like that. I've always wanted to be part of it, for my entire lyfe, it's all I think about. But now I have children and love remains here for a while now and then and then. So, I will do what I need to to prepare, and get ready for the intense journey I must take next. To help people find themselves and piece them back together again. With a new lyfe they can live with, with confidence in who they are as a person and have respect for their individual lives. Like some of my dear friends. This is part of me and I've found some of the clues to show me my newest path to journey in a trance with the LORD following me the whole tyme and showing me messages to search the quest of knowledge to assist you to *get,* the helpers. *Will you,* trust me? *Will you,* believe in me?

Everything changes when something traumatic happens in your lyfe. *Remember* the abuse, and how it changes you. To admit it, is sometimes, the hardest part. This is not a light subject in my eyes. Abuse is abuse. Whether it's because you have to sit in your closet to be able to talk to people, because you're afraid that someone could hear you. To be brutally attacked in the safety of many houses that couldn't stop your attack. Whether its mental abuse, verbal abuse, emotional abuse. Or, physical, raped, slashed, it's still abuse and I want to bring an equal ruling on this matter. To many children, ___AND___ teenagers, who are being viciously attacked and I can't do anything about it because I'm just a bystander. There should be a law protecting the innocent of mental and emotional abuse like someone who was viciously beaten and led to bleed to death. How scaring a child and threaten them of fear of finding out you've been talking to someone outside the home. How safety is a main priority with this type of abuse. Hiding from and keeping secrets from whispering protected services, for them to help you get away from your abusers. How this is JUST UNACCEPTABLE! The scars of emotional abuse scars you so deep. Just like a whip on your back. To NOT speak up, BECAUSE you're scared of the consequences, and what can happen to the victim of verbal abuse. To live with no self-esteem and when you finally reach a peace in your lyfe, that little voice inside your head, turns against you and you're reminded again what a waste of ayr I am, and if your own don't love you, who do you think will? Me. I'll love you. If your own ever told you that why couldn't you be someone else, or they wake you up and says, get up you're wasting my day, or you look for support and they knock you down, or threaten you. If you ever tell anyone, I'll deny it, and then when you're gone, you're ten times worse off. How dare I? Excuse me! How dare I stand up for rights against verbal, mental and emotional abuse? I want to change the law against verbal abuse. I pray for answers. For all of you who were scared by words, that tore your mind out in your agonizing screams, to save you from oozing infection from your heart and soul and how it's clouded your mynd of your own judgements of how this type of criminal is punished. For the wicked who supports abuse, I pray for your soul and have mercy on your soul. But hey, it's just my opinion. But this has to stop. It infuriates me. I'm so angry about this. Bullies. I'm *sick* of them. And they come in all shapes and sizes. Both young and old. They think that they can just push you around, and become a coward behind their own masks. To show you their cowardisms through their own traumas and push you down in the process of their paving the wheels that flattens you and crushes you, and makes you die inside. It makes you bleed and makes your head bow in utter sadness. And know that they can never get away with abusing you again. Whether you're a child, whether you're a teenager, whether you're an adult, mental abuse is just as harmful as a bullet to your head, or a monster brutally raping you. It's not physical abuse, no, but why do you think some children commit suicide? The scares, the threats, the underwhisper under their breath when they walk away from you. The fear of telling a bully anything, can lead to more mental anguish of a future mental beating across the head. Just put a gun to my head, instead of a slap across the body part that you've chosen for this particular insult, your lies, your betrayl, your games. I want to pass a new law, to protect children against verbal, mental, emotional abuse; The Natia Law.

I . . . slap across my face. I love . . . slap. I love you . . . slap. Give me wings to make me fly. Suicide. Someone of, someone in suffering. Suicide, something that I can't have. I can't accept that box with a pretty red velvet bow. It's gone *way* beyond repair. God, give me my future trances, I beg. As I put my praying hands upto my mouth, bow my head and close my eyes. LORD, not even love, can keep me here, but I do it, every day. As one day, this will be demolished. Okay, now laugh . . . Just kidding. I'm great. He can't run *fast* enough. He stumbles and carrys it when he needed it to. He runs, to the edge of the building and screams to God. Why *can't* I commit suicide? Who am I to come because of this? Just a tip and loss of balance. I can't get away from here fast enough, as he thinks of his fiancé. How she would never understand LORD! She's the only one I live for. I walk away from the edge for a moment and do some pretty hard praying tyme happen here. LORD! I'm scared of everything! I yell to the sky. I'm not anything to me. It's gone way *beyond* repair. She only loves what she *thinks* I am. She doesn't know me deep within. I run back to the edge. I look down and the streets were filled with cars honking and rushing to wherever they're going. Somebody! Look up! Catch me when I reach the bottom! To stand against something with no red letter. The letter is never red again for me. Where the world in my shoes are from a narcissistic view from the clouded judgement from getting drunk two nights ago. Who am I now? I stand on the edge of the ridge. I think of all the people who'd pat me on the back and say well done, Geoff. Slice it open a bit. Open up now, swallow the medicine. And I raise my hands towards God. LORD! Why can't love not exist?! My tears blur my vision. Why does love matter so much? No wonder the world is at war. Some of us are so maddened with sin and judgement and with everyday abuse. How can this change me, LORD?! I can't *repair* this damage! I yell and I start going horse. Why should I care when everything in lyfe is so wrong? Why should I care about my lyfe?! Hey LORD? Only bad can come from the seething anger my enemys feel for me. To never be aloud to come to the boil I need to feel! As I forget for a second as I stand looking down. It's so far down. Is it true? Will I think about my lyfe? As it flashes in front of me? Will I think about all the people I've sinned against? Will I think only of my fiancé? Where is my net, so when I fall, it won't hurt? Where my heart won't explode on impact of a car or a truck, or a garbage truck? Where my bones will explode and fracture in fragments and my head will split and bleed my selfunlove. I'm just a man. A person, that doesn't deserve a red letter. Standing ontop of a roof waiting my pending death, my suicide that I shouldn't be joining. I step down from the ledge and I sit on the pavement. I put my sobbing head into my hands. I sob. Why should I live? Why should I live? LORD! Answer me! I repeat those words in my head. The missteps I have taken to reach this last straw that took my lyfe. Do you understand now? How this, can be the only answer? That being just a man won't be a stereotype and for me to be strong all the tyme. How being just a man can be as rough as being a child dying from burning to death. Burning flesh, screaming in agonizing pain until I die from burning to death. To die with such scum build up throughout the years, that no red letter will ever be said to harm me from unprotected love. I show you that I am vulnerable, just because I'm a man. Do You get it God? I'm done taking pain from a colour of making me feel suicide about myself.

I'm so tired. Can I write a full Letters? I don't know. With a peek of interest, I continue to send you a message of renewal, of serene peace and tranquility. Knowing that it never left me in the first place. But I always feel this way when I get like that. Unpeace. Unserene. And the rest of the un's. So, I want to escape into your world. Tell me about your lyfe. Are you a student? A business professor? A lawyer? A mother? A parent in any form? A scientist? Tell me in your thoughts what you are and what you do? Are you tired too? I sit on a seat in the boat, as it goes mock one. Crashing into the waves. The sun shining down on my face that's blowing in the speeding by wind. I close my eyes. The boat speeds forward and we turn and the wind changes. To feel nothing except the cool breeze, the light of the sunshine, with all the hands that will hold me when I go, and make a statement as I leave. The sun of the sin for others out there. As I shove them down your throat and make it choke up. Damn, the rutter is going fast today. It's doing it's job in running the boat in that directions, out there in the ocean, with sailboats sailing by us. So many people are out on the water today, with their own reasons for being on the water today. Don't take care of me anymore with your ways of being a surf as I run from getting my feet wet, and I run to the beach. I laugh as I fall to my wet towel, and the sand kicks up from my feet. Everyone was building sandcastles, and spilling the water out of the bucket. May you get what's coming in whishes of a terrible crash as the cars crash into each other. Oh my God! I've been in an accident. There was white powder in the car. The radio was torn out of the dashboard. My steering wheel was destroyed. I was facing in the opposite direction of when I started. I get out and somehow and wander around in the middle of the street. No protection of coming cars towards me. As the sun shines on the boat, I feel the suns giving me a sunburn so I better cover up. Plus, I'm getting cold. The captain turns around to us and asks us above all the sound on the water and sounds of nothing else. Minus my thoughts. They're always loud with wickedness of a wronged slap as they phone the police. Get out of my head and let me enjoy the sunshine of a beautiful sunny day in the middle of summer. I yell, lets dive in! I take off my jeans shorts and my tee-shirt. I tighten my ponytail and say laughing, come on! Let's go! I lift my foot to the edge of the back stairs and I reach the water on my feet. One! Two! Three! I let go and I jump in the cold ocean water. I start paddling to the top to see them jump in after me. They all yell and jump in. The tyme when it was another tyme of sadness and sorrow that I was never allowed to feel, as you feel that lies were all that came out and then I dunk my head under the water and heard everyone laughing and splashing in pure joy. I did some backwards summersaults. And then finally came up for more ayr. The ayr that was poisoned when they looked for answers and comfort and then lyfe just went on and now someone has called my name and we all swim out away from the boat. Into a more distant trance that I have created for myself in the cove where water crashes against the sides and it echo's as we reach it and climb up on the ledge and are careful that the waves don't get too big. It's so calm with the fiery of dangers of what could come, so we, everyone swim back out of the mouth of the cove. Out of the nook, that's covered from tears cryed. Don't cry. Look at the water around you. Come on. She pulls me and we climb the tower to reach the handle to help us up. That was fun! We all laugh and shake off and wrap ourselves in our towels, for warmth from the sun.

He's dead. I celebrate this day, for this death of history. How he constructed deaths of thousands. he never deserved breath. And God was going to punish him for his sins against His world. How could I *NOT* write to the people who lost a husband, a wife, a daughter, a son, a father, a mother? And everyone that follows suit? I on behalf of many, I'm sure, but from me? My words won't bring them back or ease the pain of that catastrophic, torturous day, of horrific matters. Thousands lost their lives from a mass murderer who thought he was more powerful than God HIMSELF. I shake my head and say, no. I hope that this death now brings vain to those lost who the global unity when that fateful day happened in, 200_. I remember that moment well. Well, I'm not one hundred percent, but if I were to take an educated guess, I'd guess God won't deal with him in the best fashion that this piece of trash deserves. Rot him. From the inside and his screams make us laugh as of a comedy. I celebrate with and for you. I'm so sorry for your loss so many years ago now. When clouded judgement from something other than God. I pray for justice for you. I pray for peace in knowing that he was paid his debt. I do feel that he'll be suffering for a very long time for all His children who were murdered. I pray for letting go, LORD. That the survivors of this day can finally move on and raise that child that was left for you, as a Gift of your loved ones. I am PROUD, with the person in this tyme who took care of his people. He went on the bullet for his country. For what he believed in against violence. Everyone who was involved with solving the most hunted man in history. EVERY SINGLE ONE SOLE person who was involved in the hunting and killing him deserves greatness in their lives. Not saying that we'll have one hundred percent world peace, but one down, and hopefully not too many more, but some, to go. Thank You God, for hearing their crys for punishment. So much despair and I watched with the rest of the world as this took place and we too, watched your loved ones die and be slaughtered in explosions and collapses. I was fogged, I couldn't believe what I was seeing. What is this? Oh my God! What's happening mom? What?! And now, today, he's dead, and they have taken possession. Drop him in acid. Let maggots eat his scored flesh in his rotting bathtub grave, uncovered for crows to eat his eyes. This is a day for celebration. How can I be sorry for saying any of this? After what he did? I already mentioned how I would discard him. I'm sure many of you are shocked at this from me. I have feelings of anger for this. He started as a bully and ended up in hell. He was murdered in the victims of this day. And I'm sure many sad memorys came up today for many people. So many feelings to deal with. To remember the lost ones. ALL OF THEM! EVERY SINGLE ONE SOLE person who perished. I pray for good about ninety-nine percent. Minus today for this individual death. Now, we can move on and remember the souls in our children, that came from them to live *their* lyfe and go on in lyfe. Laugh again. Feel sunshine on your shadowed heart, now released from darkness from Victory. That the whole world got the national message of his death. Thank you, for doing a nation proud. Without your lyfe and your title, this capture wouldn't have happened in the way it was. You were chosen to take care of this mass mess that evil created. I will always remember this moment in tyme. God Bless and ALL OF THEM! EVERY SINGLE ONE SOLE who rid of someone who deserved to pay for his sins against a world filled with God. But hey, it's just my opinion.

Are you pleased so far? Have I taken you on many cool rides throughout? Has this become your favourite song? Without music notes to help you musically along? I think I could consider my Love Letters, my writings like a singer and their song. To soothe them, or to rev them up. The song, the music notes, the beat, and most importantly, the words. Every word to an artist is crucial, depending if it's not. Words are everything to me. They're my lyfe. So much as to say; my arms and hands and fingers do their dandling to make every word count. Right now, you're still a fantasy. Just words behind you, showing me to believe. The words; have faith, are a quiet whisper. He loves Sandra. So come on. Move me into a lull. Send me to Paris through thought. To hope for a fly. To only have what I can and I sent it off through other vias and hope it will be accepted as completed. To move on and past this time and catch up. So, I better get writing then. To know that bloggin it out, will help. To now have to anticipate the call to inform me of the steps needed to dig in and become an published author. Could you imagine if they declined it? That would be horrible. There are important messages in here for all sorts of people. This is *my* via. So then I must pray now. How many of you like when I pray? Well, with all or some of my Letters, I pray. Do you want to know why? I pray because that's the Power in me, that Feeds me; Strength, Wisdom, Compassion, and He Feeds me when I need it, and to reach you, in the world, to show you another perspective to a similar situation. And maybe help you in the process. I'm better able to respond to an email than in person for any type of advice. But I will try to be always as honest as I can be, and give you my honest opinion. But don't take it as 'what you must do'. I just pray that you have a wonderful lyfe. That you are happy with the people *in* your life. Or maybe you don't have family near you and you need a friend. I'll be your friend. You can be my price tag that is priceless. I want to be everyone's friend, who really *wants* to be my friend. Like you, or maybe not you. I would hope for the first choice first. Why haven't you called? Are you alright? Has she hit you again? Has she found out? Maybe it's you. I miss going out for lunch. Let's go eat. Where do you want to go? Let's go The Keg! Okay, so let me change and I'll let you know when I'll be there. Cool. As the clock tyme passes by and action is taken; shower, shave, dress, hair, make-up, heels, purse, keys, and on the road. I pull in the parking spot and lock up with the beeps. Smiles, hugs and kisses. We all say how wonderful it is to cee each other. You look great! So do you! Dinner for four? Our waiter seats us. Hands us the menus and offers water and something to drink. Wine? Yes please. A red please. And you? A champagne? Very good. He smiles and walks away. So how are you? What's up? You start telling me your day with your husband and everyday boyfriend. S. If applicable. Has something happened? Is she keeping you in the closet again? No vias out? I pray for away. That she's not broken again. Oh my goodness, that could be horrible! Then our drinks came. So what can I do to help? Step on that one and that step over there to reach you within my reach. To save you from drowning, to give you compressions to restart your heart again. Yes, He loves Sandra, are very powerful words in my lyfe. Have faith. Yes as the others joined in around the table. The steak was cooked to perfection. Potato was fully stuffed to perfection. Veggie's very moist and delicious. And the conversation was extremely stimulating. Smiles, hugs, and kisses.

Just so you know . . . , I'm going crazy in not hearing from you. Send me a kind message sir, with poetic justice, with flow and such. With the earlier message of her name is; Destiny Skye S. You gave her to me, you take the name, or the mane. Ride her as she is the destiny sky that she's chasing after. You ride on your warrior horse, and we ride together to chase that sky. She will be my Power Animal. I'll take her with me when I take my transe. He loves Sandra, are powerful words combined together you know . . . but you already *knew* that. Will you smile as you read these words? Will your heart muscles that you open the envelope and see what's inside? A peak? A glimmer? Nope. That's it. Okay, so if this were it, no more, then I'm in. Let's take our horses and go riding. It's my favourite outside activity along with short hikes, both on back and on foot. Just from one sentence, I got a whole lot of Letters. Of significant importance to the one who I will always have in my fantasy. Out of this world technique of gaining my capture and has had me ever since. Waiting for *that* night. When I see him, for the first time . . . I know I'm gonna fall in love. I *know* it. I'm scared shitless of it . . . did you really think I was going to divulge that sort of information to the public? As we go from a walk into a gallop. Is this really happening? This moment in my lyfe, where *everything* changes. If it's real and not make-believe. That the words; have faith, haven't proven to be a constant thought on this. Construitive. Which means simply this; open more doors to the majical place where I place my thoughts in order and follow strict instruction to not go there today. Only mountains and valleys. That I will ride Destiny, to the future she was made for. For an instant connection—as like; He loves Sandra. I'll know your thoughts. I'll know her thoughts. My golden would be right beside me, knowing something special was going on. Happen. To close the gates and let know one share in the happen. As another fiction-non-fiction form is taking place. So how long has it been? About ten lifetimes ago ? and that seeds were planted through different ways that let us find us again. That you're my soulmate? Is it true? When I finally hear your voice and see your beyond beautiful face? To know. Immediately. I'll know. Instantly. I just *know it.* I *have* to believe this. For you to chase *your* Destiny Skye and it's rider and transe me into another lifeform. Be my drum. Be my transe. To have Destiny ready at any tyme for our tyme together. She's a fantasy too. I ride her only in my mynds eye and watch her mane flow with the wind and be my new power behind God's maybe Thoughts, that God gave me, through *my* fairy dust, as He reminds me of my secret whishes of this lyfe coming my way. This is my *dream* lyfe, in my *real* fantasys. This is where I'll find answers. So many questions, but are they trivial and unimportant? No. It comes from You. The invisible reality is *my* reality. The Invisible Reality is my Reality. Be my mountains and valleys. Be the heart transplant I need so desperately. So will you be kind to me? *Is* this real? I'm talking to you. Yes, *you.* Yes, You. LORD, bless this. This love story with an impossible shield that needs to be broken and need to take away the space between us and come together. So; He loves Sandra and the rest is us. To rescue me. To give me my deepest whish in lyfe. To love me the way my Grandfather loved my Grandmother on the female side. To be free. To ride. Whenever I want to. To look for answers and messages that come in forms of . . . secret. Sshhh. My deepest whish, to know I can be freedom wrapped up in that royal-red ribbons and show me, you.

Unbelievable . . . . mmm. To make love to him? To know that he's myn. How I have sunken into you. About fourteen years ago, I started praying, that if I ever do get married again, he must be a very special man. You are, a *very* special man. You're my dream lyfe. I need you, . . . in everyway possible. Sensual tymes are to come. Well, my mirror, I have something to tell you. Meet; He loves Sandra. Soon. I have no outside wants to already know that's it's a; no. Have faith, right? I'll know tomorrow night. If he doesn't come? I'll be really upset. I *want* this to happen. So badly. Just *one more* sleep. As I'd tell my foals if they got excited for something, we'd say; just three more sleeps, just two more sleeps, just ONE more sleep. And I'll know or not. I have butterflys floating around in their. You are my dream lyfe. You're *everything* I've *ever* wanted. To know our ratio. He's *very* special my yellow sunflowers with butterflies flying by. He's special, like me. Open some more doors to flutter to the opening. With long grass on the stoop, with sunflowers reaching their heights that you have to squint in the sunshine to cee their tops. And moulding together. Yes, exactly! Like that over there. For years I've been praying for a very special man. And he is. Meaning every word I say. To dance with you to our song. Listen for it, for it's coming, just keep reading. Cravings to cee you, hear your voice, cee what you do with your fyre. I *love* your fyre. Yes, this is, He loves Sandra. Tick, tick, tick, toc. As my soul is wresting inside me. Aching to get out and to cee him. One more day of anticipation, just one more sleep. But if not? I would be crushed, obviously. That's why I always say; soon. To know our one-way vision. Not fare. How you just walk in my thoughts and take over control inside me. My throat tickles and pins and needles. And don't forget about the butterflys. Hello, Sandra. It's Me. As I wait unpatiently. Soon. Soon. Look at what you make me feel. You feed me to The LORD. Let my prayers be answered. To find and give me, a very special man. He is special. LORD, if this is real, and You Give me to him, and that lyfe with him. I pray for forever with him. Be my HOLY Place, and calm me, bestill me within my confinement. Give me a rest assured with him. Tell him, I only think of him. Draw me to him too LORD. You know how much You mean in my lyfe. Let him, with You, cee in me, and I him. Pump him in me, like my heartbeat as I lay on my side and hear it beat. Pump more. But You, LORD, will always comes First. As I ask for forgiveness if I've sinned today. Beg for Your mercy and continue to Worship You and with Blessings, I can think of him too. To hope in a lyfe with a man again while I remain here to spread Your Words of Love and Comfort. To take flights and lift off as we jumped really hard to reach the height to give You a high five. LORD, You know how much I want to find love. To fall in love again. I'm ready. Send him to me FatherGod. I want him, and I want him and more. To accept this very special union, and everything that is in towed. Bring me myn. With him. Cee how nervous I am? I can't talk correctlyness. Will you be my forever dance under Sandra loves You? To bring our love story out and put it in my words of artistry? Will you be my dream lyfe? Will you be my stairs when I need a second floor? To hold me up when darkness comes? Will you give me my words of a story yet untold? Will you be my forever Love Letters? Will you show me the way in the dark? Will you remind me that God made us; you—me, so we can be together? Will you close the blinds when even sunlight is too bright? Soon. Love, SLS-? . . . .

"Happy 42nd Birthday"

Today is my fourty-second birthday. I got up at seven a.m. Got showered and dressed and haired up, make-up, buckle boots, keys and purse. I went over to my mirror. Talked some and spent quality tyme together. Came back and we ordered pizza. Got a cake, card and presents. I got something nice, sweet deal, thank you! When we had my birthday cake, and my mom stayed at the table with me to show me how much she loves me. I can get mighty furious with my mother, but when it comes right down to it, she shows me her love, in *her* ways. And her staying with us both meant the world to me. It was a special moment for me and her and *my* foal. A closeness that is sparadic most tymes, but when they come and I'm in the right mood, *gotta be* in the right mood, I hug her and let her joke with me and I can joke back. Rare moments, but undenyable in special. Then all my friends connected with me. Those are treasures to me. Good people on my list of friends. And texts and chat, so I've been a popular girl today. I'm still waiting for one more though. Is today the day? Will he come? You'll find out soon enough, but no reading ahead now. Tisc-tisc . . . no cheating. It takes everything I have to not look ahead in a book. I have to know the end immediately, but as I grew up into an adult, I self-contain myself under great restraints, to read it like the rest of the world. So since it's my birthday, I'm going to sing happy birthday to me, myself and I. So here we go; happy birthday to me, happy birthday to me, happy birthday dear me . . . . happy birthday toooo meee. I hope you sang along with me? Just like I would if it were your birthday. Well, now what? Just listen to my music in my ears and just write what comes tonight instead of planning it and thinking a lot about it first. What if he doesn't come? I want him to come over, so badly, but situations could be tough right now. So I have to be understanding instead of hurt and sad. Know that I will one day, and I'll wait for that day. It's okay if he doesn't come. I'll still want him. Crave him. Like I'm hungry. I want to devour the moment I cee him. Just stare at him. And I have to write fast. I have an important phone call in about twenty minutes. So I must type, type, type. I'm going to another place tomorrow for the evening with company that I want to be a part of with great importance. To know I'm loved in all sorts of directions, but not every direction. I now understand the comment once said to me when she said not everyone loves me. Totally understand that now. Not every person will get along with me. Either you love me or you hate me. I choose my friends carefully. Who's not gonna leave me, no matter what? I'm a handful sometimes, ask all my friends. Sometimes I'm high maintenance. Just like your friends, who love you, whether you are or are not. Right? Laughing. Party with me. Let's turn off all the lights and turn on all the black lights and wear white, so you'll glow. You can do whatever you want in this game. Let yourself think about what you would do in a room with black lights. I would spray neon paint on the walls and laugh at the illusions of what you're really doing. The seventies music was going on with pump full loud music with no neighbours to complain of noise past midnight. We'd spray it all over each other and laugh and jump on the trampoline and hit our heads on the ceiling, every time. Bang, bang, conk, conk. And laugh as you bounce on your butt and as you pee your pants because that's just what happened this tyme because of laughing so hard. Laugh. You gotta love it. I hope you've had fun reading. Please do come back anytime and watch for details of my night of is he coming? Or isn't he? To be cont . . . .

"Good-bye"

May 9th, 2011

I'm lost again, trying to find my way out. Of another crush of reality. Everything is so messy right now in my head and heart. Just a part of me out there again to be smashed into a brick wall and my head explodes in fractures and blood. Reality speaks very loudly when I've been deaf for a while. To just wait. For everything, but this tyme he never existed. I have doubt, as once was true, but were lyes. Along with everything it came with. Such intence feelings for an invisible forces pushing me apart. The thoughts are my food. That don't feed. Is this reality or fake? I can't tell right now. It's equal. It's so loud to my quiet thoughts. Am I in a transe? Yesno. I'll never tell you, for it's my secret along with many of them and my head is a coconut. Covered in fort knocks. As the sad music wants to put me to sleep and go away. To write and feels inside of guilt and wonder if I'm a person with no compassion and no wonder I'm alone in my own fantasy world. To be scared of going insane again. Where am I? There or here? This or that? Pull or push? Just a part of me I don't have anymore. Like the part of me that makes me starve still and again in my ownness of who am I? To not listen to His Voice in Him Saying His Words. But what are You saying LORD? Your Voice is muffled. The words; have faith are faint in in the distance. Am I lost in imaginational world that's made up? And I have to fight my way through some more darkness ahead. In grieving the loss of something that didn't even exist. To believe in everything. To never ride together on Destiny Skye. Two more entitys that don't breathe this ayr. Just me and my thoughts of another insanity. I have to save them, no matter how much blackness I must face alone. Just let me know LORD so I can prepare some. I was in a high for a couple of days before the dark ahead days to follow. To fill me with hope and desire and then it emptys just as quickly. To open me to food and let it all spill onto the floor beneath me. Then fill me with hope again then to dump it, which is how I feel LORD. What is the purpose this tyme? To once again have faith in You and test me. So with each domino falling I fall behind? To want to fall in love? In my own ideas and I'm throwing a tantrum. As I dust myself off again and just keep focused on saving the world. Praying and believing in blind faith who says have faith. Who do I believe? Always the LORD, yes. Whoa, LORD! I have to do it by the book too. I can't save her alone this tyme. To know, there's nothing I can do until and things are bad in that. I can only pray. LORD, protect her, save her. I feel so desperate in You LORD. Please, as I bow my head in prayer. Eyes closed, please God, save her. Save my other foal how's his name is Emmanuel. In this I pray, AMEN. Missing pieces of a whole are gone and you're in trouble and if she goes and has to come back, it's ten tymes worse. So I'll be praying full-time to help you and get you out of a horrible situation, and so I'll keep going on. No matter how bad, and work my fingers to the bone, and to be. Live my lyfe and try to wrack my brain to invent, created as something whether its fiction or non-fiction, so you can decide for yourself. How my insane lyfe can get you out of your prison. So, I have to let you go, even though, did you really live in the earthly realm? I have to live and go on as though you were never hear. I'll always love the fantasy of someone like you and to have a wonderful aftertale of a non visible entity. To be carried off to another place to be told that you can't go there anymore, but you go anyways. I'm sorry I never got to cee you or meet you and I hope you're okay and in the hands of the tales of your lyfe.

I will do the best I can by you. I whish you were coming back. I will always have a part of you with me and I'll learn as much as possible. I hope to cee you one day and be who we are to each other. This invisible love, is one of the strongest love possible. Cee you one day, I hope. I do love the part of you that hides you from the rest of the world. I will do my best to journey to you. I'm not sure when or how, but watch for me as I will watch for you. Thank you for so much. I miss the part of you that is invisible already. I miss you, I love you, for my love travels beyond this planet. Who sends me words from a force that one day I will cee. To love the invisible is hardest of all. Why should you? Why should I? Because its force, it's the invisible forces that keep you strong and it encourages you to pray and believe in something that was meant to be. I'm sorry I couldn't save you. From where I can't go to, beyond the curtain of normal reality from a force where someone else comes in and trys to destroy you. Please don't leave. Can I scare you to make you stay? Last night, I was so stressed out. My heart was beating out of my chest and pumping so hard and so fast. I was so stressed out with everything going on with everyone, and with my book, I started having small chest pains. How can I handle you leaving me? Please don't leave. How can I live a normal lyfe knowing I couldn't save you? I don't know if I can handle another death. How can I reverse the effects on you and everyone else that I let down? Okay mister. You better listen to me, right now! You better contact me soon. Things are happening. You better buck up and fuckin' meet me soon. Stuff is happening to me and what you said to me is coming true. Okay mister, you are needed here too you know. We need you more here than them in where you are. You send me this cryptic message, which we/I uncoded by the way. And it's been happening all night. So then I find you picked up my horse and didn't tell me, and thank you hugs and make up sex later. You better not leave us. Yes, us. You, me, our daughter, myn for starters. So, as I shake my finger at you with three pointing back to me, you better fight to get out from where you are. For us all, still waiting for you. Find your way home, I'll be waiting for you. Find your way home, I'll be waiting for you. We'll be waiting for you. I just have to let go . . . and open my door, right? Just open my screen door and there'll you'll be? Just do it. I pray for my LORD to be right there, showing me to you and my next lyfe. Meet me there. And you just tell me who and what I'm supposed to do? I listened very carefully. She's supposed to show me home where I'm supposed to be with you. Who am I there? If my foal is high up there, then that makes us, VERY important. I'm typing as I'm receiving and maybe I might stop. I have to try, right? If you have to, then I have to too. Cee, three pointing back at me. But to find you there, I have to find you here too. Who will I become ? when I open the door? Didn't I just write this? Two tyme equilibriums. Different equinox from two different tymes in tyme. To show me this way please. Hello? Are you there? I hear you knocking, and I don't need to break the door down. I open the door and cee you. For the first tyme. You cee me, for the first tyme. We take a breath and gasp in. And I run to you in such a short distance. But I have to get there first and that's why you told me I have to ride. Am I supposed to ride to you on our daughters back? That I'm the only one who can ride her. Type, type, type . . . . So to carry on thank you very much. Okay, tatata, rapraprap. As I journey and open my door and you are . . . . Just kidding.

From carrying you, and playing with you while you grew inside me, giving a part of us to the world. From hiccups in the womb, to now. I can't believe it. So a little while ago, you were born. So much has happened since then to now. So many people surrounded us as I was trying so hard to push you out. Into the world, your world. And you tried to get out too. Finally, I was cut, and then just two pushes and then you were born. Our beautiful little boy. They put you on my chest and I sang happy birthday to you, as I was trying to fight against crying and sleep. We were both tired and I remember leaving the delivery room to our room and then I think the nurses took you so I could sleep. And you too sunshine. I put a stuffed puppy dog in your bed so when I went to look for you, I'd know you. I was *so scared,* that I wouldn't recognize you, so I was smart and put a puppy in your bed, just in case. The next day I got up and showered and all I could think of was getting to you and hold you and nurse you and know you, and study your face and I'd sing to you. All sorts of nursery rhymes. Which now you hate by the way. The daytime when I saw you after you were born, I went to the nursery and went to you and picked you up and brought you back to the room. I laid you on our bed, and I just stared at you. For an hour, for five minutes, I don't remember. That has never changed. I could stare at you all day if that was normal for a mother in love with her children. Capture every visit. And just stare, into your eyes and for you to know how far we've come so far and I can't wait til then, but knowing all that I know, I would change so much. But that's not *our* path. There's always been my motherly love and you were perfect in *my*/motherly eyes. Now, from being a newborn to be turning seventeen. I can't believe it. You've made me so proud. You are such a good son. You care about strangers childrens. Sorry, that's just how I write. To when we brought you home and our disaster changing your diaper. What a mess we made. Does that happen to all first tyme parents? And now, you've become a man, right before me. How you stand so tall and gorgeously lean. And now, uhg, what a killer smile. Just breath-taking and you make me gasp every tyme I cee you. And wanting to hug you so you know how much I love you. From becoming a little boy and loosing the most important part of him becoming gone, to growing up and breaking some bones along the way and teeth corrections with now, the most gorgeous smile in the world that is part of three. Your sunshine blond hair when you were a little boy, to now a natural blonde, and feathered back, just the way I love it. I hope you never change that part of you, one of the millions I could list off. And in knowing, one day, you'll be moving away from here, and I won't get to see your beautiful perfect face everydays of my life. And now, you're so beautiful and wonderful and hilarious and great. To know, once again, I must place you gently in the LORD's Hands and He carrys you and places you go over there, instead of over here. But before I do that part of our lives, let's focus on the now of our lives. I pray for that special tyme when when you hug me a layer of me just attached itself to you, and when you need a hug, just remember that special hug in your mynd and heart from me from before, and use it for now. And now, you're so beautiful and wonderful and hilarious and great. To my seventeen year old son, I'll say, I love you, everyday. Listen for it. When you need me, when you need your mommy, imagine mommy singing to you, Amazing Grace. I love you my son, my sunshine, my air. Happy 17ᵗʰ Birthday . . . .

I make a difference. Make sure *you* make a difference too. Be someone so you can be inspired to do their best like you. Be you and in who you are, and stand for it. Become a God fan. Think outside-the-box for a minute or two during the day. Believe in something out of the ordinary. Journey to another place and tyme. Become whole as a sole bass. Let go so you can breathe in the spring ayr with fragrances from the flowers on the trees. But don't stop being you, just expand a little over tyme, to the strange things in this world, on this earth. And what about middle earth? Have you been there? Are there questions I can answer for you? Journey to middle earth but ask permission to enter from the wolf. Laughing . . . . Did you actually believe that? Hahahaha. No but seriously, you have to ask permission to enter. Here's what my journey I want. To totally relax, breathe, let myself go but hang on to the silver lining. And let your non-physical body to float above and dream of your floating soul goes to the other life forms. To ride, Destiny Skye, next to my supernatural soul mate. We will ride with me to meet our next world, but then I have to return to here. To see my now. To have both worlds together. Never forgetting my LORD in combo. Ride to the end of the beginning, then come back and do my daily chores with now. With daily tears when I have to come back and whish us to live forever in forever and in eternity. Have our song repeat over and over and when I sing, it's like the most beautiful voice you've ever heard. To go to the high, to the over there, to in that direction now. To continue to listen to my souls release in number one spot right now. To thank him and release him from wandering aimlessly and whish him well. To take him to the LORD's Hands and cradle him for his oozing lost soul. And fix him and to restore him and to invite him on closer trips. To love both of you for different reasons. To have lost that connection when I'm with another. But you'll always be my first and longest love of my lifetime of this I'm wondering. And to seek for a connection that I've let go of to carry on and to find *my* Home. Then to come back and write Love Letters to share my double love in the non-ordinary earth and bring it on. To come back and remember every bit of it, to record it for you to read. So I can be the one to help you to think-outside-the-box a little today. But if you don't want to, you don't have to. But my instructions are to deliver. My surroundings were dark and over to my right was a passage way with light coming from it. I stopped or I just couldn't walk, then I woke up. It's through that passage way, I want to go. To walk to the Light. To move, I couldn't do it. But I just stared at it, and no one came out or in. Was I at my door? Or is it the screen door? I have two doors to choose from. Which door is my supernatural soul mate and Destiny Skye ? and my savage? Could I go in both at separate times? What if one was mountains and valleys ? and the other is where my Home is? And where I've always wanted to go? What if I didn't choose the right one for that moments? What's to come? Will he meet me half way ? literally? This is the most desired lifestyle I've ever dreamt of. But then I have to return to write and let someone go on a trip with me. Let the Letters melt together and say. So, go on your own journey now. Close your eyes and melt into your couch chair and cover yourself with a comfortable and soft blanket and put on some soothing music that calms you to dreamingland. To find *your* supernatural soul mate and travel and journey. But, it's not for everyone. You have to *really* want to. To have waited your whole life for *this* moment and to come back and write about it. Please.

"Sidewards Directions"

I wonder how many fairytales in books and movYs, really live outside this earth/world? The continents and dominions of land of field and rolling hills and the oceans and lakes and streams and rivers down rocky pathways with the water rushing and pushing you in it's own directions of force and you can only move with it because of it's power it has on you and your strength. Who's to say it can't be right or correct without sounding like a fool in others eyes and secret thoughts about you and what you've experienced? The pull of desires is gravity in the sidewards directions. Is love like the ripple effect ? where when the bubble is on top, it rides with the ripples then breaks? And then the bubble is gone on their own way. They lived and died within two seconds of tyme. Is that a message of how some should never live again? For sadness could come over like a cloud that makes the bubbles. When you're sad, try to expand with the ripple and it is elastic and you get bigger. Then you divide in half and journey when you lift off and become astral twins. Then you could be there and here and you could go in the opposite directions at the same tyme. To stand in both places not in in sole. And then find him and get him to divide so we can travel everywhere at the same tyme. Is this how this works? To not think of suicide and slashing my wrists with gushing blood spurting out everywhere, so you put the sunglasses on to shield your eyes and face. Separating from that time . . . for I still carry the cross of it when I'm alone, but I want to share suicide. And to beg Him to take me in the night where all happened to me in the terrors of hell. To never remember that ever again in my journeying lyfe in where I'll find him and ride on my Destiny's back. To yell to her in the silent wind blowing past me as I ride through it. My hair trails behind me, jumping up and down in tyme of her gallops. To hold on tight to her sides for she's floating and I let go and spread out my arms and let her ride beneath me. Her strides are trancelike. I escape and ride beside. To close my eyes and let my mynd wander to the next worlds above this one. What type of distance is that? Beyond the beyond. Beyond the beyond. Do you want to try it? Does it even in known? Can there be another journey on top of this one? How far will you ride with the bubble? Expand and go into another shape and form and if it's only two seconds ? how long is *this* reality? So many tyme zones to know about and the continents and marsh where the water is clear and sand beneath and seaweed through your toes and feel. So much. I want You so much LORDGod, it's all I want in lyfe and I hope we have Your blessings for this entry into a new door, a new world, a new earth, the choices of many passage ways and the swords of warriors as you pass by them and fight to the next one in order of succession. Be the scratch on the door and ask for permission for entry after. Climb the heaven's staircases that travel in every directions that go on forever, surrounding you. And you grab my hand and run up most of the staircases. And make love on every one. And they'll be making love in the boom room, where everyone was playing on cherry red streets and apples dropped from the trees and you're able to eat it and let the sugar melt you into the twisting winds and swiff you off. To not be afraid, ever, in these places with cotton candy to supernatural taste buds and go on the rides of twisting and blowing up and become a balloon for a child's play. For us to transfer through the tunnels of speeding tymes and we slide downwards and then sidewards, and up and down. We hold onto each other and then when they'll finish in the staircases, then we'll go see God.

Hello. My name is; Vala. I am supernatural in spirit and in mynd. I come from the ordinary world but have supernatural built inside me and makes me who I am. Have you been cleared up of any confusion? In who I am? That my name is; Vala. And I have found my home away from here and I must go there as soon as possible, so I can meet this portion of who I am. I've been dry in verbal for a while and I must tell you that I may not know everything yet. And I have to learn all about it. This day is of importance of finding a new way of transport. I *will* go in both you know. I must discover my new world of discoverys I haven't seen in a while, due that I've been here accomplishing this lyfe to find this lyfe. This day is about learning and discovery. Is there music to surround us? As we ride will there be music in the sky speakers? All the songs that make me trance into another world where you are? With you I never not question this story. To not never ask you a bunch of questions and I have many query. And have just a bit of mental reservations to sit at your table and sit with you and stare at each other, and get locked in, like a chastity belt. To show you my purity and that I come in peace and bring new power from God to tell you to never stop believing. To remind you all of His Will for who He's made and makes every second. To be reincarnate over and He shows you which body to use, so He plants His individual souls to the correct form and body to learn and change the world so it keeps going on to the future of yet of what to come. To close my eyes. To whish you near me. Even if it's all a big mistake, will you love me forever? But how do you know though? To reap. To gather and nest in a dwelling of a distant shore. To ask you to change in front of me and for me to change into my next form in front of you too. Am I at my best? I could do better to tell you a tale of what could be, what possibly could. So then I talk to God and ask Him to answer the fyre and bring the legends to one spot where they use their powers from Him to make something else come into you. Hello. My name is; Vala. If you know what that means, then you know already. If you don't, then you might want to figure it out so you can be in the no. LORDGod, thank You for this tyme of; that's clear, that's clear, now I can start fresh again and hopefully not let clutter block the thoroughfare. And I am going to enter both ones you know. You can't stop me. I will pray, of course, before I go. So, the only answer is to come with me. Come on baby girl, my supernatural world of being part of him and her and Him and her of development in what you've come to shape as. So be advised in advance of when I'll be going on my way to introduce myself there so you can come here. So now I'm desperate to find dragons and fyre breath and light the way to the cave and secret spot just that we know, from somewhere on the map. Of that region, of that region and what about that region? Of that vehement. The strong emotional ties there are pulling me forward in my other lyfe. Where I'm just as strongly reside, and now I completely understand when you say you want to go home again. Now that's my whish too. To seal to the fate of taking on new lyfe. To let LORD let me. But would He? Maybe. But there's only one way and one day away to being; Vala. And yes, do please call me that, for it's who I am and what I am. To keep the esoteric in facts in where I'm going soon. To peek, and to peek more up above. Seek out news. To once again take you, my readers, into myth worlds so you have something to think about during your day of what you have to do to reach out and grab the; I love you baby. Have a good sleep.

Am I lost ? in my own world ? of sadness and despair? I feel dry in my mynd, which I hope won't last too much longer. Today will be the very first tyme trying it. Some may frown, but this is my lyfe, the day I've been waiting for. I pray over my dreammaker and ask Him to guide dreams in White Light, and ask for Help and Give me answers. Ask questions, to receive messages, revelations, visions of future. To be able to heal people. I've been preparing my entire lyfe for this night of hope I dream well and journey. For this I pray LORD. I ask for only You. Bless tonight's sleep LORD. That must remained locked down, excuse the hammering, at all tymes now. Oh, no hammering? Okay then. I will always remember this night to the next day. And know what to write immediately when I wake up and contact who I need to contact and let them know. Then I pray for dreams to bring back from there to here and heal and help lost souls. To ask for *vivid* instructions. With sounds to concur and to work together. This is what I pray for LORD. For You. Can I even pretend right now? YES! I rolled over and took the cord to hang onto for re-entry. I opened the door. Oh my gosh! What is that smell? Everything was everywhere. Piled to the ceiling, boxes everywhere. There was hardly a pathway to the next room, and dust everywhere. So unsafe. Please LORD, tell me what to say. I put my invisible on, and say what I say. The beautiful roses that stand out to you, and the butterflys and royal dark pink flowers. I love my decal with pink stone, fake obviously. The four elements; sky, ayr, earth, water. With the little birdy sitting looking up, and I excuse myself from such a girly thing to say. I'm not usually flowers and royal pink. But today is a special day, leading me to tomorrow. I need to find my other lyfe and have the best of both worlds. All worlds. Give me messages, visions, revelations. And the questions are this? An official communication given to me. I will come back and deliver it to the person needing help and heal them. Given sight to something that will come, and come back and pray and write about it. The act of revealing and disclosure of themself and coming back and healing someone and help lost souls find their way through that door, and yes, that door too sur. I trugged through the rubble and made it to the bathroom. The room wasn't useable. Piled high. The ayr was stale and musky. We turned the corner and there was a kitchen with an open wall looking to the sunlight. The kitchen was dark brown wood and very dark natural lighting from outside. To the right was the sink and counter with dark wood boarders. On the left, was the stove and fridge. I walked to the balcony and looked down, then it suddenly changed. I'm driving down the highway, but I'm not moving, but I keep moving towards the gigantic mountains and the entry. Then I'm in the graveyard at his grave again, but there is two, as I'm going to repeat myself, once again and write again about the strange mulky dirt beneath my feet. The ayr was brown in texture. Foggy. I was in a limo with someone and a plane was sitting beside the car with the car being in white colour, but inside it was a reddish colour interior. So LORD, bless more dreams. Let me be creative in writing more storys of fiction-non-fiction. For them to ask for the answer of yes or no. I was walking along a road and as I was walking, my right leg was lagging behind, and I forced it forward with pulls. Finally I looked back. I was chained to my dead husband and I was carrying his dead corpse. I looked ahead of me, and that was the end. The one where I looked out my bedroom window and you were in the neighbours yard walking towards me with a knife.

Okay LORD. What should I write about tonight? That it's done. Intake over. So, lead me in the right direction LORDGod, and to write how much I can right now. Of course I will drive the distants to cee you, my loyal readers and friends. I will go the distants. Not even a question. Questions will lead to answers and old feelings will come up and I'll have to hide them from mirror. Will she question why? Only that day will tell me. To regret so much, but I'm so glad to have had that experience and will always have that for us and our past. When our presents is each other to each other. When our precents is eech other to eech other. And now you are you and I am I and we went forward and in different directions. That's okay though. Because I was supposed to live. And to him, gone away, far away, as we sail on the separate ocean in the sailboat that we had to sail in opposite directions. Distants is our now and tyme. But we'll be together for a short tyme only coming Sunday. And to talk and hug and will it help me? I'm so urging to sleep. And maybe to take more. But I'll cee. So to just finish off telling you the story of when they sailed off together on the ocean, to sail around the world with their son. To be at the steering wheel with him behind me steering together, kissing me, and the cameras span in front of us and songs of love and commitment come on. Where the world is at our fingertips and we can go anywhere. Put the anchor down and sit on the quiet water and park there for the night. The waves were rocking/swaying under the boat. The sun was at it's peak. Do you want to go in? Hell ya! I took my tee-shirt off and went to the stairs and got the lifejacket for our son, and got him all ready. Then, we all jumped in the cold ocean water on a very hot day. We splashed each other and did a family moment together. This was our home now. The boat and the ocean. We swam away from the boat a bit and did back flips, spins, twists, told jokes and laughed as we struggled to tred water. I layed on my back and let the sun shine on me. I went under water so many tymes and let my hair sway to the under the water part. Where it's weightless in sways, and sticks to my head when I come above the water. I gasp for breath when I reach to the top. They had swam farther from me and so I caught up with them on the beach. We layed on the sand and rolled around and sand went in my mouth. But I didn't care. This is everything I could want in lyfe. So it's not good-bye, just tyme for another story. The elevator was crowded this morning. Cologne and perfume scents. Sniffles and little coughs. Every floor we made a stop. Every floor from seventeen to ground floor/parkade. To walk away from the others and walk in your own distants and to drive to your work or daily chore. As I was almost at my car, another car alarm went off and it was so loud. I got in my car and locked the doors and did my daily responsibility of buckling up. And thinking of tonights episode where she gets married. I can't miss that. I start the car, turn the radio on and go on my way. And another story begins. As we all gather around the campfire, everyone is getting high. The guys have their guitars out and were playin some mellow music with the crackle of the fire pit and the sinjer of crackles go in the ayr. Will it slip out onto the pillow tonight? Will dreams come out ? and wake me to the still? Do you still love me darling? Will you always love me? Will I turn my back on you? Will you on me? So to bring us all back to the north direction again, will this work out? What am I talking about? Just say whatevers on your mynd and I'll let it go. To sum up the day; it was awesome. I got what I wanted to get and I'm happy.

To live both lives. How I have to struggle with so much responsibility that I'm reaching for all the way. Bring it on, when it's published and bringing in humble wealth that I've worked really hard on and bring and share my faith and my Christianity levels. How I carry His name, VERY seriously. To try to live as Jesus would but living *my* life. To maybe touch someone else who feels the same way. But even if you're not a Christian, I tell good stories, right? I get you into it, right? Draw your eyes to every word. To slide them across like skates on ice. And it goes in rhythm and when the skater jumps and that He gets your attention. Right in the climax, He grabs for you to feel His Love for you. That all you have to do is bow your head and ask Jesus to come into your heart. Right now. As I pray for you. To feel the Love, and you bow as I am now. God, come into my heart and let me live Your Way. You Love them Father. In this I pray for them LORD. AMEN. I pray over this book LORD, and I pray for blessedness wealth so I can move on in my own life. This is my prayer God. To do my work in spreading The Word to His Nations upon the earth and seeing what happens. But hey, you have to choose for yourself. I'd encourage you, but this is *my* life and that's your life. We all must find our own destinys. Some people choose God. Some people don't include God. It's you. But it's all good because it's supposed to happen. Life happens the way it happens. It is Written. Let The Words, come out. Let me meditate to listen. So to move on to another sentence and to bring the next scene and in my acts that I act my life out, in stories, in tails and tales. Let me come down to the ground and beg for forgiveness for sinning today, for being an addict in writing with creations . . . . Tell why it is being sent. Be courageous. As the noise is making a racket and so I shood it away. So it's being sent because it's an important part of it. To stare at the unopened envelope, and to stare past it and into it. What does it say? I'm nervous about the letter. I'm scared to open it. I shake my head and walk away in only three steps and walk back. I pick it up and stared at it. The stamps, my address, their address, and it doesn't make it any better. My phone rang. I didn't get it. Are they phoning me? Oh my gosh. What have I gotten myself into? I'm aware of every noise. Does it say, yes or no? I continue to stare at the envelope. As I put it back down and walked away. I'll open it later. Now I have to work. You may never know. Could you handle that as a reader? Not knowing the answer, and the situation and there is none. It's a no. Sorry to disappoint you, but I had to capture you. To tease you more and more and make your eyes saliva. So what would have you wanted it to be? Cancer ? pregnancy ? a new job ? got accepted into a prestige university? It could be anything. So if it's you staring at that envelope, just open it and find out for yourself it's a yes or a no. I wish it for you, if it's meant to be that way, and if it's not, it wasn't meant to be and something better is coming. For example; about a year ago now, I was suicidal and I was going to commit suicide and had my hand on the handle and my phone rang. I wasn't meant to commit suicide. God had bigger Plans for me that I had for myself. And now, I'm writing and have goals and dreams other than wanting what I thought I wanted at that moment. Even though I didn't want to live, anymore. I had lost to life and I wanted no more, and I was reaching for the door handle to start the process of my death. I didn't care about anyone in that moment, but God saved me and a whole bunch of people that love me. Sometimes the answer is opposite.

And I pray, for all the people who are drowning down here. God, the world is sinking. How can I save my future generation? The science guys better act quick LORDGod. Send messages on how to fix the situation down here. All those people who were being flooded out with one with an island now. Surrounded by fields drowned with water. Even some of the news from research, is saying some of all the places that has been flooding around the world, which I want to see before it goes down. With all this flooding, the world may become more dense with people. Where do all the victims go? They have to find a new home, a new piece of land somewhere else and all the jobs that have to make more room and the real estate market is going to become a buyers market. Cities are going to become more full, and land is going to come at a high cost for money grabbingness unfortunately, but, it's gonna be big. Soon, land will be rare to find, and cutting down more forests to make new high-rises for all the new people to the city from their now water owned lakes and rivers and oceans, and we'll run out of land. What's to come LORD? I believe that the building with food in it needs to happen and are we supposed to make and build arcs? Are we to build cities on the water? But how would that happen? How could building on water work ? cement? But that would almost totally destroy ocean life and food that we need. Is this the beginning of the end of this age? The ice age, died. The dinosaur age, died. The man-kind age, slowly dying, and next is it the water age ? for the next generations of arcs and floating cities? Please LORD, answer these burning queries of knowledge so I can prepare and maybe think twice about. Not putting off that vacation to the Caribbean, or Hawaii or Texas. *Take* a vacation. Learn to love more. Learn to live more. Learn to laugh more, to play more. Start praying for solutions to our world growing problems. Fight for what you believe in, for what you trust in. For another life to change because of the right choices, that change someone else's. Don't wait too long anymore. Take time from the business meeting to tell your employees or your great employers how well they're doing in doing their jobs. Stop being so scared all the time. Life *will* end. But it's the legacy you leave behind, even if we all go down together, as a Nation under God. Just say something like this; Mom, Dad, even though we've had our differences, and if they really are great parents, tell them. Don't wait to make that phone call or text or telecommunicate somehow. Show you were paying attention to their dedication as a parent, siblings, cousins, uncles and aunts, best friends, who've helped shape you into the person you are today. So much is happening down here, and I just don't want you, to miss an opportunity that could be one of your last chances. Make yourself count. Stand up for another person. Put your neck out sometimes when it really matters. Even if you have a concert with thirty thousand people and you only reach a handful, you deserve applause. Be self-conscious, but it's okay to look in the mirror at your reflection and say; hi me. I'm going to be nice to me today, even if I have a million dollars or a penny, show the world your power and what you were meant to be. LORDGod, if I'm being totally honest, I'd rather not drown due to unnecessary, but It Is Written for tomorrow and tomorrow and tomorrow. I pray for the people responsible for solving earth problems stemming from what God Wrote. Say today; I love you friend, I love you friend, I love you friend. Then live your life as it was meant to be. But one thing is for sure, no matter where you are, we share the world.

I told her how I've been feeling towards this whole thing. She told me to tell you. I'm ready to give up on this whole thing. I've been praying for this moment my whole lyfe, in my deepest secrets. And when I met you a few months ago, something told me to change my mind and meet you. Praying to the LORD for journeying, for trances, for astral projection, dreams with messages, visions, healing powers, knowledge, wisdom. To pray to find you in the supernatural world, which is where my Home is. I've read so much about all this, and it's all I want. But also too, to find this very special man who would come and save me and grab my hand and lets go. Well, last week I went and got my wort. This is a herb to enhance prophetic dreams. Well, you can't do it very often because it can over toxicate your body. So I can only do it once and a while as to not poison myself. I'm being smart about things and trying to make the right choices, with some failure in that sometimes. Every decision I make, I pray about it. Is it the right decision? And that includes this situation as well. It's easy to believe in, and get wrapped up in something so wonderfully dangerous that I can live both lives. Now, tyme has passed. I've asked you many tymes, to meet me, to come to me, but you've insisted I go to you first. So, I have been trying so hard, wort, praying, trying so hard. Well, I've almost given up of any hope to meet you. When you told me you were here with her and the horses, I was very hurt inside. You come to her, but not to me and I feel that I'm not that important to you after all. I've begged you, but when I'm away at orchid ? you come back. I'm not worth it to you. And I'm not going to believe in an invisible love like this anymore. I'm glad you love her enough to come back. When I email you, I wait for days on end waiting for your response, and I don't want to hope anymore for this lyfe. I want proof. But I feel I'm not worth it to show me. So, do what you want. I don't have blind faith. Once again, it's been proven that I'm not worth it. I'm very upset about this. I'm tired, I'm in pain. So, this is the very last chance. I'm not going to wait anymore. It's not fair. I've been depressed about myself and this, does not help. So either you meet me, and this is the last chance. No more. Either you risk everything for me, or this is my last email to you or in reply. It's your choice. Why should this be fair the way it's been going? It's your choice now. Do you show me you ? or do I walk away, today? Final answer. I want this lyfe with you, so badly, but I've almost given up and not believe anymore and pop the bubbles. Why don't you open my door and pull me through? Take my hand and lead me, and never let go. But to let go if you don't exist. I can't hang on if there is nothing, is of no strings or and no ropes. He and Sandra will cease to takes it's journey, or it will have, in the next day. That power will be gone, no longer have power. Just that I'm a fool for believing in such a horrible joke. That has changed the direction in my lyfe. My focal point will be gone, and it will disappear. That this is just a me journey and everything in between isn't real. But hey, I got some great "Love Letters" from it though. Good storys to share about tails and tales. Tattling their way out, onto a loving soul full of pain and anguish and harsh and intense thoughts. Never ending or letting up. But are you? Are you? Aren't you who I thought you were? Are you the pain that keeps me? Are you the definition of my love? I'll never know, will I? You'll never show me your face. Down in my heart, I feel it. So, I will continue to write and share my open wounds of a spilt heart with freys as a fractured heart.

I feel so unworthy of any love right now. Today was a very important day. It was a day of good-byes and see you laters. The end of a quarter of a century it was a Service. In You LORD. Thank You for creating a person who was so merciful, compassionate and with Your Love. Through her, like You're using me, and using him and her, of a Nation under God, as she trys to pull everyone to everyone. Everyone to everyone. And so on. To try to remember the words that were spoken today. To move on to the next faze in lyfe. To pay-it-forward . . . . Then later on, as I tried to ignore it and put it off, but then I had to look and read it again. And I feel so ashamed to be me. What have I done? I just have self-loathing again, and feel so unworthy of anything. Have *you* ever felt like that? That why you are who you are ? and look back at you ? and know that nothing can be said to make you feel better? So I have to talk it out and see if you can guess who this is? Am I the person you waved to today? Were you the clerk at the income assistants office? Am I the judge who sentenced you to lyfe in prison because he murdered his child? Am I the homeless man outside 7/11 today? I lecture to you not to feel like this about yourself. And yet, we all did it today. To not be up on the pedestal with her tired and weary soul, and to work to the bone. So, in pain, or not, this is my top priority again after what could have been a very tragic weekend. I made a smart decision this past weekend. An old friend came into town and that night I had all night insomnia, so my sleeping aids haven't worked yet, and I hurt my back the day before, so I was on pain killers. So, instead of being too proud and stupid, I offered gladly my car keys over to my right hand. As we were driving we were approaching an intersection, and we were turning left. It was a green light in our direction with on coming traffic now going to *their* green light. Even though I wasn't driving, my foot automatically went to the gas peddle, and floored it. If I was driving, my best friend could have been VERY SEVERELY HURT. It just so affected me. It just so effected me. Even though it's hard to relinquish control on my side, I did. Because of my smart, and right choice, I saved a major car accident. And maybe a lyfe. I praise God for protecting all of us and humble forgiveness for what could have happened because I was too proud to offer and ask for assistants for driving. I thank God for making it easy for me to hand my keys over . . . . So then I'm drawn back to you. With you in my heart right now. She may get tired for working tirelessly, but my head and heart suffer so much in a day. Such intense feelings come out of me. By supper time, I'm so tired. And today was no different. You asked me what you can do for me ? and you know my answer. Come'ere. But am I worth it? Do you say yes or no to that? What would you say to your sister? Your best friend? Inside, I question myself about everything. Should I be telling you this? Probably not. Will I have to suffer and wait to see you forever? As you hear it from your mother or aunt or friend. Please validate me. As one said one day. Am I the police officer who all he/she wants to do, is protect you? Am I the fireman who climbs up the ladder to pull you from a burning building? Am I the author who was hurt so many times, I have to write to release my pain and anguish ? who needs to be loved in return for everything I come with? Who wants to tell you to meet me on, May 28th, at Starbucks at seven p.m. I'll be the one waiting for you. With sadness in maybe knowing this may never happen. With child-like wonder to cee if my knight-in-armour comes. Is that him?

You say, I always let you be you. In a heart that is *always* giving. More? You say? I can do that. You say, I love you and I don't ever want to take anything away from you. You had said to me once. *Why* are you a seven? You give me me back, in reflection and in my reflection, you gave me my words, through your heart, as you were hearing His Voice that said, you should do something with your writing. For seven years of searching, you called me after seven days after I made first contact. You gave me, and continue to give me, love the way I need on a daily basis from you. You know how to calm me from a storm inside me. Your loving raspy voice soothes me. With part of us that lives in heaven. Your side, my side, our side. When I need to heal my heart and emotional state, you whisper and say, shhh baby, it's okay, I'm here. I'm right here angel. Every time you jump in skips of happiness, I throw my head back and thank God. How your eyes shows your heart, right inside with all your tears you've cryed for me. For your friendship has given me a voice, through channels of many types and kinds. How you fill me and pump relove into me for I've deflated and your ayr fills me and makes me whole. You're my calm waters that still me. Through His Perfect Love, you know how to love me in the way only you can give me, to be chosen, to be myn, best friend above all else. You are my seven in assigning you a number from Him. He has specifically chosen *you*. And everyday you show me why He brought us back together again, after a decade of being in our own separate hell, apart from each other. And now, we conquer *together*. How we share a pedestal. High in the clouds that peek into Heaven and cee them waiting for us at The Gates. That you are in yourself a worthy servant of God's. Like I am. When I need to write amazingly, I go to you and to my second home and family, and fill up my need to tell a *great* story. To write my future books from filled up from you, my mirror. To share our deepest and darkest secrets to only us and each other. You are my seven, because, you take care of me when I don't tell anyone I'm sick, and you nurse me back to health. You make all the presences that I feel real to me. Importantly, you believe me. When I need to be touched, you heal my spirit from Him, and you team up and fix me when I'm broken. You teach me so much about lyfe and what's the next question? You gave me words. You gave me *my* words. With one sentence from a Whisper in your ears mind. And now, look at what We've all created together! You picked me up with your strength through your own pain, but you'd sacrifice yourself anyways. How your strength is super-human. Going out in the call of duty 24/7. Always being my hero. Always being my shoulder for all the secret stuff and for giving me a new perspective. Always able to answer every question I have. How I love you. You're more than a friend. You're more than a sister. You're more than and than and than. I have no words . . . I stand corrected, I have lots and plenty of words to express how much I adore you. When I'm in pain, you cover me with a blanket and you say, don't be a hero, ask for help. For you are my strength to climb at a slows pace, and you offer your body as my balance beam in my weakest moments in private that no one else cees. Where when I need something, anything, you're always there for me, going beyond the duty of any normal best friend. This "Love Letters" is dedicated to *just* you. I *am* your porcelain doll. You catch every tear and offer it up to heaven. And pray to yours, and myn, our LORDGod. Thank You, for the words to say; I love you, Angie.

You have shown me what Mighty Strength looks like. You are a one to me, for sole in standing in Christ. Living the lyfe He gave you. For hearing His Voice all those years ago in medical school to become a nurse and not a doctor. What a Calling He's given you. No matter what comes, in any day of anywhere of where you are, when I think of you, you are the pillar and the door handle in the direction needed when calling on you. You chose me, and I'll never forget when you told me. You chose to stand close to me in case I had to fall again, you were my soft landing, in cushioned love. Even though it was the three of us together, you have been assigned a one from Him. You're independent in this one and you have shown me, over and over and over again, what love you have to give me, as another soul who needed to be sewn from rags. You stood there, like God had Glued your feet to the ground in *That* moment. That unbelievable strength at the tyme was solid. Total solid. That has affected me, for my entire lyfe. That is why you are number one. Now, not only you were who you are/were and now, who you are as a mother. Powerful, isn't it? You're so dynamic in your inner strengths. That you often rely on. But you've always been strong, with a tender heart, that now has mother power. How I know that power. For it's the only reason I'm still alive. For their own reason, they both have saved my lyfe from suicide. From another tragic end, but because of who you are, you kept rescuing me. You keep throwing me the rope, and now, I'm hangin' on babe. I love you and my power in my love for you, as kept me alive and I've learnt how to be a *best friend*, because you're *my* friend and you chose *me*. How I become mesmerized when you tell me a story. And your laugh with the ha ha's. Your face lights up when you do that laugh and now it will be in number one spot for you. I'm glad I'm sitting, 'cause I'd fall to my knees. I've often spoken of you and your profession/job/career/calling/vocation. To catch lyfe and hand them over to their mother for the first tyme. You hand a child of God's to another. How does that feel? Power, right? You are my anchor when I need strong links to be who I am today. No matter who your children are ? no matter where you come from, be. To know what your friendship has meant to me. I'm not not including any type of mother. If you've adopted and you love that child, mother's love. To be blessed with lyfe, is becoming a mother. And now, God has blessed you. They're so beautiful, and myn are too. And yours and hers and his. I'm so honoured to be your friend. Your lyfe matters to me, and I've only wanted great things for you and your significant other, who is also someone so special, I can't even tell you. You have shown me many things my friend of my anchor, who on many occasions has been my interpreter. And corrected them to what I mean. You have no idea how much I need that from you. Oh my gosh! I just smile and shake my head and how can I ever thank you? I know that sounds weird. Lyfe happened and we met all those years ago and meant to live and experience such a horrific trauma. To know, that in part of the number three that I didn't give you, only one. To wonder what that was. What does that mean? To have pain when you least expected to, and where does it belong? I know where I belong and you belong with me, to help each other, to know, that no matter what, we're there for each other. LORDGod, thank You, for her. For the soft music in the background and knitting and projects on the go. For always loving me. For never giving up on me, and for being my strong anchor from a very sinking ship, saved. I love you.

It is beyond me in how I could forget to tell you such an important detail. For many years, you've been doubled in a three. But, to me, you are a one. I'll tell you why in a moment. How you invited me to the opera. And the most important moment and thing in my lyfe. Yet, I forgot about it until I was home. My sweet friend as I quote from it; Then Miriam the prophetess, Aaron's sister, took a tambourine in her hand, and all the women followed her, with tambourines and dancing. Miriam sang to them; Sing to the LORD, for He is highly exalted. The horse and it's rider, He has hurled in the sea. Exodus 15: 20-21. You gave me my Bible. When I first got it, I fell down the stairs. Well, the first major purpose of It was to protect me. When I fell down the stairs, the cover protected my hand from being scraped up, badly and probably would have to have gone to the hospital. The scratch on the cover has remained. It reminds me of when God caught me when I fell. It sits in it's own spot on my shelf and I read from it often and when I really need it. You gave me the most important Book in the entire world. The Words are always there for me. Waiting for It's/Their turn. You are so wonderful, like a chocolate bar of your favourite ones, swishing around with chocolate-sweet, and delicious flavour. I remember when we first met over a decade now ago. How when I first saw you, I never knew you, and I judged you so quickly and didn't know who you were as a person, but now, I can only say I'm honoured now, due you were called as my friend. You have made many sacrifices for me in the friendship area. You got to know me because you wanted to, not because you were forced to. How little did I know how much you've impacted my lyfe. You once called me, when you asked me to be your guest to the opera. That was amazing. I had a great time. It was once told that even if you hate opera, if you go to one, you'll learn to appreciate it more because of the effort that goes into an opera singers daily routine. So now, when I hear opera, instead of cringing and plugging my ears, I listen to it like I'm tasting a fine wine. You have given me that experience and new appreciation. How I'll never forget the song, Jesus Loves Me. Laughing . . . . That was great. We drove a long time together and I whish I remembered our conversation other than, oh my gosh! We missed the exit! Well, to share the rest of the story; We were driving another friend's car, on empty. No gas, and somehow, we took the wrong exit and had to go back a long distants to turn around with your help as a guide, even though. I have to laugh though. When I said, I'm used to having a radio, sing me a song, and laughing, you started singing; Jesus Loves me this I know, for the Bible tells me so, little ones to Him belong, they are weak, but He is strong. And the song continues on and we both laughed and continued to sing and rejoice in our friendship. I love you, so much. How we spent hours talking in the car. How your gift, of friendship has gotten us together for New Year's, and how parents took me in and celebrated with all our friends. I'm sorry I even brought in the politicians wife in the salon. I felt so bad, and I still feel horrible. So every time I think of you, I think of the girlfriend who chose me, who defended me, stood up for me, listened to me, and who pats me on the back whenever I accomplish things. I'm glad you're in my lyfe and your gift of my Bible and the opera, and being my model and being there. You are continued chocolate as the flavour, and the colours that you wear are bold and brilliant. Just like you that continues to live in my lyfe as your friend. Jesus loves me, this I know, for the Bible you gave me, tells me so.

"Portuguese Goddess"

May 31st, 2011

To the Portuguese goddess. With the long black hair. You are what artist are inspired from. You have inspired me on many things in my lyfe and you'll always remind me of The Trinity. So, you are assigned the number three. This one is different. This one is special. But I see something definitive. Always trust the first instinct. Are you resting? As you will always be my fashion girl. My guru to turn to for anything business. You're so savvy. You are well informed of many things, and so I trust you. And I hope you trust me too. Your name comes from all Three in the Word that means it. How I treasure everything you've helped me with, both personally, and business. All I want, is to help you, and try not to be me too much. But you won't let that happen, and you always tell me how important I am to you, and I trust in that when I need you. In that moment I need you, and you're always, right there. You have such love for lyfe and making it work for you. I'm so proud of you, for fighting all the way, through everything. I'm so glad things happened the way did for us to meet in school. How you told me that I could do it on my own. You gave me that hope again and to begin to become stronger in myself. You showed me a dream in me that died, that your words said otherwise. So this is dedicated to you and whoever may come. To let all past frustrations of any friendship, so it was bound to happen sometime, but I meant enough to you, that you loved me still and always. Which is why you're three. You have been chosen to live on this planet and live the way it's meant to be. You are compassionate in return. And so, whenever I think of you, you are my inspiration to be better, to paint on canvases. You gave me my paintings and any future paintings that are to come in the future to now. I love my paintings. So, thank you, for being you and giving me so much. One of them looks like this; an ordinate and bright decor frame, inside on the right, is of a woman's profile looking beyond and just under the sun. The water and sky are not separated and it looks like a cloudy day, but with the sun shining in front of it. With her brown hair curling in the frame. Another is a bright, neon, fuchsia-pink octopus. And another is one of my first, my very first pet. So not only have you given me a dream, you've continued to be my cheerleader on everything I do. You've enhanced and had visions of things for me in your creativeness of your personality. You're beautiful in pictures, as you're showing off your million dollar, flashy smile that only rich can give away. You got it girl. Your sparkling eyes and how they light up when you see your friends. How you have to be brilliant-different. Always getting into character and chasing any fears and pose. Click. And don't change anything about that, for that's the part of you we all love. Sewing something to make it beautiful with your flare and style and bring out the feminine in all the woman you want to help. How you thought of me as a phoenix. How you expressed to me, a mythical bird, of great beauty. Well, it has your reflection looking into the mirror of forever of your lyfe and your journey. I'm so glad it worked out. How I got to cee some bad days, and good days. Where the only thing I can hope for, is for continuing on being who you are to me. To have a spot in history and I tell the world about your curl when you're happy. I also remember screaming my lungs out and you were right there, front row, yelling to me; you can do it! Let go! And you hugged me every time. I will never forget how you made me feel. Important, validated, loved, and should I go on? I pray that this one, will show how strong you are as the fighter we all are, together. But in our own lyfe.

215

"Your Fase, Your Feetures"

May 27, 2011

I had to write you again. I want to cee you. So bad. To cee you face-to-fase. To hug you. To look in your eyes. To study and examine your fase feetures. To whish for this, everyday. I try to dream, but I never get to. Frustrating. And I'm taking wort. Maybe I do need to do the room? . . . maybe it might help me better ? something stronger. I don't know. But I have to be careful. So for me to continue to try to get to you, is dangerous for my earthly lyfe. That's why it hurts so much when you make deals with me. So meet me in person. I've been trying for two weeks now on wort. And if you knew about this you know it could be dangerous for me to take it all the tyme. And I'd be risking loosing because of bleeding to death. So if that doesn't make you come to me, then it's not worth my lyfe. Myn will always come first. So you choose. Am I really worth it to you? I'll cee. This is what I'm asking of you. You come cee me in person, at the high school. I'll be the only one there. And if you never show up, no more excuses. Stop making deals with me, it's pissing me off. And from now on, I'm gonna say how I feel about it, not that I haven't already. Stop asking me what to do. Figure it out. You know what I want. You, to meet me, in person, at the high school, around the corner. Stop making me wait for you. Look at me. Cee my reaction to you. You're my prey. Some come out of the darkness and see me in the Light. Okay then. Come out of the long grass blazing in the night wind across your fase. To keep hypnotizing me into your site in the burning halogen sun. To not be able to read the next continuing on story and what if I just stopped writing? Didn't write anymore? I let the pages go white. Nothing to decorate it. To make it look beautiful. So, share. To want to write you to continue on. Continue to use my words to express who I want, what I want and want what? You. To add some mystery; I'm going on a date tonight. Just a friend, and you'll read him in earlier Letters. A very special friend. What a gentleman to me, as just a friend. A very good friend. And if you don't except him, then there will problems. We've been friends for about almost a decade. It's a long time. So get to know him well, and he'll get to know you. But that's just another story to shift you off the straight and narrow. What's true? What's false? So back to your ness. So what if I wrote it again? He loves Sandra. What? I didn't hear you. Did you once again, make me a deal? Of years of arguing about it, just start now. No deals . . . okay, some maybe okay. The black of my heart. I have to keep going because of my outing tonight with my friend. Oh ya, I forgot. Don't tell them, as I hide behind the curtain of future bows from an audience. Of a certain kind. Has led to this path. Of questions of who you really are to me. Are you my only soul mate? Are you my spirit guide? Are you my spirit animal? Are you Destiny? Who are you? Do you know me in your heart? Do you understand who I am? As a human *and as a* supernatural? Please be my interior who writes on the walls and I look inside and peel it back and read it. It says; Please and thank You. Please and thank you. I never knew who I could be without you. I tried to open you and lick and heal the wounds you suffered in your lyfe. I don't want you wandering around forever. So when I can, I'll come and help your lost soul return to Light. Thank you for teaching me such valuable lessons that have changed who I was to who I am now. Your lyfe mattered and I validate you. Forgive me for I've sinned against you. Thank You LORD, for his lyfe. And thank You LORD, for his lyfe. So are you coming, or not?

"I'm Story, I'm Sorry"

The words wrote me a message and in imagination world it goes like this; Vala, stay away or ____ dies in the story. And then, And stays dead. This is a warning, to stay the fuck away from us and stop writing, about The Truth, in other words that should have been only Holy. So I say your words right back at you coward . . . you can't win! So fuck you asshole. I think in desperate needs you thought of bullying a Christian. I shake my head at you and think you're such an idiot. Oh, I'm story, I'm sorry. Did I get carried away again? Such an imagination, sometimes it's scary. I laugh in your fase and spit on your fase, and it burned your ugly skin and made you wretch in pain. Oh, I'm story, I'm sorry. you are my enemy. My LORD is The Only One. You're the coward, hiding behind fyre. Always behind something of bullying ways. Where you wouldn't understand Love. I don't want that lyfe, I want my lyfe. Watch out for devils. Oh, I'm story, I'm sorry. I'm running away again, to another place where I live. And I don't want it if. I run and splash the sand behind me in my footprints as I run to the water and splash against the rocks and gave me bruises, but I didn't care. I ran. Away from land. And I went under the wave and was tossed around and I hit bottom and hit my behind side that sometimes people say, nice ass. Ouch. I tried to catch my balance. Cee how easy it is not to talk about you? So I spit it back at you at tenfolds, and spew vomit that makes you choke and die. Where many will clap and cheer. But I shouldn't be talking about that. So lets talk about good things like kittens. How cute they are at the white kittens, with long hair. With a mew and my paw reaches for you. How I want to write in your fase. Look what I'm writing you psychotic scum. May my licks turn around and slice you and maggots will pour instead of blood and water. It is your poisonous venom. I would *hope* it would be said like that. I'm tired of the games. I'm trying to live my lyfe thank you very much. To only depend on Him and me to gets the job done. As the lenses cee something the eyes don't cee. Taking a picture makes a memory forever. And how it stays and years later you look in an album. And then you say, oh ya, that tyme. That was fun. Now it's tyme to move on and let it remain behind me, 'cause it's trippy and bad stuff can come of it. But didn't I ask for it? Okay, maybe I did, so. But LORD, I can't keep believing in this situation. And so, I thank the people who have played in this play, and staged me in front rows with stairs as the stage of up and down and middle. Which has played a huge part in this. Things are flying around like ghosts above the fyre in the story. Oh, I'm story, I'm sorry. Did he let you down? Yes. He let you down and I had to look around to cee the voices, as I shake to the music. I have to become hard against this in lyfe. And listen to the advice in the beginning, and leave it alone. As daily routine to spill out hints in messed up words in different order than in order. You open the daily newspaper and you see a headline that catches your attention and you read the advice and you don't listen to it, so it's your own fault. And it plays itself out and now to the next song. What does that song mean to you? No. That's all you said? So now you're the boss of this little game? How will it change my lyfe, when it was to his convenience? I can't let it rule me and tell me how to live my lyfe as a person. Ever. No. That's all I say. I'm going to say what I want, when I want, how I want, why I want. In every direction and never love another one and let it run it. So, it's goodbye to this part of my lyfe and say; Oh, I'm story, I'm sorry.

I'm addicted to you. How can I break free ? from something it wants so bad? The day we were set to go, to meet up, and shake hands and hugs and a voice to match everything else. How can I turn back the clocks ? that makes you safe again? I'm sorry I couldn't help you. In my heart you're real and you mean so much to me, or it's the insane part, who hears voices and noises and knocks around all the stuff. I don't want anything to happen to you. I'm drawn to you. I feel responsible for you. Even though, it's a fairytail and different fases going around in circles above. I'm sorry I had to block you from ceeing my face, but he was listening and making my heart sink into darkness and guilt for not saving you or caring enough to stop. I can't stop. I have to live, so I say goodbye to you and that lyfe that could have been. How now ? do I connect back to the first one? It's like it's gone and doesn't matter anymore. Shunned and wiped my hands of him. But what if I'm wrong? How do I go back? I'm sorry things turned around and slapped you in the fase. I didn't let you go, I let go of trouble for everyone else, with you as the pawn. I can't stand the evil but it's another story for you to hear about. To know that this really happened in fake world, made into touch and feel. I am no longer the bed you flop yourself down on and wow, so comfortable. You have fyre, pain, but only in imaginary. I never saw you. I never touched you. Only words came through the funnel of the tunnel. From someone else's tail of a tale that would never come true for me. A creature of stanse and ready in positions. Living two and I'm the one who asked him to come out. The deal was broken and spoke from sound represented, that you come out of your worlds of freedom, and now once again, you're a prisoner of heat. I'm so sorry I brought you out with grantedness to make this happen. Wrong choices has sent you back to the pit. Now you must suffer, and she must live with the guilt of knowing she brought you out of safety, and are you tired of the story yet? The end is near if not already. To disconnect and want to hide in the shelter of darkness. The circle and cycle of lyfe, continues on and I reflect on how I have affected lives of the imagination of producing ideal creations and invisible sight. Everything has ended. Ceased. Now, it's gone, to never happen again. And it's all my fault. I made up storys, to live with only a picture of a fase, with all attached, and now is unattached. To know something so huge, in a little boxes filled with flowers that only you can cee. To go to the 'next'. Now what do I tell you ? what do I write about ? that tells me how to let him out again? Do I just keep doing this? So, I look up word powers and come to agreeance of releasing the damage from another words spoken. To know of what destructive forces that change destinys of people who belong to it. I just don't understand what just happened. Goodbye, can I say hello? Listen to me. How can she rectify you? How to set right? To undo the words I want to meet you in person, but who's to say me shouldn't ? but he did and ruined it. As I close off from outside of sunshine and rain and tornado, and hail and rain. Be the key that fits in the key hole and turn it and let him go out into his world and his home, that was Letters. Open the door to make another story begin, in surrender. To look in your reflection and to cee nothing in back. You must dig, claw the dirt out in making the hole to bury him in on top of the pile already there. Do you hear the echo? The sound is muffled for there is nothing to speak back. I can't even ask if you're gonna be okay. I can't save you this tyme. I'm so sorry I suggested it, the end to another one with greed and selfishness.

"The Right Way"

You can try all you want to make me think I'm not worthy and not capable and question myself. Well, I'm too strong now to let you win me over again. I was given an answer to my worrys and stress, and I guess I prayed enough to get the answer. Thank You, LORD. For a while I was questioning myself and my destiny. I shake my head and know that You showed me the way to *not* be down. Go towards my future. Don't let my head go down. If I let it get to me, I'd probably say its such a hurtful pain, that I won't let myself go there again. Take that. In standing strong, and not question myself like that anymore. I saw it coming a mile away. But wait. Is it for that? Is it for this? It, just was, and I had to play it out, and now, I move on and concentrate on something bigger than who I was yesterday. I will never turn hard LORD. Because You Soften me. For a moment, I can cee defeat. Yes, You do want to save me. You show me, I can NOT give up. If you've ever said this to yourselves in your private prayer tyme ? like I do/did, you're not alone. People all over the world in sperts like the stars feel something like this, I'm sure, but not all. LORD, I pray, once again, for more words for me and my future in the arts direction, again, but in a different way this tyme. The RightWay. Don't go that way! Turn RightWay! Ask for Him to be your Compass. Because His Name Is Everything. And that's the only way I'll write. To show. To show nothing of fear as my words are read. When you said that I was homeless? I'm not homeless. I live in a home where love is most important with Christ as our Center-Pieces. He spreads throughout and uses us in different ways, and I sleep with softness. Thank God for that. And I'm not one. you called me one. Well, if you knew me, you'd know that was the farthest from the truth. I have lots of wonderful friends, who love me, so much, because I'm a good person. So, you're *so wrong* when you say you know all there is to no. This is where I'm saffe. So in long and short, is, you are nothing to me. As I also pray you away with my LORDGod steering the wheel away from me. I crash your reflection in broken scales. In His Holy Name. I will never deny, and I beg for forgiveness, if I ever in heart, feel like I could. I'm human and I get scared, but I have to believe that You will protect those who mean the most to me and my extended family as the world is. I also pray that I am not put in ANY situation that is due to it. Enough to isolate it and those. I pray for a peaceful clarity and clear mind. Be a butterfly and fly into my site so I can throw my hurt on it's wings and when it flys away, my pain goes too, and sits on the wings. You are that to me. So, this is me, saying I love You LORD, and thanks for having my back. Thanks for Showing me The Way, when it could have turned very ugly. And horrific in spirit and mind and sterdy lyfe. But You showed me inner strength when I needed it the most in my lyfe. This could have been everything. But I put all my trust in Him, because LORDGod, You Are. And I've been blessed with this new focal point in my lyfe, to become the best me I can be. To ride on the wave under the curl, with You letting me surf smoothly. Never will I make that mistake again. And be gone. Thank God, thank You LORDGod, Father for putting an end to it. Okay! Now go. Live my lyfe in comfort from my Father, my uppers, my joys, my mirrors, my solid ground, my readers. Who can say the same? Do you join me in this? Are you going to change the world today? Are you going to stand strong in your faith? Are you going to stand in stanse, in Strength, Loyalty, Compassion? Be a leader in Faith under One God. I win.

I can not loose myself in all this. *You,* can not loose yourself in all this. To know that this was all just a game. A cruel joke. I'm so sorry that happened to you. What happened? To hear you say; Art, cut his wrists, again. Deeper this tyme, with fyre. Feel like answering yet? Still nothing . . . wow . . . this doesn't help him at all.—How could you do this to someone? It must be a *bad* situation? To say this in jest, is NOT funny. LORD, I pray for me, be forgiving this, very quickly so as not to hurt her and crush her. Is it a him on your side? It was me as the words to slise me open. All my organs shut down and melted away. I can never tell her and I have to be normal. Not share what has happened to me. To play my best play. It would suffocate her. She'd loose her breath and she'd go in the opposite way. Never will I let her know. Do you have a secret like this? To be whole but in private ? write, my continued new pain. How words can just be written and said. In any ways. I'm not myself today. I'm definitely off today. But I have to look the part. Would she want to know? I'm still not going to tell her. We *go* to Paris, Italy, Russia, and that place I want to go with you. It's rough today. I'm not all here and I placed it there, but I don't know where it is. Oh, right, I put it there. Did you put it there last-night ? when you were so tired? I went to a place, where it was beautiful with fields everywhere with rolling hills and forests and decorated doors. Where I have two. One is lit and one is like a screen door. Oh yes, I forgot to offer a couch with pillows everywhere for you to get comfortable in your spot. Welcome, if you're just joining us. Clearing my throat. Now where was I? Oh yes, the majic doors. One is filled with tunnels that lead to bigger rooms off the main pathway. Filled with arches with Paris street lights. People walk past me and nod in politeness with the old fashion words and courteous manners. Then the next room is filled with a stage with a royal-red curtain with a popcorn stand at the back. Ten minutes to start. I took a seat and nestled in my cushions. But if I stay here, you won't get the next page. The next one, the light was neon with glow in the dark stuff on the large walls. It was loud in here. So where do you get off in here? What's in the other door? It says; looking at your lyfe I cee nothing but a failure. Is thought to be of as a loser to the rest of society. I sob. In begs, how do you go back to the other door? Where I don't have to live this pain? Some more pain to get through. As I am a survivor of defeat. I have defeated everything. Please don't take that! Don't listen. So I hope you're enjoying? Are you falling asleep? Am I boring you? I run as fast as I can. An empty page to have nothing to go from. Do you give your worrys to the LORD? Yes, you do. He will be your Comfort. If you feel that you're going to hide, hide in Him. Please don't call me today. I won't answer the call. All you'll do is lye to me. When all you'll do is lye to me and put me down. Leave me alone. How I feel so destructed. But I have to remain strong for him. There I go again, living in my authors brain. I won't say that again but only to say; hahaha. Why would you think I'm gonna let your little friend read this?—Do you really think I'm going to listen to this? Let myself be dug into another one? As I second guess myself in such a horrible things to say. As I have to be put together very soon. So quickly, pick yourself off the ground, from no matter what happened to you. Remember strength in the LORDGod. Hide this. Well. Take yourself to the hospital. Shake it off with a tasty treat and close your eyes and swish the flavour in your mouth. Fight. *Win this one.*

"My Burdens"

I'm searching. I'm looking. My eyes are wide open with closed lids in prayer for the ryt one. Is he mythical ?/ or majical? Please let him be a human man that is here on earth, that I can physically touch. Even though that was fun and everything . . . clearing my throat. But LORD, he must be special. Very special. Let me ask you some questions to cee what you'd say in return; Can you live with my storys? Both and all, fiction-non-fiction? Can you be with a creator of my own style of writing? Can you soothe my thoughts when I come down from writing? Will you make me laugh when I sob? Will you love me? Will you *really*, love me? Will you mend a few hearts in your love? Will you, and are you, a man ? or a bully? Will you reopen a broken and fragile heart ? or will you be my nyt? Am I taking a risk so big ? and being open to be cut with razors and scream in agony? Will you show me what I'm looking for? Or will you carry my heavy burdens of every day for me? Will you be my laughter ? when all I can do is crawl into a bawl, and hide and self-loathe as I'm basking in sunlight? Can you love an already made family? But with hearts of a newborns? Please respond only if you can say yes to a few of these. Take it out for a test drive, in my yellow and black jeep. But don't bump it or be rough with it. I love it, so be the passenger, my passenger, and let's go four-by-fouring. I'm taking such a risk in sending you this Letters. To shed my brokenness in open was to show you, the *right* you, a look of what you may experience along the way. Will you take me on a plane ? and let me see the world? Will you buy me flowers instead of chocolate? Alive flowers, that smell beautiful ? with no silk upon them? Will you see inside my heart and try to understand me? Will you lull me to sleep when I have a rough nyt? Will you lull me to sleep when I have a rough night? Are you my dream ? or my nightmare? Will you untie my bounded bind? And let me have waves instead of knocks. Are you patient ? and kind ? and compassionate? I want to be equal. No one is higher than the other. Never try to control me. Will you be my pillow and my towel when I cry? Can you carry my burdens? Can you love my children? Can you be a daddy to a sad little girl inside ? who never had a daddy before? Can you love and accept a young man looking for a best friend to hang out with? Can you accept me ? for all my pain ? all my burdens and lost loves in my lyfe? Will you help me through the saddest days in my lyfe? Will you make a difference in our lives ? for the good? And help us and save us and love us? Some days, I'm just wracked out with emotions. *Intence* emotions. I get broken, very easily. Are you my next heartbreak? Or are you the one God sent to find me? But please, take me as I am as I will take you the way you are in return. Every single question is that equal to me too. I'm not good at advice. I'm not good in math. I'm not good at a lot of things, but I do love the LORDGod, and who ever comes in my lyfe, must be TOTALLY okay with that, and never show me any other way. Who ever comes in my lyfe, must be TOTALLY okay with all that go with my writing and how it works for me, and never show me any other way. Respect me, care for me, be a man for me, be a friend for them. Usually I'm very poetic, and sugary words to decorate my codes and unlocking my doors, and chains, and locks with double padlocks. To share with you a story that I must tell. Once upon a tyme, there was a girl, who couldn't look in the mirror. She would see uglyness in such a delicate lyt. A Loud Voice Said; one day, a man will come and take you on a plane and help us runaway from . . . .

"Sorrow In Addiction"

The feelings of being of feelings has taken me on quite a venture. And how it's come out to make it a play and plae. Being addicted is over-whelming. It controls you, and makes you it's victims. Until you are ready? Don't even ask. Just get help. Then after a while, if you get good at it, that you can't even control it? Not even close. It's death. Eating disorders often comes with *it's* plague. That rots you from inside, out. Yes, we did say yes that tyme that started a lifetime of overdosing and serious consequences. So let's ask why you started. Abuse; physical, mental, rape, being sexually abused, abuse. Any of those reasons could seriously be a contender. Or you just wanted to try it. And it was a free choice at the tyme. Or it was pressured in some way. I just want to reach everyone in general. And continued on throughout lyfe. It consumes you. It takes over your everything. But in my own personal experience, I believe this is how being an addict has such power over you. For me, my own personal journey as an individual person in my lyfe, I've seen it. I've lived it. I have had past addiction problems in my lyfe. That have taken it's *own* journey in my lyfe. Living its consequences has had it's own lyfe *in* my lyfe. That I have done to myself. To reflect back. For me it was free choice. Some wasn't though. I choose my choices and I can't blame anyone for my addictions in my lyfe. It lives in me and I carry it, every day. So to escape that, I escape to God, and letting myself feel that day. And if I need to sob for hours ? I sob for hours. My addiction allowz me to feel, and it lets me cee how it *really* affects/effects me. But when I'm in my zone, don't even touch me, but I love you/I wuv you. I just write and pray for Words/words. I must write. Give me a computer now! But don't press any buttons that could distroy. So, get back to it. Don't let it win. Get out there! Let the echoey and off-balance-numbness. It lets you leave the pain for a little while. Addiction could be anything, that you have no control over and it has taking your lyfe. Food, drugs, alcohol, physical harm to self. Should I go on? Of every type. In each category. I should have but I was free to do it. My worst days of my entire lyfe. I don't even want to talk about it. It's that kind of pain you want to hide from when you get high in your way. Such an intence lyfe. Some may disagree on you and your story. But who lived your lyfe? You did. Don't let anyone take that away from you. Maybe another reason to dig deep and talk it out, for you. The readers and audiences. And under You. I must write. I can't get enough of it. I never knew all this imagination existed in me, as I share lies and tales, and truths and majic. Don't be fooled. Will you stand by me? Yes. Will you erase the pain? No. To be us, we have to feel, and write for some of us. LORD, I pray for the souls that have had addiction in their lives. I pray for peace in their hearts, and forgiveness on any issue that has lived in your lyfe. I pray for those so lost in addiction, that You save them, from total devastation. That You will Heal them with sometimes so catastrophic storys of how they became an addict. But there's always room for healing and recovering. You must recover. If not for anyone who is number one ? you. Heal. Have a peace that you've never felt before. Let God. Find Him. Find a Higher Power and seek what you have been seeking. The LORD, is my Everything. He is Faithful, Loyal, Compassionate. Follow His Path for you. Listen in the nyt. Say good-bye to addiction, and I pray that when you do, that you will live sobriety over your heart and shoulders. That you ask only for Him to heal all your pain and sorrow in addiction.

"Because You Were Born"

Because you were born:

. . . . Over the many years of your lyfe, things have drawn you to a different experience, that will teach you, help you, guide you. Foren countrys have always been a shadow over your heart and mynd. This is something you've always wanted for your lyfe. You've always wanted to help out in a foren country as you grew up. This is where you're being called to. And your heart is calling you to pay close attention to Africa. Over the years, you've read books, and articles, leading to the decision to pack up and go. You plan to help a suffering community, and help them build new houses, and restore water to them and their community. And now, this is your lyfe. Make it count. Make it matter. Change the world as you look in the mirror. After that mission trip, you plan to travel and let come what may. You assisted the other missionaries and now, a family can sleep in their own home and drink water.

. . . . You're running late for work today. You got very easily distracted today when you checked out the pizza menu in your mailbox this morning. As you mentally and out loud say to yourself, I'm having pizza tonight. The time was ticking on when you finally closed the front door and started towards the bus stop. When you were crossing the street, you looked around and noticed by chance, a car was coming and saw someone not paying attention to crossing the street. You yelled out, **hey, look out!** They looked up in the direction of your voice, and they stopped. Just then, the cab ran the yellow light. You saved her, for she is a first time mom, who's going back to work today. Her baby is at the sitters and she's just scraping by. A lyfe was saved and a baby doesn't have to grow up without their mother.

. . . . A week ago, there was a knock on your front door. It was a Police Officer. I was stunned. Can I help you? He said words of; there was an incident with my son, and that there was gunfire and my son was shot and killed. I don't remember any other words other than mumbles of, I'm so sorry, can I call any relatives for you ? do I need to talk to someone? I don't remember much after that. The week past and I sit in the court room where my sons killer sat and talked to his lawyer. The door opened to the court room and the judge comes in. Then the jury comes in. The judge asks what's the verdict is. The jury member stands up and hands the piece of paper to the judge. Hands it back and the jury has passed it as; guilty. Manslaughter, lyfe in prison. That judge put away a killer, and now I must go on.

. . . . In the following year, you find a long time friend that goes way back to high school. In casual conversation, I mention all the poems and letters and storys I've done throughout the years of my lyfe. Then, suddenly, I'm drawn to her exact words. She said to me; you should do something with your writing. So, I started writing, Letters of love that has been waiting to be told. With God as Front-Runner, the author starts telling storys, of storys of real recovery, sadness, make-believe, and now becoming an author. To make a lyfe better and to make a lyfe for her family. All because, _you_, were born.

"Echo In Response"

June 3rd, 2011

So, it's tyme I prayed to You again LORD. In this I pray. This is *everything in my lyfe. Please,* bless this book. I pray to You, in bows in worship. Please bless the readers who *wanted*, to buy my book because it kept them on their seats 'cause I'm just about to spread it around a bit. And to ask for forgiveness in my sins and ask that this will be *a great blessing to all who read it*. To her and him, so they can continue to become an independent employer in her lyfe. People love her. She's bizarrely wonderful, and unique. Her dedication will pay off one day.—And so he can ride by himself in his expensive leather jacket. Puts on his sunglasses and helmet and off he rides to his lyfe's next step to show them who they are in You. Shine through me LORD. Let Your words flow out and make it beautiful for them. The words like, eloquent, intelligent. In my forceful expressions to cee where this goes. I pray for success, and the end goal, to live not so . . . and things just don't work out in the way we want them to. Can't use that solely as a word. Just won't work. Some things aren't just supposed to work out. Always for a purpose though. If you are everybody, and you can't exclude that, due to this, in other people's views. Hard to walk around it. I pray LORD, for *Your* Words, through *my* eyes. Through *my* heart. Through *my* mynd. Through *my* skin and soul. Through *my* lyfe. I don't know *how many people* will be reading my book. If I can just tell you how important your lyfe is to me, but I know I've mentioned that before. But I think it's something worth mentioning again, don't you? Lyfe matters. Death matters. Start matters. End matters. It matters. No matter what the 'it/It' was. Just try to, always tell it with passion and devotion and dedication. It was your lyfe. Live it. Grow in it. Party. Drive. Ride. Hard and fast. Deliver it with vengeance. Whether you can walk or you're paralyzed, use your mynd, your heart, your voice. Live a good lyfe. To please the Higher Power in *my* lyfe, my LORDGod. My heart sits on His Pages and scribes, where the professor pulls out his blueprints with his cap with the hanging tassels. The rope cord end. Tied together with a little ball with tons of tassels. To roll out the scrolls and bring out his royal-purple-feathered-pen with plenty scribes. With Him as The Writer. With songs created on earth to sing to You upon the sun on their faces/fases. Fawls ? or truw? Blahhhh, tongue out and thrusting words; words are composed of one or more morpheme. Something that cannot be divided into smaller independent grammatical parts, as the, write, as they say from the word expert. And the scribe keeps looking up once and a while, while you can take it back from in your thoughts. And so the thoughts keep moving forwards and horizontal. Push. Look to Him. Let the scribes of today, be opened tomorrow in their world, let them burst. 'Cause then the information and as one mynd. Take me away to another world. Wateing for me. But I have to pull my head back down from thear. To continue to pray. For everyday blessings. Protect loved ones. To communicate my thoughts, in a continue. And repeat and give me some credit. I know when not to, you know. Is he conscience? Yes. Very. Has to be. And she must be perfect in her thoughts and his thoughts. I started praying and I always get distracted in another storyline. Another sentence of flowing rivers of Letters. To go through the A, B, C's to learn to read. To learn how to write an expressive pronouncement. To make a formal statement. Trust Him. Live His way. Why not? Cross boundarys to open and echo in response. That would be so cool. In all this I pray. AMEN LORD.

"Bully Of Depression"

I loved you both. In order too. First there was him, the first love of my lyfe. Then there was the second love of my lyfe. But first I'll tell first, first. From the moment he looked in my eyes and he flashed me his smile and his gap, I was in love instantly. Because he was who he was, he was invited and it was a tragic end. But in the beginning it was amazing. So much fun. We went on car trips. I'd fall asleep on your lap and when I woke up, we were, somewhere. You did your best at getting me to do things. Just flash your smile and your spontaneousness, and you got me to do incredible things that I would never do otherwise. Our road trips with you at the wheel. The only way I liked it. Maybe you liked it? I'm not sure, but we did it a lot, so I can only say yes in that from my perspective and educated guess. Right hun? How we made love in public places and in private, but you were such a boy in happyness knowing that now you're a man and you could put those thoughts to rest. Right? To whish I could go back and to enjoy them like you did. You loved surprising me. I never appreciated the effort enough. If I could. Right? But you can't turn back the clock and do it again. You get a one shot deal with a major decisions. Either you keep the baby or you have an abortion. In that heavyness of a decision that some people are faced with, on a very serious note for a moment. Either you're a Christian or you're not. Every decision is this important. Do you fix your marriage or get a divorce? Do you have the surgery that gives you another's blood or do you let them die? You go to your sons funeral or you don't. It's your decision. You're either a courage or a coward. Either you're a fighter or you give in. So in all this, to say, if I could, I'd make all the right choices next tyme. With all the pain that comes with it and the guilt that followed your death. It was my bully of depression. It would beat me. Everyday. Every night. I was it's prisoner. I was it's captive. I saw hell. I found hell. Along in finding God in my isolation along with the worst days in my lyfe and such heavyest depressions of my lyfe. I couldn't find daylight. I was in his shadows and I was dead. The nights were filled with torture. Thoughts of guilt and love as SUCH A HUGE burden. I carryed and trudged behind me, heavy and dead-weight chains of a gravity I didn't want. But I was given the gift of lyfe, even though I didn't want any part of it. For a long tyme. And in this tyme, I had fallen in love again. Trying to fix who I was as a person I didn't want to be. Never satisfied, never right. Always at odds with lyfe. Fighting against the current. Resisting everything and breaking my own heart over and over again. To go into an abusive manner towards myself. And still now, I still struggle with my person at tymes. Even in knowing God as the front and main focal point in where I lead others in my lyfe. I still struggle with self-identity abuse. And I wonder, if I knew that ? and what I know now? I still would have been the way I was. It was who I was. I didn't know who I was. I don't know if you knew who you were either. And the loss of each men, was catastrophic events in my entire lyfe. But, in the end, things worked itself out and I live with everyday struggles in being who-I-am. To survive all this love has been unbelievable. And now to be able to write about it? This is where today was to lead me. To not talk about the blade of grass yet. And one day I'll get there, but today it's about the only loves of my lyfe. Beloved and various other aractnids. You moved away, then you came back. It was your immediate engagement of a task that sent me into finding God and not let myself drown in another bully of depression.

Am I going to do better ? now that I know that my book is a memoir? To repeat things as necessary to explain what this is. To spill it out, that I'm in recovery. Are you in recovery too? That from my point of view and my perspective, in talking it out and talking it through, writing a Letter to you to shower wisdom and love and my own knowledge and perspective. As I lay on the blades of grass that will later itch my skin due to it's texture and ingredients. As the sunflowers are in full bloom and so tall. I wonder what it's like to be a blade of grass? To enjoy the buzz of the café under my feet and around me. The sweet and hot taste of the caramel. And ooo, that's hot. But so good. Once a week, I should come here and just enjoy the café and the sun on a sunny day. To embark in a situation that has you studying why things are the way they are. It's quiet but loud with a soften tone. How can that be? To have people walking on you and squishing you when they lay down and roll down the hill. Why is the blade of grass with a sharp tip at the top? Why does it grow that way? The top has to criss-cross in the invisible continued line in the sky. And so that's just the way it is. And hello gorgeous. Tall, nice smile and I'll never know him. Mmmm, the flavour of banana that swishes with my tongues demands, to go this way to taste the flavour, go that way to taste the flavour. So I have things to say. I have to control my taste buds, for they're very thirsty and hungry for the recent flavours in my mouth. Control it! Control it! Control it! Until halfway done, and even then, control it. Do you want strawberrys? Do you want blueberry? Peaches and cream? Just tell me and let me know. Even here, I'm isolated myself. Biggest, medium, small, and super big. What do you want? In apparitions of enduring more. To chew more than you can bite off. So now comes a long next saying from my mynd that wanders around in the space of someone's brain and I talked to them and I did it. To watch them go in and out of the door which swings open just to let you know. Oh, look at him. Wearing shades on a sunny day. But that's to be expected, write? Have a great day. What do you wander about? I wander and wander and wander, at a pace of snails because they're so good to swallow that it's soaked in garlic butter and I drink it for my taste buds. Oh, look at him. Oh, look at her. Do you know what to say ? As you remember some more memorys from way back when, when you'd sit in his office and not talk all the appointment tyme. And write on his chalkboard and write the word; myn. He loved me and loved him like a best friend. He was my best friend and I missed him when I moved to somewhere far, far, far, far away. Do you still miss him? Yes. I do. Instead of saying that, I said, I will. I should have said the other way around. Sigh, I'm almost done with the bananas and I'm sad. Do you need your receipt mamme? No thank you. And she walked away. He listened to me so intently. Like I was the only one in the room. And he looks like him. On an angle look-alike. I shouldn't have told you all that because then you're going to judge me and tell me your likes and dislikes. But that's okay though. I don't mynd listening to you. As my mynd wanders to the end result of both things that are going to change my lyfe. Again/again. I want to ask you something so bad, but you're busy, so I won't ask you to say a random, and bizarre sentence or words that don't make sence to the innormal person. I wonder what you'd say in response to the burning question I can't ask. So I'll move on. As the blades of grass grows, let it itch you and laugh and jump in the water to make shadows in my write.

Our first dance together, and I don't remember the song that was playing. Do you? How you held me so tight. And I sunk my head into your chest. You loved when I did that. I would look up to you and you caved every tyme. Instead of just saying, okay, with a heavy sigh and let him go. It would have saved everything of such complications in our tumultuous relationship that was at lightening-speed-fast-forward. And when we broke up the very first time, and when I moved back home and I sat down and wrote him a suicide letter, and I told him about it and I asked him how he'd feel if I did it? He said he would be sad. Just like when he did before *he*, died. How it turned around eh? So I'm gonna go it alone for now hun, and one day maybe ? if it happens for me again. I don't know. I like being single sometimes. It definitely has it's benefits, that's for sure. But yes, I would love to fall in love again, for real. And he'd be in love with me. Just as much as I would like him as well as loving him and him feel the same way. Maybe? One day? Who's to know? I should right? I can cee both lives; single and remarried. But, remember my imagination. So I can create many and any images, that I want, but God has a Plan for me and whatever it leads to, it leads to. I'm okay single. I know what I want. A certain style. He must be to me in every way and in every where. Say God-bless-you and you and you too as I wave my finger at him. God bless you. It's gonna happen soon, but what you say? Everything that's coming. So be a leader in your plaes of lyfe. So write about it already; I'd write more "Love Letters" and write plays for the stage and build and create some really off-the-wall shows and come up with very unique ideas. I'd write a Letters and bring it to lyfe on stage. Have friends help and let them create sometimes too or add to this one. And write lines. And hire new actors from school and hire them on full-time and have our own theatre or rent and have costumes and directors, fresh from school. I'd call colleges and universities and give me their best students name and phone number and call them for an interviews. Give them an opportunity to decline if they so choose to. But this would be special. Tell them the ideas of the plays they'd be acting for every show. Hopefully they'll take us on as permanent and maybe rent-to-own. I'm so glad she understands that about me. Never have to give it another second thought. I'm interrupting, call me later. Thanks babe. Love you. And then that could be a part in the play. Don't you think so? You don't have to answer if you don't want to. Thank you for respecting this part of me and you understand. And then the next scene is this; breathe deep and blow out and . . . oh, I'm just kidding. Back to the story. But wouldn't that be awesome and then have a studio in my other tyme of my day. Can I have both worlds? An on stage ? or/and an art studio with my sculptures and "Love Letters"? and hire someone to make frames. That will hang in my studio. That will have mustard yellow velvet fabric covering the walls that have frills and gimmicks and spot lighting so they can read my Letters before they pick one, and will have ornate stools under each piece and I will have a matching runner that goes with the décor. And in between would stand my sculptures. With a mirror on the wall so they can cee the back with lights shining directly on top of them with halogen-spot lighting. Then I would have a curtain and in the back would be my wheel and art supplies so I could paint and make flowers and pretty bold, Christian and controversial pieces, to show my personality. And to live my dreams just like you are. To create anything, for forever.

Panic! Oh my gosh! I need to vent it out. You *must*, listen to me! So now that I have your attention, it's the only one I cee really. I'll find it and when I cee it, I'll know it. That's how it always works with me. When I see my studio, I'll know it. When I see my theatre, I'll know it. With my sculpting, I'm going to inject different colours of clay and mould them and marble them, and pin-stripe effect with a shiny with fading shine into the matte. I'd get shapers and different designs and wave them out with sewn effects, with bold paints that run together and make it original and edgy with a high collar neckline. Inside would be mustard yellow, with black stripes as Crosses and put a sculpture on the black stripe with a hanging swagart curtain with tassels and rope ends. With a mirror with an abstract feel and look. It would look like you were in Paris, France. With the lights lighting the path in the middle of the studio and have little tiffany lamps and unique and vintage feel with an edge. I will not hide my Christian faith, so there will be beautiful Crosses as art or look. I'd have my art, and I'd support new artists who I love. Who really wanted to be an artist for the joy of doing it, but with a few deadlines to be met. To make them perfect in my eyes. The desk will be somewhere in the back. I want you to walk the gallery, to feel it, to read it, to cee it, to live it. And then the phone rang and I bent down to pick it up from the passengers side. Bam. Smash. Bang. Crash. Would you rather I not go on with this terrible eruption from Paris, France? What's it's name? Destiny's Edge. ? Yes? No? Inside it'll be dark and mysterious and serious with only necessary lighting will be on with soft yellow lighting/ incandescent lighting. And shine with elegant details. Where would I find this person? To tell the story of it's contents on the outside to show inside and the story. And place them randomly in a properly fashion in an asymmetrical-balanced-orderly-way. To have soothing music with water sounds and birds chirping and have everything just right. No errors in placing things just right. And have not proper shaped frames. Have the frame in angles and shapes and boldness to catch attention to a particular and usually it's owner, first shot deal. Some won't happen like that, but some will and I can't wait to cee who goes with who. Shine and go; blingbling, knock on your heart and say; this one please. I'll ask where you're going to put it in your home. And either you'll answer me and be more than happy to tell me, or you simply don't want to divulge that kind of privacy, or you just don't know yet. I'll never ask if you want. But I'm a curious person and I'll want to imagine it so I can be inspired to do more art. Given the day, I'll be; writing, sculpting, and painting. And the other side to me will be creating more "Letters" to put on a stage play, from a memoir perspective. To somehow write a stage play and put on productions for the public to also know me as. I know where I want to be in my city. Hopefully, one day? I hope? Send a prayer up to heaven and ask Him to bless me and know that I couldn't do anything without Him. And to never forget Him. Don't go anywhere without Him. You'll need Him to help make your dreams come true. To take your hand as you step up and down so not to loose your balance and fall. He's being a Gentleman, so take His Hand. Live your dreams. *Be* your dreams. Don't dream in a crate. Dream in the ocean. Look at the coverage between the two. Cee the difference. One is small, safe, confined. The other is vast, amazing, lyfe altering. Don't go down in walking down the faux Paris street and browse with whatever piece you fall in love with and take home. I thank you, good day.

It's my burden for the coming months in the trialness of my brain and let's me think of nothing else, but finishing and getting the word out. Ya know? I must fly by this tyme then. So pray with me. So this can take on a lyfe all in it's own. A memoir. To remind you of someone's lyfe once a time ago. And it goes on and on and on . . . what do you want me to say? I just want to straighten him up a little. Scare him. Shake him up. Get his attention and listen to me with your ears and your heart, because sometimes threw the eyes, sometimes sight doesn't help you all that well. And I need you to listen to me! Do you know how lucky you are? You have everything and you just throw it away, like the garbage that doesn't get taken out. I mean, come on already! Make sense of your lyfe. Take an analysis of your lyfe. You don't challenge yourself enough. You don't care about anything in your lyfe right now. Just look what she has done for you. Everyone suffers from some features that we don't like about ourselves. So **deal with it**. Live with it, because obviously, it's going to follow you everyday and anywhere and anywhere. So don't make *her suffer* for it. Don't be so *selfish*. Your health is nothing to sneeze at. So you can live lyfe, you better take care of yourself. The stress will kill you. Eventually. Grow up. Be a man who the most important people in your lyfe don't have to worry about you so much. Be more *responsible*. Take action on making your lyfe a better place to live. So you get comfortable and work. Go to school, go into the field of your passion and work hard at it, to perfect it for when it's *really* important. Grow as a Christian, since it's part of your lyfe and what it's based on in principles and knowledge, but be vast in your knowledge. Don't *grow up* in a crate. Don't *live* in a crate. Don't *be* a crate. Be the ayr you breathe everyday. Smile when your heart is overflowing and wants to love. Smile because you're you. Just be really good at it. Like a full-time job. Feed it with good and healthy nurturance. Learn lyfe, about lyfe. 'Cause, you're gonna need it along the way to find your destiny. Listen to good advice. Take it with you. Carry it as a power to fight the jaws of lyfe. Give a little. Don't be so selfish! I'm very disappointed with the way you look upon your lyfe. Things are in your way on your way, I know. I know the drill. But in so in order, you needed what you got to get to today. Whether here and now, or there and then. Just kick up some shit with who you are as a person. If you're weird and you're a nerd and you have tape in the middle of your glasses, you listen to me, right now! Do you know and to my knowledge so far, you guys are the smartest people in the world along with many others. Scientists, Doctors, Researchers, Best Selling Authors, and so important, Artists, and *everything* in between and here and after. Learn what interests you most. Why only limit that ? when someone else can not do it for you. If you want to, do it. But have a purpose. Have a passion for it. Live your lyfe to the fullest, because one day it could be taken all away from you, in a flash. Be good to the earth. Because one day, it will pay you back with wrath. Pray to the LORDGod, in those little moments where you take your sigh, and breathe out and say thank You LORD, for letting me be me in this world. Right? I've pretty much announced how I feel. So come on. Grow up a little bit. Help out more. Take pride in who your family are if their really good and kind and compassionate people, who really care about you. Cee what they can do for you to help you on the path you must walk. Be punk, or cool, or the socs. Be whoever you are, just announce in your way to show her, yes mom, I do love you.

It would be only fitting that I end my book with you on my mynd. Thank you for giving me you. I hope, that we can finally move on in our different worlds and carry on in different realms and tymes and plases. I just want to say, I love you, to you. You and being so savvy and swavae. So military now that I notice, again. Now I add a spark of myself added from you. You saved my lyfe, Andrew. You gave me a lyfes. You gave me two of the best kids out there, and I know other mothers say the same thing, and that's good. They're my reason for surviving suicide. For my every breath of ayr that keeps me alive. I pray, when I could be going down again, to relive those days all over again in past memorys that have resurfaced. No other love besides my mother could have saved me. So many years in burden love. To get payback, I went into darkness and hid behind a pictures reflections of two fases, looking at each other, behind a flat piece of glass, and stared at me the entire tyme, so much so, that I didn't have to look away. As it once sat on your casket and on your coffin. From horrors I can't even tell you. What it had done to you. God, hold me up as I want to fall down. Keep me standing firm ground and not looking back into the mirror of tortures, as it goes on forever in it's own reflection. Don't break the glass. I can't have his picture fase look like his dead face. LORDGod, continue to heal my heart and my soul and my mynd. Don't let dreams of hauntings and hell and horror me again. Let it be stripped away, by the Power of Your Love. Is that how it goes? How have you recovered suicide? Did you or do you get high ? to ease the coping in your mynd? Do you get high in drunkenness? That makes you fall down the stairs ? and wake everyone up? You **must** survive suicide, because that's how part of your heart died, and you carry that with you, always and forever. So many unanswered questions. The guilt. In my own situation, I live the guilt. Sometimes, it owns me, and I have no control on a bad day. When all you want, is the same thing. If you were me. But now, the past has come back. My last connection to him. And it's making me say what I need to. It would never come to me succumbing to death yet. I say yet, because I still don't have any desire to harm and abuse myself, but I know I still do it sometimes. Doesn't everyone at some point? I want to say, thank you, Andrew. For giving me their lyfes. Thank you for marrying me, and loving me *that* much. I think you had way too much faith in me back then. We all make some terrible choices and we all have to live them throughout their stages. Of whatever it is in your lyfe. There are consequences to your actions. Pray for forgiveness if you know, like I know for me, the sins that I've caused. The knowing of what I did. Changed lives. Forever. Forever to be haunted daily of your mistakes that you whish you could take back. To change the past. But you can't change the past. It's always Written like it is. Please don't commit suicide. There are other choices. Trust in God above. Or search for something that fulfills you and gives you hope. For a better future than what could have happened, but this happened instead. I can only hope in my heart that you adored your children as a pair, and as an individual, but you died instead. So, I get to watch their lyfes take off, into the world and find their own homes so we can travel to visit and walk around to cee our far away comrades. So, while you're still waiting for me, I'm going to live a bit now. So I send you on a mission of waiting and going to plases thear. Meet some friends and float around the solar system a few tymes. Thank you, for your lyfe, thank You, for this book.

I wanted to get started on lyfe. So, *push me out already*! I want to start living and make a hell of a noise doing it. Break out of your womb so I could go in my way as you try to find me as a child. What a lyfe I'd live, as you as my mother. I dedicate my lyfe to you and all that's included in being your daughter. As I live my lyfe, you come into conversation many tymes and on many occasions. As I say, thank you, mom, for loving me the only way you can love me. All the challenges we've fased, in yelling and loving and explaining math at the level I can understand. Lots of explaining what we mean to each other and go in our together road and you live in that place and I live in this place, but, I love you mom. How sometimes I forget to remind myself how ? if I'm a mom and I love my kids, and I cee mirror with that reflection, then you must love me that much too. You gave me lyfe. You gave me unconditional and difficult on my part, always fighting with me to you show me your love. You allowed me to be able to find my destiny, so I could repay you, in dedication past death and love you and be proud of surviving me. All the cartwheels that you'll remember from my childhood, and other things that you remember from me mom. How your parents gave me summers and how your heart must have broken by our tyme apart and how I missed you, my mommy. To be strict with bedtimes which I always rebelled against you. How we both love the song that makes it *rocky* under our feet, and go back to yesterday and remember the younger years. How misunderstanding of your love sometimes, but always being dedicated and devoted to you. Sometimes anger grabbed a hold of me and I lost the real love shown. Thank you, mom, for helping me with my children and raising them with God as the Purpose of our lives. That you and dad, made so many sacrifices, and frustration as me as your daughter. I may have not had everything I wanted, but I had what anyone *could* want. As the words start to our song with *rocky* feelings of ups and downs as I grew and you grew. I got to watch you fall in love with my dad, who carryed me and carryed me when we buried my husband and how your heart must have pained with the most catastrophic and your ruined daughter and had to see darkness under your roof. As you carryed me through raising my children, who love you, for taking such care of them for the most important childhood memorys that were taken away, by suicide. The many tears that shed were uncountable. They were as much as the grains of the sand on the beach and the blades of grass on the ground. He swept in, and took over my lyfe, at my will, with your dedication that I wanted to repay you and live my lyfe as He has shown me. I will never forget. You gave me freedom with letting me go away. All those tymes where you never stopped being the mom you wanted to be. Even though we disagreed on many things, no one could ever understand in knowing that you come with the package and my undying love for you. The songs of dedication for you that you dedicated to me on the radio and by my hospital bed of all those tymes when you had to be. And how your love was divided many tymes on your journey as being a mom. Two daughters, two opposite-ended daughters who one fled and ran away and left you with a catastrophic and lyfe changing moment that I can never could imagine, but you fought for your cubs. All five of us. How you gave your grandchildren all your loyalty and have given tirelessly to assist us in showering with love like a thunderstorms that you held my hand and comforted me with your hearthands. I will live my lyfe as you do, with Christ in me.

"Father's Day"

Knock, knock, knock, was the knock of an unexpected father to take his role in my lyfe. Hi Trudi. I'd like you to meet, Vic. Vic, this is Trudi. Trudi, this is, Vic. It was July 10th, 1976, and that was the day you had two little girls to look after, to love, and when you and your fiancé got married, that's when you had the title and role of my dad. You had your thick dark brown hair, and your loving fase, that would love me through some of the most tragic days in your lyfe as my dad, and *as* a dad. To look back, remembering the tymes when how you took me for a ride as a child, who's hands were always in your back pocket, for I craved for a daddy. Your daddy smile, your daddy eyes, *my* daddy's heart. The day you knocked and mom answered, if you only knew what trials you would and her come to face being the husband that you would become. To love her children who are also, *your* own. From a past I know nothing about in how and not understanding your love for me, and I thought that you didn't love me because I wasn't your own child. In the weaknesses of your lyfe before us, became your and my greatest strength. You have shown me; deep and real loyalty as a husband, with a few bumps and bruises, honour in your hard work and how you've consigned your commitment on your wedding day on May 29th, 1981. The day I called you dad, for the first tyme and will never end. It must have been difficult with such a rebellious me? How we've had our thunderstorms and gusty winds that almost blew us into oblivion. But over tyme, in becoming a woman, I'm so proud to call you my father. Even though I didn't always love you on full speed, you have shown me over and over and over again how much I still have that child's heart in your hands. When you cry of sadness and despair, I hold you up to God and thank you in remembering the everyday mundane dutys. Worker, husband and beloved, cherished and daddy, grandfather, son, brother, uncle, friend, and most important, a true man of God and devoted Christian. I've got to sit in church as you play the drums and I brag at your talent and I'm so proud of your participation in your, in our church. How you love all the little children. You help them make things with wood, and you're tender in love and teaching and protecting them so they won't get hurt. Your priorities are in the right order as a man of God. To build up His children, so they're *your* children too. On this Father's Day, remember how much I love you. On this Father's Day, remember how much your children love you. On this Father's Day, remember how much your grandchildren love you and how much we embrace you as a member of lyfe. Our lyfe. For so long, I've been scared to give you every part, because of all the pain growing up and becoming who I needed to be away from you and apart from you and with you. On April 8th, 1997, my world ended. I died. From suicide, from a father who didn't have your strength, who suffered differently than you did. And when I couldn't cee, you stood there, like a cover to protect me from the cold, only I had to cee it from a distants because I was going down a hell tunnel. On the day we buried our beloved, Andrew, when it was tyme to go, you said; come on sweetie, they have to do their job. And you put your left arm under me and as I sobbed and fell to the ground, you held me with a force that wouldn't let go. Happy Father's Day, for you, to be acknowledged, by a woman that you've rescued and erasing all the past wrongs and celebrate your lyfe along with a list of men that I carry and know and hope that all little girls, love their daddy, as much as I love myn. From all the words like up, down, and sidewards. For loving me. Your way. Happy Father's Day.

I'm definitely not going to take the sister-of-the-year award in this sentence. I'm a bad sister to my little brother. I have to work on that area and may he know, forever, how much I love him. The day he was born, was the destiny that would follow us in our path together and our distant relationship. How he has to know, he's one of the loves of my lyfe and may these words find you. I watched you grow before my eyes. Into this remarkable man, who's talent is unbelievably your style. Be *everything* you can be. Let my love for you, push you forward in your career. Be the *best* you. Show the world who you are. Party hard, but you must work hard too for the rewards to show themselves. I love you, my little brother. Be strong in the LORD. Never let anyone sway you away from Him. Be His leader, so you can be rewarded there too. Be a good man of God and find love in the way He leads you. I'm sorry you have felt I didn't love you sometimes, you just change those words around sweetheart. As one tyme, when you were a baby, you were about one, and let me publically tell this cherished and engrained-in-my-heart-forever-moment that I shared with you as your sometimes erupted sister. You were one, I was crouched down in the gally of the kitchen and you ran from the hallway into and through the kitchen. You had your diaper and a white shirt that went above your cute and adorable belly. You had your right index finger on your bottom lip and you just ran past me and said, hi Wawa. You didn't even turn to look at me, you just ran to the dining room and ran past me. I regret so much with you. I don't know how to make it up to you. Even though we were in the next room, we were so distant. In our own worlds. Living our lives, separately in our together roof. I want *so much for you*, but I don't know you the way I could know you, but I never know what you're thinking, so that scars me into just loving you the way I do. Let you live your lyfe and watching you as you go. Take the rare moments to tell you, I love you. One tyme, when you were little, we were sitting together on the top stairs of the sunroom, and we were laughing so hard at something that mom said. And I laughed, and I hit my knee. You watched me and started laughing and you copied me and slapped your knee as you laughed. Then, along time in the future, I watched you graduate high school and college and watch you become this marvel in his industry. I have *so much faith* in you. I love you, to the little boy who called me, Wawa, into a man who can only become, ultimate. On the happyest day in my lyfe, you were there, seeking love, and you gave me love when you kissed me on my right cheek three tymes. How you were showing who you were back then, and I whish I had more patience with you and how you wanted to show your talent with your plaes and work that will lead you one day. Be a devoted man to the truth. Lies will get you nowhere. Be honest in who you are and always be true to yourself. Learn the world and The Word forwards and backwards in the way He is showing you. Listen to His voice when He calls you to start being His missionary in His Light. When you take that walk down the isle one day, and I pray for the tyme when you're fully ready to give your heart and lyfe to the woman of His choice. To watch you fall in love, to *really* fall in love, I'm going to embrace her and welcome her into my home. Because if she loves you, because if you love her, then I'll love her too. To the little boy who grew into a man, and watched you scrape your knees into the man with the beard. From a little boy who I pushed away, to a man, who will together work with me on a Great Stage. I love you. To Antonio; Love, Wawa.

Don't you dare lye to me when you say you love me. Don't you dare lie to her when you say you love her. I will never let you lie to her ever again. If I'm wrong, forgive me Father, and I'll seek forgiveness for eternity and push it down. your lyes are puss. Never speak her name again you foul bastard. Let The LORD have His Wrath with you. All I breathe is Him. So in His Power in me, I spit in your eyes as they disintegrate. your payment will Come. Very convoluted and may His Coil strangle you. But I must let you go into His Hands. I shake you from myn. you take advantage in the dark so you can't be seen. Where you touch and rape. Where you pretend to be an angel when you're the opposite, and if I'm wrong, forgive me Father, for such angry words making an announcement over my intercom. This past year has showed me many things. Spiritually, physically, mentally, self. Somedays weren't all that great. But somedays were the best in my lyfe. Finding my words has helped me in my recovery from suicide, one-way love, who I've become in the LORD, how I've developed as a mom, a daughter, a friend. And in this year, I have found my anger. I have voiced my anger, I've raged my anger, and I seathed in anger. I have asked for the LORD to make the guilty be punished in His Discipline. I know it's to please me, but also to seek punishment for theirs, his, her, them, crimes. And knowing that every tyme I point my finger at them, my enemys, three fingers are pointing back to me. So I should be punished too, but I seek forgiveness for my sins, and I learn from them, into something good, to show my children a good role model. Be strong in the LORD. But being strong in the LORD, doesn't mean that we as humans don't make some tragic decisions for our lives. And even in anger, I want to show love, because as the saying goes; What Would Jesus Do? Even Jesus got angry. God got angry and shook temples and made them crumble to the ground. So, I get angry and want judgement on my wrongs for the wants I want for the world around me. Take lessons from my mistakes, and use them to better yourselfs in your world, and what you need to do to get things done in your lyfe. Obey the laws of love, and love, even in devastating anger. Even when tsunamis hits and you've lost love, feel how you need to feel, under rape, strangulation of self-identity abuse, of someone who says they are the closest to you. Gain strength and find strength to remain strong and do some research on finding out the truth before you find out if they've shot you or hugged you. Don't let the coil of his death is upon him, the death of something that was thought to be true and real, ruin you, smother you into a darkness that you are alone. Watch the Light, for it's the Flashlight that leads you to a better field of wild weeds running with your real best side that you cling onto and you run together to find each other, in your blue eyes and your brown eyes. Don't you dare lye to me when you say you love me. Don't you dare lie to her when you say you love her. I will never let you lie to her ever again. If I'm wrong, forgive me Father, and I will seek revenge on other crimes that fill my heart, and pray for the truth. Her innocent belief for such a good disposition with her natural lookout for a friend but was not. If I'm wrong, forgive me Father, and I'll seek forgiveness, and never look down upon it again. For the man who raped her and her and her over there, for the lyes of a trusted friend and let her believe something that wasn't true in the heart and mynd and soul and took her on your lyes and circled them around her and if it's true and you've hurt my cub, may I never be soft on my prayers to the LORD.

So he's my guardian angel eh? I don't know what to say. To drown my sorrows in a glass of whiskey and rum and vodka and get high to oblivion. To be isolated in my pod waiting for departure. To loose the cravings for sugar and rotten fats that consume my body. To not get lost into darkness again, and I thought is was over, but I guess not. In both worlds. In both lyfes. As it goes on and on and on and on, ya know? I couldn't do it. I couldn't go through that pain again. Until my past pain has lived on in my tears and pain and runs in my blood, please don't put me in that situation again. I had to walk away, but now. She says he's my guardian angel. To exchange a lyfe for a lyfe. I just couldn't win. I had to run and fight-or-flight mode, I took flight. To let go of a world I couldn't reach, in all my tryings to. And then to wake up to, nothing. And fighting for the right thing, to only have it slapped back in your fase over and go around in circles with this. I had to let my fyr go, and know that lyfe was over. I had to refocus. To hear slit his wrists deep, more pain, until she caves and sacrifices her own. I couldn't deal or cope in such a slashing and whipping of my heart to cause it physical pain and thoughts of death, to show how much I loved in return. Just suck everything from me and blow in self-identity abuse, and only Jesus was flogged in this one. To have to bargain with the opposite and begging in prayers, for lyfe to be given for lyfe. The evil unleashed was my torture in fear. Why shouldn't I be angry? To feel her pain inside like I'm her. Soaking the mirror inside her with me there looking for a way out for her, for any outside light, to push her through, to release her pain into another world of not feeling pain at all. Why don't you trust me? To not release anything, but trust, is not even an option for me. You're you and you needed me and I was there, every time, to not destroy her heart and let bad and dark reach her, for I couldn't do that. So truth must happen, once and for all. To tell me he's my guardian angel, so why did what happened ? happen? Why could you tear me in every wincing agony pain of not being put under? To prey me like that? In words and picture? And fake love? To feed me puss of enemy territory, that makes me vomit and spew in your fase. Pray that God is brought into this and pray for the correct punishment. That He know what to do. To prey on the innocent? In your darkness of shadows in the night where you creep and tear at shadows of the young and vulnerable. To steal a child and use them against loving each other. Mother and child is the prey in the word of a forest with her deer lost to man. That heaven is forgotten about in a world full of snakes and black widows and backstabbing your childhood lessons in Sunday School, in your church with The Pure Love. No matter how we go together as a Nation under God, as familys, as sole, as a pair. How you sneak inside someone at night and rob them of sleep to be able to function in their lyfe if sadness is everyday? The dark spirits enter when she's alone and she can't look in the mirror for self-esteem lives there, and whipping inside the voices that love taunting you and make you slash your skin to let go of your pain and you vomit under secret covers not to show hiddenness. How you forget to love you like you love, your closest loves, and how you say I love you to them as they leave? Words repeated in your head, of words that no one should ever know under secret. Say over and over again to the LORD, don't let evil win me LORD. I can not live without You, and I will conquer over him with You and show him who the Boss really is in all this. Right? I pray for comfort away from where she's normally be, I love her.

Hey world. How's it? Are you having a bad day? Are you just fed up? Or ? are you happy today? Everything is going your way? Or ? is it a self-mutilation day? Are you like me today ? where, everything you felt you did, was a total failure to you? She says you're my guardian angel. Are you? I can't hear you. Can you speak louder? Where you think of, if you just did it, if I just committed suicide before, then none of this would be happening and all the pain around me, wouldn't happen. Now, that doesn't mean I'm going to. I'm just saying. And since I found my voice this year, I'm going to speak what's on my mynd. I have every right to . . . it's my book. Right? How can you have an argument with a page in a book, right? If you just let me talk it out, I'll probably feel much better. I want a voice. And I want to have a loud voice, in my views upon touchy subjects, like my faith in God, suicide, rape, abuse, addictions, self-identity/mutilation abuse. And you tell yourself that you're not worthy of anything, and it just makes you cry harder and harder. That's so sad. *It's* so sad that people do that to themselves. Or always want to be someone else. But some can tell you, the grass isn't always greener on the other side. As the saying goes. Give or take a few words. Answering all those questions yesterday was brutal. I'm in the process of doing my bio for this book. To tell you all about me, so I'm interesting enough to you to pick it up and read it and make me want to make you buy it. So thank you if you did/do. I do appreciate that. As I live in the future and the past, to learn from the future to heal from my past. So would you like to have a seat ? as I tell you woahs from my lyfe after all the years I have lived? Reality check please! As she would say, yahuh. And nod and smile at me, and then jump and do her hop that she does. She's the happy part of my reflection. And she treats me well. Let her, be a lesson on how to be someone's best friend. If there was a picture of a real best friend, yours and myn, myn and yours, hers would be there. Right beside me up way up high on the pedestal. Where she becomes the child and she plays with her doll. Wraps her up in her arms and pouts and with a soft childlike voice into my head and says, we're never going down. I'm sorry to bring you back, but I must keep on. So what to do you want to know? What do I need to change about myself? My self-identity abuse. To learn to appreciate how *much,* I've come through to get to where I am today. To let the possibility of death of a loved one not invade my constant thoughts and crowd my day with sadness and mental anguish, of; what if? To remember that I *am* strong. And not let the bad feelings take over and tell me I'm worthless, and that I don't have to crawl under a rock when I make a mistake. I look in the mirror of glass, and I'm always fixing myself; my hair, my glasses, my skin, my teeth, my make-up, my clothes . . . and the list goes on and on and on. Saying to myself I have to be more than I am. Always sad when I look at myself. To pay back all the love that was given to me, so freely of others. They *chose* me. All my friends, they *chose* to love me and to take care of me. How can I ever repay that? By trying to love them back. And I do. I love my friends, including my family of course, I love them too, just talking about my friends right now. How they've all fought for me and showering them with after effects, that would be thumbs up. So, for *you*, today, not for anyone else, look in the mirror of glass and say; today I will smile at one person. Today, I will bend down to smell that pretty flower I saw the other day in front of that red and yellow LEGO house. Say; AMEN.